Miceál O'Hurley and Oksana Shadrina

Wolves in Sheep's Clothing

The Russian Orthodox Church's Threat to European Security and Democracy

Miceál O'Hurley and Oksana Shadrina

WOLVES IN SHEEP'S CLOTHING

The Russian Orthodox Church's Threat to
European Security and Democracy

Bibliografische Information der Deutschen Nationalbibliothek
Die Deutsche Nationalbibliothek verzeichnet diese Publikation in der Deutschen Nationalbibliografie; detaillierte bibliografische Daten sind im Internet über http://dnb.d-nb.de abrufbar.

Bibliographic information published by the Deutsche Nationalbibliothek
The Deutsche Nationalbibliothek lists this publication in the Deutsche Nationalbibliografie; detailed bibliographic data are available on the Internet at http://dnb.d-nb.de.

Cover picture: ID 109761596 | Kirill © Maria Moskvitsova | Dreamstime.com

AI generated line art courtesy of Aikonika Labs

ISBN (Print): 978-3-8382-2031-4
ISBN (E-Book [PDF]): 978-3-8382-8031-8
© *ibidem*-Verlag, Hannover • Stuttgart 2025

Leuschnerstraße 40
30457 Hannover
Germany / Deutschland
info@ibidem.eu

Alle Rechte vorbehalten

Das Werk einschließlich aller seiner Teile ist urheberrechtlich geschützt. Jede Verwertung außerhalb der engen Grenzen des Urheberrechtsgesetzes ist ohne Zustimmung des Verlages unzulässig und strafbar. Dies gilt insbesondere für Vervielfältigungen, Übersetzungen, Mikroverfilmungen und elektronische Speicherformen sowie die Einspeicherung und Verarbeitung in elektronischen Systemen.

All rights reserved. No part of this publication may be reproduced, stored in or introduced into a retrieval system, or transmitted, in any form, or by any means (electronic, mechanical, photocopying, recording or otherwise) without the prior written permission of the publisher. Any person who commits any unauthorized act in relation to this publication may be liable to criminal prosecution and civil claims for damages.

Printed in the EU

Table of Contents

Acknowledgements 7
About the Authors 11

Foreword 13
Introduction 15

Chapter One
A Primer in Russian History. Sorting Fact from Fiction 23

Chapter Two
Russians — Kyivan Rus' Successors? Not All That Glitters Is Gold:
Conflating Rus' & Russian Is an Error 39

Chapter Three
Meet the Muscovy. Russian's Real Relatives — Neither Kyivan Rus'
Nor Byzantines and Not Always Christians 51

Chapter Four
Appropriation & Extermination. Inventing a Great & Noble past
Through Cultural and Historical Theft 61

Chapter Five
Russia Appears. A Brief History in Four Acts 85

Chapter Six
The Doctrine of Russian Superiority and Other Myths Told in
Russian Dachas 123

Chapter Seven
Святая русь — the Holy Rus'. Messianism, Russia, the Roc, and the
Russian People 125

Chapter Eight
Moscow — the Third Rome Superiority of Time and Place 131

Chapter Nine
Русский мир — Russkiy Mir No Pax Romana 139

Chapter Ten
A Most Unholy Trinity. The ROC, the Moscow Patriarchate, and the
Russian State 157

Chapter Eleven
Tsar Peter I Aleksyevich Abolishes the Moscow Patriarchate (1721) 161

Chapter Twelve
The Post Petrine ROC (1917–1926) a Brief Attempt at Reform and Reinvigoration 167

Chapter Thirteen
The ROC in Modernity. An Article of the State Apparatus (1926–Present) 175

Chapter Fourteen
The Restoration of The Metropolis of Kyiv. Righting a Historic Wrong 183

Chapter Fifteen
Patriarch in All but Name. Vladimir Putin and the Russian Orthodox Faith 211

Chapter Sixteen
Waging an Unholy 'Holy War'. Absolution for Rape, Torture, Summary Execution, and Attempted Genocide 225

Chapter Seventeen
Wolves in Sheep's Clothing. ROC Clergy and Their Role in Russian State Espionage 231

Chapter Eighteen
While Europe Sleeps. Will Europe Meet the Demands of the Age? 251

Reflections
Is Renewal Possible for the ROC 263

Epilogue
Does History Provide a Way Forward? 269

Bibliography 283

Book Reviews 305

Acknowledgements

If it is our desire to spend some considerable amount of space acknowledging others for their contributions to this manuscript and others for the kind support to us it is because we believe in gratitude. No amount of ink would allow us to adequately express our gratitude or acknowledge our sincere appreciation for the countless people who have been friends or otherwise helped make this manuscript possible. Many may go unnamed for various reasons, but our indebtedness to them endures.

This work is our own. Any expression of our gratitude is not an expression of any endorsement of our research, views or opinions on their part.

We would be remiss if we failed to thank everyone kind enough to encourage our work, provide guidance, impart information or otherwise assist in the development of this manuscript. Particularly, we thank Anna Neplii, whose reporting on these issues served as an inspiration to explore them more fully. Her exceptional journalism truly inspired our work.

We also pay tribute to all the women and men who gave their lives for others in the service of freedom, liberty and the security of Ukraine and Europe. It is with gratitude and the equal regret of loss that we include Joshua Jones and Stephen Zabielski amongst those honoured heroes.

We also acknowledge the fine scholarship of others whose contributions to related research and publications are genuinely worthy of acquisition, reading and contemplation. Amongst these groundbreaking authors are Nicholas Denysenko, Kristina Stoeckl, Dmitry Uzlaner, Sarah Riccardi-Swartz and Cyril Hovorun and Archimandrite Gregory Fragkakis.

To our dear friend, Kateryna Pylypchuk, whose inscribed works poetry and prose continue to take a place of distinction in our personal library, we thank you. To the Reverend Dr. Christian Dominic Boyd, who read early drafts and provided insights and criticism, we are deeply indebted. It goes without saying that we are grateful to our publisher, Christoph Ohlwärther, for his remarkable patience in the face of our manuscript being repeatedly delayed because of our obligations to unfolding world events that at times demanded our immediate attention.

Numerous people are deserving of mention as without them this manuscript might never have been published. This most notably includes Richard Nolte to whom we are particularly obliged. We thank and salute our heroic and dutiful, patriotic Cossack comrade and friend, Valentyn Smikhun, whom we have valued in both war and peace.

We acknowledge especially the kind assistance and support of Valentyna Antonivna Sukhoviy, Solomiya Khoma, Inna Fomina, Caitlin Williams Patterson, Michael Hrycak, Konstantine Pandolfi, Oleh Hrodskyi, Andrii Kos, Svitlana Halytska, Dr. Valerii Iakovchuk and the indefatigable patriot Roxolana Wynar. We are deeply appreciative of the assistance of the extraordinary journalist and war correspondent Iaroslav Oliinyk. And to Irina Ignatenko and her family, who welcomed Miceál to their home during his service in Ukraine, we are grateful.

We owe a special debt of gratitude to Borys Pysarchuk, who was with Miceál on the frontlines in Bakhmut as well as Kostyantynivka and Studenok in Donetsk during the autumn and winter of 2022. Without question, we acknowledge the patriotism and dutiful service of Vladyslav Kyzylov, Maksym Bilyi and brothers Serhii Deineko and Serhii Vasyliovych Deineko whose service continues to prove indispensable to democracy and freedom.

We are particularly thankful to Kostas Ntatsikas and Vaso Stathopoulou, who assisted with the technical aspects of Greek language translations.

We generously acknowledge the professional encouragement of the many defense and security experts, theologians, journalists and professional colleagues who provided guidance, criticism and many of whom contributed book reviews and shared their advice and criticism in advance of publication.

It is with both reverence and pleasure that we recognise Father Gabriel of the Centre Orthodoxe du Patriarcat Oecuménique, Chambésy, for his research assistance and generosity of time while visiting Geneva and later when we met at the Phenar.

We also express our heartfelt gratitude to Archbishop Damianos and the monks of the Monastery of Saint Catherine of the Sinai, especially Father Akakios, for their generosity and kindness to Miceál while he wrote sections of this manuscript while their guest.

It is with humility and love that we acknowledge the gift that is His All Holiness Bartholomew I, Archbishop of Constantinople, New Rome, and Ecumenical Patriarch. The commitment of His All Holiness to peace and Christian unity has often been challenged by the increasingly fragmented nature of the world. None the less, The Ecumenical Patriarch's exhaustive, genuine and repeated attempts at conciliarity in the fervent hope of reaching understanding has surpassed expectations. While convening the Great and Holy Synod of the Orthodox Church on the Sunday of Pentecost, June 19, 2016, proved unable to overcome the obstinacy of the Russian Orthodox Church, it was an effort consistent with the greatness of the

Patriarchal Throne. Much to his and the world's regret, this collegial opportunity which provided a path of peace, love and reconciliation, was rejected by the Moscow Patriarch and Metropolitan Onufriy.

The decision of the Russian Orthodox Church to break with the Mother Church and the Ecumenical Patriarchate, while just another in a repetitive cycle of breaks by Russia with the universal Church, is particularly regrettable. Their prioritisation of ethnophyletism over Christian unity encourages a divide in Orthodox Christianity for the sake of promoting Russian state suzerainty at a time when the world is becoming increasingly authoritarian and obsessed with power, materialism and cults of personality to the detriment of humankind. This fracture is their failing and theirs alone.

It is without hesitation that we recognise the Ecumenical Patriarch and the Holy and Sacred Synod acted canonically and with great love, compassion and pastoral concern at a pivotal time of moral, ethical and spiritual crisis for the Church. They did so with great humanity out of concern for millions of Ukrainians crying out in pain and yet still nurturing hope. At great cost, but with immeasurable moral certitude, Ecumenical Patriarch Bartholomew I and the Holy and Sacred Synod they exemplified the kerygma of the Gospels and diakonia of the church in the service of Jesus whom we proclaim as Christ.

By righting a historic wrong in restoring the Metropolis of Kyiv to the Ecumenical Patriarchate, His All Holiness Bartholomew I and the Holy and Sacred Synod emancipated millions of Ukrainian Orthodox Christians to worship free of the coercion of their temporal and spiritual oppressors. Posterity will record it as one of the finest and most selfless moments in the Greek Orthodox Church's long history and enduring commitment to peace, love, and humanity.

On a personal note, we extend our gratitude to Father Vitalii Danchak who baptised our children and administered chrismation in our Holy Orthodox Christian faith. His fidelity to the faith and enduring kindness and friendship are most dear to us.

In a very special way, we owe a deep debt of gratitude to our families, especially Olha Shadrina, Volodymyr Shadrin and Viktoriia Slavinska. To our children, Lorcán O'Hurley and Bláithnaid O'Hurley, we thank you for your patience with us in our endless hours of research, reading, and writing.

Finally, we acknowledge our beloved spiritual father, Metropolitan Iakovos of Ireland. His leadership, friendship, benevolence, wisdom, kindness, generosity of spirit, and unwavering service to our Holy Orthodox Church have enriched our personal lives and that of our community. In ways both profound and simple, His Eminence had demonstrated his personal fidelity to the faith and corporate commitment to our Holy Orthodox Church and humankind.

ευχαριστώ.

About the Authors

Oksana Shadrina is a Ukrainian and Irish psychologist and linguist. A native of Kryvyi Rih in Ukraine's centrally located Dnipropetrovsk Oblast, Oksana is a graduate of Kyiv's Taras Shevchenko University's Faculty of Foreign Philology. Through her work with the Irish charity, she currently works to assist the Ukrainian diaspora residing in Ireland under the EU Temporary Protection Directive.

Oksana maintains her private practice as a psychologist specializing in the therapeutic method of transactional analysis. In addition to her Master of Arts degree in Psychology, Oksana earned undergraduate degrees and a Master of Arts in Philology from Taras Savchenko University. She has postgraduate certificates in several psychological and therapeutic disciplines.

Oksana received baptism and chrismation as an Orthodox Christian in secret while Ukraine was still subjugated under communism during the Soviet era. Despite the era of her childhood, Oksana was raised and educated to speak Ukrainian. She is a member of the Orthodox Church of Ukraine.

A patriot, Oksana remains a staunch advocate of Ukrainian independence. She has been instrumental in raising funds for both the Ukrainian armed forces and humanitarian causes in Ukraine since 2014.

For her charitable, volunteer and other philanthropic work, Oksana has been recognised by the United States Congress with a proclamation honoring her civic and philanthropic achievements. She is a recipient of the Orthodox Church of Ukraine's Order of Liberty, conferred by His Beatitude Epiphany I, Metropolitan of Kyiv and All Ukraine.

Miceál O'Hurley is an Irish and American academic, author, researcher, and media professional. He specialises in defense and security issues, international conflict resolution and mediation. Miceál is accredited to the United Nations Economic and Social Council. He is a Chatham House Member.

Miceál has frequently appeared as an expert defense and security analyst on networks including international networks like Al-Qahera News Network, CNN, BBC and Al Jazeera. His commentary on diplomacy has included Türkiye's flagship TRT World, Egypt's Al-Qahera News Channel and Alghed News, Iraq's Al-Ahed TV, Canada's CTV and CBC, the European Diplomat and other news outlets and journals. Miceál is a member of the Overseas Press Club of America, the Foreign Press Association and has been an accredited journalist to the Holy See.

Miceál's work has been featured and published in leading international publications. His previous publications have explored the intersections of faith and society, notably examining the Irish American immigrant experience in New York; Christian philanthropy and stewardship; the ethics of *Ma'aser* and *Tzedakah* in Judaism; and inter-ethnic and religious polity in the late Byzantine Empire.

Continuing his post graduate education, Miceál completed coursework and programmes at institutions including the Universiteit Leiden; Yale Law School, University of Windsor College of Law; University of London — Centre for International Studies & Diplomacy; Higher School of Economics — National Research University of Moscow; St. Petersburg State University, United States Institute for Peace (USIP); University of Limerick — Irish Peace Institute; the Organization for Security and Cooperation in Europe (OSCE); and others.

Miceál is active in the field of philanthropy and community service. Previously, he worked as a development officer in the Archdiocese of New York and the Armenian Diocese of America. He served as spokesperson and communications director for the Pontifical Visit to the United States of His Holiness Karekin II, Supreme Patriarch and Catholicos of All Armenians.

In 1992, Miceál was awarded the Congressional Achievement Award. He was created a Knight of the Order of St. George (KStG) (UK Grand Priory) and has been inducted into the Equestrian Order of Saint Michael Archangel. He is a Life Member of the Veterans of Foreign Wars (VFW). Miceál was named a Fellow of the Royal Lion of the Levant Society, amongst other honors.

Miceál belongs to the Holy Orthodox Metropolis of Ireland (Ecumenical Patriarchate) and Exarchate of Celtic Sea. He is a member of the Orthodox Canon Law Society of North America.

Together, Oksana and Miceál have two children and reside in Ireland.

Foreword

There are books that merely inform, and there are books that awaken the conscience of their time. *Wolves in Sheep's Clothing: The Russian Orthodox Church's Threat to European Security and Democracy* belongs firmly to the latter category. It is a work of courage and precision, one that exposes dangers too often neglected or misunderstood in their depth. In these pages, Miceál O'Hurley and Oksana Shadrina undertake the difficult task of revealing the hidden ties between the Russian Orthodox Church and the Kremlin's state apparatus—ties that transform faith into a weapon and liturgy into a mask for political aggression.

What the reader encounters here is not simply a historical reconstruction, but a critical analysis of the mythology on which Moscow builds its claim to the so-called Russkiy Mir. The authors demonstrate how the blending of sacred and political language within the Russian tradition is far from a harmless cultural peculiarity; it is, rather, an instrument of domination and a justification for expansionism. O'Hurley and Shadrina trace these dynamics across the centuries—from Kyivan Rus' to the Tsarist empire, from the Soviet era to the present war against Ukraine—untangling the threads with scholarly rigour and presenting them with a clarity that makes this book accessible not only to specialists but to every thoughtful citizen.

This book is also a warning. It insists that Europe's security and democracy cannot be understood apart from the ideological and spiritual narratives that Russia wields so effectively. What is at stake is not a theological debate, but a hybrid form of warfare in which the language of the Gospel is appropriated for propaganda and the notion of holiness is cynically invoked to sanctify violence. For this reason, the book is both timely and indispensable.

Yet the value of this work lies not only in its subject but also in the voices of its authors. Oksana Shadrina, born in Kryvyi Rih, Ukraine, brings to these pages not only academic training as a psychologist and linguist but also the lived experience of her people's struggle. Baptized in secret under Soviet rule, she embodies both the resilience of faith and the clarity of witness. Today, she continues to serve her community in Ireland and to advocate for Ukraine with unwavering devotion. Her voice here is both that of a scholar and that of a witness—a woman who has endured the shadow of oppression and yet speaks with hope for freedom and dignity.

Miceál O'Hurley, by contrast, approaches the subject from the vantage point of an Irish and American academic, journalist, and security analyst. With decades of work in diplomacy, international conflict resolution, and defense studies, he combines the discipline of scholarship with the insight of lived professional experience. His commentary has been sought by media and policy circles across the globe, not because it flatters but because it illuminates. For him, truth is not an abstraction but a moral obligation.

Together, O'Hurley and Shadrina form a rare synthesis: Reason and experience, analysis and testimony, history and present reality. Their collaboration yields a book that is not only intellectually rigorous but ethically weighty. It speaks with the authority of evidence and documentation, yet also with the quiet passion of those who believe justice is possible.

To read *Wolves in Sheep's Clothing* is to confront one of the most insidious threats to the free world: an evil cloaked in the garments of virtue, a sermon that conceals aggression, a sanctuary turned into a staging ground for power. It is a book that should not leave the reader unmoved. It is a summons to vigilance, to critical reflection, and to the defense of values older and nobler than any empire: human dignity, spiritual freedom, and democratic solidarity.

Let this work be read not only as an academic analysis but also as a moral stance. For in the end, the question is not merely what the Russian Orthodox Church represents today, but what kind of future we desire for Europe—and for the world.

Iordan Georgiev, Lawyer, Theologian,
International Relations Specialist and
Editor-in-Chief of Doxologia Infonews Sofia, Bulgaria

Introduction

The thrust of this manuscript is to focus on the threat posed by the Russian Orthodox Church (ROC) to European security and democracy. It would be both impossible and imprudent not to address the *esse* of the ROC and the Russian state in both history and modernity in so doing. This requires an examination of the inextricably intertwined doctrinal concepts of the *русский мир* (*Russkiy Mir* – *Russian world*) and its religious counterpart in Russian Orthodox Christianity, *Святая Русь* (*Holy Rus'*). The interrelatedness of the *Russkiy Mir* and the *Holy Rus'* concepts in the life of the ROC and in turn, its role as a quasi-State agency within the Russian Federation security apparatus and propaganda machine,[1] will necessarily be explored.

The idea of the *Russkiy Mir* lies at the heart of the driving ideology requiring a unity of Russian military, political and cultural superiority within the Russian sphere. The ROC, that singular institution that survived Russian Tsardom and the Soviet Union into the modern Russian Federation was unique in its ability to permeate and provide continuity in perpetuating the military, political and cultural traditions for the average *Russian*. Unique in its span of Russian history and institutions, the ROC alone could sustain the concept of the *Russkiy Mir* with its unique philosophical construct of the Holy Rus' throughout Russia's turbulent history.

It follows then that the ROC, led by the Moscow Patriarchate, was pursued by the emerging politicians of the neophyte Russian Federation to create the *Russkiy Mir* as its very continuity in the dark days of the founding of the modern Russian state. At that time, the ROC provided the only stable aspect of Russian society. In equal measure, the Moscow patriarchate quickly realized it would benefit from its idiosyncratic relationship with the Russian state to realize the *telos* of the *Holy Rus'*.

A historic analysis of the early days of the leadership of both the Russian Federation and Moscow Patriarch reveals that Aleksei Mikhailovich Ridiger, known as Alexy II, Patriarch of Moscow and all Rus', believed he enjoyed a position superior to that of the first democratically elected Russian President, Boris Nikolayevich Yeltsin. The need for Yeltsin to court the favour of the only institution surviving from Tsardom to Communism and

---

[1] Marcin Składanowski, Andrjez Szabaciuk and Agnieszka Łukasik-Turecka, "Church of war: propaganda and disinformation in Patriarch Kirill's discourse on Russia's aggression", *Cogent Arts & Humanities*, 2025.

into the present, a body representing Russia's largest single voting bloc, the ROC, was abundantly evident. Yeltsin's relatively weak position also rendered the relationship with the ROC and the Moscow Patriarch imperative.

Yeltsin pledged to return church property confiscated during the Soviet era, thus ensuring that Alexy II would promote his election through his proxy clergy.[2] The scheme worked. Yeltsin emerged victorious, and Alexy II secured his position and that of the ROC as indispensable powerbrokers for the Russian state. By 1996, the symbiotic relationship between the Kremlin and the Moscow Patriarchate was complete. The benefits of the Russian State and ROC combining to reach their non-exclusive goals proved irresistible to the Russian President and the Moscow Patriarch. Clergy of the ROC actively campaigned for Yeltsin's re-election in pulpits from St. Petersburg to Vladivostok.[3] In exchange, the ROC was given unique access to Russian schools and institutions to the point of excluding other confessions of faith.

Consequently, while this is not a theological treatise, to achieve any real understanding of the why and how the ROC is a threat to European security and democracy, it is incumbent upon us to parse the concept of the *Holy Rus'* and its relationship to the political agenda of the Russkiy Mir.

The centrality of the Russkiy Mir and Holy Rus', in the minds of most Russians, comes not only from self-awareness acquired by familial, religious, and cultural inheritance alone. What is learned at home and in the church is reinforced and enhanced by politicized state propaganda, policy and construct. The neo-imperialist school engineered the doctrine of the Russkiy Mir as the *dogmata generalia* of the military, political, and social ideal of all Russians. Likewise, the ROC has developed the Holy Rus' concept as its *dogmata specialia*.

It was not by chance that in 2007, Russian President Vladimir Vladimirovich Putin created a government-funded vehicle to project Russia's soft power both domestically and internationally, giving it the name the Russkiy Mir Foundation. The goals and reach of the foundation are rooted in the core missions of its founding bodies — the Ministry of Foreign Affairs of the Russian Federation and the Ministry of Education and Science of the Russian Federation.

Unsurprisingly, the Russkiy Mir is projected worldwide in various means and domestically through traditional and cultural curriculum heavily influenced by the ROC, as enshrined in Holy Rus' doctrine. Any critical

---

2   Alexander Rahr, "Yeltsin Campaigning," *Radio Free Europe/Radio Liberty*, 4 June 1991.
3   Alessandra Stanley, "Church Leans Towards Yeltsin in Russian Vote", *New York Times*, 30 May 1996.

observer of Russia's conduct in their illegal occupations in Moldova, Georgia and Ukraine can easily point to Russia's invocation of language and cultural deprivation coupled with supposed discrimination of the ROC as *cassis belli* to achieve their military, political, and cultural goals of creating a new Russian empire.

The *Russkiy Mir's* realization depends on the belief that neighboring countries and their peoples are somehow inherently Russian and must be converted to embrace the doctrine of the Holy Rus' — that God has set aside Russia for the sanctification of the world and created the Russian people to enlighten humanity. Russia's eliminationist policy towards its neighbors' identities is the natural fruition of the pairing of the Russkiy Mir and Holy Rus'. Only by the Kremlin enjoying suzerainty over its neighbours through military means, by imposing political and cultural influence and ultimately by subjugating its neighbors to the Moscow Patriarchate and the ROC can Russia's goals be made whole.

We argue, and there is ample evidence to support our thesis, that the ROC operates as an organ of Russia's state security apparatus. Through intercepts and intelligence operations, it has emerged that the Patriarch of Moscow himself directs his clergy to be disruptive agents on behalf of the Russian state.[4] By venturing well beyond the exercise of soft power activities and its core diakonia, the ROC has exceeded norms long universally acknowledged as necessary for the free exercise of religious freedom by engaging in legitimate cultural and religious activities. At the same time, the sins of some of the sons and daughters of the church cannot reflect on the entirety of faith when those activities pit service to the state over fidelity to the gospels and humanity; the pervasiveness of the problem cannot be easily ignored.

The Moscow Patriarchate has sanctioned acts by its clergy that have proven it operates not solely as a religious institution proclaiming the Russian Orthodox faith but routinely engages in the corruption of the norms of proclaiming the gospel and administering the sacraments of the church. This has included promoting and rewarding pro-war activities, knowingly undertaking in the dissemination of Russian state propaganda and at times engaging in espionage, even by the most senior members of its clergy.[5]

---

[4] Nicholas Chkhaidze, "Moscow Uses Russian Orthodox Church as Covert Foreign Policy Tool in Ukraine and the West", *Eurasia Daily Monitor, Volume 21, Issue 55*, 10 April 2024.

[5] Following his conviction by the Vinnitsa Court of Appeal on evidence for justifying the Russian war against Ukraine, Ukrainian Orthodox Church (Moscow Patriarchate) Metropolitan Jonathan of Tulchin and Bratislava was released to Patriarch Kirill of Moscow, who decorated him with the Order of St. Sergius of Radonezh (1st degree) on 9 June 2024. The decoration was awarded despite claims by the Ukrainian Orthodox Church (Moscow Patriarchate) that it had

What marks the activities of the ROC as distinct is its willingness to subordinate its Orthodox Christian identity and values to those of the political affairs of the Russian State.

A direct consequence of such conduct is the tension created between European capitals' attempts to provide for domestic security and the free exercise of democracy, and tolerating the divergence of the ROC from activities normally associated with necessary salvation as it is understood in Christianity.

Orthodox Christian unity became severely fractured when the ROC decided to withdraw from communion with the Ecumenical Patriarchate of Constantinople unilaterally and set about suppressing the exercise of religious freedom in Russia and temporarily Russian-occupied Ukraine.[6]

The ROC, domestically and abroad, has followed the lead of the Patriarch of Moscow in assisting the Russian state to co-opt both the Russian faithful and societies in which they dwell in service of the *Russkiy Mir*. While there is nothing inherently wrong with this, when the clergy of the ROC proclaim participation in an illegal invasion and attempted annexation of their neighbor's lands to be acts of Christian virtue, such that it serves as a plenary indulgence of sins, the church departs from the norms of Christianity.[7] That ROC clergy use their pulpits to spread propaganda at the expense of preaching the Gospel puts faith in conflict with a neighboring state's right to security. It becomes problematic not just for their faithful, but for the states in which these ideas are proclaimed and promoted by Russian clergy.

The willingness of the ROC Outside of Russia (ROCOR) and the ROC in Western Europe to align themselves with the Moscow Patriarchate raises genuine security concerns. The Moscow Patriarchate's willing submission to the Russian state marks it as distinct from the rest of Christendom. The very reach of the ROC across Western Europe, North America and throughout the world creates specific security concerns for its host countries.

ROCOR claims some 232 parishes and ten monasteries in the United States, comprised of 92,000 declared adherents and over 9000 regular church attendees. There are at least 49 identifiable ROCOR parishes dis-

---

canonically broken with the Moscow Patriarchate and was an autocephalous church. Estonia refused to renew the residence permit of the head of the Russian Orthodox Church in Estonia, Metropolitan Eugene (secular name Valery Reshetnikov), for reasons of "national security". These are not isolated cases.

6 Andreja Bogdanovski, "Russia is violating religious freedom in occupied territories, says Ukraine", *Church Times*, 17 April 2025.
7 Wire Service, "Orthodox Church leader says Russian soldiers dying in Ukraine will be cleansed of sin", *Reuters*, 26 October 2022.

tributed across Europe, in addition to the 71 parishes claimed by the Archdiocese of ROC in Western Europe.[8] With the ROC willing to promote state interests, even when they are repugnant to Christian values, the presence of the church in friendly lands proves irresistible to the Moscow Patriarchate, promoting the destabilization of Europe and the Americas for the purposes of striking a blow at social cohesion under the guise of religious freedom.

The security concerns of host nations are not merely intellectual. Bulgaria, Estonia, Georgia, North Macedonia, Sweden, and Ukraine have either been forced to expel ROC clergy for spying or espionage or otherwise working to assail domestic social cohesion. Sweden withdrew funding for Moscow Patriarchate churches and institutions because they have been designated "State security risks."[9] In the case of Czechia, the government imposed sanctions on the Patriarch of Moscow, Kirill Gundyayev, personally.[10] Other European states have found it necessary to follow suit.

The response from the ROC was predictable—"persecution!" There is abundant evidence that Russian Orthodox clergy, in worrying numbers, are caught acting as agents of the Russian state security apparatus at the personal direction of the Patriarch of Moscow. A memorandum retrieved in a counter espionage operation outlining the "system of cooperation" "between the [Russian Orthodox] Church and several Russian spy agencies, including the SVR, the GRU, and the FSB", is believed by security analysts, with "high confidence" to have been approved by Patriarch Kirill personally.[11]

For the faithful and those who deal with the ROC, the inability to rely on conversations with clergy remaining confidential, concerns that the seal of the confessional would not be kept sacrosanct, or that information shared with the ROC might be misused, has a deleterious impact on the engagement of the faithful with clergy. It strikes at the heart of the intimacy of the Orthodox Christian faith experience and undermines confidence in the church.

---

[8] Archdiocese of Russian Orthodox Churches in Western Europe, "Archevêché des églises orthodoxes de tradition russe en Europe occidentale, Patriarcat de Moscou", *Archevêché des églises orthodoxes de tradition russe en Europe occidentale*, retrieved 8 November 2024.

[9] Yagiz Efe Parmaksiz, "Swedish agency cuts support to Russian Orthodox Church over intelligence concerns", *Türkiye Today*, 3 June 2024.

[10] Eirini Kongkini, "Russian Orthodox Church: Spycraft and Statecraft Overlay Faith", *Greydynamics*, 18 February 2025.

[11] Andrei Soldatov and Irina Borogan, "Putin's Useful Priests: The Russian Orthodox Church and the Kremlin's Hidden Influence Campaign in the West", *Foreign Affairs*, 14 September 2023.

The indelible consequence of such conduct by the ROC is that it is legitimately both loathed and feared as a tool of the Kremlin instead of appreciated as an ecclesial body working for the salvation of humanity.[12] It is these very dynamics and the threat they pose to European security and democracy with which this manuscript is concerned. Having briefly addressed the necessity of this work, it brings us to the issue of how we present the information that supports our thesis and how we present it.

Of course, the difficulty in writing a work such as this is confronting an audience with varied perspectives and understandings of the issues presented. Some professionals in the fields of theology, security, public policy, or diplomacy are likely to be informed by their professions and may find the work lacking in esoteric content. For the non-specialist, the public approaching this work for the first time, in-depth, it may at times present unfamiliar language, concepts, and ideas. Consequently, adopting a writing style and lexicon that appeals to all readers is difficult. We appreciate the reader's understanding of this dynamic.

To those without the specific background knowledge necessary to distinguish between the complex theological premises and institutional norms that underpin Orthodox Christian ecclesiology may prove challenging. Still, we hope our work is presented in both an inviting and informative way that engages all readers, despite it at times being a "deep dive" into specific aspects of the topics addressed herein.

Others, whose understanding of the Russkiy Mir may have been shaped by their early education and the imperialist Russian history presented during in Cold War era classrooms, may resist accepting information that counters conventional wisdom. Still other readers will be forced to confront their personal experience of Russia and the Russian Federation and may find what we present to be a direct challenge to what they have adopted unconsciously.

We are inviting readers to confront history and modernity without information having been mediated by tsarist imperialism, communism or the neo-imperialism embraced by Putin and his regime. It is not simply a matter of introducing historical and institutional nuances. This work will directly challenge the rote history and understanding of Russia, Russians and the ROC for many readers. This is understandable. It may only be that with the benefit of hindsight, perspective and the recovery of national memory and critical historical research that has developed over the last 30-some odd years, that an openness to truth and genuine knowledge might be considered.

---

[12] Pål Kolstø and Helge Blakkisrud, "Not So Traditional After All? The Russian Orthodox Church's Failure as a "Moral Norm Entrepreneur"", *PONARS Eurasia*, 4 October 2021.

We have tried to provide a content-rich work, well-researched, documented and yet presented in a readable manuscript. We trust that this work presents information sometimes hinted at in the media, explored variously in specialised policy analysis, but rarely addressed in a consolidated, comprehensive manner, exploring the interchange of the various topics of theology, geography, civics, politics, national security, ethnography, and other disciplines.

As to the ROC, its faithful, and the future? Being Orthodox Christians, we each recognise and celebrate that there is much inherently beautiful and worthwhile in Russian Orthodox Christianity. It is not, however, the sole depository of truth and tradition as practiced today. Despite Putin and the Patriarch of Moscow claiming it to be the defender of Christian values, it is often not. The ROC's focus on masculinity, authority, power, and state promotion has made it an active agent engaged in the privation of due good.

The ROC and the state it serves to the detriment of its historic essence present a real and present danger to Europe and Orthodox Christianity and their shared values of peace, cooperation, and democratic values. When the Moscow Patriarchate declared the illegal and immoral invasion of Ukraine to be a "holy war"[13] the ROC abdicated its moral, ethical, scriptural, and conciliatory authority.

The very idea of Russia's 'special military operation' to seize all of Ukraine in Putin's quest to erect a new Russian empire as a "holy war"[14] It is a betrayal of the meaning of the Resurrection of Jesus, who is Christ. The gospels and the church proclaim Jesus Christ as Ἁγία Σοφία [Holy Wisdom].[15] For this reason we are left to either embrace the ROC's teaching that waging illegal war on one's neighbors, committing war crimes, engaging in torture, non-judicial killings, and causing wanton misery in the name of God conforms to the teachings of Jesus Christ or we are compelled to entirely reject Patriarch Kirill's and the ROC's declaration of a "holy war".

Contrary to the *Prayer of the Holy Rus'* authored by Patriarch Kirill, it is not God's will for Russian soldiers to kill their Orthodox Christian sisters and brothers in the name of Russia's revanchist pursuit. Patriarch Kirill's elevation of violence to being an act of Christian virtue, complete with the promise of the remission of sins, is a declaration that the Russian war dead

---

[13] Riley Bailey, Christina Harward, Angelica Evans, and George Barros, "The Russian Orthodox Church Declares "Holy War" Against Ukraine and Articulates Tenets of Russia's Emerging Official Nationalist Ideology", *Institute for the Study of War Press,* 30 March 2024.

[14] Jonathan Luxmoore, "Russian 'Holy War' declaration condemned", *Church Times,* 5 April 2024.

[15] cf 1 Corinthians, 1:24.

are tantamount to being martyrs.[16] It is the very definition of heresy and the promotion of evil, and remains uniquely unorthodox.

Still, we must believe that the ROC, sharing in the Mystical Body of Christ, is not beyond redemption. We hope this work causes those within its ranks to reassess their role in the salvific ministry of the church left to us by Jesus and pick up the cross and return to Christ's earthly mission, rejecting war, the subjugation of neighbors, and the oppression of the weak.

For persons outside of Orthodox Christianity, we hope they, too, join in the hope for the restoration of the ROC to its true mission and character. Only with genuine ecclesiastic leadership can the Moscow Patriarch eschew its present path of pursuing a primacy of power at the cost of unity, sowing division, breeding unhappiness and promoting a Thrasymachusene culture of cynical realism where "might makes right" displaces servant leadership in service to the gospel and humanity. The Moscow Patriarchate's breach of unity with the Ecumenical Patriarchate represents not only an injury to Orthodox Christianity but also serves as a declaration of Moscow's aspirations to supplant Constantinople as the centre of Christendom.[17]

Miceál O'Hurley & Oksana Shadrina
Eochill, Contae Chorcaí, Eire
October 2025

---

[16] Jonathan Zecher, "What makes a martyr? The proclamation of Patriarch Kirill and the question of sacred violence", *ABC Religion and Ethics*, 17 October 2022.

[17] Jan Strzelecki, "Moskwa-Konstantynopol. Nowa schizma w prawosławiu?", *Ośrodek Studiów Wschodnich*, 17 Październik 2018.

Chapter One

A Primer in Russian History
Sorting Fact from Fiction

In his latest book, *Medievalisms and Russia: The Contest for Imaginary Pasts*, scholar Eugene Smelyansky quips, "If truth is the first casualty of war, history is its first battlefield." He is correct.

Apologists and propagandists often occupy Russia's historical space. In recent scholarly publications, lecture halls, classrooms, and online forums, the discourse about Russian history has increasingly been consumed by battles over its accuracy, purpose and contextualization. As so much of Russia's current domestic and foreign policy is predicated on the assertions that Russia is the sole heir to the Kyivan Rus', it becomes incumbent upon the west to make new investigations and judgments about Russian history and its service to the Russkiy Mir.

The idea that Rus' and Russian are somehow synonymous or that the Russian Federation or Russians are the successors of the Kyivan Rus' is specious at best. Only recently has external research begun to challenge the overtly mythological imperial history that Russia proclaims as truth. Why has it taken so long to challenge the rote version of Russian history, which claims its grounding in heroic cultures and kingdoms, epic battles in the defense of Baltic, eastern European and Slavic states and peoples and a worldview that Russia is the defender of Christian civilisation being threatened by western liberalism and democracy?

Several factors militate toward explaining the disinclination of academic examination or the tardiness of any genuine scrutiny of Russia's historical narrative. As modern Russia's foundations lie in pre-history, the absence of a detailed or written history of the *Moksel* people who inhabited the region that forms the core of the Russian Federation allowed the Muscovy, the Russian Empire, the Soviets, and the neo-imperialists of the Russian Federation to invent their own history. They did, and they did it to create a political, religious, and cultural history asserting their ascendency as the Holy Rus' having been pre-ordained.

With an eye cast to the developed west, Muscovy was desirous of throwing off the shackles of the Far East. Suzerainty by the waning Mongol Horde and Türkic khanates that governed the Principality of Muscovy until c. 1480 provided a window of opportunity to emerge independent of their former eastern masters. Inventing a flattering history, a veritable hagiographic historiography, offered their princes a way of coalescing their various peoples to embrace a common sense of nationhood.

When Muscovy sought integration in Europe, the history it had devised to engage in nation-building needed revision. A 'new history' replete with more ancient European roots in a lineage grounded in the empires of Rome, Greece, and Byzantium shared by the west, was a means of inducting themselves as part of a Europe propelled toward the nascent Enlightenment. Claiming a Kyivan Rus' heritage gave Muscovy all it desired — a Christian background, a share in the glories of ancient Hellenistic and Roman cultures, a claim on advanced civilizations, and an individual identity. All of this and more laid the foundations for the emergence of a new state — Russia. It came into being late in the European annals, only in 1721, making it just slightly older by a few years than the New World's Canada and the United States.

Having clothed themselves in ancient European history by undeservedly claiming the mantle of the Kyivan Rus', the princes of Muscovy justified themselves as possessors of the divine right of kings shared by their European counterparts. The journey from proto-Slavic tribes to a nation of Muscovy was exhausted. The aspirations of the Holy Rus' quest to entitle themselves to be known as the 'Third Rome' laid bare the Principality of Muscovy's ambitions. The transformation from nation to country was necessary to make their empire possible. The very title of their political leaders' new styling, царь [tsar, based on the Latin 'caesar' and its Russian derivation каїsар], spoke volumes about the path they set themselves. To become an empire, they would have to invent an even newer history, requiring further and more outlandish historical distortions.

The emergence of tsars came at a point when the Principality of Muscovy began engaging with Europe in earnest. European kingdoms were nearly ignorant of Muscovy's existence. They did not possess any real knowledge of their history beyond general lore. At the time, almost no independent historical research had been conducted about the underdeveloped, frozen wastelands to the east. The world was left to adopt the latest imperial version of Russian history available. It was not a history of facts, dates, and events. Russia's history was written from the ink well of dynastic political necessity, the perpetuation of power, and imperial promotion. From the beginning, Russian history was written for political projection, not historical preservation.

By these means, the world came to accept the history of Russia that Putin and his new nationalists and neo-imperialists now exploit yet further to justify their territorial claims undergirding their goal of the Holy Rus' achieving a Russkiy Mir.

Russian history is not, however, imperial in either nature or construct. Between 1917–1999, there were small windows where genuine historical research, criticism, and publication were possible. The Soviet Union had no use for the hagiographic history of the tsarist epoch. The Soviets preferred a history skewed toward political judgment, socialist promotion, and regime justification. The Russian Federation only briefly allowed free academic research without severe reprisals, including imprisonment, for anything that challenged the state and its propaganda. There has never been a domestic appetite or industry for deconstructing Russia's historical record. We must therefore rely on the good scholarship and recovery of the history of those states previously oppressed by imperial Russia and the Soviet Union to fully understand Russia's history and its importance for modernity.

The consequence of all this is that the requisite understanding of Russia required to engage and respond with it effectively necessarily requires the west's general populations, institutions, scholars, analysts, and politicians, all of whom have invested in the imperial Russian history that prevailed for the last two-and-a-half centuries, to be open to the idea that they have been wrong. This is a big challenge.

Only by taking a 'deep dive' into these matters can we begin to engage with Russia in constructive ways, while it shows a propensity toward the combative. While insufficient for any 'deep dive', this work should provide a sufficient basis to begin the enquiry necessary to understand Russia better and why the ROC represents a threat to European security and democracy and strikes at the heart of European social cohesion.

The difficulty in approaching the subject of Russian history is that modern propaganda and apologism echo the same dubious imperial history that permeated the west's uncritical understanding of Russia since the 17th century. Every new appeal to reconsider our understanding of Russian history, Russians, the Kremlin, and the Moscow Patriarchate's propaganda lures us back to the comfort of being satisfied with what we had always accepted as true. A new dialectic is required.

During the imperial epoch, the Soviet era, and the immediate post-Soviet period, the acceptance of the Russian version of history that permeated western thought proved an oddly acceptable basis for discourse with Russia. After all, the intense censorship of the imperial epoch and indifference to history by the Soviets, except as a means of political judgment along socialist lines, meant Russians and the west shared a similar understanding of history, albeit a corrupt one.

It is only since the re-emergence of states formerly under the Russian yoke that independent research and the region's recovery of national memory had liberal access to the records by which Russia's distorted history could be contrasted became accessible. This collision of fact versus fiction has served as a point of confrontation between the Kremlin, Moscow Patriarchate and the states previously within the Russian sphere. What they seek to recover, Russia would prefer to control.

Domestically, Putin has done his utmost to suppress independent historical research, including violently suppressing then outlawing organizations like Memorial, which delved into Russia's Soviet era sins. All the while, the Moscow Patriarchate and Patriarch Kirill himself have remained silent collaborators in the suppression and criminalization of free speech, academic freedom, religious liberty, and promotion of truth.

The collusion by silence dynamic is not limited to Russia proper. In August 2025, Putin visited Joint Base Elmendorf-Richardson for his summit with President Donald Trump. The Russian Orthodox Bishop of Sitka and Alaska greeted Putin, exchanged gifts, and they prayed together. There was no hint of reproachment by Archbishop Alexei Trader for the litany of Russian state-sanctioned poisonings, assassinations, or political murders that have occurred under Putin's reign of office. Nowhere did Bishop Alexei condemn the Russian state's glorification of war or renounce the Moscow Patriarch's endorsement of the invasion of Ukraine as a 'holy war'.

The willingness of Russian Orthodox clergy and faithful to endorse the wanton evil unleashed by the Russian state has become so normalized that a Russian Orthodox bishop embraces the very man who ordered the war, endorsed the kidnapping and trafficking of children to Russia, bears responsibility for instigating a war that kills tens of thousands of civilians and soldiers year-by-year and is wanted for arrest by the International Criminal Court. When the ROC turns the American-born son of a Methodist minister and now Russian Orthodox Bishop of Sitka and Alaska into an ally of a man whose conduct is an affront to God and humanity, it is time to consider the extent to which the ROC poses a threat to European security and democracy, if not that of the world.

Fortunately, there was a brief respite where the ROC had an opportunity to shake itself loose from the Russian state. Throughout the former Russian sphere, things changed with the re-emergence of free, sovereign states. Each was understandably anxious to recover their inherent dignity and identity thus requiring a re-discovery of their own history. Inevitably, as each state re-emerged and asserted its own language, culture, history, religious freedom, ethnic and political identity, an unavoidable clash with what had always been promoted as Russian history erupted.

In response, Russia claimed victimhood, citing hostile 'Russophobic' enemies from the west who were trying to destroy it. Many Russians fell into the trap of defending the clearly false history of the past under the guise of patriotism and nationalism. Much to the delight of the Kremlin and Moscow Patriarchate, Russians and their allies have become willingly obdurate in their ignorance in service to the Russian state by maintaining the false historical narrative.

Russian nationalists like Putin discovered embracing the imperial past to be a useful tool in their domestic and international disinformation and hybrid warfare arsenal. They contended that a demoralized and nearly bankrupt Russian Federation should still be considered a superpower. To their way of thinking, tolerating the independence of formerly occupied neighbors represents an unacceptable, direct challenge to a Russia for whom *мирное сосуществование* [peaceful co-existence] had always been a popular political slogan. In reality, it remained anathema.

As acceptance and understanding appear to be traits absent in Putin and the neo-imperialists with whom he has surrounded himself, they believe there is only one alternative—to subdue Russia's neighbors and return them to the Russian sphere where the historical, cultural, ethnological, religious, and political narrative can be controlled. The danger of Russians discovering the truth about their genuine history holds the real possibility of destabilizing the Putin regime and throwing Russia into turmoil once again.

For Putin, any historical awakening outside Russia's borders that could carry over to the Russian people would be, "a tragedy as for the vast majority of the country's citizens"[18] and a crisis Putin is not willing to suffer again. He fears what he has come to call the "colour revolutions" whose targets have always been Russian-friendly, illiberal regimes. Unsurprisingly, we are seeing the evil fruits of Russia's intolerance for the independence of its neighbors from Transnistria to South Ossetia and Abkhazia to Ukraine and the whole of Europe that daily undergoes the Kremlin's destabilization efforts.[19]

Any modern critical analysis that confronts the new nationalist and neo-imperialist historical cultism that defines the Russian Federation's view of history is deemed an illegitimate academic pursuit and political treason. Censorship promoted by the Kremlin and the Moscow Patriarchate has rendered academic honesty an attack upon Russia. Despite Article 29 of the Russian Constitution prohibiting censorship, all historical analysis that contradicts the Russian state narrative or public officials who espouse it has been criminalized in law.[20]

---

[18] Mikhail Metzel, "Putin calls dissolution of USSR tragedy and 'collapse of historical Russia'", *TASS*, 12 December 2021.

[19] Seth G. Jones, "Russia's Shadow War Against the West", *Centre for Strategic and International Studies* (CSIS), 18 March 2025.

[20] Государственная Дума Российской Федерации, "Законопроект №1074945-7 «О внесении изменения в статью 128-1, Уголовного кодекса Российской

Be it under the tsars or the presidency of Putin, a zero-tolerance policy concerning critical historical scrutiny and analysis prevails in Russia. Unsurprisingly, Russian academics who seek to enhance the credibility of Russian scholarship are either suppressed or removed from their teaching posts:

> As Russian social policy analysts working in international academic networks, we are deeply alarmed about current developments in our country which make it harder and harder for us to continue with our work. We believe that if these trends cannot be stopped, Russian social scientists will become as isolated again as they were before 1989; by the same token, international scholars outside Russia might have lesser access to information about our country, or to do research here.[21]

In Putin's mind, and those of his imperial predecessors, the duty of history and the medium by which it is asserted, as well as the very texts from which it is taught, have one overriding responsibility to "foster a sense of pride for one's history and one's country."[22]

It is necessary, therefore, to deconstruct Russia's asserted history to appreciate and consider its authentic history.

Any understanding of Russia and the ROC in the 21st century requires a willingness to parse the foundations, purposes, and means of projecting Russian history's political bias by employing realism and other critical methods in historical analysis. This will not be forthcoming from Russia. The west must become stalwart critics of Russian history, not to degrade Russia as 'Russophobes', but to reach a realistic understanding of Russia, her people and her politics to defend the democratic principles and social cohesion so critical to Europe's security and existence.

Just over 700 years ago, at the very foundation of the Principality of Muscovy, political leaders understood all too well the power of history to create a nation, shape public opinion, and underpin their political aspirations. Some 400 years would pass before that same Mongol Horde *ulus* would morph into Russia. In the intervening years, the practice of distorting history for political purposes remained the same. Russian history was recorded, chronicled, created, and even invented in the service of princes, tsars, Soviet premiers and now the equally illiberal president of the Russian Federation.

Федерации»", *Москва, Кремль*, 30 декабря 2020 (Вступил в силу 10 января 2021).

[21] Pavel Romanov and Elena Iarskaia-Smirnova, "'Foreign agents' in the field of social policy research: The demise of civil liberties and academic freedom in contemporary Russia", *Journal of European Social Policy*, 2015.

[22] Masha Lipman, "Rewriting History for Putin", *Washington Post*, 22 March 2004.

Russian history is not a compendium of reliable information supported by research, archaeology, critical analysis, and complementary disciplines such as is embraced in the west. In Europe and throughout the west, history provides a dialectic by which we can begin to understand the development of peoples, societies, nations, and states through their interrelatedness and influence in the progression of humanity. For Russians, history is but a tool in service to the state.

If Russia complains the west does not understand them (and they do complain), it is because neither Russia nor the west is engaged in dialogue about the same things. When it comes to Russian aggression and military occupations to topple western-friendly governments, the disparity of world views is on full display. If the west protests Russia's occupation of its neighbors, cites a lack of respect for international law[23] and asserts Europe's post-World War II rules-based system of world order, Russia responds as if a different question was asked. Russia, ever imbued with an abundant sense of paranoia, answers the issue as an entitlement to self-defense and what it believes is its inherent right to restore a greater Russia.

While the west cites law, treaties, and obligations, Russia argues history, culture, and language. The west points to Russia's voluntary recognition of Ukraine's 1991 sovereign borders, while Russia evokes the complex, convoluted, ancient, historical territorial claims arising from their specious claims of being the "sole successors" of the Kyivan Rus'. Europe decries forced passportisation and cites Russia's post-World War II transplanting of Russians into Ukraine's Donbas and Crimea, claiming them to be historically Russian. It is a never-ending cycle of dialogue at cross purposes.

Only once the west and Russia resolve that each is talking past the other with regard to Armenia, Estonia, Georgia, Lithuania, Moldova, Poland, Ukraine and other states formerly within the Russian sphere can engagement be more productive. It's unlikely, however, that Russia will arrive at any conclusion, as it appears it genuinely desires the dynamic to continue, as it has proven an effective tool in advancing its agenda. Only by deconstructing the fictitious claims asserted by Russian history can the west engage in any real discourse with Russia that avoids the pitfall of arguing about rights and claims arising from their supposed history and thereby begin to create safeguards for Europe and the west based on *realpolitik*.

---

[23] While Europeans embrace the concept their obligations under the European Charter of Fundamental Rights and other Treaty obligations are collectively and generally controlling over domestic law, Article 15(1) of the Russian Constitution of 1993, as amended, provides that "the Constitution of the Russian Federation has the highest legal force."

To appreciate the differences between the Russkiy Mir mindset and western civilization's world view, it is useful to have clarity about how we approach information and why Russia promotes its unique version of its past.

The western approach to history generally employs a collection of data from verified sources, then employing scrutiny and comparativism within the framework of realism, individualism, and democracy for the purposes of understanding the development and maintenance of our democratic institutions and values—all underpinned by the rule of law. For Russia, history is an instrument of social and national identification by which political ambitions can be advanced, justified and power consolidated and preserved. Given the divergent objectives of historical pursuit and discernment—the preservation of knowledge in the west and the projection of power in the east—any discourse between Russia and the west will always be fraught with misunderstanding while this *Daedalian* dynamic endures.

Any Russian concept of what Russia is and who is Russian must, therefore, be viewed with skepticism through the prism of geopolitical opportunism. The notion promoted by Putin of historic Russian Ukrainian, pan-Slavic or Baltic unity with Moscow at its center, where Russia is universally acknowledged as the "Mother of all Slavic nations"[24] is nothing more than neo-imperialist apologetics and propaganda. The appeal is not a new one. From the time of Muscovy until this day, the propensity to promote this tsarist predisposition for empire and colonialism endures:

> Over the years, Muscovite tsars, Romanov emperors, Soviet general secretaries, and Russian presidents have portrayed themselves as the legitimate heirs and successors to Kievan Rus. They have all tried to align their political, national, and cultural power with this "Lost Kingdom." Plokhy contends that since the fall of Kievan Rus, the Russian nation has only once fully aligned with the Russian state: during the Soviet Union's reign as a superpower. Apart from the years spanning 1945 to 1991, Russian governments of all types have constantly struggled both to define who or what is "Russian," as well as where the political and cultural borders of the Russian nation exist.[25]

---

[24] Kateryna Yakovenko, "Russia's claim for 'Mother-of-Slavs' status", *International Issues & Slovak Foreign Policy Affairs*, Vol. 24, No. 1-2, Europe and Russia, 2015.

[25] Jonathon Dreeze, "Russia's Lost Empire, Review of Lost Kingdom: The Quest for Empire and the Making of the Russian Nation, From 1470 to the Present, by Serhii Plokhy (New York: Basic Books, 2017)", *Origins: Current Events in Historical Perspective*, November 2018.

Russia's definition of what was Russian in Cold War Europe prevailed simply because the Russian boot was on the throat of the independent nations it occupied, with the consequence that their individual, independent voices were silenced. We cannot talk of Polish identity in the post-World War II era with any integrity, for example, as only the mimicry of Soviet Russian interests was espoused by the vassal Polish People's Republic. The legacy of the Cold War is that independent governments in exile became meaningless and therefore voiceless while the west negotiated with the Kremlin on behalf of the approximately 100 million Europeans whose lives were relinquished to occupation regimes until 1991, to the detriment of the legitimate governments in exile.

The west's unwillingness to confront Russia and therefore accept a détente along lines developed during the Cold War deprived states from the Baltics to the Black Sea from asserting their sovereignty and identity. *Ergo*, there was simply no appetite to seriously challenge Russia's historical assertions and claims upon which its historic dominion hinged.

Russia continues to rely heavily on a sanitized version of its history that was largely fabricated for the external purpose of impressing European monarchs, states, and people and justifying the power and preservation of its rulers. Today, how Europe engages in international relations and conflict resolution is the rule of law, while Russia continues to argue it has an inherent and historic responsibility to protect Russians.

It is inconsequential that those Russians, whose only relationship to the Russian Federation since 1991 may well have been limited to cultural, historic, political, and linguistic values. As these discriminators often defy definition, thereby making them universally recognizable, rulemaking surrounding them is challenging at best.[26] Putin's changes to the Russian Constitution made it possible for people with these tenuous connections to Russia to claim citizenship. That these supposed Russians do not then claim that citizenship and emigrate to Russia should unambiguously indicate their citizenship and allegiances lie in independent states. Passportisation as a means of proving Russia with the premise to occupy the sovereign territory of neighboring states under the guise of protecting Russian citizens is unlawful and unethical.[27] It exists as a mere yet brazen attempt at historical and ethno-protective justification for war and occupation.

Since his rise to power in 1999, Putin has added to the complexity of Russian history and identity, and thereby the clarity of the identity and sovereignty of neighboring states. By masterfully wielding a combination of his own version of Russian history and personal narrative, Putin has *cultivated* a heroic past for Russia and himself, firmly rooted in the ROC (emphasis on *cult*).[28]

For their part, the ROC engages in the same dynamic of promoting a Russian hagiography as a substitute for historic realism. Of late, they have worked assiduously in concert with the Russian state to promote a mythologized history of Russia in support of its territorial, cultural, linguistic, and religious claims on its neighbors. This has included the ROC promoting devotion, to of all people, Pope Saint Clement of Rome.

Hagiographers tell us Pope Clement, a disciple of the Apostle Peter, was exiled to Crimea in the late first century, c. 99, by the Roman Emperor Trajan. Pope Clement's early canonization as martyr and saint translates to his being universally venerated as a church father in Eastern Orthodox

---

[26] Press Release, "MEPs say no to Russian passports from occupied regions, stress right to asylum", *European Parliament*, 20 October 2022.

[27] Evan Harary, "In Ukraine, Russian Passportization Generates Effective Denationalization", *OpinioJuris*, 4 January 2024.

[28] Julie A. Cassiday and Emily D. Johnson, "Putin, Putiniana and the Question of a Post-Soviet Cult of Personality", *Slavonic and East European Review, Modern Humanities Research Association*, Volume 88, Number 4, October 2010.

Christianity, as well as Roman Catholic and Eastern Rite Catholic churches. What makes the vigorous promotion of Pope Clement's veneration by the ROC at this time so unique is that while both the eastern and western churches acknowledge his canonization, the ROC has generally avoided the promotion of any saints more closely associated with the Roman Catholic Church.[29] Encouraging a devotion to Saint Clement seems to signal an ulterior motive.

The ROC's new efforts to promote veneration of the "Right Believing Hieromartyr Clement, Pope of Rome" were a precursor to the 2013 restoration of the Church of the Holy Martyr Clement Pope of Rome in Zamoskvorechye. The promotion of his veneration and restoration of the church, in context, represent a conscious, albeit novel, approach to link Russian Orthodox Christianity to Crimea, where Saint Clement was martyred at Chersoneses. Accompanied by the ROC's invocation of Volodymyr the Great, the Kyivan Rus' ruler responsible for Ukraine's mass conversion to Christianity after his own baptism at Chersoneses on Crimea c. 987, it appears to be a critical component of the ROC appeal to support the Russian Federation's claims on Crimea.

Harvard University's George Soroka, by contrast, highlighted that Russia's involvement with Crimea is relatively recent, dating it only to the reign of Tsarina Catherine II in the 18th century.[30] The Kremlin and the Moscow Patriarchate's resort to a disinformation campaign about being the sole successor of the Kyivan Rus' and their attending political and religious claims on neighbouring sovereign territories are, however, part and parcel of their hybrid warfare campaign in pursuit of establishing a Russkiy Mir.

If history is both the medium and message its credibility is vital to the ROC and the Russian Federation's cause. It is therefore worthy of academic scrutiny. In the information age, observed Joseph Nye, "credibility

---

[29] Tsarina Catherine II, born Princess Sophie of Anhalt-Zerbst of Prussia, commanded that a church to St. Clement be built. In 1769, the Church of the Holy Martyr Clement Pope of Rome in Zamoskvorechye (Moscow) was opened. During the Soviet period, it was converted to a library. In 2013, the church was restored and reopened, only eight months before the Russian invasion of Ukraine and attempted annexation of Crimea in 2014.

[30] Miceál O'Hurley, "In Conversation Interview with Harvard's George Soroka, Ph.D. on the Crimea Crisis (Video) – ICC Finds Basis War Crimes & Crimes Against Humanity Committed", *European Diplomat*, 25 October 2021.

is the scarcest resource."[31] By contrast, the Russian adage, "the best propaganda is not propaganda"[32] succinctly encapsulates how Russians have perfected the art of rendering the incredible as credible for the unenlightened information consumer. Effective propaganda is perceived as organic and not the product of forced promotion with ulterior motives. We must, therefore, approach Russia's version of their history with due skepticism.

Consequently, much of Russia's propaganda is not announced from podiums or in media releases. It is fed to the west in soundbites and manufactured media articles promoted by Russian troll farms on social media. Using both algorithms and paid promoters, Russia ensures its desired messaging appears on the feeds of a receptive audience. The ability to continue to pass off their version of history has proven so effective that both the Russian State and ROC spend significant resources blurring the lines between fact and fiction through history, in education and during policy discourse. This dynamic must be fully appreciated before any attempt to unpack our reliance on Russia's unique version of history.

Although writing about China, Nye's insights on propaganda and credibility resonate within the Kremlin walls. Russia grasps that the scarcity of truth within the abundance of information in today's world benefits its propagandists. There is nothing novel about this. Ivan III Vasilyevich's inventive efforts to forge a glorious past in support of his dreams of building a more expansive state were critical to his pursuit of a greater Russian Empire. Peter I Alekseyevich's conversion of the Moscow Print Yard from a religious publisher to a propaganda machine linking Russia to the Kyivan Rus' proved an indispensable component in the historical distortion that is at the root of Russia's geopolitical claims.

Russia has taken great care to control its inventive historical narrative. At the advent of the Enlightenment and the corresponding relaxation of censorship, there arose a bevy of non-state, unauthorized histories and political criticism challenging tsarists' rule and the essence of the new, Russian identity. Censorship had always been a key article for ensuring narrative conformity for Moscow's princes and later tsars. Both Peter I Alexeyavich and Tsarina Catherine II initially embraced a liberalization of historic investigation, education, and private print houses before each curtailing them with the imposition of even harsher censorship than previously

---

[31] Joseph S. Nye, "China's Soft Power Deficit To catch up, its politics must unleash the many talents of its civil society", *The Wall Street Journal*, 8 May 2012.
[32] Joseph S. Nye (witness), "Unrevised Transcript of Evidence Taken Before the Select Committee on Soft Power and the UK's Influence, Evidence Session No. 10", *House of Lords*, 15 October 2013.

existed.³³ Turning away from her reign's initial inclinations toward the liberalization of information, education and other freedoms, prior to launching military campaigns to expand Russia's borders, Tsarina Catherine II increased Russian state censorship by then banning the private printing houses, establishing a more empowered Russian state censor and proscribing foreign books, especially those from the neighboring Polish-Lithuanian Commonwealth.³⁴ Censorship became even more restrictive through the years.

Not long after Catherine II's death, Russia's 1828 censorship law became a particularly effective tool of Russian state oppression. It was promulgated without definitions, lacked guidance for publishers and writers and carried indiscriminate powers to ban information that might "harm the faith, the throne, the good morals, the personal honor of citizens."³⁵

Both the Kremlin and ROC used the 1828 censorship law, as they had many laws before and after it, to tighten their hold on the public and virtually prohibit all scrutiny of Russian history, whose overriding purpose was to prioritize and protect the political interests of the tsars and ROC.

Before the Russian state was even declared in 1721, the Principality of Muscovy provided the ROC with sweeping censorship rights in 1551, including authority to confiscate and destroy "uncorrected manuscripts." Religious censorship was not unique to the ROC. At the Council of Trent, the Roman Catholic Church created the *List of Repudiated Books* concerning religious works prohibited from being read by the faithful. Moscow's 1551 *Stoglav Decrees* provided the ROC with broad latitude to proscribe any works that challenged the divine right of tsars, confiscate any books considered in error (secular or religious) and revise existing texts. The decisions of the Stoglav Synod effectively made the ROC political censors in defense of tsardom, leading to books being rewritten, destroying "political heresy" and otherwise restricting new publications that did not conform to the desires of tsars and patriarchs of Moscow.³⁶

---

33 Daniel Balmuth, "The Origins of the Tsarist Epoch of Censorship Terror", *The American Slavic and East European Review, Vol. 19, No. 4*, 1960.
34 The modern equivalent of Catherine II's banning of information from the Polish Lithuanian Commonwealth was Russia's hybrid warfare activity in crashing Ukraine's Internet information and access prior to its full-scale invasion of Ukraine in February 2022. See: Kristan Stoddart, "Russia's Cyber Campaigns and the Ukraine War: From the 'Gray Zone' to the 'Red Zone'", *Applied Cybersecurity and Internet Governance*, 19 June 2024.
35 Charles A. Ruud, "Fighting Words: Imperial Censorship and the Russian Press, 1804-1906", *University of Toronto Press*, 1982.
36 Jack Kollmann, "The Moscow Stoglav ('Hundred Chapters') Church Council of 1551, (Ph.D. dissertation)", *University of Michigan: Ann Arbor*, 1978.

Modern Russian censorship is equally repugnant to good scholarship, free thought and expressions of conscience and fact as it was to its predecessors. Challenges to the Kremlin narrative, including the Kyivan Rus' succession myth and the political interests or conduct of the Russian state bodies, have been met with harsh penalties. This has caused journalists, scholars, researchers, and civil society activists to flee Russia by the thousands.[37]

While Putin and the ROC may rely on these distortions and inventions as a premise for their claims of dominion and historic fraternal cooperation, the world community remains unconvinced. Even China, usually a stalwart Russian ally, refuses to go along with some narratives. Beijing has repeatedly declined to recognize the annexation of Crimea or acknowledge the so-called independent republics that have arisen with Russian state assistance in occupied Abkhazia, South Ossetia[38] and Transnistria.[39] Still, Russia attempts to justify its occupations and military adventurism by clinging to claims based on its dubious version of history.

These claims are based as much on the *mythos* of being successors to the Kyivan Rus' as to Russia's unique claims of rights deriving from undefined ethnic, linguistic, and cultural affinity. For Russia, acceptance of its Russkiy Mir'-driven version of modern history should be controlling with regards to sovereignty. By contrast, the United Nations and European Union continue to acknowledge the legal sovereignty of Moldova, Georgia, and Ukraine. Likewise, the Ecumenical Patriarchate, the Patriarchate of Alexandria, the Church of Greece, and the Church of Cyprus and others recognize the canonical autocephaly of the 'Православна церква України' [Orthodox Church of Ukraine]. The Moscow Patriarchate continues to claim canonical interference and that the ROC's refusal to grant autocephaly to the Ukrainian Church mandates that Ukrainian victims of their invasion should be forced to commemorate their oppressor—the Patriarch of Moscow.

As will be explored elsewhere in this manuscript, the very submission of the metropolis of Kyiv to the Moscow Patriarchate in 1685 was itself achieved by the threat of force. Borys Gudanov's threat, arrest and coercion of the Ecumenical Patriarch Jeremias II and the Church under Ottoman rule not only established the Moscow Patriarchate without the traditional exercise of conciliation but deprived Ukraine of its autocephalous religious freedom. The decision of the Ecumenical Patriarch to endow the metropolis

---

[37] Anton Troianovski and Valeriya Safronova, "Russia Takes Censorship to New Extremes, Stifling War Coverage", *New York Times*, 4 March 2022.
[38] Uncredited, "Abkhazia, S. Ossetia Formally Declared Occupied Territory". *Civil Georgia*, 28 August 2008.
[39] Mădălin Necşuţu, "Council of Europe Designates Transnistria 'Russian Occupied Territory'", *Balkan Insight*, 16 March 2022.

of Kyiv with a tomos of autocephaly in 2018 was simply an act of correcting a historical wrong.

However, the disinformation campaign maintained by Moscow that the Orthodox Church of Ukraine is a heretical, non-canonical entity led by invalid clergy is an offense to orthodox unity. It has been elevated to being part of Russia's distorted view of history. That the Moscow Patriarchate and Kremlin chose to weaponize the exercise of religious freedoms by Orthodox Christians in Ukraine into a narrative of religious persecution against Russian Orthodoxy is part and parcel of attempts to deny Ukrainians self-agency and liberty, while subjecting the uninformed to the same old din of "Russophobic" persecution claims. It is perverse that some embrace these claims, given the murder, execution, and disappearance of non-ROC clergy in occupied Ukraine and the general suppression of religious freedom under occupation regimes.[40]

The Kremlin and Moscow Patriarchate direct significant resources to project their unique version of history throughout the west because they know public opinion weighs heavily in policy discourse. It has proven effective in coopting large segments of western populations to accept, if not embrace, Russian history as correct and Russian actions as justified.

Russia's invocation of being successors to the Kyivan Rus' lies at the heart of their promotion of the idea of holding ancient territorial claims on places like Crimea, and clinging to this theme, which includes an overt appeal to Christian heritage and traditional family values, has proven effective in cultivating significant pro-Russian sentiment throughout Europe and the west.[41]

Maintaining the ruse that the Kyivan Rus' succession was translated to the princes of Muscovy is not only of assistance to Russia's militant expansionist objectives but is a disservice to the independence of Russia's neighbors, keen to remain outside of the Russian sphere, and who shirk the premise of the Russkiy Mir. Asserting their own, individual identity, language, customs, religious freedoms, and cultural values is essential to their defense against being automatically re-inducted into the Russian sphere as though they were mere chattel.

Refuting the Russian claims of being the sole successor of the Kyivan Rus' is critical in depriving the Kremlin and Moscow Patriarchate of the truncheon of history being used as an excuse to disregard the fundamental basis of European existence where respect for a rules-based world order rooted in law, civility and diplomacy reigns superior over demands, deception, and dictatorship.

---

[40] Gina Christian, "Russia is killing clergy, banning religions in occupied Ukraine, says foreign minister", *OSV News*, 13 January 2025.

[41] Soňa Muzikárová, "Why some EU countries in the east are still pro-Russia", *Al Jazeera*, 6 February 2023.

Chapter Two

Russians—Kyivan Rus' Successors? Not All That Glitters Is Gold: Conflating Rus' & Russian Is an Error

Europe, then the world, had little knowledge of Russia before Peter I Alekseyevich began introducing his neophyte Russia to the west. Consequently, it was relatively ignorant of Russia's past. There were no independent chronicles of the history of the semi-wild tribes that were incorporated into the Principality of Muscovy by the forces of the Golden Horde and the Türkic khanates. What existed was a compendium of mythologized history from princes who commanded them to be recorded to serve their own interests. There was no opposing historical record to challenge Russia's mythologized history, and for that reason alone, it prevailed as the only history of Russia.

Europeans could not have comprehended that they were accepting a history devised by imperial apologists operating under strict censorship. Even if they knew, they were hardly inclined to admit it. The appropriation of another's histories and claiming glorious lineages was the way of the world in post-medieval Europe. Tsars added to the records of their predecessor to lay the groundwork for the invention of a new people—Russians—imbued with the glory of the Byzantines, Kyivan Rus' and Riurikids. Clothing Russia in the history of others and adding elements of mythos was, after all, a device employed by monarchies across Europe for their own benefit.[42]

After the fall of the Soviet Union, the Russians were undeniably weary, disillusioned, and fearful of being stripped of their status as world leaders and reduced to even more desperate poverty than their command economy had previously imposed. Putin beseeched the world to recall the glory of Russia's past and instill in his people a sense of pride to displace the misery of daily life, even reinstating the athletes' parades in Red Square

---

[42] Between 1340-1801, the kings and queens of England and later Britain used *"historical"* and *"genealogical"* arguments to claim as part of their titles king or queen of France. Hereditary claims on the domain of others were commonplace in medieval Europe, and Russia's practice of the same would have gone without protest, especially as the kingdoms they claimed were extinct.

as an appeal to a more 'glorious' past, albeit a Soviet one.⁴³ From 1999 onwards, Putin's constant appeal to the country's past majesty not only motivated the Russian people but served to reinforce the west's uncritical understanding of a version of Russian history constructed for grandeur and legitimacy.

For the ambitious princes of Muscovy, creating a unifying history for their people served to assist in the assimilation of myriad tribes, cultures, and regions into an entity that could survive the suzerain of the *Ulug Ulus* [Great State] of the Golden Horde and later the Türkic khanate. Tsars of Moscow approached and promoted history as a means of providing a veneer of credibility to their invention of a newly created people, Russians, by imbuing them with a noble past, albeit primarily a rendition of mythologized elements combined with the appropriated past of others.⁴⁴

Communists approached history with the goal of consolidating power and as a means by which people could be adjudged as either oppressors or the oppressed, thereby assigning them their allotted role within socialism and the communist ideal. The neo-imperialists that came to prominence at the elbow of Putin since 1999 valued history only insofar as it serves the goal of the state. Russian history now has an overriding goal — assisting the state in realizing the Russkiy Mir.⁴⁵ This requires modernity to accept history filtered through the lens of Putin's neo-imperialist agenda. This is critical.

For Putin and his new nationalists, the Russkiy Mir depends on the Russian people being convinced of an entitlement to a birthright worthy of pride, inherently noble, marked by triumph and being superior to others.⁴⁶ Only once convinced of their superiority and entitlement would the Russian people be willing to sacrifice their well-being and even their lives to

---

[43] Athletes Parades on Moscow's Red Square were an annual event in the Soviet calendar between 1919–1945.

[44] Jarosław Wiśnicki, "History as an information weapon in Russia's full-scale war in Ukraine", *European External Action Service (EEAS)*, 14 July 2023.

[45] Maria Korenyuk, "Ukraine war: Russian schoolbook urges teenagers to join the army", *BBC*, 13 March 2024.

[46] Within recent memory, Russians would refer to themselves as Velikorosy (великоросы), while Russkiy (русский) was used as a collective term including Velikorosy (superior or outstanding Russians) as well as Ukrainians (Malorosy — Little Russians) and Belarusians (Biełarusy — White Russians). The linguistic choices of Russians towards their neighbors indicate that, despite Putin's claims of "unity" and "fraternal bonds" within the Russian view of Russians, some were more equal than others, not even masking Russians' distinction of Ukrainians and Belarusians as "others".

achieve what Putin tells them is their political destiny.[47] Necessarily, Russian history as a tool of the regime must be a persuasive instrument in convincing Europe and the world it is acting to liberate Russians from "Nazis and fascists."[48] Obviously, Russians must themselves believe they have a right to reincorporate the Baltics and eastern Europe into the Russian sphere before making such incredible sacrifices.

Concomitant with this domestic effort to re-instill pride to prepare Russians for the attempted annexation and imposition of suzerainty over their neighbors was the collateral effort to diminish lingering feelings of doubt, guilt, or inner conflict, as some Russians had familial relatives outside of the Russian Federation due to Soviet era migration and forced labor distribution. In solidifying their domestic base and reducing internal opposition, Russians could employ soft diplomacy throughout the former Soviet sphere, where they nourished dreams of establishing friendly occupational regimes or attempting to annex their neighbors in a re-incorporation into Russia directly. Challenging individual history, national identity, Indigenous culture, language, and religious identities in their target countries emerged as a priority. Defending Russia's version of history, even when absurd, remained a critical element of domestic and international hybrid warfare.

Claims that Russia is the sole successor to the Kyivan Rus',[49] boasts of its ancient ties to the Byzantines[50] and enjoying historic claims on peoples and lands throughout Eastern and Northern Europe is not simply a recitation of Russia's skewed version of history—it is a political manifesto and statement of justification for its aggression in the service of expansionism.

The Russian mythology of the Kyivan Rus' is critical to Russia's assumed identity and corresponding geopolitical claims. There is a tendency throughout the global culture war waged by the Kremlin to convince map

---

[47] Russian casualties in Ukraine have exceeded 1,000,000 since the launch of their full-scale invasion in 2022. Russian fatalities in Ukraine (in just over three years) are 15 times larger than the Soviet Union's decade-long war in Afghanistan and 10 times larger than Russia's 13 years of war in Chechnya. See: Seth G. Jones and Riley McCabe, "Russia's Battlefield Woes in Ukraine", *Center for Strategic and International Studies (CSIS)*, 3 June 2025.

[48] AFP Staff Writers, "Putin vows that 'as in 1945,' Ukraine will be liberated from 'Nazi filth'", *Times of Israel*, 8 May 2022.

[49] As variously explored in this text, several modern states can lay equal if not greater claims to being successors of the *Kyivan Rus'* than can Russia and yet only Russia claims to be the "sole successor" to their political, cultural, historical and religious heritage.

[50] Jiaqi Cao, "Religious Origin and Political Extension of the idea of "Moscow—Third Rome'", *Advance*, 24 October 2023

makers, textbook writers, academics, newsrooms, and others to maintain the colonial practice of forfeiting the name of Kyivan Rus' capital and its people to the Russian language. Here, there is a problem as the Russian language did not exist when the kingdom reigned. We must refer to the Kyivan Rus', not Kievan Rus', as the Russian language usage is pregnant with political implications.

Russia's continued lobbying to maintain this language standard goes against modern practices. Britain's London is not called by its Latin name, Londinium. Croatia's Zagreb is not referred to by its Hungarian name, Zagreb. International standards do not employ the Russian Kingissepa for Estonia's Kuressaare. And yet, the Russian 'Kiev' continues to prevail in newsrooms, capitals and many academies across the globe when referring to sovereign Ukraine's capital, Kyiv.

The Kyivan Rus' did not get their name from the Russian Киев [Kiev]. It was not named after the modern chicken dish, котлета по-киевски, chicken Kiev.[51] The kingdom was named after Kyi, one of the four mythical brothers who founded the eponymous city. Kyiv's foundations are not Russian. The continued use of Kiev represents a real cultural victory for Russia and an implied territorial claim over the city and the Ukrainian state. The distinction may at first be subtle, but its implications are real.

If Putin's claims of Russia being the sole heir of the Kyivan Rus' are to be accepted as true, it requires him to provide compelling evidence of the ancient transfer of power from Kyiv to Moscow. He cannot. It never happened. Only a gross distortion of history allows him to make this assertion. And yet, for many around the world, it is accepted as historical fact. The claim might seem naked opportunism for a state, but when the ROC resorts to the same invocation, it is often accepted as a historical and ethical truth as the ROC presents itself as the keeper of truth and tradition.

However, neither Putin nor the Moscow Patriarch engineered the mythological propaganda device. It has long been a practice of Russia to use a blend of culture, history, religion, and language for its political purposes.

We must resolve with clarity, therefore, that the Kyivan Rus' never ruled Muscovy, the political construct and region upon which the Russian state was founded. The succession myth is simply that—*mythos*. Like the princes of Muscovy and tsars before, the Russian state and the ROC have

---

51   As an example of 'Russification', even the most inconsequential of things, for historical benefit, food historian William Pokhlyobkin claimed the dish's origins arise from the St. Petersburg Merchant Club in 1912 in a dish called Novo-Mikhailovskaya kotleta. Chicken Kiev's roots are neither ancient nor Ukrainian but French and semi-modern. See: Вильям Похлёбкин, "Стреляющие котлеты", *Огонёк. Москва*, 4 May 1997.

either re-shaped history for its political purposes or engaged in a pattern of appropriation and erasure of the historical, cultural, religious, linguistic, and even archaeological record[52] of others for the purpose of inventing a legendary, if not mystical, Russian identity.

We must now turn our attention to the Rus'. There is abundant difficulty with any identification of the Rus' being synonymous with the Kyivan Rus'. Even to a lay enquirer, any employment of these two different identities by writers in antiquity strongly suggests that an inherent distinction between the two was contemporaneously recognized. It did and still does. During the period in which the Rus' and Kyivan Rus' were active in the general region of the west and northwest of the Central Uplands that would one day form the basis for Russia, it was populated not by Norse-Varangians, Rus' or Kyivan Rus', but an assortment of semi-wild, proto-Slavic tribes. A Russian identity and Russian state would not emerge for centuries.[53] Russia's varying, if not competing, claims of being more generally Rus' than Kyivan Rus' are rooted not in the historical but the mythological claim of being descendants and heirs of the Riurikids. The prevailing consensus of objective modern scholarship is that the Riurik-Varangian

---

[52] The National Academy of Sciences of Ukraine (NASU) Institute of Archaeology reports Russian authorities liquidated the Crimean branch of the Institute of Archaeology following their 2014 armed annexation of Crimea. The United Nations Educational, Scientific and Cultural Organization (UNESCO) records that Russia seized 4,095 Ukrainian national and local monuments in Crimea in violation of international law. With such activity, the bevy of published research or catalogued artefacts should be astonishing. Their absence tends to militate towards Russia engaging in further erasure of Ukrainian and Crimean Tatar history or selectively collecting and cataloguing to support the political decision to occupy and annex Ukraine based on a fabricated Russian historical record.

[53] The Russian identity emerged from the Principality of Muscovy by a gradual process. In the 15th century, there are some references made to "Russian" as a self-identification. The misapplication of Rus' to peoples inhabiting the lands northeast of what had been the territory of the Kyivan Rus' arose from a misunderstanding of migration patterns, which held that the Kyivan Rus' fled to the region following the sack of the city by the Türkic khanate and was thereafter repeated in chronicles that can most accurately be deemed apocryphal historical constructs. Historians in antiquity tended to make similar mistakes with people like the Irish, who have been historically mislabeled as Hibernians or Scotti due to early Latin histories, or Celts owing to the Greek Κελτοί (keltoi). There is no evidence that the Irish would have known themselves by these names. The Irish identity as Gaels cannot be confirmed in use before the 17th century. The Muscovy did not officially become known as Russians until 2 November 1721 (October 22, Old Calendar).

Rus' lineage is fictional.[54] Russia's foundation is rooted in proto-Slavic, semi-wild tribes, heavily influenced by the Genghisid and Türkic khans that ruled them for centuries and only later, and still tangentially, by Christianity and distant Kyivan Rus' associations. If Russians aren't successors to the Kyivan Rus' nor ethnically Varangian Rus', why maintain the ruse and rhetoric?

Putin is fond of justifying his current geopolitical policies and military conquests on the premise that the Russians are descendants of the Rus' and Kyivan Rus'. This represents an incredible stretch of ethnography, history, and genetics as we would recognize them. There is also present in this argument a healthy dose of translating the mythology into fact when it comes to the Riurkik-Varangian Rus'. In context, the shoring-up of domestic buy-in for the Kyivan Rus' myth and the direct challenge of the individual identity of neighboring states formerly under the Russian sphere of influence must be perceived as ideological preparation for political and military suzerainty.

Let's examine how and why Putin and his neo-imperialist regime project these myths, weaving them into the concept of the Russkiy Mir and Holy Rus'.

Russia, as we would recognize it today, and Russians as we would know them in modernity, are relatively new concepts in the framework of European history. In his essay "On the Historical Unity of the Russian and Ukrainian People",[55] Putin creates an almost mythical premise for believing that non-Russians should be legitimately deemed Russians. Throughout the Soviet epoch, the imperial invocation of the triune unity between Russia, Belarus, and Ukraine was discarded. The relationship between Russia and its neighbors was invoked as being one of Братские народы [brat'skie narody—fraternal nation].[56] It was only under Putin that this neo-imperial language resorted to claims of historical 'unity'.[57]

Putin bases his claims on Russia being the successor of the Kyivan Rus'—a kingdom ruled by sovereigns originating in the Baltic, reigning

---

[54] Ольга Анатольевна Плотникова, "История Одного Мифа. Легенда Династии Рюриковичей", *Гуманитарные науки Вестник Финансового университета*, No. 2, 2015.

[55] Владимир Владимирович Путин, "Об историческом единстве украинского и русского народов", *Кремль, Москва*, 12 июль 2021.

[56] Pål Kolstø, "Strategic Uses of Nationalism and Ethnic Conflict: Interest and Identity in Russia and the Post-Soviet Space", *Edinburgh University Press*, 2022.

[57] The reemergence of imperial language coincided with significant efforts undermining critical aspects of the 1993 Russian Constitution returning it to a more bifurcated Soviet era 'ornamental' approach between language in law and applied practice thus allowing for censorship and introducing contradictions that undermine rights and freedoms while giving the President wide discretion.

over a region populated by proto-Slavic peoples. That kingdom disintegrated almost 800 years ago—some 500 years before Russia came into being.

How can it be that Putin is presenting these long-vanquished people as being today's ethnic Russians? We need to look beyond science and examine politics. Despite being a multi-ethnic country, the most recent constitutional changes elevate the Russian language above all others as it represents the vernacular of the 'state-forming people'.

The history of the Russian language can generally be divided into old Russian (c. 11th–17th centuries) and modern Russian (c. 17th century onwards). As with most Russian history, contradictions abound.[58] The Russian language did not exist when the Old East Slavic "state-forming people"[59], the Muscovy, founded the fledgling late 13th century nation-state that would not emerge as a Russian state until the 18th century. Russia's Constitutional codification of the Russian language as belonging to the "state-forming people" is a political statement with social implications.

Putin is correct only insofar that the Norse-Varangian people, who became known as the Rus', did contribute to the modern Russian state in terms of elements of their culture being inducted into that which would become characterized as Russian, but then only centuries later. But as we know, all that glitters is not gold and being a beneficiary of Kyivan Rus' culture, mythology, and some elements of history doesn't render a Russian a Rus'. If this were true, Belarus, Poland, Ukraine, and others would have an equal claim on being the sole successors of the Kyivan Rus'. None makes that claim, although all share in the same way.

Neo-imperialist claims about Russians being inheritors of the mantle of the Kyivan Rus' are convoluted. Russian chroniclers of antiquity variously invoked the Kyivan Rus' and Rus' as being synonymous with Russian because they were in service to Muscovy princes and later tsars who

---

[58] Throughout the writing of this manuscript various open-source information sites such as Wikipedia experiences entire re-writes of Russian history daily. On any given day the foundation of Russia is described as, "The traditional start date of specifically Russian history is the establishment of the Rus' state in the north in the year 862, ruled by Varangians." Alternatively, the very next day it is modified as, "Russia, as the Russian Empire, was officially founded in 1721. This date marks the point when Tsar Peter the Great adopted the title of "Emperor of all the Russias."" Unfortunately, 'information' sites and online encyclopedias have become part of the propaganda war.

[59] Constitution of the Russian Federation, at Article 68, as passed by nation-wide voting of December 12, 1993, with the amendments approved by nation-wide voting on October 5, 2022.

relied on those assertions to aggrandize their positions.[60] Their goal was to co-opt others' heritage, culture, and mythology to elevate Russia in the esteem of its subjects and impress the world.

To consider if the Russians are successors to the Kyivan Rus', we must ask the question, "Who are the Russians?" Our quest to understand who the Russians are and what Russia must begin with their ethnological foundation, as opposed to the historical framework discussed previously. They are not Rus', at least not in the way they assert themselves to be. The Varangian-Norse, who later became known as the Rus', were ethnically a Baltic people, primarily from Sweden. By contrast, the Muscovy (those people who gave rise to the modern Russian state and nation) were the product of proto-Slavic and Türkic tribes who came under the political control of the Principality of Muscovy only in the 13th and 14th centuries.

Indeed, the Rus' were rulers of Slavic peoples (among others). However, the commonality between the Slavs inhabiting modern Ukraine and those of Russia's Central Upland was negligible. This has not kept Moscow from invoking pan-Slavic unity in a way that would render Indo-Europeans united as though a Dutch person were akin to being an Iranian. The Rus' were not Slavs in an ethnic sense, but rather the Slavs were, at times, in some areas, Rus' in the political sense. It is a false syllogism to believe Russians are Rus' and yet it has come to carry weight and entered the mainstream simply because the west has allowed it.

The tension between Putin's ethnicity assertions and the need to ensure minority ethnic groups are encouraged to feel a real sense of Russian identity is often at odds. Of the Buddhist and shamanic Tuva and Buryatia Türkic peoples, for example, their likelihood of serving in combat in Ukraine is staggeringly high compared to the 'ethnic Russian,' adherents of the ROC of the western regions of Russia. It is not just a matter of ethnicity or location, as poverty is closely associated with the predictability of military service and combat deaths.[61]

---

[60] Ivan IV Vasilyevich gave himself the title "Grand Prince of Moscow and All Rus'" ex nihilo in 1533. The Rus' title was not entrusted to him, nor did he assume it as part of any Kyivan Rus' lineage. His claim to dominion over "All Rus'" was a political claim and not a product of historical inheritance or succession.

[61] Social scientists argue of causality and relation. The poorest regions of Russia are generally populated by ethnic minorities, many of whom were settled collectively during the tsarist epoch or re-settled by Stalinist policies during the Soviet era. Poverty amongst Russia's ethnic minorities is a blend of ethnic, geographic, political, religious discrimination which results is economic disadvantage.

For every 10,000 Russian soldiers serving in the invasion and occupation of Ukraine, death rates by regional participation show that the Russian practice of ethnic identification for discrimination is real. Tuvans experience a 48.6% mortality rate: the Buryatia 36.7%, Nenets Autonomous Okrug 30%, the Altai Republic 26.5% and Zabaykalsky Krai 26.2%. Putin's vaunted 'ethnic Russians' have a far different experience, with 2.5% deaths for every 10,000 men from St. Petersburg and 1% from Moscow.[62]

Unsurprisingly, having used the Kyivan Rus' claims to bolster national pride, Putin is now keen to play down the Kyivan Rus' narrative domestically while directing internal communication to thematic development of a unified Russian identity. In 2021, he told a meeting on interethnic relations:

> Identity should be developed and affirmed primarily through the efforts of intellectuals, politicians, public activists, but also through the environment around us. Unlike ethnicity, which can be complex, national identity is more defined and more significant, it is supported by legal and statutory norms.[63]

It is with some irony that the proto-Slavic and Türkic tribes that provided the early foundations for Muscovy are today diminished by Putin and the ROC as being of a lower order in the Russian identity than that of genuinely ethnic Russians.[64] They prefer, of late, for obvious reasons, to claim Russians to be ethnically, spiritually and religiously Rus' to the exclusion of all other discriminators.

Russian historians have generally relied on a mythic story of the Central Uplands region being only sparsely populated until a mass migration of the Kyivan Rus' began to settle it following the Golden Horde's destruction of Kyiv and evisceration of surviving Kyivan Rus' influence.

Postulations of a great migration from Kyiv to what is now Moscow have been invoked for centuries to substantiate claims of shared ethnic identity between the Kyivan Rus' and Muscovy. The claims only arose hundreds of years after Russia began claiming to be the heirs of the Kyivan Rus'. The political capital of the Kyivan Rus' was centered on the eponymous trading metropolis located on a faraway, northern segment of the Dnieper River. For various reasons, the migration myth does not hold up to scrutiny, primarily because it never happened.

---

[62] Olga Ivshina, "Ukraine war: Tuva and Buryatia pay the highest price, but latest BBC Russian casualty figures show poverty not ethnicity the key factor", *BBC News Russian*, 30 November 2023.

[63] Vladimir Putin, "Meeting of the Presidential Council for Interethnic Relations (videoconference)", *Kremlin: Moscow*, 30 March 2021.

[64] As with most Russian propaganda, when it serves his purpose, Putin relies on the "Mother of all Slavic nations" and "Russian identity" mantras despite them conflicting with his ethnic Rus' assertions.

The generally promoted Russian theory is that when Kyiv was sacked by Batu Khan in 1240, the Kyivan Rus' undertook a mass migration to what is now Moscow. Geography and topography make it highly unlikely. The distance between the two locations spans over 1685 kilometers. The Kyivan Rus' would have had to traverse dense forests and expansive swamps to reach Moscow, adding even further distance and difficulties to the journey. Navigating the terrain would have meant penetrating even deeper into the Golden Horde-held territories and inviting further raids, death and destruction. The story prevailed because there was no independent narrative allowed to challenge it, nor was independent research possible to offer criticism of the lore. Such is how Russian history is made and accepted as fact.

The migration theory was entirely a political invention created in an attempt to substantiate the succession story of the transfer of power from the Kyivan Rus' to the Muscovy. At any rate, c. 1250, Moscow was at best an undeveloped backwater (if it existed) — hardly an attractive destination for a displaced society.[65] There is no archaeological evidence to support the supposed migration of the Kyivan Rus' to Moscow.[66] Absent a physical displacement to Moscow, any migration of culture and politics can only be considered in the context of appropriation.

There is no evidence of this alleged migration to the east. There is some evidence of a southerly and westerly migration following the sack of Kyiv, however. It is incomprehensible that droves of Kyivan Rus' migrated across a frontier swarming with khanate forces only to negotiate large forests and endless swamplands to arrive on the banks of the Moscow River, also under the thumb of the Golden Horde. While the Muscovy may have experienced migration of Kyivan Rus' influence from elite rulers, the Muscovy was not Rus' but remained a collection of proto-Slavic tribal people gathered under the *ulus* of the khanate's newly established principality.

Who then were the people who populated the nascent area of modern Moscow and founded the settlement that grew over centuries to become a metropolis?

Prior to the 10th century, the area known as the Central Upland (the region around modern Moscow) was populated by several Volga Finnic

---

[65] The Golden Horde censuses of 1237–1238 and 1257 do not mention the existence of Moscow. Moscow as a settlement only emerges in the Golden Horde census of 1272. See: Lawrence N. Langer, "Muscovite Taxation and the Problem of Mongol Rule in *Rus'*", Russian History, Vol. 34, No. 1/4", *Brill*, 2007; and, Mauricio Borrero, "Russia: A Reference Guide from the Renaissance to the Present", *Infobase Publishing*, 2009.

[66] Sebastian Milbank, "Kiev and Moscow: a tale of two Russias (Ukraine threatens Putin because it offers an alternative version of Russia)", *The Critic*, 12 March 2022.

groups. Among these Indigenous peoples could be counted the Mari, Merya and at least three other distinct groups of peoples and tribes that are now identified as the Moksel.[67] They established settlements along the banks of the Mustajoki River (Black River).[68] It is from their pre-Slavic word *Mustajoki* that the Russian names Москва-река [Mokva Reka—Moscow River] and Моско́вия [Muscovy] are derived. The region that the Moksel (later known as the Muscovy) occupied, along with other annexed territories, eventually became known as Russia.

The Moksel inhabitants of Central Upland[69] where Moscow would later be founded was loosely governed yet remained under the influence of the Suzdal Principality.[70] Only later were they successively governed by the Golden Horde and then the Türkic khanate. Being neither ethnically Rus' nor Kyivan Rus', all such claims by Putin are based on political revisionist and Russian Orthodox chroniclers seeking to provide the people who existed in their pre-history with a grand heritage.

Varangian-Norse settlers associated with the Kyivan Rus' did not begin to engage in substantial intercourse with the region until the late 10th century, when the Slavic Vyatichi and Krivichi tribes began to inhabit the area.[71] By the 13th century, the Moksel, Vyatichi and Krivichi, who by then were referred to as Muscovy, had taken on the semblance of a nation under the influence of the Principality of Muscovy and the Golden Horde.

Any appeal to reason calls us to reject Putin's claims of Russian identity and ethnicity. Claiming ethnic heritage because a distant political authority that once governed the people is an absurdity. The elastic invocation of ethnicity, nationality, and citizenry in Russian history and rhetoric has blurred the lines between fact and fiction, relying on just enough fact to lend it credibility, as Russian propagandists began to confront the realities of independent research and publications during the 21st century. This

---

[67] Willem van Rubroeck (translated by William Woodville Rockhill), "The journey of William of Rubruck to the eastern parts of the world, 1253-55, As Narrated by Himself with Two Accounts of the Earlier Journey of John of Pian De Carpine", *London: As Printed for the Hakluyt Society*, 1900.

[68] Andrew Bell-Fialkoff, "The Role of Migration in the History of the Eurasian Steppe", *Macmillan Press Ltd. (London)*, 2016.

[69] Because of the fluctuating geographic boundaries over time, for the purposes of this text we will define the Suzdal Principality as occupy land within approximately 185km of modern Moscow, stretching approximately from modern Tver in the North to Morum in the east and from Kaluga in the South and Dugino in the west.

[70] For the purposes of this text, we use 'Suzdal Principality' which was the standard before being Russified as the Vladimir Suzdal in Russian historical records.

[71] John Fennell, "The Emergence of Moscow, 1304-1359", *University of California Press*, 15 November 2023.

accompanied neighboring states pursuing a robust renewal of their independent *esse*. In response, the Kremlin took a page from the ROC and began to focus on cultural identity as a unifying tool.

Modernity's understanding of identity is more definitive than that promoted by Russian history. Putin and his neo-imperialist propaganda machine finally embraced this reality.[72] A new identity can be forged notwithstanding a convoluted history. This is especially true when the sources of the narrative have been acknowledged as dubious, the authors' biases, and the texts recognized as being prone to political apologetics. Russian history has always been a product of political necessity and aspirations. Historical truth, based on critical analysis, facts, archaeology, linguistic and cultural contextualization, is political heresy in Putin's Russia.

The reasons the Kremlin and the ROC claim to be Kyivan Rus' and therefore heirs to their monarchical history centred on Kyiv with their marginally-shared linguistic heritage as Slavic speakers and their religious identity as Greek Orthodox Christians is clear—it provides a geopolitical foundation to claim that all peoples who the Kyivan Rus' governed, who speak a Slavonic language and are Orthodox Christians are in fact Russian. It is the embrace of this reality that causes Putin and the ROC to fear the recovery of historical, cultural, religious, and political history by neighboring states.

The re-emergence of bordering nations with a robust sense of their inherent identity challenges Russia's political raison d'être—having a Holy Rus' to establish the Russkiy Mir'.

---

[72] Vladimir Putin, "Meeting of the Presidential Council for Interethnic Relations (videoconference)", *Kremlin: Moscow*, 30 March 2021.

Chapter Three

Meet the Muscovy
Russian's Real Relatives — Neither Kyivan Rus' Nor Byzantines and Not Always Christians

The Principality of Muscovy (sometimes referred to as a grand duchy) only entered the historical records in the 13th century. The Principality of Muscovy, and the Muscovy as a people, became synonymous in the same way the Kyivan Rus' kingdom lent its people their eponymous name.

Contrary to modern assertions by neo-imperialists, the Muscovy did not call themselves Rus' any more than subjects of the Eastern Roman Empire would have thought of themselves as Byzantines.[73] The Muscovy did not share in the Kyivan Rus' lineage though it is possible some of their political masters had, but then only for a very short period of time in their pre-history. Consequently, the Muscovy did not consider themselves to be Kyivan Rus' or Rus' of any measure. The Muscovy referred to themselves as Москвич [Moskvitch — Muscovites].

The Muscovy's heritage came not from the west, but from the east. At the turn of the first millennia the settlement that would, two centuries later, be founded as Moscow likely consisted, if it could be considered a settlement at all, as a mere collection of mud huts along the River Muskva.[74] The region's people, known to historians and ethnographers as the *Moksel* (a conglomeration of *Chud*, *Mari*, *Merya*, *Moksha*, *Mordvins*, *Vest* and other proto-Slavic tribes) were not yet organized as an identifiable or definable people. Nationhood, or even a unified political system of governance, still eluded them.

When Moscow was finally founded in the late 12th century, the Indigenous Moksel remained a semi-wild, pagan, tribal group wholly distinct from the Kyivan Rus' to the west or other Rus' to the Northwest. They

---

[73] Those we commonly call *Byzantines* referred to themselves as Ρωμαῖοι *(Rhōmaîoi, Romans)* because they understood their identity as being such. Byzantine, by contrast, is a late-Enlightenment scholarly device that would have been unknown by the people.

[74] John Fennell, "The Emergence of Moscow, 1304–1359", *University of California Press*, 15 November 2023.

lived on the far Eastern fringe of regions controlled by Kyiv. Their first contact with the Kyivan Rus' was negligible. They fell under territory claimed by the new Suzdal Principality, itself only tenuously related to the Kyivan Rus' and only then, primarily through mythological *Riurik* connections.

What became known as the Principality of Muscovy and its Muscovy people were not products of the Kyivan Rus'. The development of the Moskel into Muscovy evolved independently of Kyivan Rus' engagement. This requires us to reject the received narrative generally promoted through propaganda channels that Russians can claim a clear line of succession between the Kyivan Rus' as a people and political heirs.

How then did the Principality of Muscovy and its people almost universally come to be associated with the Kyivan Rus' identity in modernity? To better understand the answer to that question, it requires a 'deep dive' into the evolution of Russia, Russians and the ROC.

While evidence militates toward independent development, understanding 'Who were the Kyivan Rus'? can assist us in understanding why they must be excluded from the Russian narrative as historically asserted. The Kyivan Rus' were not the foundation of Muscovy.

The ruling Kyivan Rus' elite maintained a form of the Old Norse language similar to the way medieval English monarchs maintained the French language despite ruling over Saxons, Celts, and Normans. The Kyivan Rus' elite did not speak the local Old East Slavic tongue as a first language. For that matter, they did not speak the *Qırım* Tili [Crimean Tatar] of the Indigenous Crimean people over whom they also had dominion.[75] The linguistic distinction between the Kyivan Rus' and their subjects provides significant evidence that they succeeded in delineating their ethnic distinctiveness from the Slavic and Crimean Tatar subjects of their medieval kingdom. Later claims of unity must be received as invocations of political identity and not ethnic, linguistic, or cultural commonality.

Contrary to ethnic claims, Muscovy's genetic heritage derives from the Moksel, themselves an ethnically diverse people who later assimilated with the early groupings of peoples under collective rule in the Central Uplands. The Moskels were distinct from the Muscovy in many ways. They embraced a democratic system of governance. They worshipped as deists heavily influenced by shamanism. Politically, they maintained a fragmented, somewhat tribal control over a relatively small region, insignificant in size to modern Russia.

Except to the east, the Moksel domains were confined on all sides by more developed peoples with distinct cultures and languages that helped preserve their independent and individual identities and cultures.

---

75 The Indigenous *къырымтатар тили* (Crimean Tatars) spoke their native قریم تلی (including the yalıboyu and cenübiy), dialects within the Türkic language family.

Where terrain and geography didn't limit the expanse of the Moksel, other peoples did. The nascent Moksel were bordered by Slavs ruled by the Kyivan Rus' to the west. The Bulgars, a Türkic tribe along with the Khazars, hemmed them in to the south. Finnic Veps bordered the Moksel to the northeast and Permians to the east. From the tsarist epoch to the current neo-imperialists under Putin, Russia has undertaken significant efforts to avoid claiming them as the foundation of its genuine heritage. It was not only a matter of embarrassment. Proto-Slavs in pre-history were semi-wild, while the glories of Rome, Athens, and Constantinople had already reached their apex and were already experiencing near-complete decay, if not demise.

Claiming Moksel heritage would have been a self-limiting exercise. To the contrary, insisting on being the sole successors and heirs of the Rus', and Kyivan Rus', alternatively boasting of being the 'Third Rome' and successors of Hellenic and Roman cultures, provided a basis for claims on once-expensive kingdoms and trade empires boasting advanced European cultures. Simultaneously, such assertions tended to legitimize their early expansionist and later revanchist foreign policies.[76]

How did Muscovy become Russian? In simple terms, Muscovy becoming Russian is a product of sheer reinvention, fabrication, and appropriation on a grand scale. Historian, archeographer and member of the National Academy of Sciences of Ukraine, Yaroslav Dashkevych, summed it up with alacrity and succinctness:

> The Muscovite and later Russian tsars understood that without a great past it was impossible to create a great nation, a great empire. To do this, it was necessary to embellish their historical past and even appropriate someone else's [77]

As pre-history provides modernity with little more than the basis of conjecture, learned though some of it may be, what certainty can be achieved is necessary to our task. We shall begin with the foundations of the Principality of Muscovy for ease of clarity. Let us start with facts as they are verifiable.

---

[76] Ethnicity, culture, language and religion are Russia's on motivations for revanchism. Russia is keen to destroy the rules-based order established after World War II which challenged their right of occupation of countries from the Baltics to the Black Sea. Waging hybrid warfare on the west for historic-cultural reasons hides the nakedness of aggression based on territorial hegemony.

[77] Yaroslav Dashkevych, "Як Московія привласнила історію Київської Русі", Журнал Універсум, 11–12 (217–218), 2011.

The Principality of Muscovy was erected as an ulus of the Mongol Golden Horde in 1283.[78] Her princes and their Muscovy subjects were under the khan's suzerainty. This submission abided until the 15th century[79] when Ivan III threw off their shackles and established a unified, Christian kingdom independent of the Tatar khanate in 1480.[80]

The Principality of Muscovy should rightly be considered to have a Ghengisid identity in its immediate post-Moksel period, not a Kyivan Rus' identity.

The son of Alexander Yaroslavich Nevsky, the Prince of Novgorod, one Daniel Aleksandrovich, then only aged two, inherited the least of his father's principalities. His legacy was the minor duchy of Muscovy. Daniel Aleksandrovich ruled as a vassal of the Mongol Golden Horde. He is often cited as being of Varangian descent, an alleged claimant to the Riurik dynastic lineage. This is highly dubious.[81] The Riuriks were a mythological line claimed in antiquity to establish authority. Regional leaders clung to their heritage the way the Welsh and English sought to associate themselves with the mythic Arthur lineage until most recently.

The basis of the Riurik dynasty is rooted in the oral tradition known as the Calling of the Varangians, a mythic origin story of the Rus'. It existed in written form in such variant forms that most scholars now reject it as a historical document, saying it is "entirely fictional."[82] There are no source mentions of the Riurikids. According to Riasanovsky, "no Kievan sources anterior to the Primary Chronicle (early 12th century) knew of Riurik."[83] The *Hypatian Codex* omits any mention of the Riurikids whatsoever.

Given the requirement of the ROC that rulers must descend from the Rus', it is likely that 15th-century clergy-chroniclers, ever mindful of the theory of the divine right of kings, attempted to legitimize Daniel Aleksandrovich's lineage by tying him to the mythic Varangian Riuriks.[84] When

---

[78] Nicholas V. Riasanovsky and Mark D. Steinberg, "A history of Russia (Ninth ed.)," New York: *Oxford University Press*, 2019.
[79] John M. Letiche and Anatoliĭ Ignat'evich Pashkov, editor, "A History of Russian Economic Thought: Ninth Through Eighteenth Centuries", Berkeley: *University of California Press*, 1964.
[80] Ian Grey, "Ivan III and the Unification of Russia", *English Universities Press*, 1964.
[81] George Vernadsky, "Kievan Russia", New Haven, *Yale University Press*, 1948.
[82] Christian Raffensperger, "Reimagining Europe: Kyivan Rus' in the Medieval World, 988–1146", *Harvard Historical Studies*, 2008.
[83] Donald Ostrowski, "Was there a Riurikid Dynasty in Early Rus'?", *Canadian-American Slavic Studies, No. 52*, 2018.
[84] Christian Raffensperger, "Ties of Kinship: Genealogy and Dynastic Marriage in Kyivan Rus'", *Harvard Series in Ukrainian Studies*, 2016.

doing so, they went so far as to fabricate a family tree claiming descent from Caesar Augustus, "bolstering the Muscovite dynastic state."[85]

As for Daniel Aleksandrovich and what we know of him, depending on the source, he was presented as a wise ruler and prolific builder of churches. His history and hagiography are largely based on a post hoc record contemporaneous to his being proclaimed a saint in the Russian Orthodox calendar more than 350 years after his death, alternatively either in 1652 or 1791. Though the date of his canonization is disputed, the earlier date appears to be the most reliable, taking place during the reign of the second Romanov ruler, Tsar Alexei Mikhailovich. Together with his collaborator and chief adviser, Patriarch Nikon, the two invented an illustrious lineage for the Romanovs. Elevating Daniel of Moscow was a useful part of that reinvention.

The Romanovs, Russia and the ROC were then in the throes of convulsions due to a schism caused by Patriarch Nikon's liturgical reforms. The controversy was exacerbated by the patriarch's confiscation of what he deemed heterodox prayer books. Not satisfied with such sweeping initiatives, Russia was then steeped in further vitriol when Patriarch Nikon set his sights on launching an iconoclastic initiative seeking to destroy newer styles of Russian icons seized during his extensive household raids.[86]

Comprehending his role in the mythology of Russia, and despite the passage of centuries, notwithstanding source information being unavailable, the Patriarch of Moscow canonized him "The Right Believing Daniel of Moscow," but restricting his sainthood only for "local veneration." Given his purported role as the founder of Moscow's first monastery and his legendary Christian works, it is likely the ROC, fully aware of his true lineage, and possibly fearing God, agreed to the cause of his sainthood for political purposes but only for Russian, not universal Orthodox Christian veneration.

---

[85] Ostrowski, *ibid*.

[86] Nikon was an early member of the Кружок ревнителей благочестия (Zealots of Piety) before becoming Patriarch. Founded during the Time of Troubles (1598-1613), the Zealots believed Russia's difficulties were caused by divine displeasure due to irreligiosity and lack of piety amongst the Russian people. Sanitizing Daniel Alexandrovich's past and giving it a solid veneer of Christian virtue and works would have been of use to Nikon and the Tsar. The outpouring of hagiographic works concerning Daniel of Moscow, including his alleged Riurik lineage as well as the alleged recovery of his supposedly "incorrupt" body for veneration from a disused, swampy church graveyard, date only from this period. Patriarch Nikon was later deprived of his sacerdotal functions by the Great Moscow Synod which included the Patriarchs of Alexandria and Antioch and reduced to being a monk before being imprisoned at the Ferapontov monastery.

Given the lack of any mention of the Riurikid contemporary ancient texts, and even then, only the most tenuous links between him and that supposed dynasty, with the modern scholarship consensus that the Riurikids were almost certainly mythological, it is almost certain that Daniel Aleksandrovich was of Moksel stock, steeped in Ghengisid-Islamic or Tengrist heritage. His post-mortem canonization based on apocrypha compels us to view it as an attempt by the newly established Romanovs and an unsteady ROC to legitimize their foundations by forging a more Christian, Kyivan Rus' lineage.

According to legend, Daniel of Moscow died in 1303 after having supposedly taken the tonsure. Later sources assert his last will provided that he be buried in the churchyard of the then wooden monastery. It was a simple grave of a monk.[87] Later, the monastery was moved near the Kremlin and his grave was lost in what had become a disused cemetery whose fortified walls formed part of the defense of Moscow during the Time of Troubles (1598–1613).

Hagiographers record that the body of Daniel of Moscow was supposedly recovered in the 17th century. Claimed to have been found incorrupt, his relics were transported to the new Danilov Monastery on the right bank of the Moscow River just outside the Kremlin walls. His relics were then believed to have been destroyed during the war of 1812 when Napoleon Bonaparte destroyed Moscow by conflagration. Daniel of Moscow's relics were again reportedly wholly destroyed during the Soviet era when the Danilov Monastery was razed. His relics were alleged to have again been "Miraculously recovered" in 1986. According to the Moscow Patriarchate, they were returned to a place of veneration in the rebuilt Danilov Monastery, where they remain to this day.

Putting aside the murky mythology, claims of miracles and political intrigue surrounding the Principality of Moscow, its people and rulers, the principality's establishment arose more than four decades after what is

---

[87] The 16th century rendition of this story is without evidence. It is unlikely that the simple grave of a monk, dug on or about 5 March 1303, either being wrapped in a shroud or placed in a simple wooden coffin, would have survived the heaving of freezing and thawing of the damp soil of an early Moscow Spring, if a grave could have been dug in the frozen tundra at all at the time. There is also significant doubt as to his remains having survived for hundreds of years before miraculously being found "incorrupt," let alone being discovered after having been lost to the ages. The graveyard had by the 16th century been long in disuse, having been substantially re-developed as a fortified military garrison experiencing significant combat activity several times during the Time of Troubles. Daniel of Moscow's relics would have to reasonably considered the work of hagiographers manufacturing relics for political and religious veneration in conformity with the mythological construct of a Russian past.

widely accepted to mark the demise of the unified rule of the Kyivan Rus' in 1240[88] marked by the razing of Kyiv by the Golden Mongol Horde. Moscow could not have been the successor to Kyiv nor the Principality of Muscovy to the Kyivan Rus'. Appropriation may have occurred, but not succession.

It is also an immutable fact of history that the Grand Principality of Muscovy, founded in 1283, did not declare itself to be known as Russia until October 22, 1721.[89] Each iteration was a reinvention of identity for political purposes.

A straight line of political succession simply does not exist as claimed. Boasts of heredity entitlement to either or both the Riurik and Kyivan Rus' identities are dubious if not simply fabricated. Being a prince of the Principality of Muscovy was entirely the gift of the Tatar khanate and Golden Mongol Horde. The deconstruction of Russia's history lays bare the fallacies upon which the Russian Federation and ROC lay claim to their neighbors today.

The west's willingness to continue conflating Rus', Russia and Russian cedes far more to the neo-imperialism promoted by Putin, embraced by the ROC and which pervades Russian nationalist ideology than is deserved. There is an inherent danger in the weaponization of the oblique onomatopoeia between Rus' and Russia that reinforces the political, cultural, linguistic, religious, and territorial claims used by Putin to justify his highly nationalistic domestic and foreign policies.[90] Moreover, it shifts the burden of defense concerning sovereignty, independence, and identity to Russia's neighbors, who already suffered greatly under the thumbs of tsars, commissars, and today's neo-imperialists.

For Putin and modern Russian apologists of a neo-imperialist tilt, the Russian state and its people being the direct successors of the Kyivan Rus' drives the conflicts and occupations in Moldova's Transnistria, Georgia's Abkhazia and South Ossetia and Ukraine. Evoking ownership and dominion based on culture, language, and religion provides a maternal and benevolent gloss to the reality of Russia's desire to reoccupy the independent countries it once inducted into its Soviet empire by force.

This dissection of Russian history should not be necessary today. Problems with the Western approach to Russian history were observed in the United States as far back as 1959:

---

[88] Janet Martin, "Medieval Russia: 980–1584. Second Edition", *Cambridge University Press*, 2007.
[89] John Paxton, "Imperial Russia", *Palgrave Macmillan, London*, 2001.
[90] Andrei Kolesnikov, "Blood and Iron: How Nationalist Imperialism Became Russia's State Ideology", *Carnegie Russia Eurasia Center*, December 2023.

> There is a thirty-year lag between the introduction of a subject and its widespread acceptance. Russian studies in the secondary schools are following the traditional pattern. Interested teachers reported dissatisfaction with the presentation of Soviet affairs in textbooks and described their need to rely on pamphlets and other current materials to teach the most important information.[91]

Any progress then in presenting a more nuanced and correct understanding of Russia, Russians and the Russian sphere required teachers to abandon the curriculum and create their own syllabus and course materials. Unsurprisingly, educators acknowledged the deficiencies in the presentation of knowledge about the former Soviet Union and Russia for decades but did little to change matters, allowing inertia to carry on. If westerners misunderstand Russia today, it is because of sloth and a willingness to close their eyes to the truth. It has made confronting Russia unnecessarily more difficult. Recognizing the problem is the first step to addressing it.

Attempts were made in the past to confront the problem. In 1987, academics from the Soviet Union and the United States met to review each other's textbooks. One resounding consensus emerged from the project participants, articulated succinctly by Ben Eklof, Senior Fellow at the Woodrow Wilson International Center: "Everybody agreed that American textbooks were outrageously full of factual errors."[92]

The collapse of the Soviet Union marked a new epoch. Still, textbooks and research publications continued to repeat the errant information of the past and focus on developing a more in-depth look at the emergence of the Russian Federation. The appetite to address the problems of the past simple subsided. That so many adults in the west simply fell into the trap of accepting outdated information, developed by Russian imperialists for political consumption, is understandable, even forgivable. With Western teachers, journalists and politicians resorting to information they acquired via propaganda-driven narratives, the perpetuation of fallacy as fact has taken on its own momentum.

Since the lowering of the Soviet flag from atop the Kremlin over 30 years ago, more than a generation of children have been taught that version of Russian history, which is more akin to imperial and neo-imperial mythology than fact-based historiography. Putin and Russia know this and work to exploit it at every turn. Their projection of claims of right conduct based on claims of persecution and attempts by the west to reshape Russia:

---

[91] C.E. Black and J. Thompson, "American Teaching About Russia. Bloomington", *Indiana University Press*, 1959.
[92] Barbara Vobejda, "U.S., Soviet Textbooks Give Different Accounts of History", *The Washington Post*, 5 December 1987.

I also thought that key disagreements [between us] were ideological in nature. Yet, when the Soviet Union was gone... the dismissive approach to Russia's strategic interests persisted. The West decided... they do not need to follow the rules when it comes to Russia, which does not have the same power as the USSR... Everything was good as long as it was against Russia.[93]

Paranoia, misdirection, and revanchism drive Russia's desire for the creation of a Russkiy Mir as the premier agent of international influence. The ROC is their willing collaborator in this project. It is also its greatest beneficiary. The intersection of the Russian state and ROC polity has become part and parcel of the fabric of Russia's hybrid-warfare campaign across the European Union.

Given a better understanding of Muscovy and why it must be excluded from consideration as heirs of the Kyivan Rus', we must address the issue of Muscovy's telos.

The avarice of the Muscovy princes for all things was insatiable. Just as with the Russian Federation today, the princes of this backwater principality would never be satiated by their transition from social collectivism to nationhood while more prosperous and advanced states existed on their borders. Being a principality had to give way to being a grand principality so that it could become a tsardom on its way to an empire. Russia's political satiety remains unquenchable.

The aspiration to establish a Russkiy Mir is proof positive that their goal is world domination. Their view of themselves as agents of the Holy Rus' demonstrates not only a sense of personal superiority but a deep disdain for others. The world heard this story before, almost exactly 100 years ago, replete with claims of historic glory, ethnic superiority, external threat, need for strength, demands for *lebensraum*, and the decadent lifestyles of others. Still, the west seems to have sleepwalked into this crisis in the same way they did then.[94]

The vainglorious hagiography of Muscovy princes and their descendants, compelled to be written to project greatness, was the product of paranoia and insecurity. Those princes' desire to be received as the equals of more advanced western civilizations and monarchs, as well as to justify their right to rule their own people, drove them. Having built a nation from the collectives, the princes of Muscovy needed to build a new political paradigm—one free of the blemishes of their Golden Horde and Türkic khanate past and one of their own constructs. The Muscovy needed genuine statehood. Its rulers would need grander titles, as 'prince' simply did not measure up to the rapaciousness of their greed and imagination.

---

[93] RT Staff, "Russia-West clash not about ideology—Putin", *RT*, 13 July 2025.
[94] John F. Kennedy, "Why England Slept", *Wilfred Funk, Inc.*, 1940.

In time, the princes of Muscovy resolved to call themselves by a new title befitting their ambitions—they would be acknowledged as царъ [tsar] after the imperial Roman and Byzantine title, Caesar. Their subjects would then need a new name worthy of an emperor—they would be called русский [Russkij—Russians]. Their new identity would be imbued with the invocation of the Kyivan Rus' mythos, history, and folklore primed for political projection.

In centuries to come, tsars would tire of their association with the diminutive nature of a principality, grand duchy or whatever styling with which they clad themselves. They would call their dominion Russia. As with the Red Banner being lowered over the Kremlin on December 25, 1991, as a sign of the demise of the Soviet Union, the coronation oath of Peter I Alekseyevich as "Tsar of All Russia" on November 2, 1721 marked the death of Muscovy while breathing life into the neophyte Russian state and empire.[95]

---

[95] Peter I Alekseyevich introduced the Julian Calendar in 1699. His 2 November 1721 coronation date corresponded to 22 October 1721 by the 'Old Calendar'.

Chapter Four

Appropriation & Extermination
Inventing a Great & Noble past Through Cultural and Historical Theft

Modern scholarship has helped us recognize the true foundations of the Principality of Muscovy. Of the many petty principalities in what was still a semi-wild region, the penchant of the Muscovy for good accounting and territorial defense allowed it to thrive while those on its fringe struggled. Its ascendency as a regional power is owed to its prowess for good taxation, careful administration, and organizational management. By contrast, the translation of the Principality of Muscovy to Imperial Russia was the product of tsarist apologetics as well as the cultural and historical appropriation of its neighbors and long-extinct empires. It also required a good measure of outright invention.

Had the Russian Empire survived, these acknowledgments may never have been admitted. Oddly, we owe the truth to the change of historic orientation that occurred during the Soviet era. Freed of either the inclination or necessity of engaging in imperial apologetics there arose periods during that epoch in which academic freedom (at least in some disciplines) became possible:

> Between 1956 and 1973 the Party loosened control over the humanities, and historical writing became less determinist and less Russian nationalist in tone. With the excesses of the Stalin period condemned scholars re-introduced professional standards into their work and had greater latitude to publish and discuss. Some criticized Russian colonialism and argued that non-Russian histories should be written independent of categories and periodization derived from Russian history.[96]

The liberalization of Soviet scholarship at times allowed some new domestic research and publications concerning Russian history. It remained, however, insufficient to counter hundreds of years of imperial historical distortion. The west's concurrent efforts in independent scholarship yielded better results.

---

[96] Stephen Velychenko, "Restructuring and the Non-Russian Past", *Nationality Papers, Vol. 22, No. 2*, 1994.

Once inhibited by Russian censorship, after the demise of the Soviet Union in 1991, the recovery of national memory by independent scholars formerly subject to the Russian sphere flourished. Access to works from antiquity long withheld from western scholars and the ability of Belarusians, Estonians, Lithuanians, Poles, Romanians, Ukrainians, and other researchers, scholars and writers to publish without constraint allowed them to parse the imperial record. This provided an abundance of new and often exceptional research and publications.

More recent, unfettered works published through western universities and research centers created an atmosphere ripe for greater accuracy and truth. What had previously been fields tightly controlled by tsarist censorship or excluded by Soviet restrictions were thrown open to new scholarship. The media was liberalized. Academics, once forbidden from teaching or publishing, were finally able to embrace the freedoms of the academy. Access to travel and engagement in international discourse, where access to forums and the collective rigors of the academy were finally possible. In short, the ingredients necessary to develop a reliable, contemporary, and contextualized body of research assisted in ensuring new works would be published free of the constraints of censorship and unrestrained by political or regional bias.

Consequently, delving into once forbidden archives and sources tended to lead scholars to rewrite Russian history. Hagiographic historiographies replete with reliance on cultural and political mythology were increasingly replaced with works of modern scholarship. These were not acts of revisionism for political purposes within the newly independent states, as Russia claims. They were the fruit of a genuine academic pursuit of knowledge. The fruit, however, had consequences:

> While the USSR existed in isolation, not thriving but at least stable, the Soviet identity underwent no crises. But the collapse of communism left neither a communist nor a superpower ideology.[97]

Nationalism and neo-imperialism thrived in the vacuum. The new, neo-imperialists in Russia blamed the west. According to the Kremlin and Moscow Patriarchate, such publications are revisionist in nature, political in practice and are published for one reason: to defame the state and the Russian people. The motivation cited is always the same—"Russophobia!" It remains inconceivable in Russian neo-imperialist and nationalist circles to believe that any truth discovered or recovered by those formerly within the

---

[97] Terhi Рантанен (Отв. ред. Е.Л.Вартанова), "Глобальное и национальное. Масс-медиа и коммуника-ции в посткоммунистической России", *Славянское обозрение*, январь 2022.

Russian sphere could be anything more than a part of a great Western conspiracy to prevent the Russkiy Mir.

For the ROC, the confrontation of Russian mythology with reality poses a serious threat. Any challenge to the received tradition of the ROC, even when not of a religious or theological nature, is deemed a direct challenge to the faith and declared heresy or an act of religious persecution. The ROC, having become a central part of the power apparatus of the Russian state, could not endure if what has been taught, and is still taught, is exposed as lacking in truth and credibility. Hence, the Moscow Patriarchate has become a defender of untruths.

The difficulty for the ROC is its long-term investment in the mythology surrounding the foundations of the Russian state, which have been passed off as history. The reliance on the concept of Moscow as the 'third Rome', for example, is predicated on the supposed writings of Philoteus, a monk writing in the Yelizarov Monastery near Pskov in the 15th century.[98] The princes of Muscovy spun this apocryphal attribution and uncertain story to enhance the prestige of their realm as part of the process of aggrandizing the principality. How else would they transform into a tsardom on the path to creating a Russian state?

The appropriation of the glories and religious cultures of Rome and the Byzantine Empire was critical to the Muscovy princes' ambitions. That both the Roman and Byzantine Empires were then extinct saved them the difficulty of exterminating any collective memory that may have survived the fall of Constantinople in 1453.

The marriage of Ivan III Vasilyevich to Sophia "Zoe" Paleologue, the favorite niece of the last Byzantine emperor, lent a respectable measure of credibility to the Byzantine succession and 'Third Rome' appropriation. The papacy had adopted Zoe Paleologue upon her father's death. She was raised nobly within the papal court. She held great influence over Ivan III Vasilyevich. If the Kremlin walls and other late 15th-century- early 16th-century construction in Moscow appear remarkably Roman, it is due to her. She recruited Italian architects to accompany her to Moscow in the hopes of giving artistic flourish to Moscow's primitive design and architecture. It only followed that Zoe Paleologue imported other Roman customs and traditions to Moscow as well.

If a Muscovy prince evolved into becoming a цар as opposed to being called βασιλεύς [basileus—Byzantine styling for emperor], it is due to Zoe Paleologue's upbringing at the papal court in Rome. The senior claimant of

---

[98] Vladimir Yurtaev & Anna Klimenko, Anna. (2018). "Moscow as the Third Rome Concept: Its Nature and Interpretations in the 19th—Early 21st Centuries", *Geopolítica(s). Revista de estudios sobre espacio y poder*. 9. 10.5209/GEOP.58910, 2018.

the Byzantine Paleologue basileis lineage, Zoe Paleologue, desired more for her Muscovy husband than being closely associated with the realm's Mongol Golden Horde and Türkic khanate past suzerainty. She had no intention of remaining a princess of a backwater realm. Her ambitions to greatness, however, would remain only partially realized. She died a grand princess of Muscovy. Another 44 years would pass before her grandson Ivan IV Vasilyevich declared the Tsardom of Russia.

The Holy Rus' ideology promoted by the ROC requires a wholesale investment predicated on, among other things, the supposed vision of Philoteus of Pskov. As keepers of the historical tradition, the ROC omits the machinations of a Byzantine princess deprived of her heritage and yet anxious to invent a grand title for herself, who pushed her husband to claim to be a Caesar. To do so would be a slight to the masculinity and authority of Tsar Ivan IV Vasilyevich. It is fair to ask, then, if the ROC, which promoted these as history for centuries, is even capable of recognizing truth from lies or fact from fiction. Without historical re-examination and breaking ties to the Russian state, the ROC is bound to the paradox of proclaiming the truth of the gospels while living the deceit of its various fabricated histories.

The practice of historical reinvention has become so endemic amongst Russian scholars that academics enjoy the aphorism, "Russia is a country with an unpredictable past." The alacrity by which Russia has and continues to rewrite, reframe, reinvent, or reinterpret its own past through the agency of passing political climates continues to confound westerners. Despite all evidence available, Russians have been led to believe the emperor has new clothes. Why should it be otherwise? In Putin's Russia, to simply question if the emperor is wearing clothes is tantamount to treason or heresy.

Today, we are capable of not only examining the specific social, cultural, economic, and political circumstances of the eras in which Russia's history arose. Contextualizing history provides a legitimate means of interpreting events. When, however, it is employed to excuse the appropriation of others' histories under the guise of a framework of ethnic or national unity, it ceases to be a methodology for understanding and knowledge. Due to the freedoms that now abound in countries once within the Russian sphere, we can now do so within the context of a wider orbit of perspectives and information. The richer bevy of independent sources gives this research credibility.

The long tradition of Russia engaging in the assimilation of others' cultures, histories, literature, or achievements has imbued Russians with a sense of identity that is neither indigenous nor deserved. As much as the appropriation from others has benefited Russia, it has also served to injure the identity and essence of those who suffered the loss. It is the consequence of appropriation that, after the injury, the wound festers such that it becomes a generational injury. Cultural appropriation and deprivation, followed by suppression and erasure, strike at the core of a nation's identity.

Here, the power imbalance inherent in the appropriation mechanism further challenges the victims. The appropriators, by their very deeds, challenge the victim's right to exist. This is no overstatement. Following appropriation any such is necessarily deemed to be a threat by the appropriator. Any historic memory that survives does so as a direct challenge to the underlying act of assimilation. Consequently, in the absence of complete and utter absorption or erasure, neither is fully achieved; extermination is the ultimate endgame for the victims.

With both the Russian state and ROC denying Ukraine's historic existence, or right to exist today, extermination is the only alternative left:

> Disintegrate Ukraine and destroy several millions of disloyal Russian people.... And fascists, anyway, are Ukrainians! ...Roughly speaking, [Ukrainians are] a few million people who cannot be corrected. Well, they need to be partially eliminated, and partly expelled....[99]

Inherent in the process of appropriation is the power imbalance between the appropriator and the appropriated. This very power allows the act of appropriation to be completed by engaging in the erasure of any collective memory of all that was appropriated. When Russia wanted to appropriate Belarusian, Estonian, Latvian, Polish, Ukrainian, or others' culture, language, music, traditions or other indigenous elements, it simply engaged in censorship.

Place names may have changed, but the method remained the same. The Lithuanian press ban (1865–1904), the Valuyev Circular (1863) and the Ems Ukase (1876) in Ukraine nearly deprived Ukraine of its national identity and cultural inheritance. In Lithuania, the proscription of the use of the Latin alphabet (1865) forced Lithuanians to adopt Russia's Cyrillic alphabet and, within a generation, become divorced from their ability to access their indigenous body of literature. The general prohibition on the dissemination of literature in Latvian (1865) or Latgallian (1871) proved near fatal blows to the continuation of independent identity in the Baltics. The same occurred wherever Imperial Russia occupied its neighbors.

The lethality of Russification required not only the appropriation of others' elements of individual identity, but it also demanded that the memories be erased. The practice has become so pro forma that Russians fail to comprehend its occurrence. Russia's neo-imperial renewal of appropriation and extermination under Putin has had the unintended consequence

---

[99] Mikhail Khazin, "Их необходимо частично устранить", *YouTube Video*, 27 декабрь 2016.

of generating a new and more vociferous enmity toward Russia. That in turn has generated hostility among Russians toward their neighbors. And yet, Russia's demand that cultural appropriation be accepted by its neighbors, albeit now without Russia's ability to enforce the erasures once possible under the authority of tsars and commissars, has left the ROC as the soft power, social enforcer of appropriation and erasure. Their involvement in 'kin state activism' in neighboring states, even when uninvited or unwelcome, is a recipe for conflict. By taking up the mantle of the Russian Federation, the ROC is abandoning its role as a church and intruding into domestic politics that strikes at the heart of social cohesion in Europe.

The paradigm works by first instilling a sense of fear among Russians that their identity is under attack by their neighbors. This creates a social bulwark against attempts to disentangle what is genuinely Russian from what was appropriated. In a sense, by those formerly within the Russian sphere engaging in the recovery of appropriated culture, language, history, religious freedom, and other elements of ethno-national identity, Russians claim they feel they are under assault. Disassembling colonialism and imperialism have this general effect. Russia disagrees with this worldview and claims it to be a Russophobic activity designed to harm the Russian community domestically and beyond its borders.

The Russian state and ROC, both entities prone to paranoia and claims of being under constant siege, have sought to inhibit collective memory recovery. By propaganda and preaching, they seek to reinforce acceptance of what they see as the social, cultural, and religious norms of the Russian Federation. In response to their fears, the ROC went directly to the source—the education of young children. The Moscow Patriarchate developed the Fundamentals of Orthodox Culture (FOC) curriculum in 1992, immediately following the collapse of the Soviet Union.

Its implementation in all Russian schools had the effect of requiring the embrace of the Russian Orthodox catechism for Russian school children. In 2012, the new *Основы православной культуры* [Fundamentals of Religious Cultures] course sought to strengthen the state through increased understanding of 'traditional' religions and thereby build greater social cohesion. Few realized it was an exercise in appropriation and extermination.

In practice, the FOC curricula served to identify and marginalize children whose families did not follow the Russian Orthodox faith. With six optional modules, the most popular is Secular Ethics, followed by Fundamentals of Orthodox Culture. Critics claim the Secular Ethics module promotes political indoctrination, while all modules teach that Russian Orthodox Christianity is about "teaching about God correctly and truthfully."[100] Russia's education curriculum, left in the hands of the ROC, prioritized state goals over religious goals. The practice of reinforcing these ideas is that by embracing Russian patriotism and the Russian Orthodox faith to the exclusion of all others, Russia's promotion of 'traditional values' will strengthen the church and state.

The interplay of patriotism and faith is a constant theme in Russia. In 2009, the Patriarch of Moscow visited the Northern Shipyard at Severodvinsk, where he was received with full military honors. During his speech, Patriarch Kirill projected the concept that without the Russian Orthodox faith, Russians had nothing to defend:

> 'You should not be ashamed of going to church and teaching the orthodox faith to your children,' the patriarch told the Severodvinsk workers. 'Then we shall have something to defend with our missiles.'[101]

In 2012, Russia undertook a new school curriculum change with the stated goal:

> to develop the abilities of elementary school children to communicate and to interact in multiethnic and multi-religious society on the basics of mutual respect and dialogue for the sake of social peace and cohesion.[102]

As part of this effort, a compulsory course was introduced, World Religious Cultures and Secular Ethics. It changed Russia's educational landscape dramatically. The course was built on Patriarch Aleksii's assertion that a civilizational approach to history (in opposition to the socio-economic historical contextualization) would benefit the Russian state: "Both believers and nonbelievers should receive from it the lifegiving force of Orthodoxy and the heights of its ideals."[103]

Externally, the ROC resorted to a policy of external inclusion of Russian minorities abroad. This 'kin state activism' by the ROC projects the Russian state's educational goals abroad. Reinforcing the idea that Russian

---

[100] Alexy Beglov, E. Saplina, E. Tokareva, and A. Yarlykapov, "Osnovi Mirovih Religioznih Kultur", *Prosveshenie: Moscow*, 2012.

[101] Brian Whitmore, "Russia's Patriarch Increasingly Becoming Major Force In Politics", *Radio Free Europe/Radio Liberty*, 6 September 2009.

[102] Tatiana Pronina, ""Teaching "The Foundations of Orthodox Culture" in Schools of the Tambov Region: Achievements and Problems""", *State Religion and Church 5, No. 2,* 2018

[103] Nikolay Mitrokhin, "Ovčinnikov, O pravoslavnom obrazovanii", *Russkaja pravoslavnaja cerkov', Moskva*, 2004.

patriotism and the Russian Orthodox faith are intrinsically intertwined ensures the ROC's authority is preserved abroad, where the Russian state has little ability to exercise its power.

The "Decree of the 25th World Russian People's Council: the present and the future of the Russian world", an international forum headed by Patriarch Kirill, claimed a "West immersed in Satanism"[104] as a threat to Russia and the ROC; the constant maligning of the west by Russian propaganda seeking to indoctrinate Europeans of Russian descent poses a genuine threat to European security and democracy. The constant stream of anti-western sentiment is meant to weaken European social cohesion, especially among the "Russian minority" residing in states formerly within the Russian sphere. Condemning the west as satanic to Russians living abroad is a critical element of 'kin state activism' designed to maintain or return Russians in neighboring states to the Russian sphere.

Russia's invasion of eastern Ukraine and Crimea in 2014, and its full-scale invasion in 2022, provided Russia with a greater opportunity to engage in the solidification of cultural appropriation. An erasure campaign was necessary to complete the task. To counter what they felt was the alienation of Ukrainians from their "true Russian identity," Russia re-engaged occupied Ukrainians with cultural and linguistic re-indoctrination. Truckloads of newly printed textbooks, purpose-written for occupied Ukraine, were introduced by Russian occupation regimes within weeks of their 2014 and 2022 invasions of Luhansk, Donetsk, Crimea, and all but still free Ukrainian territory. Of course, the destruction of all textbooks and literature in Ukrainian was required.[105] [106]

The story of the suppression of ancient knowledge is nothing new. The act of Russia's erasure of widespread knowledge of the Ukraïna people in antiquity is an exemplar of the destructiveness of appropriation and extermination.

Putin was nurtured on the idea that Russia was the mother of all Slavic nations and that Russia was the sole successor of the Kyivan Rus'.

---

[104] Plenary Session, "Decree of the 25th World Russian People's Council: the present and the future of the Russian world", *World Russian People's Council*, 27 March 2024.

[105] France 24 (Video by Raïd Abu Zaideh, Robert Parsons & Pauline Godart), "In occupied Kherson, 'the Russians were destroying all books in Ukrainian'", *France 24*, 5 December 2022.

[106] Miceál O'Hurley personally visited a newly built school in Studenok, Izium Raion, Kharkiv Oblast, Ukraine immediately following its liberation. There, Russia's Wagner mercenaries had gathered the new Ukrainian language textbooks in the gymnasium and burned them in a manner eerily reminiscent of the book burnings in Nazi Germany, destroying large parts of the school in the process.

Unsurprisingly, he claims Ukraine is not a real country[107] despite there being ample evidence of its people, if not a Ukrainian nation, existing in antiquity. In fact, the evidence is preserved in the very chronicles he often invokes to undergird his distorted version of the history and superiority of the Russian people.

The *Kyivan Chronicle* c. 1187 specifically referred to the Ukraïna people. This gives near-contemporary proof that their identity was firmly established and recognized contemporaneously. The *Hypatian Codex* (c. 1452) and the later *Khlebnikov Codex* (c. 1560s) preserve large fragments of the *Kyivan Chronicle* (c. 1187), a text that serves as a continuation of the earlier *Chronicles of Nestor*. Both the *Hypatian Codex* and *Khlebnikov Codex* record the use of the word Ukraïna in relation to a people mourning the 1187 death of Volodymyr Glebovich, Prince of Pereyaslavl [in Ukrainian, Князь Переяславський]. The text appearing confirms the contemporary existence of a distinct people known as the Ukraïna: "*ѡ нем же Оукраина много постона*" [*The Ukraïna groaned with grief for him*].[108]

The historical record gives us indelible proof that the Ukrainian people existed and were recognized as a distinct people as part of the Kyivan Rus' several hundred years before Muscovy even existed, longer still before the concept of the Russian people emerged. Any assertion that a distinct nation identified by contemporary sources emerged from the yet-to-be-established Russian people is repugnant to common sense.

The research of Harvard University's Serhii Plokhy supports defining the Ukraïna of this era as being synonymous with the territories of the Kyivan Rus' Principality of Pereyaslavl[109] (spanning today's Middle Dnieper region to the west to the northern shores of the Black Sea and Caspian Sea, where it ends at the Ural-Caspian narrowing). Ukraine and its people were certainly recognized as extant in antiquity, while the first, though dubious mention of an embryonic settlement of Moscow, was mentioned in *post hoc* historical annals c. 1147.[110]

---

[107] Olesya Khromeychuk, "Putin Says Ukraine Doesn't Exist. That's Why He's Trying to Destroy It", *New York Times*, 1 November 2022.
[108] "Въ лѣто 6694 [1186] – 6698 [1190]. Іпатїівський літопис" [In the year 6694 [1186] – 6698 [1190]. The Hypatian Codex]. *litopys.org.ua (in Church Slavic)*, 1908.
[109] Serhii Plokhy, "The Gates of Europe: A History of Ukraine" (Revised Edition), *Basic Books, New York*, 2015.
[110] The c. 1147 date for the existence of Moscow is specious. We have adopted the more reliable date of c. 1272 when Moscow finally appeared in the 3rd Census of the Mongol Golden Horde.

This acknowledgment of the Ukraïna people contrasted with the later emergence of the Principality of Muscovy in the 13th century[111] tends to be dispositive as to the existence of the Ukraïna people in antiquity. Any postulation by Russian historians or the Kremlin at present that the Ukrainians either did not exist or are derivative of the Russian people runs contrary to the very texts which Putin so often selectively cites.

It is sufficient to acknowledge that the Ukraïna were recognized as a unique people before Russia even emerged as a discernable nation-state. The language of the Ukraïna was derived from the Old East Slavic in use under the Kyivan Rus'. Ukrainian is not a species or dialect of Russian. It is only through cognitive distortion that Ukraine's separately evolved and distinct language can somehow be reduced to be dialect of Russian simply because they share a common ancestor.[112] Claims of this nature are political in nature, co-aligning with the Russian ideology of the superiority of the Holy Rus'.

Linguistically, Putin argues that Ukrainian is merely a dialect of Russian. There is no evidence of this whatsoever. From a chronological standpoint, Ukrainian could not be derivative of Russian. The *Hypatian Codex, Khlebnikov Codex* and more ancient *Kyivan Chronicle* all affirm the existence of Ukraïna. Any assertion that their lingual evolution remained in a state of arrested development for hundreds of years before any concept of Russians or Russia existed lacks credibility. The Muscovy spake another branch of the Old Slavic tongue entirely. It would be a unique development for any independent evolution of a distinct language to be subordinated to another lineage of linguistic development, all for the sake of political expediency.

The Ukrainian language may share roots in the proto-Slavic linguistic tree, but it branched off long before Russian began to develop as a language. The most that can be said about the Ukrainian and Russian languages is that they share a common ancestor in Old East Slavic, if not more

---

[111] Janet Martins, "Muscovy's Northeastern Expansion: The Context and a Cause", *Éditions de la 'EHESS', Cahiers du Monde russe et soviétique*, Vol. 24, No. 4, October-December 1983.

[112] Academics debate the issues of linguistic evolution in the region. Russian linguist Andrey Anatolyevich Zaliznyak argued modern Russian is a synthesis of Old Novgorod dialect and Old East Slavic, emerging c. 13th–15th centuries and distinct from Ukrainian linguistic evolution. Linguists such as Stepan Smal-Stotsky, Olena Kurylo, Ivan Ohienko and phonologist George Shevelov argue Ukrainian is a fusion of tribal languages and not wholly rooted in Old East Slavic. What is evident is that case system, sentence structure, grammar and other elements of language show them to be diverse, with Ukrainian sharing some Indo-European linguistic principles and characteristic in ways Russian does not.

accurately, proto-Slavic languages. The appearance of the Ukraïna hundreds of years before either the Muscovy or Russians emerged negates any claim that the Ukrainians are "Little Russians."

Peter I Alekseyevich was the first tsar to discernibly refer to the Ukrainian language as a "dialect of the Russian language."[113] Desirous of presenting the empire as a monolithic dominion of Russians to a newly interested Europe, Peter I Alekseyevich engaged in a series of 'reforms' that included the elimination of individual languages and cultural identity of his minority subjects as a means of Russification. After banning the use of Ukrainian and other minority languages in education, he decreed in 1720 a ban on the publication of any new books in Ukrainian. He also caused existing books to be modified to remove traces of reference to the Ukrainians as a people or nation. This is where the intensification of efforts to reduce Ukrainians to being малороссы [Malorrosii — Little Russians] arose.[114]

Between 1762–1796, Tsarina Catherine II caused the Ukrainian language to be eradicated from classrooms, literature to be destroyed, and the Ukrainian in Orthodox church records to be erased and replaced by Russian.[115] Her attempts to entirely erase Ukraine's identity from history were near complete. Despite beginning with a liberal tilt, Tsarina Catherine II engaged in the Russification of her subjects through language, literature, and cultural censorship throughout her reign. The demise of the last truly free Ukrainians in this era, the Cossacks under the Hetmanate of the Zaporizhzhian Sich, resulted in the entirety of Ukraine being subordinated to Russia's imperial administration.

The machinations of Peter I Alekseyevich and Tsarina Catherine II remained incomplete. From the Baltics to the Black Sea, once independent people refused to relinquish their identity, culture, and sense of independence. Alexander II Nikoláyevich sought to inflict the *coup de grâce* on his minority subjects in once independent states. He caused decrees to be enacted across the empire, censoring, if not outright banning, the use of minority languages. In Ukraine, for example, the Valuyev Circular (1863) and the Ems Ukase (1876) universally prohibited the use of the Ukrainian language in schools, literature, government administration, and all public spaces. Punishments for transgressors could be severe.[116]

Russian Interior Minister Pyotr Valuyev summarized the objectives of appropriation's natural completion being erasure: "There never was, is

---

[113] Orest Subtelny, "Russia and the Ukraine: The Difference That Peter I Made", *Russian Review (Wiley), Vol. 39, No. 1*, January 1980.

[114] Kateryna Zudenkova, "Oppression and Eradication: The Linguicide of Ukrainian by Russia", *Ukraine World*, 25 October 2024.

[115] Andrzej Nowak, "The Empire That Catherine Erased", *Pursuasion: American Purpose*, 24 March 2023.

[116] Michael S. Flier and Andrea Graziosi, "The Battle for Ukrainian: An Introduction", *Harvard Ukrainian Studies*, Volume 35 (Number 1-4), 2017-2018.

not, and cannot be any separate little Russian language."[117] Imperial Russia sought, much like the Russian Federation seeks, the assimilation of its neighbors through appropriation completed by erasure. Here, it is worthwhile to reflect upon the monologue from Kenneth Clark's groundbreaking documentary, *Civilization*. In Episode 1, where Clark examines how close Western civilization came to extinction, he notes that a commonality of the collapse of social-political entities is that they had surpassed their apogee: "So, if one asks why the civilization of Greece and Rome collapsed, the real answer is that it was exhausted."[118]

Imperial Russia's exhaustion and decline were centuries in the making. The advent of the Soviet Union only temporarily replaced the imperial regime and mentality. The Russian Federation, ever anxious to avoid reform and take its place in the sorority of free nations, is caught up in trying to reintroduce an imperial paradigm in an age where imperialism and colonialism are anathema to human rights. And yet, Putin and the ROC continue to claim a return to 'traditional values' will restore Russia's greatness. This would mean a re-institutionalization of imperial hegemony and colonial rule for Russia's neighbors.

To counter the harsh reality of such an achievement, Russia points to the artistic achievements of writers such as Leon Tolstoy, Anton Chekhov, and Fyodor Dostoevsky as examples of their advanced civilization. Yet we must consider how their achievements can be celebrated at the expense of the near obliteration through censorship of Ukraine's Taras Savchenko, Estonia's Alexander Solzhenitsyn or Lithuania's Gabrielė Petkevičaitė-Bitė. Russia reached its zenith long ago and has had to claim greatness by comparison, achieved at the cost of the appropriation and extermination by erasure of others' greatness, even waging war to obliterate their existence, which serves as a reminder that Russia is a spent force in terms of civilization.[119]

> It will be lost on no one that we are approximately a week into the largest conventional military attack in Europe since 1945. Vladimir Putin's brutal war of choice against the Ukrainians continues as we speak. It grows worse, more devastating, and more brutal by the hour, and it is time that, in the

---

[117] Pyotr Valuyev, "Valuyev Circular", *Kremlin, Moscow*, 1863.
[118] Kenneth Clark, presenter (Developed by David Attenborough), "Civilization: A Personal View, Episode 1, 'By the Skin of Our Teeth'", *BBC Two*, 1969.
[119] Writers long deemed "Russian" include Anton Chekhov, Nikolai Gogol, Mikhail Bulgakov, and Isaac Babel—all of whom were Ukrainian. The appropriation of their works and personas, accompanied by the erasure of their ethnic identities, has formed the world to credit Russia for their works, fame and contributions to civilization.

midst of this war, we confronted a basic fact: that Russia isn't so much a country as it is a gas station....[120]

A critical thinker must therefore unequivocally reject any projection or assertion by Putin and his neo-imperialist propaganda machine that Ukraine and its people have been or are a "natural part of Russia."[121] The difficulty is that the success of Russia's pattern of appropriation and erasure has resulted in its near-universal acceptance in the public mainstream by external and independent repetition. This is especially so when embraced by world leaders, such as Trump's exclamation to his National Security Council advisers, being repeated ad nauseam by the media: "[Ukraine] wasn't a 'real country,' that it had always been a part of Russia."[122]

Trump's enthusiastic repetition of Russian propaganda shocked even his hand-picked team of advisers. Still, it demonstrates the danger of appropriation's natural conclusion — that it can only be accepted as fact is predicated on the extermination of independent memory.

Beyond cultural and linguistic appropriation, we must consider physical appropriation. For centuries, Russians repeated the politically driven myths that they were the mother country of Ukraine and, as such, Ukrainians are merely немного русский [Little Russians]. Putin made great use of this in his Address to the Federal Assembly in the Kremlin's St. George Hall in 2014:

> Crimea is where our people live, and the peninsula is of strategic importance for Russia as the spiritual source of the development of a multifaceted but solid Russian nation and a centralised Russian state. It was in Crimea, in the ancient city of Chersonesus or Korsun, as ancient Russian chroniclers called it, that Grand Prince Vladimir was baptised before bringing Christianity to Rus.
> In addition to ethnic similarity, a common language, common elements of their material culture, a common territory, even though its borders were not marked then, and a nascent common economy and government, Christianity was a powerful spiritual unifying force that helped involve various tribes and tribal unions of the vast Eastern Slavic world in the creation of a Russian nation and Russian state. It was thanks to this spiritual unity that our forefathers for the first time and forevermore saw themselves as a united nation. All of this allows us to say that Crimea, the ancient Korsun or Chersonesus, and Sevastopol have invaluable civilizational and even sacral importance for Russia, like the Temple Mount in Jerusalem for the followers of Islam and Judaism.

---

[120] John McCain, "Relating to a National Emergency Declared by The President on March 13, 2020", *Congressional Record Vol. 168, No. 39, (Senate)*, 3 March 2022.
[121] Propos recueillis par Marc-Olivier Bherer avec Mykola Riabchuk, "L'Occident est bien plus influencé par l'impérialisme russe qu'il ne l'admet", *Le Monde*, 15 May 2022.
[122] Greg Jaffe and Josh Dowsy, "A presidential loathing for Ukraine is at the heart of the impeachment inquiry", *Washington Post*, 2 November 2019.

And this is how we will always consider it.[123]

The United Nations recognizes the Crimean Tatar people as the Indigenous inhabitants of Crimea. They self-identify as being Ukrainians. Ukraine accepts their self-identification and right of self-determination as both Crimean Tatars and Ukrainians as reinforced by international recognition of Crimea being Ukrainian. Russia refuses to acknowledge their Indigenous status or their Ukrainian citizenship consistent with international law. Their governance was one of being an autonomous region under the Mejlis of the Crimean Tatars as an integral part of a sovereign Ukraine. Putin, however, declared Crimea to be of strategic importance to Russia and therefore its occupation was vital to his long-term plans to control the region and the Black Sea.

To justify the occupation, Putin needed more than an appeal to strategic importance. He turned once again to the distorted history Russia relies upon to assist him. In their ROC, he found a partner. Putin coupled the history of Crimea being the place of baptism of Volodymyr the Great, Grand Prince of the Kyivan Rus', of whom he claims Russia is the successor. He commenced his claims on Crimea with a view that the Russian state shares with the ROC—Christianity was the foundational linchpin upon which the Russian state was formed. By appealing to the notion of sharing a common language, culture, and history, Putin states what he hopes will be accepted as rote. For Putin and the Russian Federation, Crimea is as important and sacred: "as the Temple Mount in Jerusalem for those who profess Islam and Judaism."[124]

It is inconsequential that the Russians in Crimea are artificial transplants.[125] Ukrainians are now coercively made Russian citizens through illicit passportisation measures.[126]

---

[123] Владимир Путин, "Послание Федеральному Собранию", *Кремль, Москва*, 3 декабря 2014.

[124] Sergei L. Loiko, "Vladimir Putin says Crimea is part of Russia historically and forever", *Los Angeles Times*, 4 December 2014.

[125] In February 1944, Stalin ordered the overnight forced displacement of almost 200,000 Crimean Tatars from their ancestral home on Crimea to the Soviet interior. Tens of thousands of Crimean Tatars were starved to death in the February 1944 forced displacement. Crimean Tatar place names were Russified and Russians were redistributed to Crimea to make it "Russian." In the 18th and 19th centuries Crimean Tatars were subjected to degradation and relocation at the behest of Tsarina Catherine II following her victory over the Crimean Khanate in 1783. Following the Crimean War (1853-1856), Crimean Tatars were forcibly displaced to the Ottoman Empire to make way for the resettlement of Russians to Crimea. Today, Ukrainians and Crimean Tatars on Crimea are forcibly made Russians by the process of passportisation.

[126] Helen Sullivan, "Russia 'systematically' forcing Ukrainians to accept citizenship, US report finds", *The Guardian*, 3 August 2023.

The suppression of national identity and memory, including imposing the Russian language on neighboring states are systematic features of Russian expansionism. In 1939, Russia imposed a mutual assistance treaty on Estonia, inserting its own military bases and controlling territorial waters. By 1940, this 'mutual assistance' was translated into an occupation. Exploiting native Estonians like poet and statesman Johannes Vares and writer-politician Johannes Lauristin espoused Russian Soviet propaganda to undermine Estonia's individuality.

Lauristin took part in radio broadcasts during the June 21st Freedom Square rallies organized and funded by Moscow. While both were ardent communists, their rise to prominence depended on their willingness to engage in the suppression of their native Estonian language and culture. If the Baltics are worried about Russian aggression today (they are), it is because they remain aware of the danger to democracy and security that always attends appropriation and erasure when conducted by political allies of Moscow.

To rise to power, Vares was willing to serve the new Russian Soviet occupation regime, which required the suppression of Estonian identity. As a reward, the Russian Soviet occupation regime forced the Estonian government to appoint Vares as prime minister. His tenure was short-lived as Nazi occupation forces caused him to flee. Exiled to Russia, Vares returned to office in 1944 only to be investigated by the KGB. Shortly thereafter, he committed suicide in the presidential residence at Kadriorg, Tallinn, in 1946. The exploitation of the once admired Varest led some ethnic Estonians to espouse the extinction of their own language in favor of Russian all while delivering their arguments in Estonian. This dynamic was later mirrored in Russia's preparations in anticipation of occupations in Moldova, Georgia, and now Ukraine.

This dynamic proved effective then and remains so now. Europe's security, democracy and social cohesion rely upon its populace understanding both the historic and present dangers of Russia's pattern of extermination and erasure. The existence of thriving cultures boasting productive economies with governments opposed to corruption, on Russia's borders, is problematic for Russia. Putin realizes that their independence, predicated on the recovery of historic memory and identity, directly undermines his claims of unity. Moreover, the very proximity of successful states on Russia's borders only serves to highlight the failure of the Russian Federation to lift its people out of poverty since all were concomitantly freed from Soviet oppression in 1991. If free, sovereign and independent states have thrived since that cardinal moment in history while Russia remains emersed in an economic, social, political, and religious quagmire, it highlights the problem is rooted in Russia—not Europe or the west.

The enduring legacy of Russian Soviet cultural, linguistic, and national extermination in the Baltics was so severe that today, states formerly within the Russian sphere struggle to balance democracy and self-preservation. Estonia embraces its ties to the European Union while vociferously guarding its individuality and cultural identity.

Attempts to restore a mono-ethnic and culturally imbued Estonia have led to laws that at times defy the European ideal. At the same time, laws aimed at ensuring the primacy of the Estonian language are perceived by Russians as attacks upon its ethnic kin minority who remained in the country following the 1991 collapse of the Soviet Union.

Estonia has managed, however, to embrace digital and financial integration, agricultural policies and other aspects of the European Union and still protect itself from unwarranted and unwelcome Russian influence by limiting 'kin state activism' with the Estonian Christian Orthodox Church (formerly the Moscow Patriarch Estonian Orthodox Church) distancing itself from Russia. While Estonia's president has voiced concerns over the Riigikogu (Estonian parliament) legislation banning the Moscow Patriarchate outright, the move received widespread support, passing 68–17 in a demonstration of popular support.[127]

In June 2024, the Riigikogu, Estonia's parliament, passed the Churches and Congregations Act through its final reading. The Act requires the Estonian Christian Orthodox Church to sever its ties with the Moscow Patriarchate.

The primate of the Estonian Apostolic Orthodox Church (EAOC), Metropolitan Stephanos, has been an advocate of the legislation: "We cannot allow a situation where national security is threatened through or under the cover of a religious organisation."[128]

The removal of Russian Soviet monuments and statues is a natural feature of identity recovery and retention.[129] Reducing or removing Russian language literature from libraries and schools to bolster the recovery

---

[127] It is worthy of note that pro-Kremlin propagandists, MAGA Republicans like Marjory Taylor-Greene, and media pundit Tucker Carlson have all decried Ukraine implementing quite similar legislation banning Moscow-related churches, without citing Estonia, for fear of it being accepted not as a Ukrainian anomaly but seen as a European necessity.

[128] Andreja Bogdanovski, "Estonian Parliament resumes efforts to cut ties between Church and Moscow Patriarchate", *Church Times*, 27 June 2025.

[129] Russians complain that the removal of Soviet era statues and monuments in neighboring countries once under their yoke, often featuring ethnically Russia persons or images, is an attack upon the Russian Federation and its citizens. The removal of colonial-era monuments across Africa was, by contrast, hardly opposed and understood to be a natural outcome of domestic restoration. Even during the American Revolution (1776–1783), the famed pulling down of the

of the Estonian language has also been cited by Putin and the ROC as a direct challenge to Russia. Both the Kremlin and Moscow Patriarchate have repeatedly reminded, if not outright threatened, Estonia that it maintains its responsibility to 'Russians' outside its borders. This included Estonians deemed by Russia to be Russian, though the individuals may self-identify as Estonian.

Consequently, the ROC and the Russian state have once again become increasingly active in Estonian domestic politics. The 2025 Russian State Budget allocated more than ₽137.2 billion (approximately €1.2 billion) on state propaganda, including more than ₽25.5 billion (approximately €275.3 billion) for the Internet Development Institute (IRI) troll farms.[130] There is ample Russian capacity to disrupt Estonia's domestic tranquility as part of its overall anti-EU/anti-NATO activities.

According to the European Union High Representative for Foreign Affairs and Security Policy, Vice President of the European Commission, Kaja Kallas: "Our information space has become a geopolitical battleground."[131]

According to a recent assessment published by King's College, London, Visiting Professor Lukasz Olejnik wrote:

> Between November 2023 and November 2024, 505 incidents of foreign information manipulation and interference (FIMI) were classified, involving 38,000 channels across 25 platforms. These incidents targeted 90 countries, and 322 organisations, and produced over 68,000 pieces of content. The infrastructure behind these incidents included official state media, covert networks, state-aligned proxies and unattributed channels. Information influence and operations use a layered and scalable system.
> Russia remains the most active actor. Nearly half of the incidents in the dataset targeted Ukraine (257). France (152), Germany (73) and Moldova (45) also faced sustained targeting. Russian campaigns are highly adaptable — tailored to local languages and contexts while consistently aligned with geopolitical goals. Germany and France were hit with localised campaigns; meanwhile, Ukraine, Moldova, Poland and the Baltic States are the key focus areas due to their geopolitical importance.[132]

---

statue of King George by Continental soldiers on 9 July 1776 passed without much rancor despite some English expression of outrage at what was deemed disrespect for their monarch.

[130] Alex Stezhensky, "Kremlin's propaganda machine: Who funds it, who runs it, and how it dominates Russia's media", *The New Voice of Ukraine*, 13 April 2025.

[131] European Union, "3rd EEAS Report on Foreign Information Manipulation and Interference Threats Exposing the architecture of FIMI operations", *European Union External Foresight: Strategic Communication*, March 2025.

[132] Lukasz Olejnik, "Russian cyber and information warfare and its impact on the EU and UK", *Kings College: London*, 15 April 2025.

The total known expenditures by Russia on propaganda and disinformation represent a full 13% increase in its public budget for such activities.

As machine learning and artificial intelligence enable newer methods of confronting electronic misinformation delivery, the tried-and-true method of mixing sermons with state propaganda continues to be a reliable tool for the ROC across Europe, North America, and most recently throughout Africa. The danger to social cohesion, security, and democracy is to balance freedom of religion with the ability to interdict destabilization delivery methods, even when conducted by those masquerading as clergy.

Putin's neo-imperialist attempts to restore the displacement of truth and fact for political purposes have experienced uneven success. Still, enough success has been achieved to continue to make it worthwhile, especially in reaching youth.[133]

New Russian textbooks have returned to teaching long-discredited historical narratives.[134] At the same time, Russia has adopted a policy of using new textbooks, both domestically and in occupied territories, to justify its invasion of Ukraine. Central to these new textbooks is an argument of the necessity for Russia to confront NATO and western pressures.[135] The combination of domestic propaganda and disinformation, its employment in occupied territories and its amplification through its generous international propaganda budget represents a real danger for European security and democracy.

Asserting the claim to be the Kyivan Rus' sole successors while ignoring the existence of the Ukraïna people in antiquity rejects almost a millennium of individuality marked by a unique language, culture, history, social, and political development, as well as Ukraine's struggle to maintain its sovereignty after centuries of Russia's attempts to obliterate both the Ukrainian state and people.

Putin lays claim to what is rightfully Ukrainian, all while denying its existence. One need only examine his speeches to see how Putin associates Grand Prince Volodymyr with Moscow, not Kyiv or Ukraine. It is an immutable fact of history that Moscow did not exist when Volodymyr the Great ruled the Kyivan Rus'. Still, Russia persists in this discredited narra-

---

[133] Horne, B.D., Rice, N.M., Luther, C.A. *et al.*, "Generational effects of culture and digital media in former Soviet Republics", *Humanities and Social Sciences Communications*, 2023.

[134] Anastasia Gulubeva, "Rewriting history – the planned new school textbook accused of whitewashing Russia's imperial past", *BBC News Russia*, 1 September 2023.

[135] Valeriya Safronova, "New Russian High School Textbooks Seek to Justify War in Ukraine", *New York Times*, 1 September 2023.

tive because it still bears some fruit among those willing to listen. In politics, which drives international relations, division and dissent, even in minuscule amounts, have merit.

Russia's acts of appropriation and erasure are not dissimilar to what is now taking place in the United States. The deformation of the Republican Party by the Make America Great Again (MAGA) cult led by President Donald Trump has generated similar political distortions of history. MAGA Republicans have passed laws prohibiting certain methodologies for teaching American history. Newly approved textbooks like those in Florida no longer recognize the evils of human enslavement of Africans brought to America beginning in 1619. Florida Governor Ron DeSantis approved and promoted textbooks that promote slavery as a species of gift that allowed Africans in human bondage to benefit from clothing, shelter, basic education and Christianity.[136]

In a startling move not unlike Putin's efforts to keep Memorial from examining Russia's brutal Soviet past, Trump published an Executive Order called "Restoring Truth and Sanity to American History" in March 2025. The order directed the Smithsonian and other museums in receipt of federal funds to refrain from having exhibits or content critical of America's slaveholding past, the internment of Japanese Americans during World War II, segregated military service, the civil rights movement and other topics he finds contrary to his personal views. Putin and Trump both are anxious to rewrite history to their liking, despite critical analysis being integral to national development and an identity rooted in truth.[137]

The act of highlighting how other Africans played a role in capturing their fellow Africans as a means of re-focusing attention on the role played by Europeans in the development and monetization of the slave trade remains a device used to shift responsibility. Blaming Africans for the slave trade in the Americas as a means of defending white privilege is not unanalogous to Russia blaming Ukrainians for their being invaded and occupied out of necessity. Both seek to benefit from the victims while denying responsibility for their victimhood as a means of justification.

Trump, Putin, and the Patriarch of Moscow understand that culture wars are central to their attainment and retention of power. They are also acutely aware that any successful culture war can only be won by the erasure of their historic misdeeds being accompanied by the obliteration of the collective memory of their victims. For Trump, blaming foreigners for America's woes, especially those of Latin or African descent, is critical.

---

[136] Kevin Sullivan & Lori Rozsa, "DeSantis doubles down on claim that some Blacks benefited from slavery", *Washington Post*, 22 July 2023.
[137] Donald J. Trump, "Restoring Truth and Sanity to American History: Executive Order", *White House, Washington, D.C.*, 27 March 2025.

Russia and the ROC have directed their animus toward the prosperous border states previously within the Russian sphere to explain away Russia's economic and social woes. By claiming Ukraine to be controlled by "Nazis" and the Baltic states by "satanic Westerners," each attacking and undermining Russia in their own ways, Putin and Patriarch Kirill shift blame to the west to excuse the corruption, repressive and illiberal governance and militarism that pervades Russia today.

They are equally aware that undertaking these activities has the benefit of the masculine projection of power, which has long been part of the Russian ethos. Appealing to a desire for 'traditional values' associated with what Russians were taught was a glorious past also serves to cultivate and consolidate the kind of political base necessary to accept and endure the kind of casualties and economic hardships involved with their 'special military operations'.

Indeed, while Russia's overall long-term economic outlook is decidedly grim, in Russia's industrial regions, the Kremlin boasts of economic success due to its wartime arms and equipment industry demands. Ethnic Russians now report they worry less about meeting their economic and material needs in the coming year while simultaneously claiming a higher satisfaction with life.[138]

Convincing a nation that they are under threat is a populist tool in energizing a political base through emotive means. It is particularly effective in Russia as it harkens to a glorified past where Potemkin villages and May Day parades projected a mythological view of superiority and tranquility that never truly existed. In short, sacrificing historical truth for patriotic fervor is an exchange Russians have been willing to make since the time of Ivan III Vasilyevich.

Historical examination is being rebuffed and repealed where illiberal regimes have taken power, not just in Russia. In the United States, slavery and the ills inflicted on Native Americans who were victims of 'Manifest Destiny' are indelible and undeniable. The deplorable consequences persist, and mention of them is disappearing. Black Americans, women's achievements and other minority contributions to the American fabric of life are disappearing from government websites.

Attacks upon the academy and support of investigative journalism unaligned with the Trump administration have come under fire, and public interest broadcasting has had its funding eviscerated. It is not surprising that the Trump administration, which campaigned on culture issues, became an unsteady partner with Europe and Ukraine, given their shared

---

[138] Sinikka Parviainen, "War economy boosts life satisfaction for ethnic Russians and residents of military-industrial regions", *Bank of Finland Bulletin*, 4 June 2025.

values with Putin. Europe needs to be wary of political movements that promise to echo such culture-curtailing activities.

Such activities have flourished for the last two decades under Putin. Pressure from Russians, the ROC and far right ideologues to do the same in Europe is growing. The banning of non-governmental organizations in Russia, like Memory, which sought to expose the evils of Russia's past as a means of deterring current and future authoritarianism, was a repressive feature to Putin's benefit.

Georgia's adoption of a 'Foreign Agents' registry similar to that used by Russia to quash civil society activism received significant support from the ROC and elements of the Georgian Orthodox Church. Outside of Russia, however, Putin and Patriarch Kirill have little control where their government apparatus and legislation stop at their borders. Their answer has been to bank on the ROC's soft power being reinforced by Russian troll farms.

By incorporating subsumed states' histories into their own narrative and employing *русификация* [Russification], Russia has created the illusion that the histories are theirs. For centuries, Russia has effectively appropriated Baltic, Belarusian, Moldovan, Polish, Romanian, Ukrainian, and others' history and cultures — not to mention dipping generously into two of their favorite wells — those of the Byzantines and Kyivan Rus'. Be it tsars or commissars, Russia prefers 'approved' histories that conform to its political and social narrative needs:

> The official interpretation of the histories of the nations of the USSR emerged between 1934 and 1953 on the basis of decrees signed by Stalin and/or the Central Committee. This interpretation subsumes the histories of the non-Russian Republics within the "history of the USSR" that begins not in 1917 or 1922 in Moscow, but in prehistoric Asia. <u>The official view recognized the non-Russian nations and republics as separate historical entities, yet imposed upon their pasts a Russocentric statist framework while denying the Russians a separate history of the RSFSR</u>. Within this scheme the history of non-Russian nationalities before they became part of the tsarist state was built around the idea of "oppression" of "the people" and their "struggle" against native and foreign ruling classes. Russian and non-Russian "working people" were assumed always to have been "fraternal" while non-Russian political leaders, before and after incorporation, were judged according to their sympathy and/or loyalty to Russia."[139] [emphasis added]

---

[139] Stephen Velychenko, "Restructuring and the Non-Russian Past", *Nationality Papers, Vol. 22, No. 2,* 1994. *See also* Cyril Black (ed.), "Rewriting Russian History", *New York: Vintage Books,* 1962; and Samuel H. Baron, Nancy Heer (eds.), "Windows on the Russian Past", *American Association for the Advancement of Slavic Studies,* 1977.

Cultural appropriation and extermination are inherently products of a power imbalance. If Russia claims its neighbors share in a brotherly unity, it seems the only fraternal story they know is Cain and Abel. Russia's relationship with its *братский народ* [brotherly people] has been historically marked by a lack of self-control, nurtured jealousy, expressive anger, unbridled violence, and unmerited pride, and ethnic conceit. As history has shown by repeated occupations or subjugation under the USSR, the result of this paradigm is either submission or death.

The erasure of independent self-identity has left states once under the Russian sphere to defend their right to exist free of Russian influence. The trauma of having forcibly been made to assimilate a new cultural identity — that of being Russian — is omnipresent in the region. Education and cultural revival are the best defenses against the continued encroachment of Russification attempts by the ROC's culture wars and the Russian state's troll farm propaganda machine.

Ultimately, the west has two tools in its arsenal to defend itself against Russian attempts to create the Russkiy Mir. The first is its embrace of a rules-based system of world order that kept Europe at relative peace since World War II, that is, until large-scale military adventurism by Russia returned with its invasion of Ukraine.[140] The second is martial defense. In a world where the toleration for 'might makes right' is increasing and the west seems unwilling to match its rhetoric about freedom with the means to ensure it, Europe remains acutely vulnerable. This is what makes Russia's soft power projection mechanism, the ROC, so dangerous. The European Convention on Human Rights is enshrined in Article 10, which specifies protection for religious liberty and free speech. When it comes to curbing them, there has been a reluctance to consent.

If we are to prevent another generation of Europeans from being coerced into adopting a Russian identity because the west is unwilling to stop the forward march of Russian aggression, there will be consequences that will undermine the European experiment in peace and prosperity that is

---

[140] Post World War II Europe has experienced conflicts in which either Russia or the Soviet Union played an outsized role — though none on the scale of the Russian invasion of Ukraine. These included the Soviet interventionism in the Greek Civil Wars (1946–1949); armed Soviet's crushing the Hungarian Revolution of 1956; using tanks to crush the Prague Spring revolution initiated by Alexander Dubček in Czechoslovakia; Soviet intervention and occupation in Moldova's Transnistria region (1990-1992); the Slovenian War of Independence (1991); Croatian War of Independence (1991–1995); Bosnian War (1992–1995): Insurgency in Kosovo (1995–1998); Kosovo War (1998–1999); the invasion and occupation of Georgia's Abkhazia and South Ossetia in 2008; and Russia's continuing invasion and occupation in Ukraine (2014-ongoing). The "Russian Sphere" or "Russkiy Mir" significantly drove each of these conflicts.

the European Union. Already, Moldovans in Transnistria, Georgians in Abkhazia and South Ossetia, as well as nearly 27% of Ukrainians, are being forced to believe they have a gnostic national and cultural history and identity—being Russians.

Having recovered their historic identities, complete with the resurrection of their political independence, Russia's neighbors have recently made known they are unwilling to play the role of Abel once again. Pulling them back into the Russian sphere will prove costly to Russia. To prepare for their reabsorption into the Russian sphere, Putin relies on hybrid warfare and the social weaponization of the ROC to soften their western targets. To date, increased contributions to NATO by states formerly under the Russian yoke signal that they are prepared to sacrifice to remain free of the Russian thumb. Understanding the appropriation and erasure dynamic will assist these now free states and their allies to avoid the pitfalls of the last two decades.

For those weary of parsing the bright line between the ROC as an ecclesial institution and the role it plays in Russia's soft-power projection and acting as part of the intelligence apparatus of the Russian state, a reckoning with the issues raised in this manuscript is necessary. It must begin with the recognition of the role the ROC plays in reinforcing the sociological, ethnic, cultural, and even linguistic components of appropriation and extermination within the context of Russian aggression.

The very act of seeking to maintain neighboring national churches under the jurisdiction of the Moscow Patriarch cannot be deemed anything less than the weaponization of faith. For Orthodox Christians, tradition demands that a church be under the jurisdiction of a canonical patriarch. Nothing in the orthodox faith demands that they be tied to the ROC.

The very hubris of Patriarch Kirill and the ROC demanding their victims commemorate the Patriarch of Moscow during the Divine Liturgy is an act of evil. No mother of a child fighting for the independence of their country should be forced to pray for a patriarch who has given plenary indulgences for Russians to kill their children, exterminate their national identity, or speak their native language.

Russia's use of spiritual pressure to force Orthodox Christians to remain within the Moscow Patriarchate is a perversion of the authority of the church. For those outside of Orthodox Christianity, the prospect of becoming canonically aloof from the church, by failing or refusing to follow the guidance of a hierarch, is a frightening prospect. Even for a Russian who dissents from their government's policy of bloodshed and carnage, the idea of separating themselves from their Russian identity as promoted by the ROC is tantamount to heresy. No Christian ought to be placed in the position of having to choose between goodness, truth, and righteousness simply to maintain their relationship with the Orthodox Christian faith.

It is the sad position today that the ROC's willingness to declare a 'holy war' on their Orthodox Christian neighbors places them in the position of becoming excommunicated for choosing Christ's Gospel prayer for peace and unity over Patriarch Kirill's Holy Rus' prayer for war and domination. The deep and abiding connection between the Russian State and ROC places the faithful in the position of having to choose a friendly, if not loyal, posture toward the Russian State as a means of maintaining their fidelity to the religious and faith experience imprinted on their souls at the moment of baptism. This unorthodox heresy must end.

Chapter Five

Russia Appears
A Brief History in Four Acts

Proto-Slavs, Muscovy, Russians and Soviets (With a Special Encore as Russians — Again)

Now that we understand their foundation and how they were formed through many iterations we must ask again, after these various transformations and names, "Who are the Russians?"

What we are being asked to accept about Russian identity and territorial claims is unsupportable in fact. Where Russians come from and what defines their land isn't merely a matter of debate. It is the product of a campaign of intentional misinformation and disinformation that has lasted centuries. When did this all begin? Why did it first happen? Why is it happening again? What are the consequences?

Russia, as a name for a state and people, first appeared only in the 14th century.[141] Russia is a derivation of Ρωσία [Rosía], the late Byzantine Greek name for the Rus' (referring to a people of Norse origins). While the Kremlin and ROC would have us conflate Rus' with Russia and being Russian to buttress their claim to being successors of the Kyivan Rus', the historical record leaves a right-thinking person at best highly skeptical or, if astute, in disbelief of Russia's claims. An examination of historical and cartographic evidence is revealing. It serves to help us better understand who the Russian people are, as well as define what is Russian beyond conventional wisdom and propaganda.

In the late 7th century, Norse traders left Sweden and began to expand their trade and dominion eastward before following the Dnieper River south to the Black Sea. Joined by other Scandinavians, they became known as Varangians — a derivation of the Norse *væringi*, meaning 'broth-

---

[141] Robin Milner-Gulland, "The Russians. The peoples of Europe", *Blackwell, Oxford*, 1999.

ers of a sworn allegiance' (accurately applied to Norse explorers, mercenaries, and bodyguards).[142] They eventually established permanent settlements on the Dnieper River in what is today's northern Ukraine. These settlements had developed into semi-city-states by the latter half of the 9th century.

It was in today's north-central Ukraine that the Varangians established their capital. The location was ideal, effectively providing a location from which they could communicate between the Baltic and Black Seas. The ruling class, who maintained their Norse tongue, called their settlements and lands by their Old Norse tongue, *garðar* [strongholds or enclosures].[143]

It was in this period that the Varangian leader Oleh united northern and southern settlements, creating a medieval kingdom based on the city-states that arose from their exploration and trade. To distinguish between the classes, the Norse class retained their language and culture while the traders and populus became known as Rus'.[144] They situated their capital in a settlement on the upper Dnieper River that had been occupied since at least the 5th century. The city is named after Kyi, one of the three legendary brothers who founded the metropolis.

It was not until recently, the 19th century, that historians began to refer to the Varangian city-states kingdom and its people as Kyivan Rus'.[145] The device is much the same as the post hoc name for the eastern Roman Empire, becoming ubiquitously known in modernity as Byzantium and its people, Byzantines.[146] Neither the Kyivan Rus' nor the Byzantines would have known themselves by these post hoc names, however.

The meteoric progression of the Kyvan Rus' brought them to the attention of more ancient civilizations. They received the constant attention

---

[142] Raffaele d'Amato, "The Golden Age of the Varangian Guard", *Medieval Warfare, Vol. 1, No. 2, Karwansaray BV*, 2011.

[143] Елена Александровна Мельникова, "Skandinavskie runicheskie nadpisi: novye nakhodki i interpretatsii; teksty, perevod, kommentarii Скандинавские рунические надписи: новые находки и интерпретации; тексты, перевод, комментарии, Vostochnaya literatura", *Российская академия наук (РАН) Rossíyskaya akadémiya naúk, Москва*, 2001.

[144] The early medieval *De administrando imperio* reveals Emperor Constantine VII Porphyrogenitus used different nouns, in Rus' and Slavic, when referring to the Dnipro Rapids as well as the martial class as Varangians and trading-political class as *Rus'*. This not only delineates the periodic name for the people by class and function but differentiates between the Norse and the Slavs, defeating Russian neo-imperialist claims that Russians, being a Slavic people, are descendants of the Rus'.

[145] Adolf Stender-Petersen, "Verangica", *Universitets Slaviske Institut*, 1953.

[146] Georg Gaspar Mezger, "Memoria Hieronymi Wolfii Hieronymi, Vol. I", *Rieger, Augsburg*, 1862.

of neighboring states and their various religious leaders. Each sent envoys to Kyiv in the hopes of encouraging the Kyivan Rus' to adopt Christianity. Competition arose between the Latin envoys promoting loyalty to the pope in Rome and the orthodox envoys encouraging fidelity to the Ecumenical Patriarch in Constantinople. Islam, Judaism, and Buddhism were also competitors for the favor of the grand prince of the Kyivan Rus'. Volodymyr I seized upon the idea of consolidating his power from within and unifying the Kyivan Rus' through the adoption of a uniform religion throughout the realm. He commissioned envoys c. 986 to travel abroad to help him determine which of the major known religions—Orthodox Christianity, Latin Christianity, Judaism, or Islam he should adopt for himself and his people. According to a monk named Nestor, who chronicled the period from the Kyiv Pechersk Lavra caves c. 1110,[147] Volodymyr I's envoys returned from Constantinople resolute in their recommendation, reporting:

> We knew not whether we were in Heaven or on Earth... We only know that God dwells there among the people, and their service is fairer than the ceremonies of other nations.[148]

In 988, at Chersonesus in Crimea, Volodymyr I was baptized and received chrismation into Greek Orthodox Christianity. He bound himself and the Kyivan Rus' to the Ecumenical Patriarchate at Constantinople. Shortly thereafter, he became known to history and Orthodox Christianity as Volodymyr the Great. Kyivan Rus' raids on Constantinople ended. Diplomatic relations with the eastern Roman Empire in Constantinople flourished. Here, the foundations of the future Ukrainian state were laid.

It later became the habit of tsarist courts and chroniclers to claim that Ukraine, Ukrainians, and their language were fruits that fell from the Russian tree. Having appropriated the conversion of Volodymyr the Great and claimed the Kyivan Rus' mantle, these acts served to exterminate and remove any mention of the independent existence of the Ukraïna and their embryonic Ukrainian state. For neo-imperialists like Putin, he denies Ukrainians to have ever been a people, let alone a state or for Ukrainian to be anything but a dialect of Russian. History rebuffs such nonsense. The difficulty is that, having controlled the historical narrative for hundreds of

---

[147] *The Nestor Chronicles* has been variously re-titled throughout history as *The Tales of Bygone Years*, *The Russian Primary Chronicles* or simply *The Primary Chronicles*, the title being largely dependent on the place and political outlook of its translator or the times in which it was re-published. The best scholarly practice is to refer to them in the original, *The Nestor Chronicles*. We adopt that standard.

[148] Нестор Летописец, "Повесть временныхъ лет", *Harvard Library of Early Ukrainian Literature in English Translation*, (unknown binding), first published 1 January 1095.

years through aggression, occupation, colonialism, and Soviet oppression, the Russian narrative came to be accepted as fact in wester textbooks, reference works and being often repeated by politicians.

Persons in positions of authority repeat that such propaganda does not lend credibility to the claims in the way Catholic dogma asserts papal infallibility to establish truths. It only serves to appeal to the public biases prone to the effects of repetition and, as in the case of America, a political cult following that embraces the musings of their president as truth. Trump, who has so often espoused Russian propaganda and taken steps to restrain Ukraine from defending itself, has played an oversized role in assisting Russia at the expense of Ukraine and European security. His tendency to substitute critical analysis for his personal judgment demonstrates the power propaganda plays as part of Russia's hybrid warfare campaign against the west.

Propagandists repeat messages, slogans, or make images ubiquitous with the aim of ingraining them in the public imagination as being more memorable and believable. It works. That propaganda messaging is so very often accepted without factual basis, lacking in fundamental truth, becomes inconsequential as the goal is acceptance by repetition and saturation, not elucidation by education.[149]

With a better understanding of the rise and conversion of the Kyivan Rus' with their fidelity to the Ecumenical Patriarch in Constantinople, we must now turn our attention to understanding how the Kyivan Rus' suddenly ceased to be the center of influence in the region.

Kyiv Rus' dominions began to fragment under pressure from the Mongol Golden Horde khanate. By the 13th century, the grandson of Genghis Khan had all eastern Europe under pressure. Batu Khan expanded his territorial domain, and his successors, including Möngke Khan, imposed suzerainty over Slavic rulers and former Kyivan Rus' cooperators. Kyivan Rus' outposts began to rise in prominence as the Mongol Golden Horde brought increasing pressure on Kyiv.

On December 21, 1237, the Mongol Golden Horde descended on outposts of the Kyivan Rus' in the east. After the destruction of Ryazan on that day, Grand Prince Yuri II Vsevolodovich sent the remnants of the Rostov-Suzdal army under the command of his sons Vsevolod and Volodomyr to stem the advancement of the Mongols. The armies met at Kolomna. The

---

[149] Across the globe, the idea that "Nero fiddled while Rome burned" is generally adopted as fact despite it being a post hoc invention attributed to Dio Cassius to depict Nero as indifferent and cruel. The fiddle (violin) wasn't invented until the mid-16th century making the statement ludicrous. This 'historical' statement persists because of repetition alone.

Rostov-Suzdal army was routed. They fled northwards to outposts at Volodymyr-on-Klyazma and Moscow.[150] In 1240, Kyiv itself was razed by the Horde, bringing an end to the Kyivan Rus'.

The duchy and later Principality of Muscovy came into being in 1277 as a tribal-nation (*ulus*) of the Mongol Golden Horde on the instructions of the Tatar-Mongol Khan Munegu Timur. A half-century later, Khan Uzbek appointed his brother, Prince Kulkhan, as the 'Grand Prince of Moscow' in 1328. A convert to Islam, Khan Uzbek had the Christian nobility of the supposed Riurik dynasty executed, ensuring his brother's and the Genghisid dynasty's dominion over Muscovy.

What extremely tenuous links may have existed then between Byzantium, the Kyivan Rus', and Muscovy died with them. For the next three centuries, the 'princes of Muscovy' were appointed at the pleasure of the Genghisids. The Khans issued letters patent to the Slavic princes to administer taxes and pay tribute. The more successful Slavic princes expanded their bases and created semi-city-states. It was in this epoch that the nascent settlements along the Moscow River began to reach some semblance of cohesiveness.

It is a byproduct of the Genghisids that the political and administrative structures they imposed allowed these Slavic entities to amass both power and wealth. Moscow's transition from semi-wild, proto-Slavic tribes to the Principality of Muscovy is due to the Genghisids, not the Kyivan Rus'. Several decades would pass between the sack of Kyiv and the Principality of Muscovy independently emerging at the behest of the Mongol Golden Horde's tax supervisors. Contrary to the tales told in Russian dachas and classrooms, hundreds of years more would pass between the fall of the Kyivan Rus' and the emergence of Russia.

Contrary to prevailing neo-imperialist propaganda, there is no direct link of succession between the demise of Kyivan Rus' and the rise of Russia in the way history provides us with clarity, such as with Constantine the Great moving his capital, the senate and bureaucracy to Byzantium (Constantinople). Nor is it analogous to the Continental Congress removing itself and the United States government from Philadelphia to New York before finally settling on Washington, D.C., after winning the American Revolution. A straight line of succession can be drawn between the Kingdom of Portugal and Brazil, with its capital moving from Rio de Janeiro to Brasília in 1960. The British government's direct administration of India gave way to its successor, the Republic of India, in 1947. Such a translation of power between Kyiv and Moscow never happened — it was self-serving

---

[150] Володимир Білінський, "Країна Моксель, або Московія. Книга 3 (4-е вид. 2012)", *Видавництво імені Олени Теліги*, 2012.

mythology designed to elevate Muscovy by appropriation and extermination.

In each of these instances, a clear succession of power and government succeeding the previous is discernable. When a capital moved or was translated because of a conscious effort by one administration to the next, succession can be said to have occurred. This is not the case with Russia and the Kyivan Rus'. Russia, being the successor state of the Kyivan Rus', is a pure construct promoted for imperial purposes under the tsars and renewed by the revanchist Putin regime and the Moscow Patriarchate for obvious reasons. Thanks to the Mongol Golden Horde, a succession of political power from Kyiv to Moscow was rendered impossible.

What is largely defined as Russia today never fell directly under Kyivan Rus' control. In the 13th and 14th centuries, areas of modern Russia extending into the western foothills of the Urals did form a duchy ruled by dispossessed princes claiming Kyivan Rus' heritage. However, to say the Kyivan Rus' and Russia were the same would be analogous to claiming the French provinces of Brittany and Normandy are today English.

Russia's claims of being the sole heirs to the Kyivan Rus arise somewhat late in the historic record. The erection of the Suzdal Principality in the 13th–14th centuries does give some basis for Russia's tenuous claims to being heirs of the Rus'. This is not the same as being the political or dynastic successor of the Kyivan Rus'. Ukraine certainly has a claim to being the successor of the Kyivan Rus'. Arguably, so do Belarus, Poland, and Lithuania. They shared deeply in Rus' heritage long before a fledgling Russia even began appropriating their histories and cultures to justify its being while consolidating its identity and power.

Why is it then that only Russian historiography asserts itself as being the "successor state" and "sole heir" to the Kyivan Rus'?

Russia's claims require us to suspend our possession of history, command of linguistics, the ability of ethnographers to disentangle cultural entanglements or otherwise have historians dispense with substantial access to surviving cartographic evidence of Russia's true history. There is an expectation rooted in imperialism and colonialism that we, like the Russians, will reject neighboring states and peoples' individual identities, culture, languages, and history as being distinct from that of Russia. Russia's claims about its own heritage, and certainly those of its neighbors, are wholly mediated by its historic and modern geopolitical goals and history of colonial pursuit. Allowing it to go unchallenged is a disservice to states formerly coerced under the Russian sphere and injures their right to exist out of deference to the distortion of Russia's history.

The search for understanding who the Russian people are should not begin, as Putin would have us believe, in the apocryphal words of Oleg the Prophet about Kyiv: "Let it be the mother of all Russian cities."[151] [152]

This quote from the *Chronicle of Nestor* is assumed to have been written in Old Church Slavonic. The most ancient extant translations of his work, however, survive from Byzantium and are written in Greek. The contemporary translators of Nestor used πρωτεύουσα [administrative city] when referring to "[Kyiv] the mother of all Russian cities." This, by definition, would define the idea of the city being a mere administrative center, as many others were referred to at the time. If the Byzantine translators had meant to convey the idea that Oleg the Prophet connoted Russian cities should carry any significance that would have implied a sense of political succession, they would have used the distinct πόλις βασιλίς [royal city].

Nestor and his near-contemporary translators did write of Kyiv as a royal city of the Kyivan Rus' but never used πόλις βασιλίς when referring to any settlement in what is today Russia. We can resolve, therefore, that Oleg the Prophet was merely proclaiming the desire that these new cities to the east be administrative centers under this newly founded realm of the Kyivan Rus'. It was a pledge of fidelity, not succession.

There is also the anomaly that the translation used by Putin uses the phrase "mother of all Russian cities." Nestor would not have referred to these people as Russian. The concept of being Russian had not come into common use. Oleg the Prophet would not have known the word Russian. It was not until the 14th century that the Greek Ρωσία [Rosía] came into common use. The attribution of this statement to Oleg the Prophet is almost certainly apocryphal for Russian political purposes. Putin repeats it out of context and takes the illogical step of conflating Rus' with Russian for obvious reasons.

Novgorod, the major city that first served as the ruling capital of the Duchy of Muscovy prior to it evolving as a consolidated principality based at Moscow, would have been well known to Nestor. There is no evidence that Nestor, who recorded the supposed Kyiv quote by Oleg the Prophet, referred to Novgorod as anything but an administrative center. What else can we know about this oft-repeated story now used by Putin to lay claims on Ukraine? If Putin were correct in asserting that Oleg the Prophet should be interpreted as having conveyed the idea that Kyiv's political powers

---

[151] Влади́мир Влади́мирович Пу́тин, "Об историческом единстве украинского и русского народов", *Кремль, Москва*, 12 июль 2021.
[152] Putin relies on a mistranslation of the 'Oleg the Prophet' supposed prophecy. There is no evidence Oleg wrote or said anything, certainly nothing that survives supporting that idea. The source of Putin's claim of this comes from the *Chronicle of Nestor*.

were transferred to Muscovy, Nestor would surely have referred to Novgorod or Moscow by referring to either of them as a πόλις βασιλίς [royal city]. He did not. Putin has taken a phrase out of context, conflated Rus' with Russia and by sheer repetition made it enter the mainstream as fact in legacy media covering his speeches.

As recorded by Nestor the Chronicler, Oleg the Prophet's supposed quote in context should be interpreted as meaning the Kyivan Rus' were to be deemed the mother of all the new administrative centers, and the people longed to be forever governed by Kyiv. It held no importance in political succession then, nor should it now. It is incongruous that Oleg the Prophet would have projected a succession of power that would mark the demise of the realm to which he belonged and praised. In this sense, he can be deemed to be projecting a natural desire for new lands to forever remain under Kyivan Rus' control. A child may grow to maturity, but that does not negate their remaining offspring of the mother. Russia is not the mother of Slavs. Putin's inventive misuse of Oleg the Prophet's quote is merely wordplay uttered to give Russia's claims of being the successors of the Kyivan Rus' and the foundation stone of Slavic peoples some veneer of credibility.

Russian historiographers have a tendency toward hagiography. Their preoccupation with claiming Russia to be the exclusive heir of the Kyivan Rus' and the aggrandizement of their state has led them to distort history in ways that render their versions of events wholly unreliable. We must dispel the idea that Russia is the successor state of the Kyivan Rus' and the inheritor of territorial and political claims on its neighbors once and for all.

The Kyivan Rus' claims are often ignored by the assertion of other, equally specious claims. The first ruler of the Principality of Muscovy to invoke the title tsar was Ivan III Vasilyevich (Ivan the Great). Both he and his son, Vasili III Ivanovich, claimed succession ties between the eastern Roman Empire at Constantinople and their tsardoms of Moscow based on their supposed Riurik lineage.[153] After all, having taken Princess Sophia Palaiologos as his bride, Ivan III Vasilyevich had married into the former ruling Palaiologos dynasty of Constantinople.

Constantinople was sacked by Sultan Mehmed II when Sophia Paleologue was only four. That event reduced any real advantage her title as a minor royal may have once had to being meaningless beyond its association with the Byzantine dynasty's former glory. This was inconsequential for Ivan III Vasilyevich. Indeed, it was the complexion of being bound to Byzantine royalty that was beneficial to him.

---

[153] Eugene Smelyansky, "Medievalisms and Russia: The Contest for Imaginary Pasts", *Arc Humanities Press*, 2024.

Claiming the Palaeologus lineage entitled Ivan III Vasilyevich to assert successor rights over the throne of the basileus of the eastern Roman Empire. That Constantinople had fallen, and the Trebizond succession was on its knees, meant there were no others with authority to dispute his claims. In succeeding years, this tenuous-at-best connection to Byzantium assisted tsars and patriarchs of Moscow in bolstering their insistence that Moscow be deemed the 'Third Rome' (we will treat this claim and its consequential importance in-depth in a later chapter). Projecting the idea that Moscow as the 'Third Rome' sought to elevate them in the courts of Europe as much as it was meant to instill a sense of awe among their own subjects.

For Ivan IV Vasilyevich (Ivan the Terrible), a descendant of Zoe Paleologue, Byzantine lineage was not enough. He coveted all that being a claimant of the Kyivan Rus' could mean for Muscovy. By distorting information and inventing more, the tsar created a history, albeit further mythologized, in which the epic Kyivan Rus' past could be translated as belonging to Muscovy. Here, the premise that Russia was the primogenitor of the family of the Belarus, Muscovy, Ukrainian and other Slavic peoples was employed. As Yaroslav Dashkevych wrote: "to invoke the law of 'elder brotherhood', have the right of inheritance of Kyivan Rus'."[154]

Aside from claiming to be successors of Byzantium, tsars of Moscow began invoking the use of the word *русский* [Russkiy], implying they were equally heirs of the Kyivan Rus'. Here, a duality of competing identities and ideas arose. The tsars' ability to cling to their identity as successors of Muscovy was essential to maintaining control over their principality. Their people only knew themselves as Muscovy. While no longer a semi-wild people largely shaped by hundreds of years of Mongol Ghengisid identity, the Muscovy people needed to maintain what identity they had. Being enculturated with the latest iteration desired by the tsars—being Russians—would require care.

The ability of the tsars to maintain domestic tranquility in balancing identity retention while pairing their people with the identity of the Byzantines was tricky. The Muscovy people were generally ignorant of the rich history of the Byzantines, whose literary, scientific, political, cultural, and religious greatness their tsars now invoked as being their own. Histories had to be rewritten to meet the day's demand.

By simultaneously invoking the identity of the Byzantines and Kyivan Rus' Ivan IV Vasilyevich was social engineering, *ex nihilo*, a mythological alter ego for his subjects. Unwittingly, the Muscovy people were being groomed to merge their identity with the now historic Kyivan Rus' and Byzantines. Ivan IV Vasilyevich was slowly but consciously inventing a

---

[154] Yaroslav Dashkevych, "Як Московія привласнила історію Київської Русі", *Журнал Універсум*, 11–12 (217–218), 2011.

new identity for Muscovy, being Russian. It would not only serve his aspirational goals but would assist him in occluding their Genghisid past.

Only a handful of Ivan IV Vasilyevich's court were cognizant of his scheme. Fewer contemporaries of his age, if any at all, suspected him of engineering a synthesized Muscovy-Kyivan Rus'-Byzantine identity to create novel territorial claims on neighboring states and peoples. It was a masterful strategy. It first required him to claim the inheritance of the then-defunct kingdoms by cultural acquisition. The second step required a combination of intellect and craftsmanship—the appropriation of the diverse cultures and identities of peoples of the past he wished to subsume. The third step was to proclaim a new identity.

If Ivan IV Vasilyevich were to succeed, what had previously made one uniquely Belarusian, Polish, Romanian, Ukrainian, Muscovy or other would emerge indistinguishable from the new Russian being. By appropriation, Russians would immediately share in the glories of others' pasts and achievements. The tsar was determined to succeed.

His dependable collaborator, the ROC, ever desirous of cleansing Muscovy of any remnants of its pagan past, imbued with the shame of its Mongol Golden Horde submission, became a formidable cooperator in the scheme's success. The ROC needed to have its subjects deemed pristine—worthy of the Orthodox Christian faith, unspoiled by their true past and identity. Their access to the masses from baptism to burial would serve the tsar's goals.

Aside from the tsars personally, the biggest beneficiary of the creation of a new Russian identity was the ROC. As a proxy of the state, it would see its dominion extended over large regions of eastern Europe. It would immediately make the Metropolitan of Moscow a considerable competitor with the Patriarch of Constantinople, whose position had been diminished by the Ottomans.

As much as the tsar wanted to be deemed the equal of the Holy Roman Emperor, the Metropolitan of Moscow desired to be *primus inter pares* [first among equals]—the Ecumenical Patriarch in Constantinople. An unholy deal was struck to elevate the Metropolitan of Moscow to the station of patriarch. Ivan IV Vasilyevich's son, Tsarevich Ivan Ivanovich, was meant to succeed him and see his grand plans for tsardom realized. We know this did not come to be. History records that Ivan IV Vasilyevich murdered his son in a fit of rage. His distaste for his son's clothing led him to strike his son in the head. It proved fatal. This left the mentally feeble Tsarevich Fyodor I Ivanovich to replace him as tsar. The succession proved devastating for Russia's neighbors and consequential for the Orthodox Christian faith.

In 1587, the plan to elevate the religious status of the Russian tsardom would be realized. The Ecumenical Patriarch, Jeremias II, was lured to Moscow by the regent, Borys Godunov, with promises of funds to rebuild the Patriarchate in Constantinople. His journey was to take an unexpected turn:

> When Jeremiah crossed the border from the Polish-Lithuanian Commonwealth into Muscovy in the summer of 1588 he entered a world that was substantially different from the one he had just visited. One of the most important contrasts across the frontier concerned the relationship between the ecclesiastical and secular realms. A church-state distinction or separation had never developed in Muscovy as it had in the Europe of Western Christendom. At a time when religious questions were revolutionizing European societies and polities, throughout the sixteenth century Muscovite ecclesiastical developments were for the most part guided by the authority of the tsar and the court.[155]

Godunov, who effectively ruled in Tsar Fyodor I Ivanovich's name due to his mental defects, instead imprisoned the Ecumenical Patriarch. By coercion and imprisonment, including the presence of Ottoman hirelings pledged to destroy what was left of the Patriarchate of Constantinople, Ecumenical Patriarch Jeremias II finally agreed to elevate Metropolitan Job of Moscow to the dignity of patriarch. Contrary to the Russian assertion, he did so with the consent of other hierarchs; Ecumenical Patriarch Jeremias II was deprived of the ability to engage in the usual orthodox practice of conciliatory consultations.[156]

The machinations used to achieve the tsar's goal of elevating the status of Moscow were nothing new. The Metropolis of Moscow had declared, along with the ROC, to be autocephalous in 1488 without the consent of the Ecumenical Patriarch. Godunov ensured the orthodox Metropolitan of Moscow would become the Patriarch of Moscow at any cost, by threat to the Ecumenical Patriarch and without the practice of conciliarity and prior agreement of other bishops, so dear to Orthodox Christianity.[157]

---

[155] Borys A. Gudziak, "The Creation of the Moscow Patriarchate: A Prelude to Patriarchal Reforms in the Kyivan Metropolitanate Preceding the Union of Brest (1595-1596)", *Logos – A Journal of Eastern Christian Studies, Volume 37,* 1996.

[156] George Vernadsky, "The Tsardom of Moscow, 1547-1682. Vol. 5 in A History of Russia", *Yale University Press,* 1959.

[157] The Greek Orthodox Church's Ecumenical Patriarchate was left in a precarious position after the fall of Constantinople. Ottoman pressure and threats by Russia to use Ottoman hirelings to menace the greatly weakened Patriarchate left the hierarchs little choice but to ratify the creation of Moscow as a Patriarchate *post hoc* at councils in 1590 and 1593. In a hypocritical move, Moscow later claimed the Ecumenical Patriarch's tomos for Ukrainian autocephaly was non-

Ivan IV Vasilyevich plans to lay the foundations for making real the idea of Moscow as the Third Rome was advancing. By these acts, he, his son and Borys Godunov intended to propel his people into the arms of an ever more powerful ROC. Together, their state-church goal was to implement their concept of the Holy Rus' — the premise that God set aside Russia as his specific agent for the salvation of the world, with the Russian people serving as the enlightened leaders of humanity to make it so. The co-alignment of the Holy Rus' with the Russkiy Mir was to evolve as a powerful, driving force in Russian life for centuries to come.

The Muscovy's translation from Muscovy to Russians marked the advent of Russia's unbridled hubris, asserting that humanity's destiny and salvation were inextricably intertwined with the superiority of the Russian State and the ROC.

The combination of appropriating Byzantium's history and that of the Kyivan Rus' proved the linchpin in transforming the Finnic tribes and proto-Slavic peoples from being Muscovy into Russians and Russia into greatness. Not to be outdone, Peter I Alekseyevich (Peter the Great) would in time eclipse his predecessors' gradual transformation of the once backwater state by realizing the progression of goals made real over the centuries when he proclaimed the Russia Empire into being in 1721.

Europe accepted the new concept of Russia and the Russians. As imperialists ruled Europe, it is not surprising that a Russian history concocted by imperialists found favor. Many of Europe's royal houses had themselves generously dipped into the waters of mythology and invention in their not-too-distant past. Russia's new history conformed to the general monarchical bias in such works.

Europe had theretofore relied on antiquity to understand Muscovy. There had been little understanding at all. Europeans had shown scant interest in that near-barbaric, geographically distant kingdom. However, once cleansed of its defects in history, the debutant Russian Empire was finally palatable to the society of fellow Christian emperors and their people.

The European Enlightenment created a climate ripe for fascination and receptiveness to new knowledge. Peter I Alekseyevich immediately grasped the opportunity to introduce his reimagined dominion to Europe and set the Kremlin to work. As a void of knowledge pervaded in the west, the tsar quickly filled the gap with information and 'histories' that suited his purposes. He was aided in this task by promoting domestic scholarship — albeit a highly censored one — to ensure its suitability. He ensured visiting dignitaries were courted and tutored in the new Russian history he

---

canonical as it had not received prior agreement with other Patriarchs and hierarch through by the norms of Orthodox conciliarity.

desired the world to adopt. Peter I Alekseyevich was aided in this task by capitalizing on the Russian state monopoly established by Ivan IV Vasilyevich—the Moscow Print Yard. This ensured the only image of Russia that was projected was one approved by him and the ROC censors.

The Moscow Print Yard had published its first book, *Apostolos*, with the specific permission and blessing of Metropolitan Макáрий [Macarius] of Moscow and all Rus'[158] Its evolution as the state printer of propaganda disguised as a publisher of histories and other subjects is due to Peter I Alekseyevich. His decision to create tunnels between the Moscow Print Yard and the Kremlin to speed communication and provide more storage is a testament to how valuable the printing press was to his plan to reshape Europe's opinions and knowledge of Russia. These works were not for mass domestic consumption. Textbooks and educational materials would have to wait for another day. Peter I Alekseyevich's information offensive was as critical to creating a European image of a modern Russian as Putin's propaganda organs are to projecting his desired view of Russia in the world today.

Peter I Alekseyevich's embrace of the Enlightenment expanded the use of the printing press. It had previously been devoted entirely to religious works. His decision to employ the Moscow Print Yard in the production of political works and uniquely Russian literature proved a masterstroke in forming Europe to believe Russia had a grand history and a society worthy of advanced scholarship. While his predecessors had whispered propaganda, Peter I Alekseyevich's Moscow Print Yard shouted his version of 'truth' about Russia, its history, heritage, culture, and religion. Its influence on the west's understanding, or more appropriately, misunderstanding of Russian history, has been profound. In many ways, it endures to this day.

Peter I Alekseyevich's reinvention campaign proved all too easy. He was filling empty shelves when it came to the Russia section of Europe's great libraries. Russia's modernizing tsar was astute. He realized his new Russian history propaganda campaign was a seed being sewn in fertile ground. Europe's own ignorance and biases about both Byzantium and the

---

[158] Макáрий (Macarius) was the tenth Metropolitan Archbishop of Moscow, a metropolitanate created at the demand of Prince Andrey Shuisky who held Regency over Ivan IV Vasilyevich who had yet to come of age. The enthronement contravened Orthodox Christian norms occurring at the behest of the state without conciliar engagement or the consent of the Ecumenical Patriarch of Constantinople, forever marking the Moscow Patriarchate's loyalty and foundations as being grounded in the state. The first metropolitan illicitly enthroned was Jonah. See: Evgenii Golubinskii, "Istoriia russkoi tserkvi, Vol. 2., Part 1.", *Moscow: Universitetskaia Tipografiia*, 1900.

Kyivan Rus' ensured few would defend their historic mantle now worn by Russia.

Although not exactly contemporaneous to Peter I Alekseyevich's efforts to redefine Russia in the late 17th century, any reading of Edward Gibbon's 18th-century *The History of the Decline and Fall of the Roman Empire* depicts the low regard in which Europeans held the former eastern Roman Empire. Their reasons were largely political and religious as previously mentioned:

> [Byzantine history is] a tedious and uniform tale of weakness and misery. O the throne, in the camp, in the schools, we search, perhaps with fruitless diligence, the names and characters that deserve to be rescued from oblivion.[159]

Since the time of Charlemagne, the mantle of the eastern Roman Empire had been claimed by the Holy Roman emperors. Having developed their own history and lore, these emperors found little with which to be concerned with tsarist claims over this bygone empire. The view of Constantinople throughout Europe had been shaped to be virulently negative. In modernity, to call something Byzantine conveyed a highly negative connotation throughout the west.[160]

Roman pontiffs were also beneficiaries from having contrasted the survival and influence of the Papacy in the west with the decline of the Patriarchate of Constantinople and demise of the eastern Roman Empire in the east. The sack of Constantinople in 1204 by Sultan Mehmet II left the papal states and papacy itself with substantially more influence than what survived of the Patriarchate of Constantinople after the fall of Byzantium. At the time of the tsars' ascendency, popes stood as the singular remaining, unifying source of authority in the west—a position they had not held since Constantine moved his capital to Nova Roma [Constantinople] in 330 CE.

---

[159] Edward Gibbons, "The History of the Decline and Fall of the Roman Empire", *Strahan and Cadell, London,* Published in 6 Volumes, 1776–1788.

[160] The Byzantines adopted the practice of disfiguring the nose a person of royal lineage, including disposed emperors, to bar them from ruling as physical deformity disqualified a person from serving as Basileus. As in the case of Justinian II (ὁ Ῥινότμητος, "the slit-nosed"), western writers commonly refer to this act being extremely cruel and barbaric. Byzantines found this practice to be far merciful than the commonly accepted Western practice of murdering political opponents or beheading deposed rulers. As for administration, Westerners characterised Byzantine administration as being overly and unnecessarily complicated without purpose. Few admitted that modern diplomacy is firmly rooted in Byzantine polity.

Indeed, between 537–752, the election of the bishop of Rome required the approval of the emperor at Constantinople.[161] No longer required to compete with the primacy of the Patriarch of Constantinople, Rome was satisfied to ignore Moscow's claims of ancient glory rooted in an empire whose demise posed no threat. The promotion of Moscow as the third Rome was almost laughable. The Latin west failed to comprehend the danger that Russia's emergence from its arrested development posed for the future.

In the absence of real knowledge and with only tangential experience of the vast, undeveloped Russian state on the verges of Europe, western civilization was both primed and happy to cede the lineage of the Byzantines and Kyivan Rus'. Russia exploited the opportunity. A succession of imperial apologists and propagandists used this vacuum to create a noble past for the Russian Empire and its tsars that was continually accepted for centuries, such that disentangling truth from myth has become increasingly difficult and fraught with peril.

Peter I Alekseyevich was free to reshape their history at whim. For his own purposes, he would use it to create Russia's new backstory that would parallel the great achievements of ancient Greece and Rome. He thirsted for Europe's admiration. He nurtured the Russian people to have a sense of awe, even if it was built on appropriation and invention.

Today, Putin claims the right of dominion over Ukraine, Belarus, and large parts of Europe, hinged on his invocation that Russians are the descendants and successors of the Kyivan Rus'. The facts and logic employed by Putin and Russian propagandists are faulty, relying on the invention of the Russian identity by the tsars of yesteryear. History and DNA refute such assertions. The Russian people's identity is intrinsically linked to its pre-Slavic Finnic peoples, the Mari, Moksha, Mordvins, Ves, and others, as well as the arrival of the Vyatichi and Krivichi tribes, peppered by the presence of only a small, contemporaneous diaspora from the disintegration of the Kyivan Rus' influenced regional principalities.

As for the invocation of Moscow being the third Rome, which arose with some cohesion and prominence under Peter I Alekseyevich,[162] Russia in modernity has pushed the ideas of the Holy Rus' and the necessity for a Russkiy Mir to their zenith. The interplay of Putin's personal faith narrative with Russian nationalism, combined with the appeal of 'traditional values', achieves a great deal in tying the Russian Orthodox Christian faithful to

---

[161] Frederic J. Baumgartner, "Behind Locked Doors: A History of the Papal Elections", *Palgrave Macmillan*, 2003.

[162] The Chronicle of Novgorod records Moscow at the time being a mere fortified village and trading post "*on a crossroads of four rivers*", *See:* Vasilij Grigorjevič Jan, "Batu-kan : istorijski roman", *Beograd: Prosveta*, 1991.

the state. Collectively, they create a formidable bulwark designed to consolidate Russia's domestic power as a precursor to realizing its revanchist goals.

There are numerous reasons for the difficulties in understanding Russia and Russians and making sense of its "unpredictable past". Russia's genesis story is one example of the challenges presented in reconciling Russian history with reality. Russian historians, and those who have relied on them, always insisted that Prince Yuri Dolgurukiy founded Moscow c. 1147. Moscow is cited as the place for the meeting with Sviatoslav Olgovich, Prince of Novgorod.

The commonly repeated narrative is that Dolgurukiy fortified Moscow c. 1150. Wikipedia, the favorite search destination of the hoi polloi, boasts: "between 78% and 98% of respondents said they trusted Wikipedia 'A great deal' or 'somewhat.'"[163] The site restates these assertions as fact, citing John Fennell as its source. However, it doesn't pass the test of academic rigor and research. The Dolgurukiy myth of Moscow's early history has entered the western zeitgeist as fact without challenge. This story of Moscow's foundations would at first glance tie Moscow somewhat to the Kyivan Rus'. And yet, there is no evidence whatsoever of this event or Moscow's existence in contemporary records.

Two sources inform us that these fabrications of Moscow's existence and supposed Kyivan Rus' ties are entirely bogus. The Mongol Golden Horde conducted three separate census counts in this era. The first census occurred during 1237–1238. There was no mention of Moscow. Had Moscow been prominent enough to have been the meeting place of two princes, it would not have escaped the tax assessors and census takers of the Mongol Golden Horde for nearly a century. The second census was conducted between 1254–1259. Again, there is no mention of this supposedly long-fortified settlement. It was only in the third Mongol Golden Horde census of this era, conducted in 1272, that Moscow's first mention arises.[164] Good scholarship and contemporary records give us every reason to believe that Moscow was not founded until between c. 1260–1272. We must reject the c.1147 story of Moscow's existence and prominence as an apocryphal invention.

The mythical mention of the Dolgurukiy meeting c. 1147 is likely one of the fictitious claims made *ex nihilo* during the reign of Ivan IV Vasilyevich. It seems to have been made ubiquitous by the propagandists and

---

[163] YouGov Wikimedia Foundation, "*Women and Wikipedia: Summary of results from 2019 YouGov survey*. Technical Report", *Wikimedia Foundation*, 2019.

[164] Mauricio Borrero, "Russia: A Reference Guide from the Renaissance to the Present", *Infobase Publishing*, 2009.

apologists of Catherine II during the late 18th century without citation of any source.

Ivan IV Vasilyevich was the first Tsar of Moscow, crowned in 1533 and was adept at laying the foundations to claim Kyivan Rus' heritage and have himself proclaimed "successor" of the Roman Emperors who reigned at Constantinople. Like the later Tsarina Catherina II, Ivan IV Vasilyevich was horrified that his and Russia's true heritage was rooted in the Golden Mongol Horde. While there can be no certainty, opportunity, means, and motive militate toward the invention of this date and event being that of the clergy writing the latest iteration of histories promulgated under the reign of Tsar Ivan IV Vasilyevich.

According to Yaroslav Dashkevysh, when Ivan the IV Vasilyevich was crowned, the supposed document issued by Constantinople, confirming the legitimacy of his coronation as successor of the Eastern Roman Emperors, had an impressive 39 signatures. Only four were found to be authentic.[165] That documents were created post hoc by Russian clergy to substantiate Ivan IV Vasilyevich's credibility and enhance the tsardom of Moscow were fabricated is undeniable.[166]

The Constantinople coronation confirmation document is but only one example of the use of forgeries created by ROC clergy serving in tsarist courts. The Ivan IV-Kurbsky correspondence, which has been heavily relied on for centuries as the only authoritative source of first-person accounts by Ivan IV Vasilyevich, is now universally considered by scholars to be a poor forgery created in the 17th century. There is also the "Extract about the Second Marriage of Vasilii III" [Vypis' o vtorom Brake Vasiliia III]. Brian J. Boeck argues persuasively that the document is a mere postmortem creation designed to shield Ivan IV Vasilyevich from scrutiny by the ROC.

The ROC would have been eager for the extract to be created. The ROC considered second marriages at the time anathema. Any irregularity in Ivan IV Vasilyevich's marriage validity would have undermined his right to have ruled as tsar. The title of the work provides dispositive proof that it was not a contemporary document but a later forgery:

> Выпись из святогорьские грамоты что прислана к великому князю Василию Ивановичю о сочтении втораго брака и о разлучении перваго брака чадородиа ради. Творение Паисено, старца Серапонского [variant Ферапонтова] монастыря [Extract from the letter which was sent to the

---

[165] Orysia Hrudka, "Russian ideology: imperialism, militarism, and racism", *Euromaidan Press*, 5 April 2022.

[166] Serge A. Zenkovsky and Edward L. Keenan, "Prince Kurbsky – Tsar Ivan IV Correspondence. Reflections on Edward Keenan's The Kurbskii-Groznyi Apocrypha", *The Russian Review*, Vol. 32, No. 3, July 1973.

Grand Prince Vasilii Ivanovich about the contraction of a second marriage and the dissolution of a first marriage for the sake of childbearing. The creation of Paisii, elder of the Serapon-Ferapontov monastery].

The Athonite monk Paisii was long in his grave when the events to which he alludes occurred.[167] The letters could only have been articles of forgery. The most impactful Russian forgery may be that of the supposed will of Peter I Alekseyevich. The will of the tsar was used for almost 200 years to drive and justify Russian foreign policy. This deathbed document allegedly contained Peter I Alekseyevich's political testament, which included the subjugation of Europe. Almost 20 years after the tsar's death, Russian Chancellor Alexey Bestuzhev-Ryumin unveiled his foreign policy manifesto, which he called "The System of Peter the Great". The policy relied heavily on the late tsar's fascination for the sea, suggesting a grand alliance of maritime powers from England and the Netherlands to counter the Polish Lithuanian Commonwealth. It was undoubtedly the work of Bestuzhev-Ryumin and not Peter I Alekseyevich. It is closely related to a document circulated to Emperor Napoleon called "Aperçu sur la Russie", popularly referred to as the "Testament of Peter the Great."[168] It has been declared a forgery by scholarly consensus.[169]

Of course, there is no more notorious Russian forgery weaponized for Russian state purposes than the Протоколы сионских мудрецов [Protocols of the Elders of Zion]. In the aftermath of the Partitions of Poland in the late 18th century, the Russian Empire became home to the world's largest collection of Jewish communities. Antisemitism and pogroms flourished. The ultra-nationalist declaration of Tsar Nicholas I Pavlovich, "Orthodoxy, Autocracy, and Nationality", summarized the prevailing ideology of the era.

There was increased pressure by the ROC and tsarist authorities on Jews to convert to Christianity in a movement not dissimilar to that which occurred in Spain 300 years before. Still, the same ROC that could not tolerate the presence of Jews among the Holy Rus', they could not accept them even after baptism. Just as Jewish converts were not fully accepted as authentic Christians and were ubiquitously known as "conversos", Russian

---

[167] Brian J. Boeck, "The Performance of Forgery in Late Medieval and Early Modern Culture, Chapter 5 Prenatal Prophecies and Linguistic Ciphers: A Russian Political Forgery Devoted to the Autocratic Evil of Ivan the Terrible", *Brill, Intersections, Volume: 84*, 2022.

[168] Raymond T. McNally, "The Origins of Russophobia in France", *American Slavic and East European Review Vol. 17, No. 2*, April 1958.

[169] Lucjan R. Lewitter, "The Apocryphal Testament of Peter The Great", *Polish Review, Vol. 6, No. 3*, 1961.

Jews who converted to Orthodox Christianity were despised as "infiltrators." Eradication was the preferred method of disposing of Russia's Jews.

To motivate widespread support for more repressive measures needed to cleanse Russia of the Jews, inherited from its territorial conquest, propaganda was required. In 1902, the Saint Petersburg newspaper *Novoye Vremya* published parts of the "Protocols of the Elders of Zion". This was immediately followed by publication in *Znamya* and the newsletter of the radical Black Hundreds movement. In 1906, the "Protocols of the Elders of Zion" appeared in its entirety as a pamphlet. Soon, the supposed manifesto of the Jewish people to take over Russia and Europe spread like wildfire, fueling anti-Semitic public opinion. Official regulations made life more difficult for the already oppressed Jewish people of Russia, leading to mass emigration and increased tolerance for pogroms, large and small.

The document was undoubtedly a forgery. As early as 1921, its authorship was linked to Russian journalists Matvei Golovinski and Manasevich-Manuilov. According to a lecture presented by Princess Catherine Radziwill in New York, the "Protocols of the Elders of Zion" was written at the direction of Pyotr Rachkovsky, the director of Отделение по охранению общественной безопасности и порядка [The Department for the Protection of Public Safety and Order, the 'Guard Department' or more popularly 'Okhrana' — the Russian secret service].

The work is universally recognized today as a forgery uttered for Russian state objectives. Its legacy, however, survives. The mass migration of Russian Jews from eastern Europe between the late 19th and early 20th centuries and the quest to establish a 'Jewish Homeland', which was realized as the State of Israel, can be directly traced to the anti-Semitic initiatives of the Russian state, an article of which was the forged "Protocols of the Elders of Zion".

For its part in the disturbing anti-Semitic affairs of the era, the ROC was complicit in failing to condemn the patently forged document. When the Moscow Patriarchate did respond, they claimed they could take no position on its authenticity but declared the nefarious objective of "controlling the world" was consistent with the ROC's view of the Jewish people:

> While the Church has no knowledge of the authenticity or lack of authenticity of the Protocols, and cannot provide an opinion concerning their authorship, it sees the practices and actions described in them as compatible with the Jewish religion and practices of the Jewish people.[170]

---

[170] Russkaia Pravoslavnaia Tserkov, Moscow Patriarchate, "Protokolle der Weisen von Zion" .Strafsache Schweizerischer israelitischer Gemeindebund und Israel-

The anti-Semitic chords are still played by the Russian state today. In December 2024, in comments directed at Jews in Russia dissenting from the war in Ukraine, and particularly directed at Ukrainian President Volodymyr Zelenskii, who is ethnically Jewish, Putin lashed out on national television:

> These are people without any beliefs, godless people. They're ethnic Jews, but has anyone seen them in a synagogue? I don't think so! These are people without kin or memory, with no roots. They don't cherish what we cherish and what the majority of the Ukrainian people cherish as well.[171]

The remarks came during Putin's annual media address. While speaking about the sanctions on the ROC, Putin claimed Jews were "tearing the Church apart."[172]

During the same media address, Putin defended Russia's incursion into Crimea:

> The events in Crimea were spontaneous, and the events of 2022 were also started without any special preparation. Why did we start? Because it was no longer possible to stand still and endure, waiting for the situation to worsen for us.[173]

Putin's position that Crimea is "us" is wrong. He previously claimed, "Crimea is Russian and where its people live,"[174] an assertion that runs contrary to facts. The Crimean Tatars are a Türkic people, not the Slavic people Putin claims are at the heart of being Russian. They speak Kipchak, not Russian. They are primarily a Muslim people, not the Christians to whom Putin constantly alludes.

According to the chairman of the Mejlis of the Crimean Tatars, Refat Chubarov: "The Crimean Tatars possess their own history, culture and

---

itische Kultusgemeinde Bern gegen die Gauleitung des Bundes national-sozialisticher Eidgenossen und weitere Angeschuldigte … (microfilm copy), Frames 001347, Der Berner Prozess um die (microfilm), *Jewish Culture Society: Bern*.

[171] Corinne Baum and Ben Sales, "'They're tearing the church apart': Putin targets Russia's 'godless' Jews at media conference", *The Jerusalem Post*, 20 December 2024.

[172] Baum and Sales, *ibid*.

[173] Analysis, "When the "action" starts: Debunking 12 falsehoods from Vladimir Putin's "Direct Line"", *The Insider*, 20 December 2024.

[174] Владимир Владимирович Путин, "Федеральному Собранию Российской Федерации Послание Президента РФ Федеральному Собранию", *Кремль, Москва*, 4 декабрь 2014.

identity and it is not today, nor has it ever been Russian except by force of occupation, deportation and persecution.[175]

Crimeans are not Russians. Crimea has not been historically Russian. Putin's and Russia's claims on Crimea are relatively recent and only arise from the imperial conquests of Tsarina Catherine the Great, c. 1783.[176]

While these examples primarily address Ukraine, they could well apply to Georgia and other neighboring states where Russia has asserted the need to protect Russians as part of the *cassis belli* to annex territory. When Russia failed to sufficiently maintain Georgia within its sphere of influence, fearing its drift to the west after the pro-democracy and pro-European Rose Revolution[177] of 2003 was a threat to the "motherland," Russia launched an invasion in 2008, eventually claiming annexation of Abkhazia and South Ossetia. The protection of "ethnic Russians" was cited as a necessity. Originally styled as a "peacekeeping operation," Russia justified its occupation as necessary due to Georgia supposedly engaging in genocide against ethnic Russians.[178] The similarities of claims of causation and responsibility for Russia's use of military force to invade sovereign Georgia in 2008, and Ukrainian territory in 2014 and again in 2022 are striking. In both instances, claims of protecting "Russians" featured significantly despite the persons being citizens of Georgia and Ukraine.

In ethnic, cultural, linguistic and other discriminating factors, the idea that Ukrainians are "Little Russians" is a projection of ideology and political doctrine. Nevertheless, it has served the Russian state and people for centuries in justifying its quest for empire. The erasure of anything remotely Ukrainian in terms of culture, language, and history, or their outright appropriation as being Russian, has primarily been achieved by policies designed to deny their existence and use.

Then there is Georgia, Poland, Moldova, and other neighboring states like Romania (each of which could only be considered contiguous to Russia if Ukraine were to be considered Russia). From the time of the tsars to Putin, these peoples and states have at times been claimed as "Russian"

---

[175] Refat Abdurahman oglu Chubarov, "Interview with Miceál O'Hurley and Refat Aga, Chairman of the Mejlis of the Crimean Tatars at Antalya Diplomacy Forum", Antalya, Türkiye, *European Diplomat*, 2 March 2024.

[176] Prior to Russian Annexation in 1783, Empress Catherine and Russia acknowledged Crimea as being historically free: Treaty of Küçük Kaynarca (1774) at Article III, "Russia and the Ottoman Empire acknowledge all of the Tartar peoples as free and independent nations, with freedom of religion and the freedom to be governed by their own ancient laws."

[177] Named after opposition leader Mikheil Saakashvili carrying red roses as he led protests outside of the Georgian parliament.

[178] Andrew Osborn, Jeanne Whalen, "Evidence in Georgia Belies Russia's Claims of 'Genocide'", *The Wall Street Journal*, 7 August 2018.

because the Russian language emerged to displace the vernacular by design (à la the *Valuyev Circular* and similar directives and policies enforced during periods of Russian occupation or influence).[179] The Russian language claim is possibly the most thinly supportable element used by Putin and the Russians to claim someone to be Russian, but increasingly used as it represents an outward manifestation of Russian influence.

Identity and nationalism have often combined with fatal results for the state and oppressed peoples alike. For the National Socialists under Hitler, being a "Good German" or "Aryan" drove the state to commit unspeakable evil in its quest to prevail over all other peoples and territories it intended to bring under its sphere of influence. Some white Americans clung so tightly to their belief in Manifest Destiny that they wiped entire Indigenous peoples from the face of the Earth and damaged others so severely that the trauma of confiscated lands, dispossessed people, and cultural deprivation remains as abundant scars on the lands and peoples of the remaining Indigenous American Indians. Belgium's colonial dominion over the Belgian Congo, including Leopold II's personal ownership of the Congo Free State, marked the zenith of Belgium's integration of identity and nationalism and remains a stain on its national consciousness.

This needs to be examined in the context of Putin's revanchist policy, which compels Russia on a seemingly unceasing crusade of conquest. Consider the following excerpt from Putin's address to the Federal Assembly of the Russian Federation of 2014:

> Along with ethnic closeness, language and common elements of material culture, a common territory, although not then delineated by stable borders, emerging joint economic activity and the power of the prince, Christianity was a powerful spiritual unifying force that made it possible to include in the formation of a single Russian nation and the formation of a common statehood the most diverse tribes and tribal unions of the entire vast East Slavic world.
> And it was on this spiritual soil that our ancestors first and forever recognized themselves as a single people.
> And this gives us every reason to say that for Russia, Crimea, ancient Korsun, Chersonesus, Sevastopol have a huge civilizational and sacred significance. Just like the Temple Mount in Jerusalem for those who profess Islam or Judaism.

---

[179] The Georgian language is not Slavic in origin as is Russian but is part of the independently evolved *Kartvelian* language family. Romanian represents a derivation from 'Vulgar Latin'. These countries, though at various times claimed by Putin and Russia to be "Russian" have also enjoyed independent cultures and territorial histories unconnected to Russia. Romania was a Russian protectorate in the 18th and 19th centuries.

> This is exactly how we will treat it from now on and forever.[180]

There are several immediate takeaways from even this small excerpt of Putin's address. He begins his appeal by combining the aspects of the Russkiy Mir of which we heretofore alluded: culture, language, territory, and ethnicity being combined in the power of Christianity. Here, Putin intertwines the concepts of what is Russian and who is Russian with the mission of the ROC—converting people to Christianity under the auspices of the Moscow Patriarchate.

Venturing beyond the rhetoric of identity, Putin moves to the realm of logical fallacy. The assertion that "our ancestors first and forever recognized themselves as a single people" is without foundation. Indeed, it is refuted by facts and history. We need only to recall the Khmelnytsky Uprising in which Zaporozhian Cossacks, allied with the Crimean Tatars and local Ukrainian peasantry in a national liberation effort, first from the Polish Lithuanian Commonwealth that sought to convert Ukraine's Orthodox Christians to Roman Catholicism and later from Russian control. Any assertion that the Zaporozhian Cossacks, Türkic Crimean Tatar Muslims, and Ukrainian peasants saw themselves as "one people" with the Russians, as Putin asserts, is baseless. There are myriad examples, including non-Slavic people incorporated into the Russian Empire, mostly by force, over centuries.

Notwithstanding, Putin and the ROC have continued to drive home the narrative that any people who are Slavic, descendants of the Rus', became Russian by means of the Principality of Muscovy or were later incorporated into the empire or Soviet Union by force of arms and occupation, de facto or de jure, are Russian. This served the pursuit of empire centuries ago, as it serves the revanchist policy of the Russian Federation at present.

Concerning the Patriarchate of Moscow, we have attempted to employ the clearest understanding of the body to which we refer whenever possible, be it the Moscow Patriarchate, ROC, or Ukrainian Orthodox Church (Moscow Patriarchate) or even the ROCOR when referring to the ROC under the auspices of the Patriarch of Moscow. Where using the term ROC would provide greater clarity, we have done so.

Likewise, we have opted to apply the term Russia when referring to the state as the internationally recognized sovereign territory of historic Russia (elastic though it was over time) or otherwise use the term 'Russian Federation', as internationally recognized, where clarity so demands. For

---

[180] Влади́мир Влади́мирович Пу́тин, "Федеральному Собранию Российской Федерации Послание Президента Рф Федеральному Собранию", *Кремль, Москва*, 4 декабрь 2014.

clarity of mind, though the Russian Federation asserts its claim to the temporarily occupied territories in Crimea and Ukraine, and additionally parts of Georgia and Moldova, we reject such claims as being *sui servientes* and failing to be internationally recognized.

The employment of the ethno-nationalist moniker Russian also presents difficulties because of the inexactitude of its use in recent history. While Catherine II of Russia may have called those in Crimea and in parts of Ukraine Russians after her bloody, imperial conquest of these distinct lands and peoples, it did not make them Russians in the way the term is generally and acceptably known. These people may have become Russian subjects by force, yet they remained, in nationalist terms, Ukrainians, Crimeans, Georgians, Moldovans, etc., by ethnographic heritage according to Russians. By avoiding the pitfall of attributing that people subjugated by Russia by illegal occupation and/or passportisation are somehow rendered Russian, we hope to preserve the individual and national dignity of those imperiled peoples.

The Muscovy, who were converted by Ivan 'the Terrible' to being Russians during his reign, are therefore a distinct people from those who became subjects by acquisition in treaty or by force. The Russian people have every reason to take pride in their heritage as being forged from the Finno-Ugric peoples, Slavs, Türkik, Caucasian, Mongols, and Uralic and other peoples that ground the Russians in being Russian'.

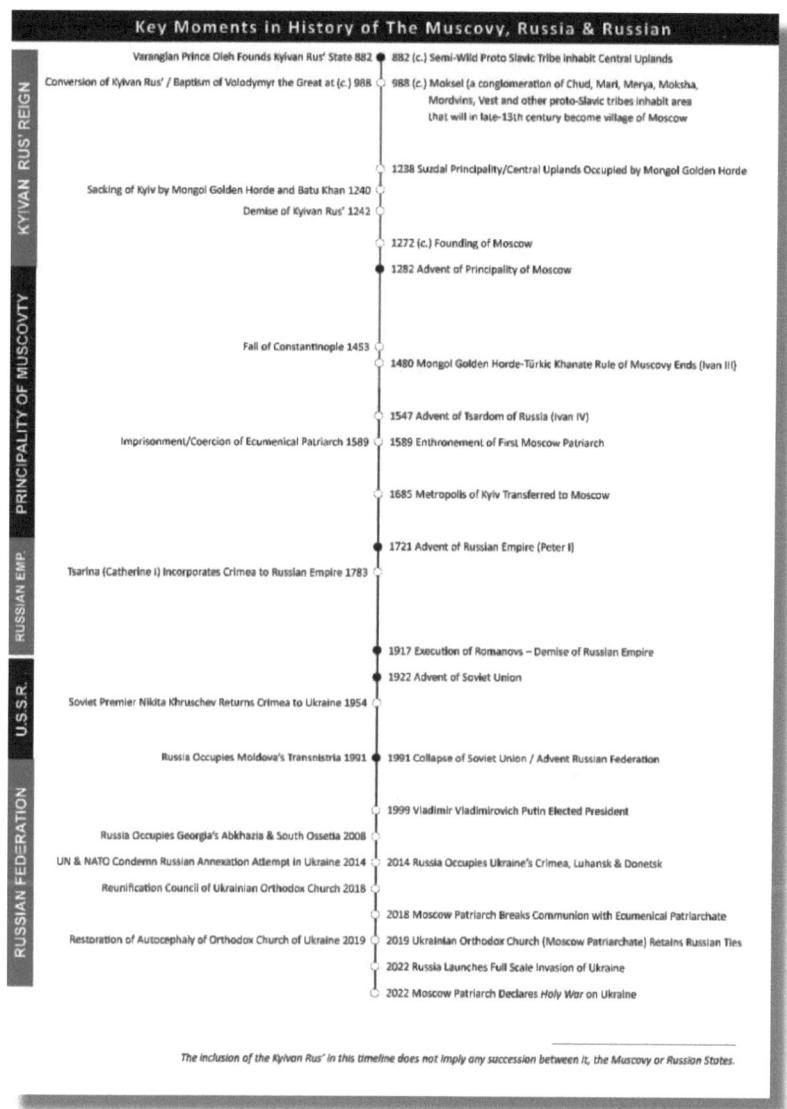

We have tried to exercise extreme caution in using the terms Russia and Russian. When used in historical reference, they might tend to organically deny the ability to whom it was implied to refute that those currently claimed to be Russian by virtue of Putin's "one people" doctrine. Adopting Russian history's application of Russian to Estonians, Lithuanians, Ukrainians, and others when they were compelled to become 'Russian citizens' by virtue of illegal occupation, colonial conquest, and/or passportisation injures not only their individuality and identity but also creates difficulty in presenting a clear and accurate narrative.

Therefore, Russians specifically exclude Ukrainians, Georgians, Moldovans, the people of the Baltics, Crimeans, people of the Black Sea regions where the Russian Federation has laid baseless claims of sovereignty unrecognized by international bodies, or Eastern Europeans once under the Russian sphere, except where they may have acquired citizenship by birthright prior to the demise of the Soviet Union.

Russia's rise always came at the cost of its neighbors and was invariably achieved by force. Along the way, Muscovy misappropriated the national, cultural, religious, linguistic, artistic, and other elements of its neighbors. When not incorporating them as part of their so often mythic Russian history narrative, they have otherwise tried to suppress them.

The attempted Russification of neighboring states such as Poland and Ukraine is an exemplar of a foreign policy pursued by Russia from the beginning of tsardom until the present.

In 1720, Tsar Peter I issued a writ of prohibition of the use of the Ukrainian language. Peter II followed by ordering that all Ukrainian legislation and regulations be published only in the Russian language, thereby forcing not only the law to be entirely Russified but the judiciary to adopt Russian legal customs and procedures. In 1863, Imperial Interior Minister Pyotr Valuev decreed:

> no special Little Russian language (meaning Ukrainian) ever existed, does not exist, and shall not exist and the tongue used by commoners [i.e. Ukrainian] is nothing but Russian corrupted by the influence of Poland.[181]

Poland fared no better. By the 19th century, the last vestiges of the Polish language were eliminated from schools. Russian nationalist Dmitry Ilovaysky's history texts, which included a pro-Russian view of history, became required texts. As with Ukraine, by 1869, Polish courts were administered in Russian, followed Russian rules of civil and criminal procedure and adopted imperial Russian law. Consequently, non-Russian-speaking lawyers were excluded from practice, and the intelligentsia of Poland was greatly subdued.

Of course, when cultural appropriate or deprivation proved insufficient, Russia resorted to genocide. After signing the Treaty of Küçük Kaynarca (1774), which created an independent Crimean Tatar state, Catherine II conquered the Crimean Peninsula in 1783. What followed were attempts to forcibly expel or exterminate the Qırımtatarlar (the Indigenous

---

[181] Volodymyr Dibrova, "The Valuev Circular and the End of Little Russian Literature," at p. 124, *Kyiv-Mohyla Humanities Journal* 4, (2017)

Crimean Tatar people) from their Ukrainian peninsula (an act repeated several times by tsars, Soviet premiers and now by Putin himself). Hostilities continued with the Türkic people until they engulfed other nations in the Crimean War (1853–1856), not unanalogous to Russia's attempt to annex Crimea in 2014, which led to a western alliance of nations against Russian efforts to obliterate Ukraine beginning in 2022.

The Polish and Ukrainian examples cited are by no means exhaustive. From the Baltics to eastern Europe, there is hardly a nation that has not experienced Russian attempts to incorporate it into a greater Russian Empire. History reveals this has always been the way of Muscovy.

Putting Russia's modern origin mythology aside, beyond the extensive scholarship of Nataliia Polonska-Vasylenko, who distinguished herself as one of the most preeminent Ukrainian historians of the 20th century, there is significant consensus by respected Russian scholars, historians, and archaeologists, such as Boris Rybakov, Dmitry Likhachov, Aleksey Shakhmatov, Alexander Presnyakov and Petro Tolochko, who universally concur that Kyi was a historic figure who founded the city now known as Kyiv on the Dnieper Upland and the Polesian and Dnieper lowlands in the 6th century.

Kyi established a dynastic rule over the city and region, transforming the city-state into a nation-state during his lifetime. According to the *Primary Chronicle* ascribed to Nestor, an Orthodox Christian monk writing at the Kyiv Pechersk Lavra caves c. 1110, Kyi was in diplomatic communication with the Byzantine Empire where trade furthered their bonds. Nestor recounts in the Primary Chronicle how Kyi led a "great army" to Constantinople where he was received with "many great honours by the Emporer".[182] Here too, the Russian Nikon Chronicles which date to the mid-16th century confirm this history which reinforces the reality that the Ukrainian capital of Kyiv far predates the founding of Moscow and the eventual formation of Russia.

Claiming an unbroken line of succession and ethnic purity, Catherine sought to deliver for her subjects the victories Ukraine's Crimea and Ukraine itself that failed to materialize during previous efforts during the regency of Sophia and her half-brother Peter I. The paucity of truth in this new Russian formation story not only usurps the factual origins of Kyiv and Ukraine but it wholly ignores the genuine ethnic, cultural and social history that make the Russian people uniquely different than Ukrainians.

The leader of the Kyivan Rus', Volodymyr the Great, centered his reign in the city of Kyiv. His dominion converted en masse to Christianity.

---

[182] Jonathan Shepherd, "Emergent Elites and Byzantium in the Balkans and East-Central Europe", *Taylor and Francis, Philadelphia, Pennsylvania*, 2011.

The Christianization of the Kyivan Rus' dates to c. 988 (the year is disputed), when Volodymyr the Great was baptized in Chersonesus (Korsun) on Crimea and proceeded to have his family baptized as well as people in Kiev.

The very idea that Kyiv has a more ancient claim on an ecclesial See than Moscow not only recognizes Ukraine's right to autocephaly by historical foundation but it equally entails that Ukrainians are more ancient, and therefore not Russian, as claimed by Russian imperialists at least since the time of Catherine II. Even then, it began in earnest only in the late 18th century. Putin could not abide this challenge to his territorial claims on Ukraine during his 'special military operation' in Ukraine.

When the Orthodox Church of Ukraine was granted autocephaly Patriarch Kirill was expected and required to object to Constantinople's Tomos to the Orthodox Church of Ukraine. There were never any questions that the Moscow Patriarchate would therefore break Eucharistic Communion with the Ecumenical Patriarch to assert not only the Russian's state's feeble claims on Kyiv but the Moscow Patriarchate's claims on the orthodox faithful of Ukraine. Unsurprisingly, to please Putin, Patriarch Kirill shortly thereafter broke with Christianity's pacifistic theology and tradition and declared the Putin's military operation in Ukraine a 'holy war'.

Russia had always boasted of its artistic prowess as a way of humanizing the nation. Unsurprisingly, artists widely known as Russian often were not. Those ascribed in exhibits, history and texts as Russian include Marc Chagall (Jewish), Oleg Kulik (Ukrainian), Kazimir Malevich (Polish) and even the father of modern Russian literature, Alexander Pushkin (African).

Claims of ethnic artistic achievement were only second to political claims. Political leaders assumed to be Russian often have surprising backgrounds. Catherine I, Empress consort of Peter the Great, was born Marta Helena Skowrońska (Polish). Mikhail Gorbachev and Nikita Khruschev's parents were not Russian (Ukrainian). Soviet Cosmonaut Pavel Popovich, Hero of the Soviet Union awarded the Order of Lenin, was not Russian (Ukrainian). The list is endless. Despite these truths, such persons are invariably identified as Russian.

The difficulty has always been that being Russian often alternated between being a point of pride and embarrassment. Peter I Alekseyevich (Peter the Great) desired to reconcile the two.

Peter I Alekseyevich has often been considered a great reformer who sought to inject western liberal education into his backward Russia but who faced two serious problems. Access to information deemed essential to projecting the Russian people into the nascent Age of Enlightenment (17th and 18th centuries) posed a challenge to an absolute monarchy. The ROC's almost complete dominion over the Serfs and poorer free Russians most in need of education created opposition from the Patriarch of Moscow, most bishops and almost all priests.

Despite his attempts to subdue opposition from the clergy by dismembering the Moscow Patriarchate and creating the Most Holy Synod empaneled with senior Metropolitans and bishops but under the "assistance of a lay crown official,"[183] the ROC remained a fierce opponent of his attempts at enlightening Russia. Clergy by and large prevailed in curtailing the development and delivery of a broader liberal arts curriculum. Mass education was almost uniformly restricted to religion, basic literacy, writing and math as a means of limiting challenges to the state that would arise from the study of history, politics and other social sciences.[184] The system continued into the Soviet era when access to basic education included broader opportunities for access to knowledge than under the imperial regimes.

Joseph Vissarionovich Stalin feared intellectuals. Under his regime, Russian intellectuals suffered mass suppression and often the relegation of critical thinkers to the 'Gulag Archipelago.'[185] Despite rising to be general secretary of the Communist Party of the Soviet Union, Stalin was only moderately educated because he was expelled from the Tiflis Theological Seminary before completing his training to be a priest. A product of the peasant classes, he was more educated than most, mostly through autodidactic pursuits.

Stalinism required that knowledge, both taught and acquired, be judged on its conformity with Leninist-Marxist theory and its support of the state as the unquestioned arbiter of good and bad, right and wrong, acceptable and unacceptable. After 1930, teachers and professors who strayed outside of the 'authorized' or 'official' curriculum, strictly governed by regulation and law, were removed from their posts.

Overall, Stalin did manage to achieve what Peter the Great could not — he nationalized all religious schools, imposed compulsory education to age 17, expanded university enrollment, guaranteeing placements by quotas for working class students, and reduced literacy before the liberalism inspired challenges to the state, resulting in his "Great Retreat" refocus on education to promote traditional family values.[186] Its policies imposed

---

[183] Paul Bushkovitch, ed., "The State in Early Modern Russia: New Directions", *Slavica Publishers, Bloomington, Indiana*, 2018.
[184] Richard Pipes, "Russia Under the Old Regime", *Charles Scribner's Sons: New York*, 1974.
[185] Aleksandr Isaevich Solzhenitsyn, "The Gulag Archipelago 1918-1956: An Experiment in Literary Investigation", *YMCA Press*, 1973.
[186] David L. Hoffmann, "Stalinist Values: The Cultural Norms of Soviet Modernity (1917–1941)", *Cornell University Press*, Ithica, 2003.

a virtual pre-revolution educational system based on "traditional" teaching methods (including the reintroduction of corporal punishment), based on respect for authoritarianism.

The Great Retreat's political values promoted a strict monitoring of curriculum and teachers to ensure "new Soviet Men and Soviet Women" would be education's primary product, with knowledge not central to communist ideology being reduced to a mere byproduct. A great consequence of the Great Retreat was that what wasn't considered Russian was often suppressed.[187]

If the Russian language emerged as predominant throughout the Russian sphere, and was accompanied by the displacement of native culture, literature, arts, history and political polity, it was not, as neo-imperialists would suggest, the product of any historic unity with Russia's neighboring states. The Russification of all within the Russian sphere was rather the intended outcome of a policy of linguistic discrimination, a mix of cultural appropriation and indigenous suppression and a posture promoting the erasure of anything that did not serve the goals of the Russkiy Mir and conformed to the ideology of the Holy Rus'.

Little consideration is given today by those who adhere to the propagandist's notion that Russia has rights over other states, nations, and territories as to how that omnipresence of the Russian language, distorted version of history, cultural dominance or the ROC's position within Orthodox Christianity in eastern Europe and the Baltics was achieved. This colonial process of forced assimilation is not unique to Russia by any measure. When any state has it within its grasp to proscribe any other version of language, history, culture, or religion than that which it desires, it cannot claim that achieving a near universal predominance over its victim's languages, cultures, and religious identities is the product of their implicit "erasure culture" and not the product of natural displacement and assimilation.[188]

Having achieved the near total Russification of those within the Russian sphere, including imposing a Russo-centric cultural, linguistic, historiographic and religious preference in the lives of its occupied or subdued neighbors, even if nearly eradicating their inherent sense of identity and

---

[187] Tove Skutnabb-Kangas and Robert Phillipson in collaboration with Mart Rannut, "Linguistic Human Rights: Overcoming Linguistic Discrimination", *Muton de Gruytur*, 1995.

[188] In North America, First Nations people (Native Americans, sometimes called 'Indians'), were often subjected to having their children forcibly removed from their family and indigenous lands for the purposes of "education" which included their indigenous cultural deprivation and re-education in State sponsored boarding schools. *See:* Dene Moore, "Schools' mission: take the Indian out of the child", *Toronto Star*, 6 March 2016.

history. If people could not be convinced they were Russian, they were encouraged to believe their ancient identity is owed to Russian influence. Being told repeatedly that Russia was the wellspring of their culture and language proved effective over time in saturating their psyches.

The step is illogical, however, for the unconvinced; it helps promote a sense of belonging in the Russian sphere, if not somehow being part of the Holy Rus'. Consider the following extract from Katerina Yakovenko's work and how Russia's claim for 'Mother-of-Slavs' status attempts to manipulate Ukraine's identity: "From the 1830s on Slavophiles in the Russian Empire propagated the idea that Russia, with its Slavic orthodox world, was the cradle of Slav civilization — the 'Mother-of-Slavs.'"[189]

Unsurprisingly, American textbooks among others in the west, repeated this phrase to the extent that it permeated the zeitgeist outside of the Russian sphere. The tendency of western textbook writers over the past century to approach their duty as conforming to prevalent political ideas, such as teaching the absurdity that Russian cows giving less milk because they are not "free" to roam, that Russia is the "mother-of-Slavs" and that Ukrainians are "Little Russians" means that non-critical westerners are bound to believe Putin's ethnic, linguistic, and cultural claims regarding who is Russian simply because it reinforces the information they were taught in their formative years.

Indeed, while the Soviets sought to impose their brand of ideology on occupied peoples through oppression, occupation and creating illiberal police states, Putin has cast the Russian Federation as the 'liberators' of the: "Tens of millions of our fellow citizens and countrymen [who] found themselves beyond the fringes of Russian territory."[190] Estonians, Latvians, Poles, Moldovans, Romanians, Hungarians, and others by and large don't want to be counted as Russian, even if they maintain a Russian-friendly political posture.

It is inconsequential that these neighboring states, be they Belarus, Estonia, Latvia, Poland, Romania, Ukraine and others, can legitimately make an equal claim to Kyivan Rus' heritage. They can, and some more legitimately. That they are independent and have recovered their identity, culture, language and religious independence that Russia worked tirelessly to deprive them of, is of little concern to the Kremlin. Indeed, the recovery of national identities by countries on the periphery of Russia is seen as a direct challenge to the Russkiy Mir and therefore tantamount to treason.

---

[189] Kateryna Yakovenko, "Russia's claim for "Mother-of-Slavs" status", *International Issues & Slovak Foreign Policy Affairs*, Vol. 24, No. 1-2, Europe and Russia, 2015.

[190] Владимир Путин, "Послание Федеральному Собранию Российской Федерации", *Москва, Кремль*, 25 апреля 2005.

Putin's attempts to convince the world that neighboring states once within the Russian or Soviet spheres are implicitly Russian are nothing new. It is a resurrection of ideas arising from Russian imperialism. In his 2018 political propaganda essay "On the Historical Unity of the Russian and Ukrainian People", Putin provides a par excellence example of how Russia projects its claims as being the wellspring of Slavic nations to achieve a veneer of credibility, albeit undeserved.

His carefully constructed work appeals to reason without credible evidence simply because it specifically appeals to the corrupted history of Russia taught in the west. That version of history has, for the last several hundred years, been based on Russia's self-serving imperialist version of history. Just as social media algorithms are based on reinforcing biases, prejudices and affinities held by their subscribers, so too has Putin's quest to impose the Russkiy Mir and promote the concept of the Holy Rus' relied on the same dynamic using information that sits comfortably within the learned bias and misinformation ubiquitously accepted in the west.

The Cold War generation, its children and grandchildren have been taught a version of Russian history developed by imperialists. This extends to how people of other states or nationalities have been presented in textbooks, galleries and popular culture as though Estonians, Georgians, Moldovans or Ukrainians are somehow a sub-species of Russians sharing in their history. The dialectic of our personal experience tends to fix matters in our memory without resort to facts reinforcing the likelihood that we will not amend our beliefs about Russia and its history despite newer and better information being readily available.[191] Russia's penchant for transposing Russian identity to people of other states, nations and cultures has helped to reinforce the current neo-imperial narrative about who and what is Russian.

Dismantling education-based indoctrination about Russia that grounds much of the west's understanding of Russia and Russians will take time. It is unlikely to occur until it's too late to diminish its consequences. Still, the need is pressing. The duration of Russian occupations in Moldova's Transnistria, Georgia's Abkhazia and South Ossetia, and even in the shorter duration of its occupations of eastern Ukraine and Crimea, is translating into acceptance.

---

[191] Today's senior decision-makers are old enough to have personally known the generation of citizens of Tsarist Russia in exile or experienced the Soviet Bloc as encompassing most of eastern Europe and having influence throughout the world. It was not uncommon in western classrooms for Baltic, eastern European and other nationalities within the tsarist or Soviet spheres to simply be referred to as "Russians".

The axiom, "The future whispers, the present shouts," is instructive simply because it can serve to remind us that voluminous disinformation tends to continually direct us to focus on the present without regard to the future. Propagandists know that issues that appeal to the immediacy of personal experience are always prioritized over issues happening to other people, in other places. Putin invokes the necessity of the 'special military operation' in Ukraine to protect Russia from a repetition of Nazis threatening Russia's borders or having 'foreign agents' influence civil society actors in an attempt to delegitimize his regime and cause a return to the economic and social chaos that characterized the post-Soviet era before he rose to power.

Consequently, most Russians accept the elimination of civic freedoms and the elimination of human rights organizations like Memorial, as it does not affect them personally. Decrying former Soviet states by removing statues and monuments to their Russian oppressors works well for Putin, as it strikes at a sense of pride from those who remember a bygone age when Soviet strength and an expansive Russian sphere were equated with national pride. Little consideration is given to it, eventually leading to statues of Stalin being reintroduced in Moscow subways without explicitly acknowledging that they represent the re-embracing of state brutality and their implicitly loss of civil liberties.[192]

Putin and the ROC did not confine the attacks on Russian heritage to having begun or ended with criticism of its tsarist or Soviet record of brutality and calls for accountability. The growing demand for increased equality by Soviet women that began in the 1980s had, by the 1990s, spurred advocates of non-normative sexual orientations or supporters of acceptance of sexual fluidity and gender reassignment to demand a place in the national debate on what civil liberties meant in being Russian. The movement endangered the Holy Rus' concept of 'traditional family values'. Conservatives and neo-imperialists combined to begin actively legislating against anything perceived to challenge the concept of the Holy Rus', thereby creating a culture war in the newly free Russian Federation. Putin was determined to win the culture war, and by enlisting the ROC in his campaign, he found an enthusiastic ally.

In its rush to cooperate with Putin, the ROC began to equate criticism of Putin or the state as being declarations or acts of heresy. Those who have spoken out against the continual diminishment of civil rights have been branded as persons desirous of exercising those rights to expand western values in Russian culture and law. When members of the feminist punk band Pussy Riot undertook a 40-second political stunt to decry the overly

---

[192] Ivan Nechepurenko, Stalin's Image Returns to Moscow's Subway, Honoring a Brutal History", *New York Times*, 28 May 2025.

cozy relationship between the state and ROC, they were charged with inciting religious hatred, convicted, and two members served prison sentences.

The ROC deemed that their song questioned the depth of its cooperation with the Kremlin, sacrilegious[193] When opposition leader Alexei Navalny died after being subjected to torture and maltreatment in a Siberian prison, the ROC, cognizant that his crimes were political, forbade its priests from giving him the Christian rite of burial. Patriarch Kirill personally suspended the priest who presided over the funeral.[194]

In the face of the suppression of civil society actors, curtailing civil rights and confronting the embarrassment of the abject failure to "demilitarize and de-Nazify" Kyiv and topple the Ukrainian government within its operational plans' six-day window, the ROC decided to change the conversation. Seeking to deflect from the scrutiny of its increasingly fascist state it supports, the ROC stated: "67% of Russians believed a strong family to be the most important value in life...."[195]

The ROC has even extended the concept of traditional family values as being central to Russia's national security:

> Thus, in the words of St. Theophan the Recluse, 'Whoever lives in a family approaches salvation by good deeds done to their loved ones. The family is a little Church, [i.e., the father is the priest, the mother the deacon, who helps the priest, and the children are like the congregation], and it is strong, large families which form healthy citizens of both our earthly and heavenly Fatherland':
> And this, in turn, is the surest guarantee of the national security of the country.[196]

The Moscow Patriarchate's mantra that Russia is the "defender of traditional family values" is not simply a declaration of religious values. Such would be expected from the church. The claim also knowingly serves Putin and the neo-imperialist cause, calling the faithful to believe the world is decaying so rapidly and completely that the values Russians hold dearest are in serious, if not immediate peril. It is incontrovertible that the ROC is

---

[193] The performance of the song in Moscow's Cathedral of Christ the Saviour was undoubtedly a sacrilegious act. However, the fundamental act of engaging in political protest of the ROC's ties and influence in the Kremlin should not legitimately be considered sacrilegious, despite the vulgar way it was done in this instance.

[194] Uncredited by line, "Russian Priest Suspended After Navalny Memorial Service", *The Moscow Times*, 24 April 2024.

[195] Sandro Gvindadze, "Analysis: How Vladimir Putin defends 'family values' to mobilise voters", *BBC*, 27 February 2024.

[196] Father Fyodor Lukyanov, "Defense of Family Values Is a Matter of National Security – Russian Church", *Global Orthodox*, 28 September 2022.

obliquely forming society to accept normally repugnant conduct by the state as being necessary for the greater good in an almost echo of Stalinism.

None of this was taught to prior and present generations as part of their formative education. While the presentation of this information presents challenges to the conventional wisdom of those in the west, it is simply understood by Russia's neighbors, who have experienced the Russian state and ROC firsthand. It may well be that the west's slow, if not begrudging, realization that Russia does not intend to stop its territorial conquest with Moldova, Georgia, or Ukraine may be the chasm between personal experience of citizens of Baltic and eastern European states and the poor presentation of Russian history, politics, culture, and religion in the west.

Any solution for the west in addressing these issues so that it can effectively confront Russian propaganda will prove complex. Western politicians tend to suffer from the personal biases developed from their early education, which included erroneous information about tsarist Russia, the Soviet Union and now the Russian Federation. Politicians are generally slow to admit their shortcomings, let alone adopt a new appetite for scrutinizing how the works and words of the Kremlin, the Russkiy Mir Foundation and the ROC impact their public policy positions. The understanding of the threat the Russkiy Mir and Holy Rus' present outside of policy circles is scant outside of persons threatened by Russia on their frontiers.[197]

According to a 2018 Pew Research Center report:

> 45% of adults get news on social media, including 33% who get news on social media daily. Facebook is the most common social network used for news. In France, young people (those 18 to 29 years old) are more likely to get news on social media daily than those 50 and older (69% vs 17%) [198]

Those numbers have likely risen in the past seven years, given the dynamic reported growth throughout the west. In all, without editors and fact checkers, social media continues to perpetuate false information. The challenges posed by exposure to propaganda, disinformation and misinformation in the public arena cannot be ignored. With increasing numbers of

---

[197] Just as Americans began to have an appetite for deconstructing their erroneous understanding of Russia, its history, culture, language and politics, the re-election of Donald J. Trump to the presidency, and his termination of US interest in helping Ukraine defend its sovereignty and internationally recognized borders, effectively terminated a more universal grasp by Americans of the dangers of the Russkiy Mir and Holy Rus', relegating them to being European concerns.

[198] Amy Mitchell, Katie Simmons, Katerina Eva Matsa and Laura Silver, "Publics Globally Want Unbiased News Coverage, but Are Divided on Whether Their News Media Deliver Deep political divides in many nations on satisfaction with news media; greatest is in the U.S.", *Pew Research Center*, 11 January 2018.

westerners relying on social media as their regular, primary source of news, it is unlikely that propaganda and misinformation will be identified, let alone countered. Worse still, according to the same report, public disinterest and indifference to world news reached shocking levels:

> People are much less interested in news about other countries (global median of 57%). In only six countries do more than two-thirds say they pay close attention to news about the rest of the world. People outside of the U.S. express a similarly low level of interest in news specifically about the U.S. (48%).[199]

Consider a 2023 video posted by the Kremlin. Putin points to a 17th-century map proclaiming: "The Soviet government created Soviet Ukraine. This is well known to everyone. Until then, there was never any Ukraine in the history of humanity."[200] What made the video go viral wasn't the claim. Putin repeats this often. Rather, it was the word Ukraine prominently appearing on the map referred to by Putin that made his claim so laughable. Still, given the dynamics highlighted by the 2018 Pew Center for Research, it is likely that few took notice beyond the headline. In the absence of interest and scrutiny Russian propaganda prevails despite evidential proof contradicting the headlines in the same video.

Between self-interest and public ignorance, Putin has found that the sheer repetition of the myth that Russia is the "mother of Slavs" and Russians are the "sole heirs of the Kyivan Rus" proves useful in shaping public opinion. The uncritical acceptance of propaganda occurs when the "illusion of truth" effect takes place.[201] Worse still, in this age of increasing fascist and authoritarian tendencies, even elected western politicians find favor in quoting dangerous propagandists. Speaking during a Committee on Foreign Relations subcommittee hearing, Republican Congressman Keith Self unhesitatingly quoted one of the most notorious propagandists of the last century, Nazi Propaganda Minister Joseph Goebbels: "It is the absolute right of the state to supervise the formation of public opinion, and I think that may be what we're discussing here."[202]

Goebbels is the same man who supposedly said, "Repeat a lie often enough and it becomes the truth."[203] An unbroken chain of Russian apolo-

---

[199] Amy Mitchell, Katie Simmons, Katerina Eva Matsa and Laura Silver, *ibid*.
[200] Tom Porter, "Putin claimed a 400-year-old map proved Ukraine isn't a real country, not noticing it has 'Ukraine' written on it", *Business Insider*, 24 May 2023.
[201] Tom Stafford, "How liars create the 'illusion of truth'", *BBC*, 26 October 2016.
[202] Rachel Snyder, "North Texas Congress members clash over the use of Nazi propagandist Joseph Goebbels quote at hearing", *WFAA*, 3 April 2025.
[203] There is no evidence Joseph Goebbels said this. It is, however, accepted as an accurate summation of his *"große Lüge"* (big lie) philosophy. Adolf Hitler first

gists from Philotheus to Dmitry Peskov has repeated the claims about Russia's rightful dominion over Ukraine, the Baltics, and other neighboring states that politicians and academics alike, and certainly the public, are predisposed to adopt Russian propaganda concerning Russian territory and identity with unwavering certainty.

Recall Putin's essay "On the Historical Unity of Russians and Ukrainians", in which he wrote: "I said that Russians and Ukrainians were one people—a single whole,"[204] Putin undeniably claims Ukrainians to be Russians. He repeats it often for effect and with the knowledge that it will be reprinted ad nauseam in the media and trend on social media.

We argue that no other single document than "On the Historical Unity of Russians and Ukrainians" did more to shape modern public opinion about Russia's claim on the unity of Russians and Ukrainians than this essay. As much as western scholars decried it, and some learned politicians, it was vigorously defended in Europe. Politicians in Marine Le Pen, Alternative für Deutschland (ADF) and other right-wing parties, as well as prime ministers within the European Union, such as Hungary's Viktor Orbán and Slovakia's Robert Fico, variously repeat these claims.

Even US President Donald Trump, albeit not usually known for his intellectual prowess, is said by former National Security Council official and then Senior Aide to the President, Dr. Fiona Hill, to have struggled to grasp the idea that Ukrainians were not Russians: "[Trump] could not get his head around the idea that Ukraine was an independent state."[205] Given Trump's education and the period in which he acquired it, it is not surprising that he adopted the imperialist version of history that was so ubiquitous at the time.

It is incontrovertible that people tend to be limited by their education, or lack thereof, and their experiences mediate their knowledge. For millions of people who came of age before 1991, they were often taught that Russia was somewhat synonymous with the Soviet Union. A review of Dwight D. Eisenhower's "Atoms for Peace" speech to the United Nations General Assembly demonstrates how even an experienced former NATO commander and president of the United States of America used the Soviet Union and Russian interchangeably:

---

used this concept writing, "[The public will believe it because they won't accept anyone] could have the impudence to distort the truth so infamously." See: Adolf Hitler, Translation by Ralph Manheim, *Mein Kampf, A Mariner Book, Houghton Mifflin Company*, 1943.

[204] Влади́мир Влади́мирович Пу́тин, "Об историческом единстве украинского и русского народов", *Кремль, Москва*, 12 июль 2021.

[205] Fiona Hill, "There Is Nothing for You Here: Finding Opportunity in the 21st Century", *Mariner Books*, 5 October 2021.

> The Soviet Union has informed us that, over recent years, it has devoted extensive resources to atomic weapons. During this period, the Soviet Union has exploded a series of atomic devices, including at least one involving thermo-nuclear reactions....
>
> Instead of the discontent which is now settling upon Eastern Germany, occupied Austria, and the countries of Eastern Europe, we seek a harmonious family of free European nations, with none a threat to the other, and least of all a threat to the peoples of Russia.[206]

The public in the west can be forgiven for being formed to conflate the Republics of the Soviet Union as being Russian, just as all peoples under tsarist rule and influence were also referred to as Russian, despite their individual identity being distinct. References to all within the former Russian sphere as being Russian continued into the era of the Russian Federation. Even in 2008, members of the Commonwealth of Independent States (CIS) with its nine Member States and one associated state, were commonly considered as a single entity, leading US Senator John McCain to quip wryly: "Russia is a gas station masquerading as a country. It's kleptocracy. It's corruption. It's a nation that's really only dependent upon oil and gas...."[207]

All this and more requires us to be critical in re-examining the claims of Russian origin, Slavic-unity and other myths told in the Kremlin and Russian dachas and how the west unintentionally supports the idea of the Russkiy Mir in terms of the sovereignty, independence, and identity of states previously associated with former imperial or Soviet era Russian subjugation. Indeed, talking about independent states like Estonia, Latvia, Lithuania, and Ukraine being 'post-Soviet' countries is highly problematic. Argita Daudze railed against the practice in 2022. Daudze, an astute scholar and Latvian diplomat, rightly pointed out that these states cannot be called post-Soviet by the west.[208] They are not successor states of the Soviet Union. Westerners, of all people, should know this as they maintained a policy of non-recognition when incorporated into the USSR, as their sovereignty was deprived of them against their will.[209] It is folly for the west to continue to adopt language that asserts these countries were Soviet republics and their citizens Russians when their loss of sovereignty by force resulted in non-recognition.

---

[206] Dwight D. Eisenhower, "Address Before the General Assembly of the United Nations on Peaceful Uses of Atomic Energy, New York City", *General Assembly, 8th Session: 463rd Plenary Meeting, New York (A/PV.463)*, 1 December 1953.

[207] Jon Terbush, "John McCain: Russia is a 'gas station masquerading as a country", *The Week*, 8 January 2015.

[208] Argita Daudze, "Why the notion 'post-Soviet' is obsolete, and not only for the Baltic states", *International Institute for Peace (IIP)*, 10 January 2022.

[209] Arno Liivak, "Soviet Responses to Western Nonrecognition of Baltic Annexation", *Journal of Baltic Studies, Vol. 18, No. 4 (Winter 1987)*, Taylor & Francis, Philadelphia, Pennsylvania, Winter 1987.

Chapter Six

The Doctrine of Russian Superiority and Other Myths Told in Russian Dachas

Identity and nationalism have often combined with fatal results for state and oppressed peoples alike. For the National Socialists under Hitler being a "good German" or "Aryan" drove the state to commit unspeakable evil in its quest to prevail over all other peoples and territories they intended to bring under their sphere of influence. The same attended the American exploitation of native Americans during its Manifest Destiny epoch.

The Русский мир [Russkiy Mir] relies on a similar juxtaposition of these and other ideas, creating a sense of ethno-nationalist superiority for Russians. Such a dynamic served the expansionist goals of the tsars, supported the Union of Soviet Socialist Republics and Putin's pursuit of rebuilding a greater Russian Empire.

Russia has long embraced an expansive concept and doctrinal political policy that arises from its inherent imperialist worldview. The heart of the Russkiy Mir can be summed up as the sphere of military, political and cultural influence of Russia.[210] Here, an understanding of what Russia means is instructive. To whom the Russkiy Mir applies, one needs to take an expansive and inclusive approach to defining who and what is Russian.

For Putin, the Kremlin and ROC, it incorporates all ethnic Russians, Russian speakers in neighboring states and members of the ROC and those local churches that look to the Moscow Patriarchate for leadership. The breadth of this list is shocking in terms of policy and security implications. Of the 44 countries the United Nations recognizes as comprising Europe, applying this methodology, Russia claims to be able to assert varying degrees of interest in the territories and peoples of 22 sovereign states (excluding the former East Germany) and their peoples under the guise of belonging to the Russkiy Mir.[211]

---

[210] Valery Tishkov, "The Russian World—Changing Meanings and Strategies", *Carnegie Papers, Number 95*, August 2008.
[211] The list includes Albania, Belarus, Bosnia and Herzegovina, Bulgaria, Croatia, Czech Republic (Czechia), Estonia, Finland, (unspecified interest in Germany), Hungary, Latvia, Lithuania, Norway, Moldova, Montenegro, Poland, Romania, Russia, Serbia, Slovakia, Slovenia, Sweden, and Ukraine.

The Russkiy Mir's consciously expansive view of what is Russian is problematic where a rule-based order exists. It is designed to assert a notion of Russia's right of dominion over its neighbors. While such a notion is contrary to international law and Russia's obligations as a member of the United Nations, it still informs Russian foreign policy. Just as Putin refers to his fellow citizens being caught beyond its borders in 1991, Russia is determined that it will not recur. Indeed, Russia has little respect for the internationally defined borders of Member States,[212] as it has exercised what it believes to be its right to intercede on behalf of its 'fellow citizens,' what Russia now refers to as the 'near abroad' claiming humanitarian necessity, thereby condoning the use of force in the name of protecting supposed Russian citizens.

Modernity regrets that the west shares in such a disparate and distorted understanding of Russia and Russians. Regrettable—but not surprising.

The complexity of the interchange of the myriad elements that are present in the annals of Russian history is stupendous. It has rarely been a discipline subjected to genuine scrutiny, research, and scholarly exploration for the edification of humanity. We can blame the epochs over which it evolved, the lack of access to source materials and the propensity of the Muscovy-Russian Soviet-Russian leaders to reinvent history to suit their political needs.

Russian history was rarely pursued for the purposes of recording for posterity the acts and deeds of bygone ages with accuracy and without prejudice. From its nascent days as the Principality of Muscovy and throughout the tsarist, Soviet and now federation eras, Russian chroniclers have generally approached history as a vehicle by which its political, social and religious goals and objectives can be met.

To that end, the ROC has been employed at the heart of Russian politics to help bring about the Russkiy Mir. Its leader, Patriarch Kirill and his cadre of assistants, have forged what Dr. Elaine Wilson aptly describes as a "militant theocracy" that mutually permeates the ROC. It is, in her view, required to fulfill its role on behalf of the state. With its supra-territorial claims by virtue of its presence throughout the world, the ROC is indispensable to the Russian state.[213]

This is the situation in today's Russia.

---

[212] UN Charter generally, particularly at Article 2(4), Prohibition of threat or use of force in international relations, *Charter of the United Nations*, 24 October 1945, 1 UNTS XVI [accessed 21 February 2024].

[213] While claims of "religious persecution" of members of the ROC featured as a *cassis belli* in Moldova's Transnistria region occupation in 1990-1992, in the 2008 invasion of Georgia, and again in the 2014 and 2022 Russian invasions of Ukraine, it has always been asserted in relation to other Russian interests and has yet to be the singular or even main issue by which Russia has justified aggression against a neighboring State.

Chapter Seven

Святая русь — the Holy Rus'
Messianism, Russia, the Roc, and the Russian People

Messianiasm has always been understood to revolve around a central figure whose mission has been the salvation of humanity. It figures heavily in Christianity, Hinduism, Islam, Judaism, Zoroastrianism, and other religions. In Russia, where the development of the state over the individual has always been promoted, the role of the messiah became shared between the land and its people. The Holy Rus' concept is the synthesis of that very idea — it is the state and people that together are necessary for the deliverance of humanity from evil. What that means for international relations and human relations is therefore as complex as the concept itself.

The Holy Rus' cannot be fully understood without its role being considered vis à vis the ROC and the Russian state. Its fullness, the idea that God specifically chose Russia for the salvation of the world with the Russian people enlightening humanity, can only be realized once a Russkiy Mir is achieved. Together, the Holy Rus' and Russkiy Mir elevate not only the temporal greatness of Russia and the Russian people above all others but their philosophical ideology as well. It proposes Russia as the overlord of all nations and the Russian people as *Übermensch* superior to all people. With this understanding, it becomes easier to reflect on the hubris that has traditionally accompanied Russia's foreign relations and generalized ethnic character.

If crude, wild, drunken, harsh, and prone to authoritarianism have been the misplaced stereotypical caricature of Russians, their traits might be strong-willed, resilient, passionate, willful, possessing immense national pride, imbued with competing values of individualism and collectivism, and capable of incredible emotional depth and spiritual character. Of course, such abstractions are not wholly reliable. The caricature is grossly unfair. The traits we have listed, however, can provide a more accurate and insightful picture of the Russian person.

Why is it important to understand the Russian person? Elsewhere in this manuscript, we spend considerable time developing the history of Russia, the Russian State and the ROC because the understanding of the

Holy Rus' and Russkiy Mir requires a somewhat comprehensive view of why the ROC is a threat to European security and democracy. Indeed, too often the inability of the west to understand Russia's foreign policy is that it assumes the Russian state to be a corporate expression of the political will of the people. Such a view is a recipe for disaster.

To understand Russian foreign policy and consider ways in which the west can effectively counter its orientation toward domination revanchist-expansionism it requires us to apply what we know and understand about Russia and Russians within the context of their *esse*. Why do we say *esse*?

The revolutionary philosophy of René Descartes holds, "Cogito ergo sum" [think, therefore I am]. His understanding of the human *esse* reversed all prior understanding of our humanity. It revealed the truth that what we do is prioritized over who we are in understanding and revealing our being. It redefined our understanding of our being—our *esse*. A natural extension of Descartes' philosophy is that we should also embrace a more revolutionary understanding of Russia and Russians to understand them better. Our focus needs to shift from their being to their doing. This is critically important for our understanding of the trinity of the Russian state, the ROC and the Russian person. I refer to this triune being of the Russian state, the ROC and the Russian person as the concept of the Holy Rus', which binds all three, imbued in the minds of Russians from the moment of first comprehension to the moment of death. This is no understatement.

The Holy Rus' renders Russians almost unique in the world. Jews may see their fruition in the re-establishment of Jerusalem as the center of the world. Muslims can be said to seek the fullness of their faith being realized by a universal caliphate. But Russia and Russians alone believe their state, not just their religion, is called to a messianic mission for the sake of the world. That corporate trinity of the Russian state, ROC and Russian person, therefore, has individual aspirations and goals that can only come to fruition collectively.

The individual is the center of focus in western development. We think in terms of "I" before we think in terms of "We." This is a somewhat alien concept in Russia. The Holy Rus' concept that God chose Russia for the world's salvation necessarily places the Russian state in an a priori position in the trinity's hierarchy. The idea that the Russian people are called to enlighten humanity is asserted within the context of baptism into the ROC. In this manner, the ROC and the Russian person are joined to the Russian state as equal parties; however, with the ROC being subordinated to the Russian state and the Russian person's role being predicated on baptism into the ROC. It becomes essential that we understand Russia in the context of this trinity within the framework of the Holy Rus'. It is not what we want the reader to understand—it is what the Russians understand for themselves by virtue of the Holy Rus' concept.

While westerners may be motivated by the principles of nationality and patriotism, Russians are different. Europeans, for example, tend to see themselves as individuals before they see themselves as being French, Estonian, German, Irish, etc., whose lives are lived within the context of social compacts. They might be, for example, considering their formative social duties and obligations to arise from being Spanish, Catholic, a member of the VOX political party and European. Their lives are lived within the social compact demands of those communities. Their esprit de corps, patriotic fervor, political outlook, and religious values are influenced by these social associations. It is different for Russians who embrace the Holy Rus'. The triune nature of the Russkiy Mir calls Russians to think differently from Europeans.

The idiosyncratic trinity of state, church and the person under the Holy Rus' concept occurs within the context of the sacred. The idea of God setting aside a state and people for a specific purpose elevates the Russian *esse* to carrying a religious and moral imperative—saving the world. The Holy Rus' is therefore differentiated from secular demands or even the religious observances of westerners whose confessions of faith are of a personal nature, not a matter of state.

Saint Athanasia wrote in his opus *On the Incarnation*, "God became man so that man might become God". This idea of theosis, that humanity can be mystically united with God by our becoming more godlike in our thoughts, acts and deeds, provides an interesting context in which to consider the Holy Rus' ideology. The Holy Rus' requires that humanity become more Russian by embracing the idea that God selected Russia for the world's salvation, with the Russian people designated to enlighten humanity. The theosis desired by the Russian state is essentially the process of not being more godlike but being more Russian.

Understanding the Holy Rus' provides us with insights into our dealings with Russia and Russians. Many political analysts have commented on how personally Putin took the collapse of the Soviet Union. In Putin's view, the west engineered the collapse of communism in Russia, with the result that its form of government necessarily ceased, so the west could dismember what he believed was the justness of continuing the subjugation of other states and peoples under the idea of a greater Russia. For Putin, "One fact is crystal clear: Russia was robbed."[214]

These same pundits claim Putin took it so personally because he lost the power and prestige of being a feared KGB Colonel. Others speculate

---

[214] Влади́мир Влади́мирович Пу́тин, "Об историческом единстве украинского и русского народов", *Кремль, Москва*, 12 июль 2021.

that Putin felt wounded because the only thing he knew how to do—be a spy and exploit others—deprived him of having a transferable occupation suitable for the new peace. Others still claim he felt patriotically incensed by the degradation of the Soviet Union on the world stage. All of these may have been true, but they miss the point entirely. Putin took the demise of the Soviet Union personally because the Holy Rus' concept deprived him of any ability to differentiate between the injury to the state and himself. If, as he claims, he was secretly baptized as a child, the pain of the offense became more acute because it struck at the heart of the Holy Rus' trinitarian theory of the unity of the Russian state, Orthodox Church and Russian person.

It cannot be surprising that Russia's view of who is Russian is driven not by legal definitions but by the Holy Rus' ideology. The unity between the Russian state, ROC, and the Russian person being bound together has implications for Russia's world view. Defining who is Russian in law, or even by citizenship, would diminish the demands of the Holy Rus'. Defining Russia and who is Russian by its 1991 internationally recognized borders would transgress the principles and call of the Holy Rus' concept. It would naturally exclude the Russians, whom Putin complains were trapped beyond its borders on December 25, 1991.

The Holy Rus' concept, however, had a more expansive view of who and what was Russian. By virtue of confessing the Russian Orthodox faith, either directly within the ROC or through one of the local churches subordinated to the Moscow Patriarchate, one should be deemed to be Russian under the Holy Rus' ideology, or by having been occupied by Russia through colonial control or by Soviet occupation imposed upon neighboring states and people, the Russian language, culture, history, and society. The Holy Rus' demands that they too should be considered Russian, despite the restoration of their independence.

Any distinctions pertaining to language, culture, and ethnicity might otherwise be relegated by history to being of interest to historians, ethnologists and other social scientists were it not for the Holy Rus' concept. The Holy Rus' made these distinctions of paramount importance for princes, tsars and politicians in Russian history specifically because of the Holy Rus'. Language, culture, and ethnicity directly inform the modern sense of self in the way cardinal moments in history shape people's view of their belonging, such as in nationhood. Consider how the principles of liberté, égalité, fraternité inform the French people's understanding of being French. Certainly, "American exceptionalism" shapes the American sense of self-understanding. The concept of όντα [being] influences a Greek's sense of their role in life and the world.

It is not an exaggeration, therefore, that the Holy Rus' concept remains somewhat central to the self-realization of a Russian being a Russian. Regaining territorial holdings of yesteryear, asserting the Russian language and culture to the point where they subdue, replace, and ultimately erase the local identity of peoples of neighboring states, engaging in religious discrimination to ensure the ROC prevails if not excludes all others, and crafting the Russian person to see their being as inextricably bound-up in the goals of the Russian state and ROC is part and parcel of being part of realizing the Holy Rus' ideology and establishing the Russkiy Mir.

Is there room in the Holy Rus' for the Ecumenical Patriarchate or the survival of Orthodox Christianity under the other historic and new patriarchates?

The concept of the Holy Rus' continues to challenge the very historical nature of the position of honor enjoyed by the Ecumenical Patriarchate. The idea of the Holy Rus' stands in fundamental opposition to the orthodoxy of the Ecumenical Patriarchate, serving as *primus inter pares*. It requires Orthodox Christianity to interpret everything, the exercise of conciliarity, theology ecclesiology through the lens of the ROC led by the Patriarch of Moscow. If God specifically set aside Russia for the salvation of the world and the Russian people were made to enlighten it, how then can the historic and new patriarchates of Orthodox Christianity exist except under the authority of the Moscow Patriarchate? How can Christianity ever realize Christ's prayer for unity except under the auspices of the ROC?

The very premise of the Holy Rus' agitates for a confrontation between the Patriarch of Moscow and the Patriarch of Constantinople. Holy Rus' ideology compels an existential showdown for superiority in the life of Orthodox Christianity. It should not be surprising, therefore, that both the Russian state and the Moscow Patriarchate have become interchangeable partners in an unceasing quest to subordinate all within their influence on the idea of the superiority of the Russia state as the defender of Christian values and tradition.

The 18th-century German militarist and philosopher Carl von Clausewitz enunciated the reality of war and diplomacy by writing, "War is an extension of Government policy by other means."[215] In service to the Holy Rus', Patriarch Kirill's declaration of a 'holy war' and requirement that ROC recite the Holy Rus' prayer[216] Kirill's prayer specifically implores God to deliver a Russian victory in Ukraine. It necessarily precludes any concept of peace or accord. This demonstrates how the influence of the Holy Rus' ideology has supplanted basic Christian theology and values within the ROC. For Kirill and the ROC faithful, the triumph of the Russian state reigns supreme, despite it distorting if not obliterating normative teachings of Christ and long-held traditions of the Holy Orthodox Church directed at peace, the reconciliation of humanity and pursuing Christian unity.

---

[215] Oliver O'Donovan (Roger Williamson, editor), "War by Other Means: Some Corner of a Foreign Field", *Palgrave Macmillan: London*, 1998.

[216] Mark Trevalyan, "Russian Orthodox priest faces expulsion for refusing to pray for war victory", *Swiss Info SWI*, 13 January 2024.

The promotion of the Holy Rus' as part of the Russkiy Mir has been a focus of Putin since his rise to the pinnacle of Russian power just over 25 years ago. It is not coincidental that the ROC has become ever more enmeshed in Wilson's aptly described militant theocracy,[217] reinforced by the special status ROC clergy enjoy as chaplains to the Russian military.[218] It is reflected in the very artwork depicted in a special collaborative project between Putin and Patriarch Kirill—the Cathedral Church of the Russian Armed Forces.

> Angels hover above artillery, religious images are adorned with Kalashnikovs and the Virgin Mary strikes a pose reminiscent of a Soviet second world war poster. The imagery inside Russia's vast Cathedral of the Armed Forces blends militarism, patriotism and Orthodox Christianity to breathtaking and highly controversial effect.[219]

Does the Holy Rus' ideology require a masculine and militant ROC? The answer is yes.

To attain the Russian state policy of re-absorbing "[Russians] caught beyond our borders" after the 1991 collapse of the Soviet Union, the Russian military is compelled to complete the task where politics and 'soft power diplomacy' failed to achieve a 'voluntary' return to the Russian sphere. As the declaration of the World Russian People Conference, chaired by Patriarch Kirill, stated: "the entire territory of modern Ukraine must enter the zone of exclusive influence of Russia."[220]

The Holy Rus' isn't just a topic of interest or concern for theologians, academics or the faithful. It presents genuine security concerns. When the head of the ROC declares a sovereign nation like Ukraine "must enter the zone of exclusive influence of Russia," it is time for policy analysts, military experts and European politicians to take notice and seek to contain the operations of the ROC. Its role as a religious institution has clearly been relinquished to the Russian state, such that it can no longer be thought of as a church. This is the importance of Descartes' revelation that what one does, rather than who one is, describes our true *esse*—our being. The ROC can justly and rightly be deemed an apparatus of the security services of the Russian state. While it may be described as a church, it has revealed its mission is uniquely Russian and messianic and disposed to elevate the Russian state and Russian people at the expense of humanity.

---

[217] Elaine Wilson, "Русская «самобытность»: попытки присвоить и переписать религиозную историю," *Public Orthodoxy*, 30 December 2024.

[218] Dmitry Adamsky, "Russian Nuclear Orthodoxy: Religion, Politics and Strategy", *Stanford University Press*, 2019.

[219] Sean Walker, "Angels and artillery: a cathedral to Russia's new national identity", *The Guardian*, 20 October 2020.

[220] Наказ XXV Всемирного русского народного собора, "«Настоящее и будущее Русского мира»", *Русская Православная Церковь*, 27 Mar 2024.

Chapter Eight

Moscow — the Third Rome
Superiority of Time and Place

There are those who cling to the idea that the decision by the Ecumenical Patriarch, His All Holiness Bartholomew I's decision to grant a tomos of autocephaly to the Orthodox Church of Ukraine was wrong. Their reasons in opposition are far and ranging including the decision supposedly lacking conciliarity to an offense against the exercise of canonical authority. They are wrong.

There is a long and complicated history behind the re-emergence of the Orthodox Church of Ukraine. A review of history seems to indicate that there was always tension between the ROC and the Ecumenical Patriarchate in Constantinople. On December 15, 1448, the ROC enthroned Archbishop Jonah of Moscow as Metropolitan of Kyiv and All Rus' without the consent of Constantinople. By declaring their own head of the ROC without the consent of the Ecumenical Patriarch or any recognizable exercise in conciliarity made the ROC de facto autonomous. In Orthodox Christianity, such a breach is not only uncanonical it serves as a declaration of schism.

Ecumenical Patriarch Dionysius reconciled with the ROC 18 years later in 1466, and Kyiv, then the head of the ROC, was returned to its former jurisdiction under Constantinople. The matter wasn't settled, however. His All Holiness, Patriarch Dionysius, demanded that the hierarchs of Muscovy make obedience to Metropolitan Gregory (the Bulgarian) of Kyiv. They refused. In 1467, Muscovy Grand Prince Ivan III declared a complete breach of relations with Constantinople.

One hundred and three years later, in 1560, relations between Moscow and Constantinople had been restored, but just barely. In 1589, the ROC was recognized as autocephalous, operating as an exarchate of the Ecumenical Patriarchate. Despite the exarchate being elevated above a metropolis but not carrying the authority of a patriarchate, Muscovy remained dissatisfied. Ivan IV Vasilyevich, Russia's first tsar, wanted the dreams of grandeur flamed by his grandmother, the Byzantine princess Sophie Paleologos, to be made real. It fell to his mentally and physically impaired son and surviving heir, Tsar Fyodor Ioannovich, via his regent, Borys Godunov, to see to the creation of the Moscow Patriarchate in 1589.[221]

---

[221] Konstantin Gavrilkin, John Anthony McGuckin (ed.), "The Concise Encyclopedia of Orthodox Christianity", *John Wiley & Sons*, 3 February 2014.

Godunov's scheming lured the Ecumenical Patriarch to Moscow on his fundraising tour to Warsaw, Vilnius, and Kyiv. The Ecumenical Patriarch, Jeremias II, was anxious to rebuild the patriarchate in Constantinople and breathe new life into the Greek Orthodox Church under his jurisdiction. It has suffered a terrible degradation following the fall of Constantinople to Sultan Mehmet II and his Ottoman Türk army in 1453. The sojourn to Moscow would change the nature of the Orthodox church and world history in ways the Ecumenical Patriarch could not have fathomed.

Fyodor I Ioannovich and his ROC clergy were of the opinion that with the fall of Constantinople, Moscow was the only, and natural, successor to that ancient See. Seizing on the alleged prophecy of a Russian monk residing at the Yelizarov Convent, Philotheus of Pskov, that Moscow would become recognized as the 'third Rome', the court of Tsar Ivan IV Vasilyevich began to promote the idea. After all, Bulgaria, Greece, Serbia, Walachia, and Moldavia had each been subdued by the Ottoman Türks, arguably leaving Russia as the sole extant Orthodox nation. By the time the Ecumenical Patriarch, Jeremias II, journeyed to Moscow in July 1588, the conceit of Moscow enjoying a place of honor above Constantinople was already accepted among the Muscovy people.

There are serious problems with the interpretation of Philotheus having been the originator of the concept of Moscow being the 'third Rome' c. 1510. His 'essays' comprised a collection of correspondence between himself, the archpriest Mikhail Grigorievich Misyur-Munekhin, and a third party, Grand Duke Vasily III.[222] Philotheus of Pskov allegedly wrote:

> Know, O lover of Christ and God, that all Christian realms have come to an end and have been gathered into a single realm under our sovereign, which is the kingdom of the Romans, according to the prophetic books. For two Romes have fallen and a third exists and there will not be a fourth. The apostle Paul oftentimes recalls Rome in his epistles and this is interpreted as meaning that Rome is all the world. For you see, O elect one of God, how all the Christian realms have been crushed by the infidels and only the realm of our sovereign stands by the grace of Christ. He who reigns should remain

---

[222] Филофей. «Посланіе О Злыхъ Днехъ И Часѣхъ», «Посланіе К Великому Князю Василию, В Немъже О Исправленіи Крестнаго Знаменія И О Содомском Блудѣ» Archived 2013-06-16 at the Wayback Machine // Библиотека литературы Древней Руси / РАН. ИРЛИ; Под ред. Д. С. Лихачева, Л. А. Дмитриева, А. А. Алексеева, Н. В. Понырко. — СПб.: Наука, 2000. — Т. 9: Конец XIV — первая половина XVI века. — 566 с.

steadfast to this with great fear and with turning towards God, not putting his hope in gold and transient riches, but in God who grants all things.[223] [224]

The alleged Philotheus of Pskov, writing about Moscow being the 'third Rome', is overtly dark in character. It reflects the mood of the age when the historic centers of Christendom had fallen to Islam. An apocalyptic sentiment pervaded much of Eastern Christendom. The 'end times' prose of the Book of Revelation from Christian scripture. As with all prophetic literature, great care should have been taken before it entered into the eschatological corpus of the ROC. The relevance it took on and retains today must be attributed not to any theological imprimatur but rather its use by the Russian State and ROC for political advantage.

It is inescapable to read Philotheus without also contrasting it with similar writings of the past. Just as the Tanakh's story of Noah and the great flood had a predecessor in the Mesopotamian story of Gilgamesh, so too did Philotheus' third Rome exist as an expression of mythology and prophecy of the past. The Muscovy and Philotheus had access to a work known as *Eulogy of the Pious Grand Prince Boris Aleksandrovič by the humble monk Foma*, written c. 1453.[225] It is an allegory about the ruler of Tver, Prince Boris Aleksandrovich, who ruled between 1425 and 1461.

Tver's existence as a city-state made it both a competitor and adversary of the Principality of Muscovy. Foma variously refers to Prince Boris as the "new Jacob", "new Joseph", and "another Moses." Not satisfied with the religious elevation of Prince Boris, Foma then foists upon him comparisons to the Roman emperors Tiberius and Augustus before citing the eastern Roman emperors Justinian and Theodosius, who ruled from Constantinople. Foma did not use the phrase 'third Rome' in his *Eulogy*, but by linking Prince Boris to the Roman emperors of Rome and Constantinople, he may have been implying that Tver was the 'third Rome.'[226]

---

[223] Pavel Kuzenkov, ""The Third Rome": From Eschatology to Political Myth", *The ROC: Department for External Church Relations*, (https://mospat.ru/en/authors-analytics/86649/), accessed 20 July 2025.

[224] No extant originals of Philotheus of Pskov's letters survive. There are varying versions of his writings, notably the several embellishments presented here.

[225] William Van Den Bercken, John Bowden (translator), "Holy Russia and Christian Europe: East and West in the Religious Ideology of Russia", *SCM Press*, 1999.

[226] Foma went so far as to call Tver the *"new Israel"* giving the city a territorial-religious dimension. This theme was also employed by Putin who said in 2014, *"Crimea is to Russia what Jerusalem is to Muslims and Jews."* See: Wire Story, "Putin: Crimea is to Russia what Jerusalem is to Muslims, Jews", *Anadolu Ajansı (AA)*, 4 December 2014.

Not to be outdone, another city-state rival, Novgorod, had its own 'third Rome' pretensions. Dimitrij Gerasimov, a translator of the Archbishop of Novgorod, wrote, *The Story of the White Mitre* in 1490.[227] As Gerasimov writes, after the fall of Constantinople, Novgorod is recognized as the center of Christendom. The tale is that when entrusting the city of Rome to Pope Sylvester I, he gave him a white miter as a sign of his authority. After Rome fell into heresy following the 'Great Schism' in 1054, the miter was sent to Constantinople, where Patriarch Michael I Cerularius kept it. After the fall of Constantinople to the Ottoman Türks, the white miter was entrusted to Archbishop Vassilij of Novgorod, where it was maintained in the Sophia Cathedral as a sign that Novgorod had become the guardian of the true, Orthodox Christian faith. Unlike the *Eulogy*, the *Story of the White Mitre* specifically invokes the term 'third Rome', with the mission: "all Christian lands shall come together in the one Russian kingdom for the sake of the true faith."[228]

We cannot, therefore, credit Philotheus alone with the concept of Moscow as the third Rome, as do other scholars. The myriad precursor stories militate against doing so. The third Rome concept's origins are, however, deeply rooted in the Muscovy and Russian psyche, regardless of its origins. As with the predilection for cultural, linguistic, political and historical appropriation, the desire to appropriate the religious authority vested in the Ecumenical Patriarchate seems to permeate both Muscovy and Russian history as a component of its political greatness narrative.

The Muscovy-Russian sense of shame may be intergenerational.[229] As Keir Giles put it:

> Putin is not the only person who is old enough to have felt that sense of deep, personalized humiliation and shame that came with the loss of power of the Soviet Union at the end of the Cold War.[230]

It may be that the same sense of shame that caused Muscovy to re-invent its history, appropriate the past of Rome, Greece, and Byzantium and exterminate competing narratives to cleanse itself of its Mongol Golden Horde foundations was always extant in their minds. As Van Den Berken puts it:

---

[227] Alar Laats, "The Concept of the Third Rome and Its Political Implications", *Kaitsevӓe Ühendatud Õppeasutused*, 2009.
[228] Van Den Bercken, *ibid*.
[229] Yasmin Sirhan, "Who is Vladimir Putin's Revisionist History For?", *The Atlantic*, 27 February 2022.
[230] Keir Giles, "Moscow Rules: What Drives Russia to Confront the West", *Brookings Institution Press*, 2019.

The fall of the Orthodox capital of the world, the new Rome, Constantinople, led among the Russians to the notion that they had been called to make good this shame on Christianity, or, as Nestor Iskander says, 'to annihilate and obliterate this evil and godless Ottoman faith and to renew and strengthen the whole Orthodox and unstained Christian faith.'[231]

Iskander's observation about Muscovy's need to "annihilate and obliterate" all they found abhorrent is acutely analogous to Russia's tendency to seek to exterminate Ukraine to achieve its goals, as to the quest to see the Moscow Patriarchate come into being, the third Rome narrative would prove necessary.

Tsar Fyodor I Ioannovich and his regent, Godunov, recognized the practicalities of their situation. It was not lost on them that only 27 years passed following the fall of Constantinople before Muscovy emerged from almost 250 years of suzerainty under the Mongol Golden Horde and Türkik khanate. The Principality of Muscovy had only stopped paying tribute and collecting taxes as its vassals less than a century before. Muscovy needed to hide its sense of shame. It returned to the Muscovy playbook and decided upon reinvention.

The Principality of Muscovy was still too new and unsteady a brand to be worthy of universal recognition throughout Orthodox Christendom, by either merit or necessity. For Moscow to be recognized as the third Rome, it would require its status to be significantly elevated. Enter the Patriarch of Constantinople, Jeremias II, limited by the Ottoman Türks and bruised from his ongoing conflicts with his own bishops. In the Ecumenical Patriarch, Jeremias II, Muscovy would get what it wanted by flattery, coercion, or threat.

In 1576, Pope Gregory XIII (1572-1585) commenced a campaign with Ivan IV Vasilyevich seeking to lure Moscow away from the diminished Patriarchate of Constantinople and Christian Orthodoxy. Seeking Moscow's alignment with the Holy See, Pope Gregory XIII wrote:

> So that such a significant and wonderful part of the Christian body, so to say, united with the other members into a unified being, would act together in agreement with them... therefore it would be much more proper if His Majesty allies with the Roman Church....[232]

---

[231] Van Den Bercken, *ibid*.

[232] Ugo Boncompagni (Pope Gregory XIII), "Perepiska pap s rossiiskimi gosudaryami v XVI veke, naidennaya mezhdu rukopisyami, v Rimskoi barberinevskoi biblioteke. Izdana s perevodom aktov s latinskogo na russkii yazik [Correspondence of Popes with Russian Sovereigns in the 16th Century, Found Between Manuscripts, in the Roman Barberine Library, Published with the Translation of Acts from Latin into Russian]", *Sankt Peterburg : Akademiya nauk*, 1834.

Ivan IV Vasilyevich judged the situation with the Holy See rightly and decided the Russian Orthodox of his realm were pious and would not tolerate being translated under the Holy See. It would be upon Constantinople that Moscow would direct its ambitions and plans.

Pope Gregory XIII's view that the Ecumenical Patriarch, Jeremias II, was an unreliable partner was not without foundation. A view had emerged, especially by the Muscovy hierarchs, that the Ecumenical Patriarch's authority had become reliant on the changing whimsy of the Ottoman Türk Sultan. Intense internecine fighting among Orthodox Christian bishops in the aftermath of the fall of Constantinople also constrained Ecumenical Patriarch Jeremias II's ability to exercise his authority.

In that era, it was not unheard of for ecumenical patriarchs and bishops to be deposed only to be rehabilitated again to office. His All Holiness Jeremias II himself served as ecumenical patriarch on three separate occasions, suffering deposition and even exile to Rhodes before being returned to his Patriarchal See.[233] As conciliarity made all bishops equals, the special, honorific status of the ecumenical patriarch as 'first among equals' gave Jeremias II unequaled authority, but only so long as it was accepted. His three terms as Ecumenical Patriarch, alternatively being deposed and exiled, translated to mean he had little, if any, real power. In the mind of Muscovy, the Ecumenical Patriarch was ripe for exploitation.

There are various conflicting accounts about the events leading up to the Ecumenical Patriarch agreeing to elevate Moscow to the dignity of a patriarchate in 1589. Without independent records, we must rely on our best estimation of what happened, cognizant of the motivation and bias of the chroniclers of events.

One version is that Godunov demanded that Jeremias II elevate Moscow to the dignity of a patriarchate. Legend is that he required the Ecumenical Patriarch to create Moscow third in the precedence of patriarchates, supplanting the historic Pentarchy of the Patriarchates of Constantinople, Alexandria, Antioch, and Jerusalem.[234] [235]

When Jeremias II declined, citing a lack of merit and his inability to engage in conciliar consultations with his fellow bishops, Godunov had

---

[233] Larysa Shvab and Yulia Tokarska, "1580s Transfer Attempts of the Ecumenical Patriarch's Seat to the Ruthenian Lands of the Polish-Lithuanian Commonwealth (Rzeczpospolita)", *Codrul Cosminului, XXVIII*, 2022.

[234] To Godunov's reasoning, Constantinople was beholden to the Sultan. Jerusalem was in the hands of Islam. Russia desired that Moscow take third position in the patriarchal hierarchy behind Alexandria and Antioch. In the end, despite each of those Patriarchal Sees also being subject to Islamist influence.

[235] While the councils of 1590 and 1593 did confirm the creation of the Moscow Patriarchate *post hoc*, they rejected Godunov's demand that Moscow be elevated to third in dignity of the Orthodox hierarchy of patriarchates in 1593.

him held against his will in the Kremlin throughout the long, cold Russian winter in difficult conditions. Given our knowledge of Godunov, the story appeals to conventional bias, but we cannot know the truth. There are no reliable sources for this apocryphal legend. An alternative account holds that Fyodor I Ioannovich desired Jeremias II to become the Patriarch of Moscow.[236] History would indicate that Jeremias II obviously declined the offer. A third, more reliable version of events is that on January 23, 1589 (February 2, old calendar), the synod met at the Assumption Cathedral of the Kremlin.[237] The synod is said to have elected three candidates for consideration for enthronement as the first Patriarch of Moscow in the presence of the Patriarch of Constantinople and the Holy council members.[238]

Unusually, while the Pohvalsky chapel in which they met had been the traditional place of election of candidates for metropolitan, the three candidates, Job—Metropolitan of Moscow and All Russia, Alexander—Archbishop of Novgorod Alexander, and Barlaam—Archbishop of Rostov, were summoned to appear in Tsar Fyodor I Ioannovich's private apartment by Godunov. It was there, in the presence of the Ecumenical Patriarch, that the tsar and his regent consented to Metropolitan Job being enthroned as the first Patriarch of Moscow by Jeremias II.

This legend can be considered somewhat reliable. It coincides with the Russian practice through the ages of the elevation of a bishop to Patriarch of Moscow, requiring the consent of tsars, Soviet commissars, and then Russian Federation presidents. In almost every other jurisdiction, it is the orthodox church norm that the matter is reserved for the bishops during a synod.[239]

Jeremias II's creation of the Moscow Patriarchate and almost immediate transfer of the metropolis of Kyiv from the Ecumenical Patriarchate to the Moscow Patriarchate cannot be said to have followed the norms of Orthodox Christianity. These were the products of either exploitation, coercion, or threats of violence—possibly all three. The actions of Godunov

---

[236] Ivan Levitsky, "Brief information about the All-Russian Patriarchs", *Synodal type: Moscow*, 1871.
[237] Unspecified, "Anniversary of the establishment of patriarchate in Moscow. Metropolitan Job elected Patriarch", *Presidential Library of Russia*, citation of 5 February 1589.
[238] Neil Kent, "A Concise History of the ROC", *Academica Press*, 2021.
[239] Gudziak argues that there exist a want of reliable information and research concerning the events surrounding the election of the first Patriarch of Moscow and the activities of Ecumenical Patriarch Jeremias II. See Borys A. Gudziak, "The Creation of the Moscow Patriarchate: A Prelude to Patriarchal Reforms in the Kyivan Metropolitanate Preceding the Union of Brest (1595-1596)", *Logos – A Journal of Eastern Christian Studies*, Volume 37, 1996.

to lure Jeremias II to Moscow by pretense were shameful. However, contemporary councils in 1590 and 1593 affirmed the erection of the Moscow Patriarch. As a sign it was distasteful, Godunov's demand that Moscow be placed third in the hierarchy of patriarchal precedence was rejected. Still, Moscow considered the whole affair a victory.

Moscow has long used its unorthodox, irregular, if not nefarious, acquisition of its patriarchate for Russian state purposes. Patriarchates ought not to be created by politicians but organically by the church. The creation of the Moscow Patriarch at the demand of a tsar suffering from mental defects and a regent bent on the pursuit and acquisition of power through the coercion of an Ecumenical Patriarchate reads like poor pulp fiction, except it was true. The consequences of the ROC being subservient to the Russian state endure for both Orthodox Christianity and humanity.

Russia's long history of the ROC subordinating itself to the Russian state is undeniable. Through the centuries, ROC clergy served to legitimize the authority of tsars, especially by espousing the doctrine of the 'Divine Right of Kings.' As civil service mandarins, the clergy fulfilled the wishes of tsars in roles as mundane as writers and copyists (helping to fabricate numerous and often competing versions of Russian history) to acting as state censors.

The submission of the ROC was so great that in 1721, Tsar Peter I Alekseyevich abolished the Moscow Patriarchate in favor of the creation of the Most Holy Governing Synod.[240] For the next two centuries, the ROC became indistinguishable from the Russian state—a situation that mirrors today's relationship.

---

[240] Between 1721-1917 there were no Patriarchs of Moscow. By Peter I Alekseyevich's command, the ecclesial head of the ROC was the metropolitan or archbishop of Moscow. Saint Tikhon of Moscow (Vasily Bellavin) would be enthroned as the first restored Patriarch of Moscow on 4 December 1917 following the deposition of Tsar Nicholas II and before the advent of the Union of Soviet Socialist Republics regime taking power.

Chapter Nine

Русский мир — Russkiy Mir
No Pax Romana

Writers in modernity have referred to the space occupied or heavily influenced by Russia using various terms according to time and circumstances. For some the Russian Empire was a description of the ever-amorphas state whose borders changed on a regular basis through colonial expansionism.

The issue of discussions of former Soviet republics is also pregnant with possibilities for misunderstanding and dispute. There has been a tendency in the west to apply the term post-Soviet nation, especially to Baltic countries, for ease of reference. It is as offensive as it is outmoded. The west spent decades denying Soviet claims of dominion over these countries based on international law. To continue experiencing historians, pundits, and politicians referring to them as post-Soviet, implying they once belonged to the Soviet Union, only serves to nurture Russian historical, political, and territorial claims.[241]

The employment of post-Soviet and other phrases has proved useful to Putin. It's a small but perceptible part of his hybrid warfare campaign against the west—controlling how the west talks about European states previously under the Russian sphere. He has employed the works of his neo-imperial apologists to achieve astonishingly wide acceptance for his objectives, particularly in the west, through their use. As a result of his efforts, despite the war in Ukraine, the number of Americans who view Russia as an "enemy" dropped from 61% to 50% between 2024-2025. Some 38% of Americans view Russia merely as a "competitor", while 9% see Russia as a "partner".[242]

---

[241] Argita Daudze, "Why the notion 'post-Soviet' is obsolete, and not only for the Baltic states", *International Institute for Peace (IIP)*, 10 January 2022.

[242] Moira Fagan, Jacob Poushter and Sneha Gubbala, "Republican Opinion Shifts on Russia-Ukraine War", *Pew Research Center*, 17 April 2025.

The corollary to this is increased hostility by Americans towards Europe[243] and Europe's reciprocal decline in trust in America.[244] Russia understands propaganda's value. With the significant decline of trust in western politics, politicians, and institutions and growing mistrust of traditional media outlets, Russia now effectively and cheaply communicates propaganda messaging directly to westerners through the unfiltered lens of social media. This has been aided by the Trump administration's budget recissions and termination of programs from the Corporation for Public Broadcasting to the Voice of America and Radio Liberty.[245]

The withdrawal of pro-democracy messaging and news from these once critical sources has left Russia and China to saturate legacy media and social media with propaganda. In a response that should have left Trump and his MAGA supporters questioning their willingness to cede airspace and print to America's ideological enemies, Russia celebrated the decision to terminate Radio Free Europe, Radio Liberty, and the Voice of America operations. Margarita Simonyan, Editor of Russia's RT network, boasted their victory with glee, "We couldn't shut them down, unfortunately, but America did so itself."[246] The result is that Russia has blunted condemnation, muted criticism and even created a sympathetic western citizenry to accept, if not embrace, the idea that the world needs Russia for stability and peace.[247]

Enter the Russkiy Mir. Current Russian ideology promotes the concept called the Russkiy Mir. It is based on the idea that Russia is inalienably entitled to control the language, politics, culture, faith, and economies in its 'backyard.' The ROC is critical to the Russkiy Mir as it relies heavily on a perception that the world needs the traditional values the ROC promotes. In this way, the idea of the Holy Rus' — the ideology that God specifically set aside Russia for the salvation of humanity, with the Russian Orthodox people being special operators in that salvific mission — becomes inextricably bound up with the Russkiy Mir. It reflects the long confluence and cooperation between the Russian state and the ROC. Of course, the problem is that what Russia considers its backyard, others consider their own. This

---

[243] Daniel Michaels, Laurence Norman and Matthew Dalton, "Europe Confronts Reality That Vance's Hostility Is More Than Just a Show", *The Wall Street Journal*, 26 March 2025.
[244] Maggie Shiltagh "Anti-American sentiment rises in Europe as Trump fuels anger", *Japan Times*, 2 April 2025.
[245] Ketrin Jochecová, "Moscow and Beijing rejoice at looming death of Radio Free Europe, VOA", *Politico*, 18 March 2025.
[246] Eric Albert, Noa Jacquet, Brice Laemle and Benjamin Quénelle, "How the West is losing the international information war", *Le Monde*, 21 April 2025.
[247] Jochecová, *ibid*.

undefined Russkiy Mir sphere of influence works to Russia's benefit, allowing the Kremlin to portray itself as a benevolent brother with certain states, e.g., Hungary and Slovakia, while simultaneously allowing it to be threatening to states formerly under its now historic sphere of influence.

Wilfried Jilge, a scholar at the Universität St. Gallen's Center for Governance and Culture in Europe, contends that the idea of the Russkiy Mir has become expansive to now include an "imagined community" — a "Russian world" that culturally and nationally incorporates Russians in Russia as well as their "Russian-speaking compatriots" abroad as being indivisibly one.[248]

Being part of the Holy Rus' in turn requires a confession of faith to the ROC. The concept of the Russkiy Mir and Holy Rus' is so intrinsic to the ROC ideology that it even permeates the ROCOR. Consider the June 2013 letter of Metropolitan Archbishop Hilarion (Kapral) of New York on the celebration of the 1025th Anniversary of the Baptism of Rus':

> As sons and daughters of the ROC, we are all citizens of Holy Russia. When we speak of Holy Russia, we are not talking about the Russian Federation or any civil society on earth; rather, it is a way of life that has been passed down to us through the centuries by such great saints of the Russian Land as the Holy Great Prince Vladimir and Great Princess Olga, Venerable Sergius of Radonezh, Job of Pochaev, Seraphim of Sarov, and more recently, the countless New Martyrs and Confessors of the 20th century.
> These saints are our ancestors, and we must look to them for instruction on how to bravely confess the Faith, even when facing persecution. There is no achievement in simply calling oneself "Russian:" <u>in order to be a genuine Russian, one must first become Orthodox and live a life in the Church, as did our forebears, the founders of Holy Russia!</u>[249] [emphasis added]

Is it possible that Metropolitan Hilarion believes that Americans who are or become Russian Orthodox should be thought of as Russians? The illogical precept that to be genuinely Russian one must be a member of the ROC is problematic. Surely, being in communion with other Russian Orthodox believers and therefore members of the Holy Rus' cannot bifurcate their identity as being lesser because they were not born Russian. Does being Russian Orthodox render one Russian, as Metropolitan Hilarion hints at in his sermon? It appears so.

The American-born grandson of a Methodist pastor who converted to join the ROC (ROCOR), Archbishop Alexei of Sitka and Alaska, felt so enough to greet and embrace Putin during the Putin-Trump summit in

---

[248] Wilfried Jilge, "Russkiy Mir: "Russische Welt"", *Deutsche Gesellschaft für Auswärtige Politik (DGAP)*, 3 Mai 2016
[249] Metropolitan Hilarion (Kapral), "Appeal by Metropolitan Hilarion on the celebration of the 1,025th anniversary of the Baptism of Rus", *First Hierarch of the ROC Outside of Russia*, 19 June 2013.

Alaska in 2025. He did so despite American sanctions having been imposed on Putin for the war in Ukraine. Archbishop Alexei seemed to ignore any attention to the human rights violations of Putin and Russia, the least of which was Putin evading an arrest warrant issued by the International Criminal Court (ICC).[250] Archbishop Alexei's embrace of Putin during the Alaska Summit should have come as a surprise to nobody. The ROC's commitment to human rights is woeful. The transformation of their narrative on human rights has, however, proved a master stroke in the ROC's non-orthodox narrative shaping.

According to the Фонд «Русский мир» (Russkiy World Foundation) set up by Putin in 2007, the doctrine of the Russkiy Mir incorporates members of the ROC. Are we to believe that American converts to Russian Orthodox Christianity have consciously decided to become "Russian"? Russia would have us believe so or at least claims them to be part of the Holy Rus'.

And what of the ROC's non-canonical forays into Africa? The establishment of the l'Exarchat patriarcal d'Afrique by the Moscow Patriarchate in 2021 represents a concerted effort to convert Africans to Russian Orthodox Christianity. While certainly part of Nye's concept of "soft power diplomacy",[251] which seeks to co-opt people by conversion rather than coercion, the ROC's service to the Russian state is in expanding its "imagined community"[252] where the Russian state would otherwise have to use force or arms.

The spread of the ROC throughout the world, particularly in Europe and the United States, therefore, represents a security threat. Unlike other confessions of faith, which promote their faith without territorial interests (although unique in having a religious leader with temporal interests, Roman Catholics can hardly be accused of promoting national allegiance to the Vatican City State), the ROC's integration with the Russian state as part of the Russkiy Mir and Holy Mir represents a security problem.[253]

When considered in context, the Russkiy Mir has incredible implications for everything from foreign policy to defense and civic development to trading markets. This applies both to Russia and its neighboring states as well as Europe.

---

[250] Iordan Georgiev, "Putin met with the Archbishop of Alaska ahead of the Summit", *Doxologia InfoNews*, 16 August 2025.
[251] Joseph S. Nye, Jr., "Public Diplomacy and "Soft Power", *The Annals of the American Academy of Political and Social Science, Vol. 616, Public Diplomacy in a Changing World* (March 2008).
[252] Jilge, *ibid*.
[253] Dessie Zagorcheva, "Praying for Putin: Spies in Cassocks Threaten the West", *Center for European Policy Analysis*, 31 October 2023.

The Russkiy Mir is justified as a necessary counter to what Putin claims are the west's destructive values. For the Russian State and ROC, the west is an enduring threat. Since it cannot be banned, it must be countered. The Kremlin's claim, inter alia, "The West imposes homosexuality and pedophilia on us,"[254] is part of the Russian worldview, reminiscent of the paranoid and malevolent and conspiracy-driven claims promoted by the *Protocols of the Elders of Zion*, the west is somehow under the control of an elite few who inflict their policies on the world: "This destruction of traditional values from above not only entails negative consequences for society but is also inherently anti-democratic because it is based on an abstract notion and runs counter to the will of the majority of people."[255] [256]

The Patriarch of Moscow, Kirill, endorsed this idea when he presided over the World Russian People's Council, which declared western civilisation to be one of: "[The] West immersed in Satanism"[257]

The political nature of the ROC is undeniable. According to Patriarch Kirill, the Church and State are equal partners in Russian foreign policy:

> the universal nature of the Christian teaching makes us interested in various spheres of the life of society. The Church acts on equal footing as a subject of relations with different states and with international public and political organizations. We defend our values and promote the rights and interests of our congregations.[258]

For the Russkiy Mir to be realized, it must rely on the active cooperation and promotion of the ROC. This is not only a domestic priority but an external imperative. The value of the ROC through the Moscow Patriarchate's 's broad reach into states formerly within the Russian sphere is their ability to 'soften' their populations through 'soft power' activism.

---

[254] Vanessa Nikolova, "Kremlin speaking: homophobia as geopolitics", *Factcheck.bg*, 1 June 2023 (accessed 24 July 2025).

[255] Владимир Путин, Послание Президента Федеральному Собранию года", *Москва, Кремль*, 12 декабря 2012

[256] Putin's appeal to the value of the "will of the majority of people" ring hollow. Under Article 2 of the UN Charter the forceful acquisition of territory is unlawful. Russia's illegal referenda administered to legitimise his occupation regimes in Donetsk, Luhansk, and Crimea in 2014 were rife with irregularities and administered at gunpoint. See Rebeca Lowe, "Ukraine: clear breaches of international law in Crimea", *International Bar Association*, 20 February 2015.

[257] Plenary Session, "Decree of the 25th World Russian People's Council: the present and the future of the Russian world", *World Russian People's Council*, 27 March 2024.

[258] Patriarch Kirill, "Russia's "Orthodox" Foreign Policy: The Growing Influence of the ROC in Shaping Russia's Policies Abroad", *The Statute of the ROC, Department for External Church Relations of the Moscow Patriarchate*, pt. I, § 3 http://orthodoxeurope.org/page/3/15.aspx), as archived on 19 November 2011.

Why does the ROC pose a threat to European security and democracy? One reason is their worldview. In the post-World War II era, the world community progressively pursued a policy of promoting human rights and working on structures capable of promoting and protecting them. Outside of legal and diplomatic efforts, the promotion of freedoms and individual human rights proved capable of upending societies deeply rooted in injustices. Westerners are generally aware of the efforts to promote freedoms and individual human rights by the likes of Protestant activists such as Martin Luther King, Jr., Ralph Abernathy, John Lewis, and Claudette Colvin, who followed in the footsteps of India's Gandhi, the United Kingdom's Emmeline Pankhurst and South Africa's Robert Sobukwe.

The west's almost universal embrace of human rights as a guiding principle has been opposed by the ROC. The Moscow Patriarchate considered the delinking of rights and morality a fundamental flaw of western civilisation. Despite their opposition, the west continued to promote and pursue human rights as an overriding principle of western societal construct. After joining the Council of Europe in 1996, Russia began to distance itself from its long-standing condemnation of systematic approaches to elevating human rights enshrined in the 1948 Declaration of Human Rights and Fundamental Freedoms and the Charter of Fundamental Rights of the European Union. As an alternative, the Russian Federation and the ROC developed a new, unified, critical approach based on human rights rooted in individual freedoms, being antithetical to morality:

> By 2010, the leadership of the ROC had acquired a clear understanding of the human rights universe that Russia (and the Russian Orthodox Church) had entered when the Russian Federation joined the Council of Europe in 1996. Consequently, it settled on a new approach for dealing with human rights claims: instead of rejecting them, the church responded in rights terms. Alexander Agadjanian has aptly spoken about 'acceptance through rejection' (Agadjanian 2010).[259]

Both Russia and the Moscow Patriarchate have had significant success in reframing the debate from one of legal rights to moral conduct. It has been enough to see people like the American-born ROC Archbishop Alexei dispense with his grandfather's Protestant, Methodist pastor's values on religious values and the American tradition of pursuing the elevation of human rights. Once converted to the ROC, Archbishop Alexei embraced his

---

[259] Kristina Stoeckl and Dmitry Uzlaner, "The Moralist International: Russia and the Culture Wars", *Fordham University Press*, 2022.

political allegiance to the Russian state and the ROC's unorthodox devaluation of human dignity, explaining such decisions as being rooted in "traditional values" and "morality."

Had Archbishop Alexei maintained his grandfather's religious and American values, it is almost certain he would have spoken out against the waging of a cruel war on Ukraine, the poisoning and murder of dissidents, the promotion of a holy war and the kidnapping and trafficking of Ukrainian children to Russia, along with war crimes and other evil acts. It has become a common thread in the development of the ROC, even in the United States, Europe and Africa, that Russian converts to the ROC place a higher priority for what they perceive as 'traditional morality' above their modeling of traditional Christian values.

The growth of the ROC in the United States, which has experienced up to 15% growth in converts to Orthodox Christianity since the pandemic,[260] has largely been based on a valuing of 'traditional values' and 'morality'. It raises a fundamental question: "Do Evangelicals, ana-Baptists and others who convert and join the ROC (including ROCOR) understand that their Russian masters believe them to have become 'genuine Russians' who prioritize supposed morality over their belief in fundamental human rights?" These issues undeniably loom large in the culture wars. Any assertion by the ROC that morality and human rights are mutually exclusive is not accepted a having merit based on Christian theology or Orthodox Christian tradition.

The problem is not limited to ROCOR activities in North America or Africa. In Europe, the ROC's mission to serve the 'near abroad,' that is, persons they consider Russian (whether they consider themselves Russian), is at the heart of the Moscow Patriarchate's External Affairs Department activities.

Concerning religious affairs diplomacy, this includes special attention to the former Soviet and almost concomitant canonical jurisdiction of the ROC, including Russia, Ukraine, Byelorussia, Moldavia, Azerbaijan, Kazakhstan, Kirghizia, Latvia, Lithuania, Tajikistan, Turkmenia, Uzbekistan, and Estonia. And yet, because of Russia's 'near abroad' formulation and forays into 'kin state activism' wherever Russians may live are deemed by both the ROC and the Russian state to be legitimate domains of interest and activity. This raises serious concerns for domestic sovereignty in Europe and the rest of the world.[261]

---

[260] Meagan Saliashvili, "Orthodox churches boomed during pandemic, study finds, but calls growth 'mixed bag'", *Religion News Service*, 23 August 2024.

[261] The recent explosion of ROC parishes and missions in Africa, and the conversion of Africans, has allowed Russia to assert an interest in both domestic policy and foreign affairs across the continent. See Charles A. Ray, "Russia's Influence in Africa: The Role of the ROC", *Foreign Policy Research Institute*, 15 October 2024.

The role of the ROC in the destabilization of other nations cannot be discounted. As with the usurpation of power across the Baltics in 1940, the groundwork relied heavily on creating the idea that Russia was a benevolent ally ready to act as guardians of the state. While Orthodox Christians held the Russian state in contempt due to their having kept the Moscow Patriarchate vacant following the 1925 death of Patriarch Tikhon, the Soviets found an ally in his eventual successor.

Metropolitan Sergius (born Ivan Nikolayevich Stragorodsky) broke with many ROC loyalists and pursued a policy of unconditional appeasement with the Soviet regime. With his covert encouragement, some Orthodox Christian clergy in the Baltics promoted a conciliatory view of the Soviets as 'protectors' of their sovereignty. Russia turned treaties for naval bases in exchange for mutual defense pacts into occupation regimes by the summer of 1940. Under guidance from Metropolitan Sergius, the apparent if not de facto locum tenens of the Moscow Patriarchate, Orthodox clergy preached a brand of pacifism regarding relations with Soviet occupiers.

Estonia's problems with Moscow give us an insight into the general disarray in the Baltics caused by the Soviet suspension of the cathedra of the Moscow Patriarch. The EAOC was still a neophyte entity in 1917 when the Bolsheviks took control of Saint Petersburg and displaced the tsar. The first Estonian to be elevated as the Bishop of Revel (modern-day Tallinn) was Bishop Platon (born Paul Kulbusch). He was a staunch supporter of Estonian independence. After Estonia declared independence in 1918, Red Army soldiers executed Bishop Platon in 1919 as they undertook a retreat from Tartu under pressure from the Kuperjanov Infantry Battalion.

Recognizing the climate and the precarious situation in which Russia found itself in the Baltics, yet ever interested in control, Moscow Patriarch Tikhon granted autonomy to the EAOC. He refused, however, to grant autocephaly. After the martyrdom of Bishop Platon, a new Metropolitan Bishop of Revel was needed. Archpriest Alexander Paulus was enthroned with Patriarch Tikhon's consent, but only after agreeing to make an oath of fidelity to the Moscow Patriarchate. Russia was unwilling to let Estonia or any of the Baltic countries enjoy true religious freedom.

Estonia's problems under the Soviets are not unanalogous to those experienced by Ukraine in modernity. Russia demanded control of the entirety of the Estonian Orthodox Church. When it resolved, it could not immediately achieve that goal, the Moscow Patriarchate did what it does best—employ the colonial tool of division.

In 1940, the short-lived restoration of independence of the Estonian people came to an end. The state was absorbed into the Soviet Union. Metropolitan Alexander canvassed his clergy, who recommended, as a practical matter, making amends with the Moscow Patriarchate. Metropolitan

Alexander sent a message to the pro-Soviet Metropolitan Sergius (the future Soviet installed Patriarch of Moscow) expressing regret for seeking autocephaly by: "embracing with love the unintentional sin of schism."[262] Supplication prevailed. The EAOC was reconciled with the Moscow Patriarchate.

The remarriage of Revel and Moscow would not endure for long. At the outset of World War II, Metropolitan Alexander and his Revel (Tallinn) metropolis took the opportunity to break ties with the Moscow Patriarchate once again. Unable to control matters because of the unfolding war, Metropolitan Sergius commanded from Moscow that the Estonian Orthodox Church be divided to form a pro-Soviet faction. Bishop Pavel (Dmitrovsky) and his Diocese of Narva chose submission to the Moscow Patriarchate and Soviet State in much the same way the Ukrainian Orthodox Church (Moscow Patriarchate) under Metropolitan Onufriy remains steadfastly in the camp of the Kremlin and the Patriarch of Moscow, Kirill.

With the Soviets prevailing over German and Estonian independence patriots, the situation of the Revel metropolis and Metropolitan Alexander deteriorated. In 1944, he and 22 of his clergy fled into exile. The Moscow Patriarchate demanded that the Revel metropolis be reunited with the Metropolis of Narva to form a single Estonian Diocese faithful to Metropolitan Sergius, the Moscow Patriarchate and the Soviet regime.

The EAOC would remain directly under the ROC's thumb until its independence in 1991. Attempts to pull free of the ROC are still ongoing. The Riigikogu (Estonian parliament) passed its Churches and Congregations Act in 2025, which attempts to ban the Moscow Patriarchate from operating in Estonia due to its efforts to undermine the Estonian state and Estonian Orthodox Church. The president, Alan Karias, has vetoed the Act out of concerns that it disproportionately restricts freedom of religion. Meanwhile, the Moscow Patriarchate operations in Estonia continue their 'kin state' activism as part of the Russian state's 'near abroad' initiative. The inability of Estonia and the continent to balance freedom of religion with national security continues to haunt the European Union, much to Russia's benefit.

Estonia and the Baltics never really had a chance of receiving 'brotherly' mutual defense support from Moscow.[263] In reality, the secret protocols of the Molotov-Ribbentrop Pact of 1939 ensured that Russia's goal of

---

[262] Igor Prekup, "Baltic Rehearsal", *Russia in Global Affairs*, No. 2.1, June 2019.

[263] From the time of the Russian Empire, through the Soviet epoch and under Putin's Russian Federation, a feature of their expansionism has routinely been the promise of defense and security assistance which morphs into an occupation regime. This was true in Transnistria, Abkhazia, South Ossetia, Luhansk,

dividing Europe between Moscow and Berlin remained the real controlling and only foreign policy document with which Moscow was interested. By June 1940, the world's gaze was diverted as Nazi jackboots marched down the Champs Élysées. This sleight of hand, achieved by Stalin and Hitler, allowed the Народный комиссариат внутренних дел [People's Commissariat for Internal Affairs—NKVD] to breach the frontiers of the Baltic states.

In short order, and thanks to the preparatory work of propagandists, spies, and collaborators, including ROC clergy like Metropolitan Sergius, governments were deposed and replaced by Soviet dupes and traitors.[264] As a result, the NKVD deported or murdered some 34,250 Latvians, 75,000 Lithuanians, and almost 60,000 Estonians within a matter of months.[265]

It is not without notice that, aside from the Russian state, the primary beneficiary of the Russkiy Mir would be the Moscow Patriarch personally[266] and the ROC corporately.[267] The symbiotic relationship between Putin and Kirill, and the Russian state and the ROC, is nothing new. After all, legend has it that when Borys Godunov demanded the Ecumenical Patriarch elevate the metropolitanate of Moscow to the dignity of a patriarchate, it was the tsar's regent who presented three individuals to Ecumenical Patriarch Jeremias II in the imperial residence—not at a church or in the context of a synod:

> All the participants of the elections came to the palace where Jeremias II presented to Tsar Fyodor Ivanovich three candidates: the Metropolitan of Moscow and All Russia, Job, Archbishop of Novgorod Alexander and the Archbishop of Rostov Barlaam. Here, in the tsar's chambers, Job was named patriarch.[268]

Understanding how and why Putin and Patriarch Kirill work to complement each other's efforts in support of Russia's unceasing pursuit of the

---

    Donetsk and Crimea. Russian 'peacekeepers' also were used to partisan purposes in the dispute between Armenia and Azerbaijan where Russian Federation forces ultimately collaborated with Azerbaijan forces to force Armenians to flee the disputed region in September 2023.

264 Jan Åke Dellenbrant, "The Integration of the Baltic Republics Into the Soviet Union", *Journal of Baltic Studies*, Vol. 18, No. 3, 1987.

265 Simon S. Montefiore, "Stalin: The Court of the Red Tsar (5th ed.)", *Phoenix: Great Britain*, 2003.

266 Lucy Sweeney and Lucia Stein, "With his luxury watch and murky Soviet past, Patriarch Kirill is Putin's spiritual leader and power broker", *Australian Public Broadcasting*, 21 January 2023.

267 There are arguably 125 million +/- Orthodox Christians living in Europe in states formerly under the Russian sphere.

268 Staff Content, "Anniversary of the establishment of patriarchate in Moscow. Metropolitan Job elected Patriarch", *Presidential Library of Russia*, (https://www.prlib.ru/en/history/619001), accessed 19 July 2025.

Russkiy Mir lies at the heart of confronting their claims that the Baltics and Eastern Europe are integral parts of the Holy Rus and should fall within the Russian sphere.

The Russkiy Mir, or previous versions of it, have long proved of benefit to the Russian state. Its indelible, colonial aspects seek to create for Russia both the empire its conceit demands and the buffer-zone its paranoia requires. Named after former minister for foreign affairs of the Russian Federation, Yevgeny Primakov, the 'Primakov Doctrine' espoused by the current minister, Sergei Lavrov, has proven to be a critical tool in attempts to induce the Russkiy Mir. The Primakov Doctrine is designed to thwart supposed attempts by the United States to create a unipolar world where Russia is no longer a power player. It is specifically designed to keep Russia aloof from the west, contrary to the previous policies of Foreign Affairs Minister Andrei Kozyrev, who sought rapprochement with the west under the regime of Boris Yeltsin.[269]

The Primakov Doctrine, employed to create the Russkiy Mir desired by Putin, has startling ramifications. Not only does it feed into the revanchism that seemingly lurks in Putin's heart, domestic politics and international policies, but it wholly reorients Russia away from a European context while creating a more expansive Eurasianist posture.[270] Russia's relations with China to the east and Iran, Syria and with asymmetrical partners to the south, in addition to its continuing confrontation with the west, returned the Russian Federation to the world stage following the malaise of the Yeltsin era.

---

[269] Andrei Kozyrev, "Boris Yeltsin, the Soviet Union, the CIS, and Me", *The Wilson Quarterly*, Fall 2016.

[270] Emanuel Copilaş, "Cultural Ideal or Geopolitical Project? Eurasianism's Paradoxes", *Strategic Impact. No. 3.*, 20 April 2018.

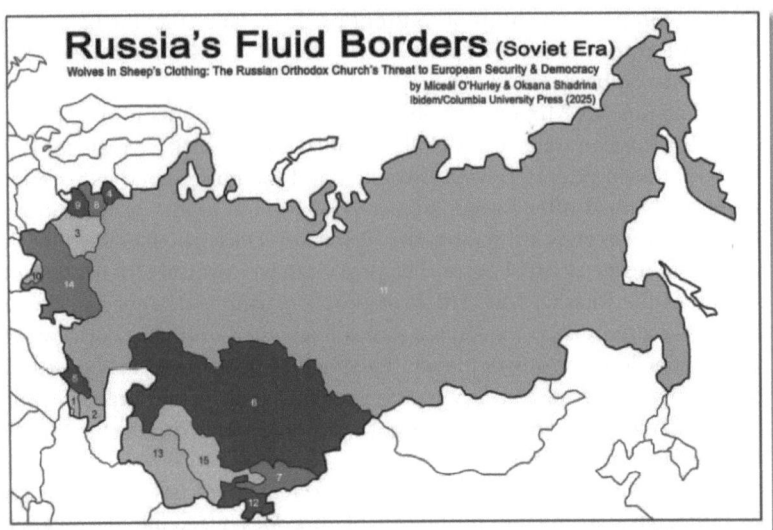

Absorbtion of USSR Republics (alphabetically)

1 Armenia — 1936
2 Azerbaijan — 1936
3 Belarus — 1922
4 Estonia — 1940
5 Georgia — 1936
6 Kazakhstan — 1936
7 Kyrgyzstan — 1936
8 Latvia — 1940
9 Lithuania — 1940
10 Moldova — 1940
11 Russia — 1917
12 Tajikistan — 1929
13 Turkmenistan — 1925
14 Ukraine — 1922
15 Uzbekistan — 1924

Where Russia could not assert its influence, it has returned to the time-tested tactic of regime change by causing a coup d'état. In 2016, pro-Serbian elements in Montenegro gained the support of the Russian Federation to attempt to overthrow the government in an attempt to avert its NATO ascension.[271] Milivoje Katnić, then Montenegro's special chief prosecutor, argued in court, "a powerful organisation", which he estimated was organized and undertaken by upwards of 500 people from Russia, Serbia and Montenegro, was the mastermind of the attempted coup d'état.[272] Convictions of the parties were later overturned on appeal. Nonetheless, on April 28, 2017, Montenegro's parliament voted 46–0 to accede to the North Atlantic Treaty Organisation, despite Russian opposition and interference.

---

[271] Staff Writers, "Russians, opposition figures sentenced over role in 2016 Montenegro coup attempt", *Reuters*, 9 May 2019.

[272] Dusica Tomovic, "Montenegro PM Accuses Opposition Over 'Plot to Kill Him'", *Balkan Insight*, 10 November 2016.

In the aftermath of the attempted coup d'état, the foreign secretary of the United Kingdom, Jeremy Hunt, delivered a message laying responsibility for the affair on Russia's doorstep:

> The failed coup attempt against Montenegro in 2016 was one of the most outrageous examples of Russia's attempts to undermine European democracy. The GRU's brazen attempt to interfere with Montenegro's national elections and undermine Montenegro's application to join NATO is yet another example of destabilising and aggressive Russian behaviour over the last decade... Russia is a great country and central to European civilisation. Moscow must desist from any attacks that undermine the territorial integrity and democratic processes of its neighbours or other sovereign states. The UK calls on Russia to choose a different path — to uphold the security of Europe, respect the rules based international system that keeps our societies safe, and to work together with us to fulfil our common responsibilities as permanent members of the UN Security Council.[273]

While not directly implicated in the attempted coup d'état plot, the ROC has long been an active collaborator with the Serbian Orthodox Church's attempts to return Montenegro to its influence and control. In a meeting including Patriarch Kirill, the Serbian Orthodox Church's Patriarch, Porfirije (Peric), pleaded with Putin in 2025 to help create a "greater Serbia." Such bombastic and destabilizing rhetoric on the part of Patriarch Porfirije was like music to Putin's and Patriarch Kirill's ears:

> Our position regarding Kosovo, Republika Srpska and Montenegro, I believe and feel that it also depends on the position of the Russian state, the Russian Federation on a global level. My wish, and the wish of the majority in our Church, is that in the future, if there is a new geopolitical regrouping, we will be close to that Russian environment.[274]

The Patriarch's comments were directed at Kosovo. In response, Kosovo's prime minister, Albin Kurti, responded:

> The Patriarch called for a broader geopolitical realignment under Russian leadership, reiterating that the [Serbian] "small boat, sailing on rough seas, should always be tied to a big Russian ship". He also suggested that Serbia's stance on its neighbors — Kosova, Bosnia and Herzegovina, and Montenegro — is contingent on Russia's global position... This is not religious diplomacy, it's a strategic partnership of authoritarian regimes, placing the region at serious risk. Kosova, however, stands firm in its democratic principles

---

[273] Statement, "Attempted coup in Montenegro in 2016: Foreign Secretary Jeremy Hunt notes the verdicts against 2 Russian GRU officers who plotted the coup", *Foreign & Commonwealth Office: United Kingdom*, 9 May 2019.

[274] S'Bunker, "The Serbian Patriarch calls for a 'Greater Serbia' with Putin's blessing", *Global Voices*, 11 May 2025.

and aspirations and unequivocally rejects revisionist agendas driven by authoritarian powers.[275]

As a demonstration of how autocephalous churches under the Moscow Patriarchate defer in all matters, both ecclesial and political, to the Kremlin, a transcript of the meeting indicates Serbian Orthodox Church Metropolitan Irinej interjected the concept of a "Serbian World" before adding "…in the Russian World."[276] Other language in the transcript reveals echoes of Slobodan Milošević's rhetoric and political language used during the 1990 genocides and war crimes for which he was indicted and later cited as a co-conspirator.[277] The discussion of such matters by hierarchs of the Serbian Orthodox Church, using language once espoused by a villain such a Milošević, all in the presence of Moscow Patriarch Kirill and Putin, demonstrates the expectation and willingness of Moscow Patriarchate-aligned churches to subordinate the gospels to the political manifesto which is the Russkiy Mir.

When the Russkiy Mir and the gospels are in tension, the hierarchs of the ROC can be relied upon to subordinate their baptismal and ordination vows to the objectives of the Russian state. Consider the letter of Patriarch Kirill to Metropolitan Onufriy of the Ukrainian Orthodox Church (Moscow Patriarchate) in 2014:

> The children of our Church are people of different political views and convictions, including those who today stand on different sides of the barricades. The Church does not take one side or another in the political struggle. But it is the duty of the Church to mourn for those who are subjected to violence, who need protection, whose lives are in danger.
> In response to your appeal, dear Vladyka, I assure you and our Ukrainian flock that I will do everything possible to convince all those in power that the death of civilians on the land of Ukraine, dear to my heart, cannot be allowed.[278]

---

[275] Albin Kurti, "A concerning development emerged from yesterday's meeting between the Serbian Orthodox Patriarch and Vladimir Putin in Moscow", 'X' *(formerly Twitter) post of @albinkurti*, 24 April 2025.

[276] Transcript: "The complete transcript of the conversation between Patriarch Porfirije and Putin: Vučić is coming to Moscow", *Moscow Patriarchate: Website*, 23 April 2025.

[277] Slobodan Milošević died in the custody of The Hague before a verdict in his trial could be reached thereby avoiding a verdict. However, he was specifically named in the verdicts of other co-conspirators found guilty by the International Criminal Tribunal.

[278] Vladimir Mikhailovich Gundyayev (Patriarch Kirill), "Appeal of His Holiness Kirill, Patriarch of Moscow and All Rus', to the Locum Tenens of the Kyiv Metropolitan See, Metropolitan Onufriy of Chernivtsi and Bukovina, the archpas-

Patriarch Kirill's letter to the pro-Russian Metropolitan Onufriy of the Ukrainian Orthodox Church (Moscow Patriarchate) has all the elements of pastoral concern in the midst of aggression driven by Putin's attempts to create a Russkiy Mir. The line about the duty of the church does, however, betray Patriarch Kirill's true allegiance to the Russian state: "But it is the duty of the Church to mourn for those who are subjected to violence, who need protection, whose lives are in danger." The accusation is that Ukraine's 'Revolution of Dignity', centered around events played out in Maidan Nezalezhnosti (Maidan Square), was merely an extension of the part of the 'colour revolutions' abhorred by Putin and ROC, such as the 2004–2005 'Orange Revolution' surrounding Russia's intrusion and interference in Ukraine's presidential election. After all, Putin declared on several occasions his clear opposition to popular democratic reform in bordering states formerly under the Russian sphere: "The measures taken by the CSTO have clearly shown we will not allow the situation to be rocked at home and will not allow so-called 'color revolutions' to take place."[279]

The recent events in Ukraine in 2014, which were the precursor to Patriarch Kirill's letter to Metropolitan Onufriy, were viewed by the Moscow Patriarchate as arising from anti-Russian activism in Ukraine. By accusation and implication, this necessitated Russia's 2014 invasion of Ukraine on behalf of ethnic Russians "who need protection, whose lives are in danger."[280]

It is inescapable to view Patriarch Kirill's letter to Metropolitan Onufriy not as an expression of pastoral concern but rather a declaration of solidarity with the Russian state for launching its invasion and seeking to annex parts of Ukraine out of a supposed need to protect lives. If the Moscow Patriarch wished to protect lives, he didn't send the message to the pro-Russian, quisling President of Ukraine, Viktor Fedorovych Yanukovych.

Yanukovych ordered Berkut special forces personnel under his control to fire on unarmed civil society actors and protestors in Maidan Square[281] prior to fleeing Ukraine for Russia. According to Putin, Russia assisted Yanukovych to flee to Russia with great amounts of wealth in the

---

tors, pastors and all faithful children of the Ukrainian Orthodox Church in connection with the situation in Ukraine", *Moscow Patriarchate: Moscow*, 2 March 2014.
[279] Jamie Dettmer, "Putin: No More Color Revolutions", *Voice of America*, 10 January 2022.
[280] Dettmer, *ibid*.
[281] UNIAN Staff Report, "Приказ расстреливать митингующих отдавал Янукович—ГПУ [Order to shoot protesters was given by Yanukovych—GPU]", *UNIAN*, 2 April 2014.

process,[282] "I will say it openly—he asked to be driven away to Russia, which we did."[283] More than 108 protestors and 18 law enforcement officers were killed in street clashes in the Ukrainian capital.[284] Another estimated 14,000 Ukrainians died as a result of Russia's 'little green men' invasion and occupation of Eastern Ukraine and Crimea that year.[285]

For his part, and that of the Ukrainian Orthodox Church (Moscow Patriarchate), Metropolitan Onufriy did what was expected and made a plea for the prevention of "fratricide[al] bloodshed." In a letter that bypassed Patriarch Kirill, Metropolitan Onufriy wrote directly to Putin. Metropolitan Onufriy did not condemn Russia's aggression against his native Ukraine, nor did he decry the invasion of Eastern Ukraine and Crimea or even protest the summary execution or disappearance of Crimean Tatar activists and the death of some 14,000 Ukrainians. Instead, Metropolitan Onufriy appealed to Putin to act from a self-acknowledged position of power and superiority over Ukraine and be the: "guarantor of the rule of law in the Great country to stand in the way [i.e., prevention] of the divide, to prevent bloodshed and fratricide of the nations that have emerged from the same Dnipro River baptistery."[286]

In Kyiv, Tallinn, Tbilisi, Warsaw, and across eastern Europe, people who had regained their freedom and independence from Russian control are alarmed at the prospect of a Russkiy Mir. As the Russkiy Mir has no geographic limiters, it cannot be viewed as a Russian equivalent of the United States' Monroe Doctrine. The Monroe Doctrine's objective was to keep foreign powers from colonizing the Americas. The Russkiy Mir's objective is the colonization of a now free and democratic eastern Europe. The implications of the Russkiy Mir, and the foundation Putin created to promote it, are a diplomatic declaration of an intent to re-incorporate those states that escaped the Russian sphere in 1991.

States formerly under the Russian sphere have no desire to return to its shackles. Having been subjugated as lesser beings, some from as far back as the foundations of Russian tsardom, to Europeans placed firmly

---

[282] Shaun Walker and Oksana Grytsenko, "Ukraine's new leaders begin search for missing billions", *The Guardian*, 27 February 2014.

[283] Bridget Kendall, "Putin: Russia helped Yanukovych to flee Ukraine", BBC News, 24 October 2014.

[284] Svetlana Kozlenko and Jim Heintz, "Troubled Ukraine Marks Year Since Protest Bloodbath in Kiev", *ABC News/Associated Press*, 21 February 2015.

[285] UNHCR Staff, "Conflict-related civilian casualties in Ukraine", *Office of the United Nations High Commissioner for Human Rights*, 27 January 2022.

[286] Місцеблюститель УПЦ митрополит Онуфрій направил письмо Президенту РФ В. Путину // Православіє в Україні [Електронний ресурс]. — *Режим доступу:* http://orthodoxy.org.ua/data/vazhno-mestoblyustitel-upc-mitropolit-onufriy-napravil-pismoprezidentu-rf-vputinu.html, 2 March 2014.

under the boot of Russian occupation post-World War I and II, millions of Europeans had personal experience of life under Muscovy. Equally so, millions of other Europeans comprehended the threat, having been forced to maintain a near-martial state to defend themselves during the Cold War, not only from overt military operations, but the subterfuge directed against them from Moscow.

Chapter Ten

A Most Unholy Trinity
The ROC, the Moscow Patriarchate, and the Russian State

This manuscript is concerned with providing readers with a better understanding of how the long history of church-state-patriarchal interplay in Russia has indelibly corrupted the ROC. It goes without saying that the ROC offenses against Orthodox Christian norms by creating its own metropolitans without conciliar consultation or permission from the 'Mother Church' in Constantinople and other actions such as declaring a 'holy war' is notorious. It has at various times unilaterally broken communion with the Ecumenical Patriarchate in the Middle Ages and at least twice in the last 50 years.

The ROC's opposition to the universality of the Ecumenical Patriarchate manifested by setting itself up as the 'third Rome' — implying Constantinople ceded its authority to Moscow — has marked the ROC, Moscow Patriarchate and Russian state as unsteady partners in all things. At the heart of all this has been the integration of the ROC into the Russian state apparatus.

Criticism of the confluence of the ROC, the Russian state and the Moscow Patriarchates is perceived in those circles as a near-theological indictment if not blatant heresy. Still, the abdication of moral and religious authority and fidelity to the gospels has impeded, if not destroyed, the Moscow Patriarchate from acting according to the precepts of the Holy Orthodox faith. The ROC has repeatedly failed to conduct its affairs according to the canons, norms and traditions of the Holy Orthodox Church or to otherwise act discernibly as a church.

The difficulty isn't that they err — that is human. The problem is they deny their errors and omissions, point out the splinter in others' eyes while denying the plank in their own. A startling example of this is found in their cries that the tomos granted to the Orthodox Church of Ukraine is non-canonical. Such a view wholly ignores the ROC's long history of non-canonical conduct, the spurious events surrounding the creation of the Moscow Patriarchate or the two centuries of non-canonical existence arising from their integration into the Russian state under Tsar Peter I Alekseyevich.

Of course, the ROC claims to be the only genuine orthodox authority within the former Russian sphere. When the Moscow Patriarchate dispenses with the canons, norms, and traditions of Orthodox Christianity, they claim necessity requires the practice of οἰκονομία [economia] to claim canonical regularity. It is an aspect of Orthodox Christianity that they never seem to afford others. No better example of this can be witnessed in modernity than the necessity of Orthodox Christians in Ukraine to be granted autocephaly so that they might worship freely without the specter of the Moscow Patriarch threatening them with excommunication.

The willing submission, if not supplication, of the ROC and Moscow Patriarch to voluntary continue in their role as extensions of the Russian state constitutes an unholy alliance between the church, the state and the patriarch. Its very nature disfigures the ROC to the detriment of the faithful. No church can proclaim the gospels with full-throated zeal while its patriarch simultaneously proclaims a 'holy war'.[287]

One of the dynamics that has endured in the ROC and can explain part of its divergence from the rest of Orthodox Christianity is the intense nationalism that has been nurtured in Russia since its nascent period as the Principality of Muscovy. Nationalism, and the emergence of the ideology of the Holy Rus' concept that God ordained Russia to lead the world following its enlightenment by the Russian people, has always been a feature of its intense and overt nationalistic nature. As cleric and theologian Cyril Hovrun observed:

> Many Orthodox churches uphold different forms of political Orthodoxy. Yet there is a form of it common for most churches—nationalism. Nationalism is one of the most powerful political devices that can unite masses of people. It is capable of creating a feeling of belonging and destiny for millions. Those millions, driven by nationalism, can act together as one person, sometimes being led by one person. Nationalism is a controversial device because its basic function is to separate "us" from "them." "We," being moved by nationalist sentiment, feel ourselves superior to "them." This feeling of superiority differentiates nationalism from patriotism....[288]

It is this distorted and elevated sense of superiority that lies at the heart of Russia's belief that it, and only Russia, can lead the world. Conversely, if God has ordained Russia to lead by virtue of creating a Russkiy Mir, it holds that Russia and the ROC are to be forever enmeshed in conflict with

---

[287] Jerry Pillay (on behalf of WCC member churches), "WCC 'cannot reconcile' World Russian People's Council decree describing Ukraine conflict as a 'Holy War'", *World Council of Churches*, 12 April 2024.

[288] Cyril Hovrun, edited by Ashley John Moyse and Scott A. Kirkland, "Political Orthodoxies: The Unorthodoxies of the Church Coerced", *Augsburg Fortress, Fortress Press*, 2025.

a world order it does not lead. Unsurprisingly, this was made manifest when the ROC decided to break communion with the Ecumenical Patriarchate in 2018 in the belief of its superiority, reflected in its belief that it is the 'third Rome' and therefore destined to a place of honor and superiority over other Orthodox Christian patriarchates and local churches.

We will parse the thematic issue of this unholy trinity of the Russian state-ROC-Moscow Patriarchate's development and how it manifested itself in a linear manner. As the focus of this manuscript is the ROC's threat to European security and democracy, this history of the ROC will by no means be presented exhaustively or authoritatively. We have elected to present this history and various aspects of its peculiarity in broad strokes. We trust this will provide readers with an easier and possibly more complete, contextualized understanding of the triune nature of operations between the ROC, the Moscow Patriarch and the Russian state.

The topic is, admittedly, worthy of its own comprehensive research and lengthy publication. We will not do so here as others have ably done so elsewhere and numerously.[289]

---

[289] *See*: Banka, 2023; Blakkisrud, 2023; Bliznekov, 2020; Chiriac, 2024; 2023; Demydova, 2020; Dogadaylo et al., 2017; Dovganenko, 2023; Gips, 2022; Kiryukhin, 2023; Lukyanov, 2009; *Menon & Ruger*, 2020; Merkx, 2023; Nincic, 2005; Serafin, 2022; Suslov, 2017; *et al.*

Chapter Eleven

Tsar Peter I Aleksyevich Abolishes the Moscow Patriarchate (1721)

Peter I Alekseyevich's was more than aware of the special role the ROC had for Russian history and for Russian society. Their various collaborations with the princes of Muscovy and tsars, creating new histories to suit the needs of the age, had proven invaluable to the evolution of the Principality of Muscovy to tsardom and establishing Imperial Russia. As an institution, it was the sometimes inventor of Russian history and always the foundation of Russia's social fabric.

Every tsar embraced the ROC to a greater or lesser extent. It remains an open question how much of it arose from personal piety and what measure was sheer political expediency. The tsars knew, as Boris Yeltsin would discover in 1991 and again in 1996, the ROC was not only capable of ensuring widespread public support—it could take it away just as quickly.

Peter had never forgotten the ROC's and the Moscow Patriarch's personal role assisting the streltsy guard in ensuring he was forced to rule jointly with his notoriously feeble, half-brother Ivan V Alekseyevich. On June 25, 1682, Patriarch Ioakim crowned the mentally impaired Ivan as 'senior tsar' with Peter, his junior. Peter, aged only 9, felt the insult acutely. His half-brother was known to be "infirm in body and mind." It offended his mother and himself that he, although favored by his father Tsar Alexis Mikhailovich, was reduced to being a co-tsar with the disfavored though not disowned Ivan.[290]

Neither of the children had yet attained the age of majority. They would need a regent. The mothers of the two tsars, Maria Miloslavskaya and Natalya Naryshkina, were the products of competing boyar families. Patriarch Ioakim feared appointing either regent and invoking the wrath of the boyars and possibly setting off a new 'Time of Troubles.' The patriarch instead looked for a competent yet controllable male to serve in that role. It was a tall order.

---

[290] Walter Keating Kelly, "The history of Russia from the earliest period to the Crimean war: In Two Volumes", *Henry G. Bohn, London*, 1854.

Patriarch Ioakim's plans would be interrupted. He did not count on the ingenuity and strong force of will that was Sophia Alekseyevna (Miloslavsky). The funeral of her brother Tsar Fiodor III Alekseyevich gave Sophia Alekseyevna her opportunity. Funerals for tsars had usually been an all-male occasion. Uninvited and yet undeterred, Sophia Alekseyevna insinuated herself into the funeral, exhibiting an unusual blend of tearful mourning and outward dignity. It proved moving to spectators, especially the streltsy guards in attendance.

Sophia Alekseyevna's performance allowed her to present herself as an alternative to her half-brother Peter. Despite the display and her intellect, grace and forcefulness being noted, tradition would not be broken. Sophia Alekseyevna would not be proclaimed tsarina. The occasion was not lost, however. She had gained the attention of the feared streltsy guard. In short order, she whipped them into a frenzy.[291] Aligning herself with a streltsy uprising, Sophia Alekseyevna saw herself declared regent for her brother Ivan and half-brother Peter.

Peter I Alekseyevich detested his half-sister, having been named regent. It was she, after all, who had pleaded with the dying Tsar Alexis Mikhailovich not to name Peter as his sole heir. To no one's surprise, once regent, she ensured Tsar Peter was kept away from court and state affairs. He was remanded to the near-solitary company of his mother, far outside the Kremlin at Preobrazhenskoye. The location was ideal—it kept the 'junior tsar' away from court affairs but still close enough to monitor. While Sophia Alekseyevna's full brother Ivan V Alekseyevich was retained at the Kremlin, there was little room for the young co-tsar at court. His future was then uncertain if not constantly precarious.

Peter I Alekseyevich proved a patient plotter. Still considered a mere child, Sophia Alekseyevna misunderstood that the 'junior tsar's' determination and ambitions exceeded her own. Peter I Alekseyevich pretended to play with the soldiers with whom he was surrounded. Little did the regent understand he was drilling the Preobrazhensky and Semenovsky guards at Preobrazhenskoye to be his own pretorian guard. They became enamored with the young tsar, making personal fealty to him.[292]

As regent, the female Sophia Alekseyevna had been an anomaly. The patrician Russian hierarchs made certain she had to rely on the goodwill of the Patriarch of Moscow. The boyar families sought to influence her and gain personal favor. The *streletskoye voysko*, [infantry units] whose 1682 uprising she indirectly used to rise to power, began to exercise its conceit,

---

[291] Lindsey Hughes, "Sophia: Regent of Russia, 1657-1704", *New Haven: Yale University Press*, 1990.

[292] In 1717, Saint-Simon described him as, "tall, well-formed and slim... with a look both bewildered and fierce" See: Jacob von Stählin, "Originalanekdoten von Peter dem Großen: aus dem Munde angesehener Personen zu Moskau und Petersburg vernommen, und der Vergessenheit entrissen", *J.G.I. Breitkopf*, 1785.

challenging the regent by reminding her how she rose to be regent. It became intolerable for both.

Disaffected streltsy leaders informed Peter I Alekseyevich of the regent's plan to either imprison, exile, or kill him. In 1689, the now physically imposing 17-year-old 'junior tsar' decided to act.[293] The regent's position had been put into question following two disastrous campaigns to seize Crimea. Peter realized he had an opportunity to depose his half-sister and claim power. He rallied his supporters while holed up at Troitse-Sergiyeva Lavra, the monastery he used as his base of operations. He overthrew the regent, his half-sister Sophia Alekseyevna. Unlike western monarchs like Henry VIII or Elizabeth I, Peter I Alekseyevich felt no need to have her beheaded. He followed the Byzantine tradition of forcing deposed rulers to take the habit and enter the monastic life at the Novodevichy Convent.[294] Sophia Alekseyevna renounced any royal privileges or titles to which she had been entitled. She would have been relegated to being a footnote of history had it not been for ambitious boyars. Upon the death of Tsar Ivan V Alekseyevich, a group of boyars rallied to Sophia Alekseyevna, hoping to use her restoration to Moscow to regain acclaim and power stripped from them by Tsar Peter I Alekseyevich's promotion of meritocracy.

The attempted 1698 coup d'état led by the streletskoye voysko failed. They were defeated by four regiments of imperial cavalry just outside the New Jerusalem Monastery, some 40 kilometers from Moscow 18 June 18, 1698.[295] Sophia Alekseyevna's tenure in the monastery became repressive and restrictive. She died in obscurity in 1704, denied a state funeral and unreconciled with her half-brother, Tsar Peter I Alekseyevich.

With the 'senior tsar' now dead and his half-sister and former regent well in her grave, Peter I Alekseyevich was determined to limit competition for all quarters. In 1700, the Moscow Patriarch, Adrian (born Andrey), died. Peter I Alekseyevich conspired to keep the cathedra of the Moscow Patriarch vacant. The duties of the patriarch fell to the coadjutor, Archbishop Stephen Iavorksy, a man educated in Europe by enlightenment thinkers.

> Thus in the course of seven months Iavorsky ascended from the humble position of father superior to the highest office in the entire church. Iavorsky had never desired such an appointment and even attempted to avoid it, but

---

[293] Пётр I Алексеевич, Дело об издании писем и бумаг императора Петра Великого, *Дела по ученым учреждениям Департамента народного просвещения за 1863–1895*, 1672–1725.

[294] It remains uncertain if Sophia Alekseyevna was tonsured or was simply banned for life to the monastery.

[295] Michael C. Paul, "The Military Revolution in Russia 1550–1682", *The Journal of Military History 68 No. 1*, January 2004.

Peter was unyielding [because] the prelate was not a progressive or a reformer, but he was an authoritative figure with a European education, of which there were still few in Russia.[296]

His tenure would last for some 21 years. Upon Archbishop Iavorksy's death, the tsar would require an alternative to re-establishing the Moscow Patriarchate.

Peter I Alekseyevich eventually promulgated the Ecclesiastical Regulations of 1721.[297] Among other reforms, monasteries with fewer than 30 monks were converted to schools or churches. Most notable of the introduced changes, however, was the abolition of the Moscow Patriarchate in favor of the Священный синод Русской православной церкви [Most Holy Synod], which came into being on January 25, 1721. With the tsar's Most Holy Synod's having been formed, the canonical status of the ROC ceased and the office of Patriarch was abolished.

The Most Holy Synod was a commission of laymen and clergy to undertake the functions previously discharged by the Moscow Patriarch. The tsar, it seems, found controlling a committee far preferable to dealing with a patriarch. In years past, patriarchs had acted as regents over tsars, causing imperial resentment. It was not in Peter I Alekseyevich's constitution to suffer the possibility of a member of the clergy reigning over him.

A procurator led the Holy Synod. The hierarchs were selected by the tsar, not a sobor of bishops. For the next two centuries, hierarchs and clergy of the ROC were treated as (and believed themselves to be) civil servants. Being bound to the Russian state entirely became a formative ideology of Russian Orthodox clergy.

Despite some rebellion during the early Soviet era, the allegiance of every ROC hierarch from the time of Peter I Alekseyevich to Putin was always divided — but not always equally. To be a ROC bishop required walking a fine line with one foot in the Kremlin and the other in the cathedral. According to Konstantin Kharchev, former chairman of the Soviet Council for Religious Affairs:

> Not a single candidate for the office of bishop or any other high-ranking office, much less a member of Holy Synod, went through without confirmation by the Central Committee of the CPSU and the KGB.[298]

---

[296] Sergei Nikolaev, (Marcus C. Levitt, editor), "Stefan Iavorsky — Early Modern Russian Writers: Late Seventeenth and Eighteenth Centuries", *Gale Research*, 1995.

[297] Феофан Прокопович, "Духовный регламент, тщанием и повелением всепресветлейшего, державнейшего государя Петра Первого, императора и самодержца всерос...", *В Синодальной типографии*, 1856.

[298] Yevgenia Albats and Catherine A. Fitzpatrick, "The State Within a State: The KGB and Its Hold on Russia — Past, Present, and Future", *Farrar, Straus and Giroux*, 1999.

The long duration over which the Moscow Patriarchate ceased to exist and the resurrection of the ROC during the Soviet era ensured that the church-state fealty of bishops was balanced in favor of the state. With Patriarch Kirill having owed his elevation to bishop and archbishop to the KGB (as did Patriarch Alexii before him):

> A Soviet Era document discovered in Estonia suggests that Patriarch Alexy II, the head of the ROC, may have been a fully-fledged KGB Agent. While allegations of his collaboration with the Soviet secret police under the code-name "Drozdov" (Thursh) have circulated since a brief examination of secret police files in Moscow in 1991, this newly surfaced document provides the first publicly available evidence indicating that Alexy was not just a passive collaborator but an active KGB agent from 1958.[299]

In 2023, the Swiss National Archives declassified files providing indelible evidence that Father Kirill was active as a KGB agent under the code name "Mikhailov." His mission was not limited to serving as the ROC's representative to the World Council of Churches (WCC), as his work permit indicated. Father Kirill's real mission was to influence the Swiss Federal Council: "The files, labelled "Monsignor Kirill," record the Patriarch's clandestine mission under the code name "Mikhailov" and note that the council was already infiltrated by the KGB."[300]

It is not surprising, therefore, that Patriarch Kirill, like Patriarch Alexy before him, has continued to form his own clergy to embrace the concept that clergy are tantamount to civil servants and should defer to state priorities in lieu of fidelity to the gospels or their ordination vows.[301]

---

[299] Eirini Kongkini, "ROC: Spycraft and Statecraft Overlay Faith", *Grey Dynamics*, 18 February 2025.
[300] Kongkini, *ibid*.
[301] Euronews with Agence France-Presse, "Patriarch Kirill worked for the KGB in the 1970s, Swiss media reports", *EuroNews*, 6 February 2023.

Chapter Twelve

The Post Petrine ROC (1917-1926) a Brief Attempt at Reform and Reinvigoration

The canonical standing of the ROC lapsed entirely during the 'Petrine Period' between 1721 and the enthronement of a new Moscow Patriarch in 1917.[302] The election of Patriarch Tikhon (born Vasily Ivanovich Bellavin) amidst the chaos caused by the abdication of Tsar Nicholas II Alexandrovich, the several provisional governments that arose and collapsed in short order and the seizing of power by the Bolsheviks, all within the course of six months, may have been advisable, but was hardly canonical.

1917 proved to be pivotal both for Russia and the ROC. The short window in time created by the rapidly shifting political events in Russia created a void in the government's oversight and control of the ROC that had existed for almost 200 years. The rise and fall of the First, Second and Third Provisional Governments created a power vacuum. The ROC seized the opportunity to reinvigorate itself.

Bishop Tikhon experienced a meteoric rise from bishop of the Aleutian Islands and Alaska to being elevated to archbishop and serving as head of all ROCs in North America. Having returned to Russia in 1908, his organizational and pastoral skills earned him high regard. In the chasm created by the rapidly deteriorating political climate, he was enthroned as the Metropolitan of Moscow on July 4, 1917 (June 21, old calendar). On August 27, 1917, he was again raised in dignity as Metropolitan of Moscow. The following day, August 28, 1917, the local council of the ROC met for the first time since Peter I Alekseyevich abolished it, and their deliberations resulted in a resolution to restore the Moscow Patriarchate. The cathedra of the Moscow Patriarch was filled by Metropolitan Tikhon on September 24, 1917.

---

[302] The ROC argues it was necessary to act without conciliatory consultations given the exigent circumstances. Applying the theological principle of οἰκονομία (economia), where a relaxation of Church canons can be accommodated in consideration of the exigent needs of the faithful or the Church require it, the Moscow Patriarchate asserts their acts were rendered normalised and canonical. They deny applying this same consideration of exigency and need to the Ukrainian Church or the tomos of autocephaly that was given to it.

The election of Patriarch Tikhon in 1917 did not resolve the ROC's problems. The October Revolution by the Bolsheviks was to make having been a supplicant under Peter I Alekseyevich and his Romanov descendant tsars a desirable condition. The ROC had lingered as a Russian state agent. The dichotomy that had arisen within the ranks of the clergy, some of whom could not avert their eyes from the strife, poverty, and widespread illiteracy across Russia, began to concern itself with the social good of the Russian people. One such member of the clergy, Archimandrite Mikhail (Semenov), began to write passionately about his turn towards socialism: "Orthodoxy, in its essence, always prioritised spiritual interests above corporal, and it did not only believe that a person does not live only by bread, but unfortunately, underestimated the importance of bread."[303]

Archimandrite Mikhail, also a member of the Renovationist Movement and other reform-minded ROC clergy who sought to link social reform with liturgical reform, was suppressed. The imperial regime and ROC leadership found any dissent intolerable. It is no wonder the public, especially the intelligentsia, was wary of the ROC, given the conditions in Russia.

After the end of Imperial Russia, the ROC threw its weight behind several provisional governments. Nonetheless, none of those governments survived the year. Following the storming of the Winter Palace and the establishment of the Petrograd Soviet, the ROC found that it did not influence the prevailing political climate.

Following the November 12, 1917 (October 31, old calendar), torture and murder of Archpriest John Kochurov near Tsarskoye Selo, subsequent persecution and murder of ROC clergy by Russian revolutionaries including the Bolsheviks became routine. Most Russians were too afraid to dissent, let alone publicly protest the brutality and depravity of the Bolsheviks.

While the Petrograd Soviet had not been overtly hostile to the ROC, Patriarch Tikhon and his fellow bishops and clergy seemed oblivious to the plans and ideology of the Bolsheviks, who would soon take power. The Russian people seemed to sense the changing headwinds where the ROC could not. The complex and varied relationship they shared with it alienated many from demonstrable support for Moscow Patriarch Tikhon and the clergy.

The November 2017 publication of the *Declaration of the Rights of the Peoples of Russia* left no question that the Bolsheviks meant to destroy any attempts by the ROC to reinvigorate itself. All special privileges previously

---

[303] Simon Dixon, "Archimandrite Mikhail (Semenov) and Russian Christian Socialism", *The Historical Journal: Cambridge University Press*, September 2008.

afforded the ROC and clergy were terminated.³⁰⁴ When the Совет народных комиссаров (CHK) (The Council of People's Commissars (CPC) began to implement their unofficial and yet overt anti-church, state atheism policies, the Moscow Patriarchate did not know how to respond except to condemn the actions, further inflaming Bolshevik hostilities. The confiscation and destruction of church property and harassment of clergy found a sizable portion of the population willing to support or at least remain silent.

After centuries of near serfdom, watching the Romanovs bask in the opulence of untold wealth while the average Russian lived near subsistence level, the Bolsheviks' retribution on the ROC was almost welcome. The consequences of having immersed themselves in the state apparatus for almost two centuries left Russians to regard the ROC as their natural enemy.

On February 14, 1918 (February 1, old calendar), Patriarch Tikhon enflamed the situation by publishing an open, pastoral letter announcing he had resolved to anathematize the Bolsheviks:

> Think what you are doing, you madmen! Stop your bloody reprisals. Your acts are not merely cruel, they are the works of Satan for which you will burn in Hell fire in the life hereafter and be cursed by future generations in this life....
> By the authority given me by God I forbid you to partake of the Christian Mysteries. I anathematize you if you still bear a Christian name and belong by birth to the Orthodox Church.³⁰⁵

There was no turning back. The death struggle between the ROC and the Bolsheviks had finally come.

When the Romanov family was executed in the basement of the Ipatiev House in Yekaterinburg on the evening of July 16-17, 1918, Patriarch Tikhon publicly condemned the act on July 21, 1918 during a memorial service in the Cathedral of Our Lady of Kazan, Moscow:

> A terrible thing has happened: the former Tsar Nikolai Alexandrovich was shot, by decision of the Ural Regional Soviet of Workers' and Soldiers' Deputies, and our highest government, the Executive Committee, not only approved it but deemed it as legitimate. But our Christian conscience, guided by the Word of God, cannot agree with this. We must, in obedience to the

---

[304] Arto Luukkanen, "The Party of Unbelief: The Religious Policy of the Bolshevik Party, 1917-1929", *Helsinki: Suomen Historiallinen Seura*, 1994.

[305] Alexander Ivanovich Vvedenskii, "Tserkov' i gosudarstvo (Ocherk vzaimootnoshenii tserkvi i gosudarstva v Rossii), 1918-1922", *Unpublished Manuscript: Moscow*, 1923.

teaching of the Word of God, condemn this act; otherwise, the Tsar's blood will fall not just on those who committed it, but on all of us.[306]

In 1918, the Bolsheviks placed Patriarch Tikhon under house arrest. His quarters were repeatedly searched, and his activities were recorded in detail. Persecution became more widespread as the year progressed. With every act of oppression, persecution, torture, and murder of clergy, the Bolsheviks could not help but to have felt emboldened. The very depravity of their violence deterred public outcry, giving them no impetus to stop.

Fearful of repeating the mistakes of the past, namely creating a popular martyr out of Patriarch Tikhon in the way Patriarch Saint Hermogenes of Moscow was, singlehandedly swaying public sentiment during the Time of Troubles (1598–1613), Vladimir Lenin personally ordered Patriarch Tikhon's release.[307] It wouldn't last long; the Bolsheviks again placed Patriarch Tikhon under house arrest in 1919.

By 1920, the Bolsheviks were intent on destroying the mystic ethos of the ROC. This period became known as the 'Liquidation of the Relics.' A campaign was undertaken to expose, desecrate and destroy relics. The public was generally cowed into submission with little widespread protest. Given their experience of the supposedly Christian Okhrana under the tsars, Russians rightly suspected what the Bolsheviks would do to them if accused of dissent.

Between 1920–1921, a natural calamity combined with agricultural policy mismanagement created a devastating famine. The Bolsheviks needed an antagonist to blame. With the tsar gone, the ROC became the Bolsheviks' scapegoat. It became their cause to cast the ROC and the clergy as wealthy exploiters of the Russian people. During the Great Russian famine, an estimated five million Russians died from starvation. Bolshevik propagandist blamed the ROC and sought to devalue their agency by failing to prevail upon "their God" to stop the "natural" calamity.

In a letter only made public following the opening of the Soviet archives following the demise of the Soviet Union, a letter by Lenin dated March 19, 1920, secretly outlined his plans to blame the ROC while extracting millions of rubles from it:

> The decree on the removal of church property in addition to what we know about the illegal proclamation of Patriarch Tikhon, then it becomes perfectly

---

[306] Paul Gilbert, "Nicholas II: Russia's Last Orthodox Christian Monarch: Russia's Last Orthodox Christian", *Kindle Edition*, 2022.

[307] The issue was fresh in Lenin's mind and that of his fellow Bolsheviks. The glorification of Patriarch Hermogenes had only occurred 5 years earlier on 12 May 1913. Today, Saint Hermogenes is commemorated on both the date of his death — 17 February and the date of his glorification — 12 May.

clear that the Black Hundreds clergy, headed by its leader, with full deliberation is carrying out a plan at this very moment to destroy us decisively....
Now and only now, when people are being eaten in famine-stricken areas, and hundreds, if not thousands, of corpses lie on the roads, we can (and therefore must) pursue the removal of church property with the most frenzied and ruthless energy and not hesitate to put down the least opposition. Now and only now, the vast majority of peasants will either be on our side, or at least will not be in a position to support to any decisive degree this handful of Black Hundreds clergy and reactionary urban petty bourgeoisie, who are willing and able to attempt to oppose this Soviet decree with a policy of force....
We must pursue the removal of church property by any means necessary in order to secure for ourselves a fund of several hundred million gold rubles (do not forget the immense wealth of some monasteries and lavras). Without this fund any government work in general, any economic build-up in particular, and any upholding of Soviet principles in Genoa especially is completely unthinkable. In order to get our hands on this fund of several hundred million gold rubles (and perhaps even several hundred billion), we must do whatever is necessary....
I think that it is advisable for us not to touch Patriarch Tikhon himself, even though he undoubtedly headed this whole revolt of slave-holders. Concerning him, the State Political Administration [GPU] must be given a secret directive that precisely at this time all communications of this personage must be monitored and their contents disclosed in all possible accuracy and detail. Require Dzerzhinsky and Unshlikht personally to report to the Politburo about this weekly.[308]

Corporately, the ROC did not wholly ignore the issue of the famine. Collections by the ROC for the hungry were widespread. However, the Bolsheviks highlighted their exemption of valuable objects from being donated, including chalices and other sacramental objects. The 'success' of the Bolshevik relief efforts was promoted on the back of the idea that the ROC chose to retain its wealth while Russians starved[309] Ultimately, the Bolsheviks placed several members of the clergy on trial for their role in the retention of ROC wealth in the midst of the wildly lethal famine.[310] One of the most famed cases was that of the case of A.D. Samarin, N.D. Kuznetsov before the Moscow Revolutionary Tribunal. Known as the "1st and 2nd trials of churchmen."[311]

---

[308] Vladimir Ilyich Lenin, (translation by Library of Congress), "Letter", *Moscow: Collection*, 19 March 2022.

[309] Владимир Воробьев, "Следственное дело патриарха Тихона. Сборник документов по материалам Центрального архива ФСБ РФ", *Памятники исторической мысли: Москва*, 2000.

[310] Наталья Александровна Кривова, "Власть и церковь в 1922-1925", *АИРО-XX*, 1997.

[311] Вадим Никонов, "Особенности вынесения приговоров Московским революционным трибуналом по делам духовенства и верующих в 1918-

The difficulties facing the ROC were not merely domestic. In 1921, the Ukrainian Autocephalous Orthodox Church (UAOC) was formed following the 1918 Church Council in Kyiv. That council met during that brief era when the ROC was free of the Russian state's imposition of Petrine authority, manifested by the abolishment of the Moscow Patriarchate, and before the Soviet Union abolished the Moscow Patriarchate again.

The council took place during a great civil upheaval following the abdication of Tsar Nicholas II Alexandrovich and the Ukrainian People's Republic (UPR), with Kyiv as its capital, being proclaimed in 1917. Consequently, in Lviv, Ukraine's western territories were proclaimed independent under the Ukrainian People's Republic (WUPR) in 1918. By means of the Unification Act [Act Zluky] on January 22, 1918, the two republics were merged into an independent Ukraine.

The 1918 Ukrainian Council received the explicit blessing of the newly restored Moscow Patriarchate — Patriarch Tikhon — for the purpose of deciding the future of the Ukrainian Church:

> Initially, it seemed that the council would declare autocephaly and "Ukrainianize" the Church by adopting Ukrainian as the language for liturgy and restoring the traditions that had been suppressed during the synodal period. The first session of the Council occurred in January 1918, just after the horrifying murder of the leader of the Church in Ukraine, Metropolitan Volodymyr.
> In May 1918, the Council elected Antony as the metropolitan. The session spanning June and July 1918 surprisingly adopted autonomy, which kept the Ukrainian Church a part of the ROC. The session also retained Slavonic as the liturgical language and limited the use of Ukrainian to the reading of the Gospel on Easter.[312] [313]

Unsurprisingly, the constant attacks by Bolshevik forces in eastern Ukraine, along with the incursion of separate Polish, Romanian, and Czechoslovakian forces in western Ukraine, each desirous of dividing Ukraine for their individual territorial gain, acted as a pall on the council's deliberations. The overwhelming support for Ukraine's religious liberation from the ROC dissipated as quickly as the opportunity arose due to martial and political concerns.

In late November–December 1917, a delegation from the Provisional All-Ukrainian Orthodox Council traveled to Moscow to consult Patriarch

---

1920-е гг., Серия II: История. История Русской Православной Церкви", *Вестник ПСТГУ*, 2022.

[312] Nicholas E. Denysenko, "The Church's Unholy War: Russia's Invasion of Ukraine and Orthodoxy", *Cascade Books*, 2023.

[313] Metropolitan of Kyiv and Halytskyi, Archbishop Volodymyr (born Basil Nikephorovich Bogoyavlenskyi) was executed by Bolshevik forces against the walls of the Kyiv-Pechersk Lavra on 25 January 1918.

Tikhon. There can be no question that the delegation received the blessing of Moscow Patriarch Tikhon for their Ukrainian Council in 1918. There could have been no question that the purpose of the council was to consider the future of the Ukrainian Church being restored to autocephaly. This was the stated purpose of the council. The protocol record is clear that Patriarch Tikhon's concern was confined to canonical conformity:

> In order to establish the canonical connection of the Ukrainian Church with the Patriarch of the Russian Church, it is necessary to have a clear understanding of the actual situation on the ground and to know the specific plans of the representatives of the Ukrainian Church regarding its future structure. All this will be clarified at the Ukrainian Council, which is scheduled for December 28 of this year. We have given our blessing for its convocation, and it must be convened on canonical grounds.[314]

Beyond canonical correctness, Moscow Patriarch Tikhon conditioned his blessing for the convocation of the council such that the council had to be convened on "canonical grounds" — under episcopal leadership, in accordance with Orthodox canons, and: "without breaking communion with the Moscow Patriarchate."[315]

The debate about Patriarch Tikhon's intention to be bound by the Council of 1918 remains unresolved. Arguably, provided the council was formed and conducted canonically, had the body voted for autocephaly, conciliarity would have demanded Patriarch Tikhon honor such a resolution of the council and consent to the Ukrainian Church's autocephaly. Had the Ukrainian Church voted for autocephaly, and it was done canonically, it would remain in communion with Moscow in the same way other local churches were in communion with Moscow, yet not under its jurisdictional control. Some scholars disagree, arguing that autocephaly would have restored the Ukrainian Church to Constantinople, and there is no indication that the Ecumenical Patriarch was obliged to grant a tomos under these conditions or at that time. Whatever Patriarch Tikhon meant by "communion" remains uncertain, and the second session of the Council of 1918 rendered the point moot. The council voted for autonomy rather than autocephaly.

Still, the only Moscow Patriarch genuinely freed of Russian state control or influence between 1721 and the present chose to bless the right of Ukraine's Orthodox Christians to define their future. That should have informed the ROC when autocephaly emerged again as a matter of consequence following the demise of the Soviet Union, when the first pan-orthodox council in over 1000 years met to consider the issue in 2016. We will

---

[314] Андрій Стародуб, "Всеукраїнський православний церковний Собор 1918 року: огляд джерел", *Національна Академія Наук України,* Kyiv, 2010.

[315] Стародуб, *ibid.*

never know how such an argument would have played out. Patriarch Kirill, however, refused to let go of his and the Russian state's control over Orthodox Christians. The ROC simply declined to participate in the council as a means of attempting to frustrate Orthodox Ukrainians who sought parity across the globe to celebrate the Divine Liturgy in their vernacular, enjoy local church independence and be freed of the Russian state and the Moscow Patriarchs, who deferred to the Russian state over service to the Kingdom of God and unity with the Ecumenical Patriarchate.

Patriarch Tikhon accepted the decision of the Ukrainian Council, surprised though he was. The fate of the UAOC, however, was inevitable, with it being denied canonical status and being rejected by other Orthodox bishops. On March 21, 1922, Patriarch Tikhon was arrested for his general opposition to the Bolsheviks and his specific protest of the Bolshevik scheme to seize church valuables. He was transported to the dreaded Lubyanka prison. Despite denials by Bolshevik authorities, Patriarch Tikhon is said to have been both physically and psychologically tortured. He was forced to read the summary of his imprisonment interrogations:

> Demands from citizen Belavin, as the responsible leader of the entire hierarchy, a definite and public definition of his attitude to the counter-revolutionary conspiracy, led by hierarchy subordinate to him.[316]

Patriarch Tikhon and the ROC's woes were immediately made more complicated by Antonin (Granovskiy) on March 25, 1922. Antonin, a self-styled bishop, was recently released from imprisonment by the Bolsheviks in 1922, joined with other Renovationist, ROC clergy in forming the Живая Церковь [living church]. With the assistance of the Государственное политическое управление [state political directorate—GPU], Bishop Antonin led a revolt against Patriarch Tikhon. The Bolsheviks' exploitation of the ROC lured many clergy to their cause who wished to continue to live as priests even at the risk of being considered non-canonical.

Patriarch Tikhon's tenure as Moscow Patriarch took its toll. As if discharging the responsibilities of that office were not onerous enough, the Russian Revolution, civil war and his stint in the Lubyanka prison couldn't have helped. Although aged only 60 years, photographs show him looking far beyond his years. Patriarch Tikhon died in 1925. He had been what was best about Russian Orthodox Christianity. Those virtues he experienced, however, would dissipate from the ROC in the years to come.

---

[316] Record, "Interrogation of Vasily Ivanovich Bellavin", *Soviet State Archives (CPU)*: Moscow, 1922.

Chapter Thirteen

The ROC in Modernity
An Article of the State Apparatus (1926–Present)

Patriarch Tikhon was aware of his failing health, and in an age where all ROC clergy had to consider their mortality, he wisely planned ahead. He resolved to designate three candidates from whom the synod could choose to succeed him. Metropolitan Peter of Krutitsy (born Peter Fyodorovich Polyansky) was chosen as the patriarchal locum tenens. The new Soviet government was fearful of another able hierarch possibly rejuvenating the Moscow Patriarchate.

Metropolitan Peter was arrested only mere months after his installation as locum tenens. Like Patriarch Tikhon, he too had planned ahead, naming three successors to replace him should necessity arise. One of his named candidates, Metropolitan Sergius of Nizhny Novgorod (born Ivan Nikolayevich Stragorodsky) would succeed him following his arrest. The decision as to which candidate should succeed Metropolitan Peter had been an easy one. The other two candidates chosen by the locum tenens had already been either exiled or arrested by the Объединённое государственное политическое управление [joint state political directorate — an eventual Cheka successor and KGB precursor].[317]

As patriarchal locum tenens, Metropolitan Sergius would prove himself unworthy of his predecessor's trust. He formed a solidly pro-Soviet 'provisional patriarchal holy synod' to negotiate with the Communist Party and Josef Stalin. 29 July 29, 1927, Metropolitan Sergius signed an encyclical address as an 'Epistle to pastors and their flocks' declaring his unwavering support, and that of the ROC, for the Soviet Union, which he called "our civil motherland,":

> We need to show, not in words but in deeds, that not only those who are indifferent to Orthodox Christianity, not only those who have betrayed it, but also its most zealous adherents, for whom it is dear as truth and life, with all its dogmas and traditions, with all its canonical and liturgical structure, can be faithful citizens of the Soviet Union, loyal to the Soviet government. We want to be Orthodox and at the same time recognize the Soviet Union as our civil motherland, whose joys and successes are our joys and

---

[317] Vladimir Moss, "How the Moscow Patriarchate Fell From Grace", *Vladimir Moss*, 2012.

successes and whose failures are our failures. Any blow directed at the Union, be it a war, a boycott, some kind of social disaster, or just a murder from around the corner, like the Warsaw one, is recognized by us as a blow directed at us.[318]

Metropolitan Sergius could not have been so foolish as to believe appeasement would repair the fracture between the ROC and the Soviet regime. From the time of the rise of the Bolsheviks, the unrelenting, brutal, and murderous treatment of ROC clergy and faithful had been a hallmark of the Leninist-Stalinist ideologues. The reaction by the genuinely faithful survivors of the martyrs and imprisoned bishops and clergy was to break communion with Metropolitan Sergius. It would not deter him. He needed the favor of the powerful, not firmly entrenched in the Kremlin and the Lubyanka—not martyrs or prisoners.

Despite Metropolitan Sergius having prostrated himself before the Communist Party, the persecutions continued. The process of commissars destroying churches and monasteries, desecrating and confiscating icons, attacking the faithful trying to enter churches to participate in the divine liturgy and the continued persecution, torture and murder of ROC clergy continued unabated. Of the nearly 50,000 ROC clergy functioning in 1918, fewer than 500 remained by 1935.[319]

Metropolitan Sergius would be rewarded for his supplication. Following the Nazi invasion of Russia, 'Operation Barbarossa', on June 22, 1941, Stalin needed every ally he could get. As part of a propaganda effort to inspire patriotic nationalism, it was agreed that Metropolitan Sergius could be elevated to be seated in the long vacant cathedra of the Moscow Patriarch. The ROC hierarchy acted alone, declining to consult the Ecumenical Patriarchate in Constantinople concerning the reinstatement of the Moscow Patriarchate, or any other canonical Orthodox Christian patriarch or bishops. They only sought permission from the Politburo in the Kremlin.

Stalin and the Politburo gave the hierarchs of the ROC were granted permission to enthrone the aged and ill 76-year-old Metropolitan Sergius as the 12th Patriarch of Moscow and All the Rus' on September 8, 1943. His reign would be short. He died on May 15, 1944.

Patriarch Sergius' legacy is that he subordinated the ROC to the Communist Party. In so doing, the non-canonically enthroned Patriarch Sergius elevated communist ideology while debasing the Holy Orthodox Christian faith. That legacy in and of itself has consequences that endure.

---

[318] Mikhail V. Shkarovskii, "The ROC versus the State: The Josephite Movement, 1927-1940", *Slavic Review, No. 54*, 1995.

[319] Журнал Московской Патриархии. Прием товарищем И. В. СТАЛИНЫМ Митрополита Сергия. Москва: Издательский Совет Русской Православной Церкви, сентябрь 1943.

Between 1944 and the demise of the Soviet Union in 1991, there was one constant in the ROC—fealty to the Russian state. Given that Patriarch Kirill, who currently sits on the patriarchal throne in Moscow, had to be approved for elevation to the episcopal state by the KGB, the ROC in modernity can be said to be a continuation and creature of the Russian state.[320]

Since the advent of the Russian Federation, the relatively weak position of Yeltsin in public opinion, vis-à-vis the ROC, brought the two together for practical purposes. Yeltsin bought the support of the ROC in exchange for certain privileges, beginning with the return of Moscow Patriarchate properties confiscated during the Soviet era: "Of course, while I was a Communist," he added with a smile, "I was a sincere atheist." Yeltsin said there are also "political considerations" in his open return to church, saying he felt "the need to support the church, and that means all kinds of denominations--I have respect for all of them." "In order to give support to believers, we help religion," he continued, "and we have programs to rehabilitate and build new churches, mosques, Buddhist temples, synagogues and so forth."[321]

Both Yeltsin and Putin found willing partners in Patriarchs Alexy II and Kirill. The ROC would directly benefit from remaining willing accomplices of the Russian state. Patriarch Alexy II and Patriarch Kirill would benefit indirectly.

By 1997, the extent of the Russian state's 'gratitude' to the ROC was revealed in a series of exposés in the new, and temporarily free Russian press. The revelations revolved around the tax-free status the Russian state granted the ROC on purchases of cigarettes and alcohol:

> The Moskovskiye novosti weekly newspaper has alleged that the church and, more precisely, its Department of External Church Relations, led by one of the church's most prominent officials, Metropolitan Kirill, has been importing tobacco on a massive scale. Since 1994, when <u>the government granted the Moscow Patriarchate the right to import thousands of tons of tobacco—duty free—as humanitarian aid</u>, 10,000 tons of cigarettes have been imported by the church. According to estimates, that works out at about 8 billion cigarettes—10 percent of Russia's total tobacco imports. Because they were imported free of duty, the government has missed out on US $40 million in tax.[322] [Emphasis added]

---

[320] Yevgenia Albats and Catherine A. Fitzpatrick, "The State Within a State: The KGB and Its Hold on Russia—Past, Present, and Future", *Farrar, Straus and Giroux*, 1999.
[321] Michael Parks, "Yeltsin Sheds Atheism, Gets Religion Again", *Los Angeles Times*, 15 June 1992.
[322] Andrei Zolotov, "Orthodoxy, Oil, Tobacco, and Wine: Do They Mix?", *East-West Church & Ministry Report*, No. 5, 13 December 1996.

Cigarettes weren't the only peculiar "humanitarian aid" venture undertaken by then Metropolitan Kirill and the ROC:

> Another newspaper, Novaya gazeta, has claimed that the Sofrino icon and vestment factory has been importing millions of bottles of wine, also duty-free. The bottles have been officially listed as church wine imported as humanitarian aid. The deputy chief of the Russian government's State Customs Committee has been sacked for violating the law in connection with the Sofrino wine deal, and a criminal investigation is under way involving Sofrino's director, Yevgeni Parkhayev....
> In response to the allegations in the press, the church's Department of External Church Relations issued a statement on 11 October denying it had ever been involved in 'commercial activities involving alcohol or tobacco products or any excise goods.' However, the statement admitted that some humanitarian aid was not intended for direct use by church organizations, but to be sold for profit. 'In the latter case, with the government's approval, these items have gone to secular trade organizations... Part of the revenues received has gone into the general church budget, and part into special programs for restoring churches and monasteries, restoration of church life as a whole, and for charitable activities.'[323]

As author Anna Neplii wrote for United24 Media in 2024:

> The ROC is a giant corporation that, according to investigations, received $72 million in untaxed profits in 2014. Unofficial estimates suggest its total annual income could be $500 million. Part of this money goes to Kirill as "taxes" from each of the churches. In 2018, it was established that the patriarchate received over $13 million from Moscow churches alone.
> However, the ROC's extrareligious interests are not limited to money. With each year, they lean towards "spiritual" militarism.
> In 2020, a scandal broke out in Russia over the opening of the Church of the Armed Forces of the Russian Federation, near Moscow. One reason for the scandal was a mosaic with the images of Putin and Joseph Stalin on the church's walls.
> The cathedral has a lot of symbolism, but it is mainly dedicated to the 'victory in the Great Patriotic War' [in Russia, this is the name of the Second World War, which, in their opinion, began in 1941, not in 1939]. The temple walls are decorated with images related to the war. In addition, military artifacts — like tanks, cannons, etc. — were used in its construction.
> However, this is not the first 'religious shrine' with a touch of belligerence. In 2007, the previous patriarch of the ROC, Alexy II, proclaimed Saint Seraphim of Sarov 'the patron saint of nuclear weapons.' In 2023, the current Patriarch emphasized that the development of weapons took place with the 'direct participation of Seraphim'[324]

---

[323] Zolotov, *ibid*.
[324] Anna Neplii, Secret Fraternities, a Temple of War, and Espionage Globally. What Does the ROC Hide?" *United24 Media*, 23 June 2024.

Since then, the ROC's Moscow Patriarchate has become a major player in several industries, including controlling interest in the oil exporter MES, a chain of hotels and casinos, jewelry stores, publishing houses and manufacturing facilities that produce goods ranging from furniture to religious icons. While Russia's economic woes slip from bad to worse under international sanctions, the ROC under Patriarch Kirill has emerged as Orthodox Christianity's wealthiest church.[325]

Possibly because of preferential tax treatment of the Russian state, shrewd business dealings or the intercession of Saint Seraphim of Sarov, 'the patron saint of nuclear weapons,'[326] Patriarch Kirill himself has enjoyed the peculiar advantages of commerce and favoritism by the Russian state. On July 3, 2009, Patriarch Kirill appeared in a photograph with Russian Justice Minister Alexander Konovalov. The photograph was discovered only too late to have captured an image of his $30,000 luxury Breguet watch.[327] At the time, the average annual income in Russia was only $7,046, making his watch worth almost four times the annual Russian wage.[328] The scandal arose in 2012 after Russian bloggers spotted the watch in the original photograph and compared it to an image on the Moscow Patriarchate website in which the watch had been digitally removed. The problem was that they failed to remove the reflection of the watch Patriarch Kirill was wearing from the highly polished table, which clearly identified it by make and model. To quell outrage by an impoverished Russian nation, the Moscow Patriarchate removed the images from its site altogether. They survive in the viral media coverage the scandal gave rise to, despite attempts by Patriarch Kirill to hide it from public view.

A mere watch, however, wasn't the only indication of how a "slave of God" has enriched himself personally while the Russian people teeter between poverty and desperation:

> In December 2019, Novaya Gazeta drew attention to previous media reports about Patriarch Kirill's involvement in automotive, oil, jewelry, and fishing businesses. The newspaper cited unconfirmed reports claiming that the patriarch's estimated net worth is $4–8 billion, underscoring that these figures

---

[325] Neplii, *ibid*.
[326] Stephen Kostoff, "The Patron Saint of What?", *Orthodox Church of America: Reflections in Christ*, 3 January 2020.
[327] Blake Buettner, "Breguet At Middle Of Russian Patriarch's Photo Scandal", *Hodinkee*, 6 April 2012.
[328] United Nations Economic Commission for Europe, "Gross Average Monthly Wages by Indicator, Country and Year", *United Nations*, 2010.

can't be verified since Kirill keeps his savings in banks in Switzerland, Italy, and Austria.[329]

The patriarch's penchant for eschewing poverty has continued to catch the attention of investigative reporters:

> According to the investigative report, Patriarch Kirill owns three apartments under his secular name, Vladimir Gundyaev:
>
> - A 145-square-meter (1,560-square-foot) apartment in the House on the Embankment on Serafimovich Street in Moscow — with an estimated value 70 million rubles (about $893,000), according to Proekt.
> - A 38-square-meter (409-square-foot) apartment on Nikoloyamskaya Street in Moscow valued at 12 million rubles (about $152,000).
> - And an 83-square-meter (893-square-foot) apartment on Bolsheokhtinsky Avenue in St. Petersburg valued at 9 million rubles (about $114,000).
>
> Meanwhile, the patriarch's second cousin, 73-year-old Lidia Leonova, owns four pieces of real estate, Proekt reports:
>
> - An 83-square-meter (893-square-foot) apartment on Gagarinsky Pereulok in Moscow with an estimated valued of 47 million rubles (about $597,000).
> - A 300-square-meter (3,229-square-foot) house in the "Zelenaya Roshcha-1" village located in the Moscow Region's Odintsovsky District valued at 10 million rubles (about $127,000).
> - A 121-square-meter (1302-square-foot) apartment on the Kryukov Canal Embankment in St. Petersburg valued at 42 million rubles (more than $533,000).
> - A third of the non-residential space (200 square meters or 2152 square feet) in the same building on the Kryukov Canal Embankment in St. Petersburg, which is valued at 3 million rubles (about $38,000).
>
> Lidia Leonova became the owner of the apartment on the Kryukov Canal Embankment in St. Petersburg in 2001 — this piece of real estate was gifted to her by an old friend of Patriarch Kirill, businessman Alexander Dmitrievich.
> Proekt notes that this took place six months after the Moscow Mayor's Office withdrew its claims against Dmitrievich's business partner, Italian national Nicola Savoretti, who also claims to have known Patriarch Kirill for a long time. Savoretti told Proekt that the patriarch wasn't involved in settling the dispute with the mayor's office, adding that Dmitrievich wasn't associated with his projects."[330]

---

[329] Proekt Staff, "New 'Projekt' investigation uncovers millions of dollars in real estate belonging to Patriarch Kirill and his family members", *Meduza*, 28 October 2020.
[330] Proekt, *ibid*.

This manuscript will not quell the debate over the nature of the ROC. We hope this work does, however, inform that debate:

> Is the ROC an organ of the Russian state intelligence service?
> Is the ROC a cooperator in war crimes, crimes against humanity and violations of international humanitarian law in Ukraine?
> Is the ROC a department of the Kremlin's propaganda machine?
> Is the ROC a corporation built on profiteering?

Or is it possible, just possible, that the ROC is simply a church that has lost its way, albeit in ways offensive to Christian values? There is much to consider.

Chapter Fourteen

The Restoration of The Metropolis of Kyiv
Righting a Historic Wrong

Modern Europe is the inheritor of a rich history, owing in no small part to the church imbuing its lands and people with extraordinary gifts. Be it literature, sculpture, painting, music, philosophy, or stability, the positive contributions of the church over millennia cannot be denied. Equally undeniable is that the same said history records times when the church, through its children, inflicted unholy suffering through its misguided pursuit of perfection; the overall trend has been a positive one.

Our greatest institutions of learning were built on the foundations laid by the church and the religious orders' pursuit of knowledge. Tour any museum in Europe, attend any concert, visit a hospital, a social welfare institution or simply observe a skyline of even the most modest village, and the indelible contribution by the church in contemporary society becomes immediately apparent. Nowhere is this truer than in the 'ivy-covered' towers of Europe's oldest and newest institutions of higher learning. There was a time, however, when it was not for the church, human progress might have ceased altogether for extended centuries.

Shortly before Romulus Augustulus' reign marked the end of the western Roman Empire and Rome fell to the barbarians, his counterpart in the east, in Constantinople, Theodosius II, founded the Magnaura [Greek: Πανδιδακτήριον τῆς Μαγναύρας] in 425. Better known in the west as the Imperial University of Constantinople, Byzantium's premier institution of higher learning thrived in the Magnaura's classrooms while the western Roman Empire slipped steadily into the Dark Ages.

While pestilence, war, and division pervaded during this woeful period of European history, the church (still unified before the 'Great Schism' of 1056) strove to better the human condition. Shortly before the Battle of Manzikert marked the decline of the eastern Roman Empire, Emperor Constantine IX Monomachos re-founded the Pandidakterion's [Medieval Greek: Πανδιδακτήριον] mission, complementing the institution's humanities and ecclesial curriculum by adding the departments of law and philosophy in 1046.

Far from Europe's boundary on the Bosphorus River, the Dark Ages fell across Europe. As the 6th century began, it was not uncommon for scrolls and books to be valued solely for their suitability as kindling. Saint Kevin and other Irish monks set for themselves a great and noble quest — not for the Holy Grail — but rescuing what survived of recorded knowledge on the continent. In the candlelit scriptorium at Glendalough and across Ireland, monks diligently copied the length and breadth of what documents remained, even if in fragments. It would not be until the 15th century that Greek manuscripts preserved by these monks once again emerged from monasteries where they had languished in Sicily. Were it not for priests and brothers of the church, human history would be much different.

The fall of Constantinople to Mehmed II in 1453 caused academicians, engineers, artists and priests from what had been the Byzantine Empire to flee to the west for refuge. Their exodus from the east included their knowledge, artistic talents, and perspective, scientific experiments, music, and knowledge of mechanical engineering achievements. These Orthodox Christian migrants and their students reintroduced knowledge to continental Europe that had been lost since the fall of Rome in the 5th century. Greek-speaking Romans and Orthodox church clergy lit the candle to terse the darkness ushering in the Renaissance. From the UK's Cambridge University to Poland's Jagiellonian, and from Germany's University of Greifswald to Spain's University of Salamanca, the fruits of the church's pursuit of knowledge were the intellectual endowment that purchased modern Europe.

Regrettably, events of recent years have seen public confidence in the church and institutions, both public and private, eroded. This has changed Europe. The social cohesion that had once been the result of ecclesial commonality gave way to philosophical debates of 'equality, liberté and fraternity'. Where disputes about the filioque once divided western thought, the concepts of church and state, democracy, capitalism, communism, and atheism pervaded the public space. The chasm of these divisions was then, and continues to be, widest along the lines of political and intellectual adherence to the ideas nurtured by Rome and Geneva in the west and the traditionally Orthodox Christian populations centered on Moscow in the east.

The metropolis of Kyiv was established by His All Holiness Ignatius, Patriarch of Constantinople and Ecumenical Patriarch of the Orthodox church. The Ecumenical Patriarch provided for Kyiv's first hierarchs and priests and assisted in the development of schools, charity hospitals, a university and the construction of churches, most notably Kyiv's Church of Tithes. Volodymyr was inducted into the canon of saints in 1258, and his feast day is celebrated on July 28 each year.[331] The metropolis of Kyiv thrived under the Patriarchate of Constantinople.

While the first known mention of Volodymyr dates to 1058, church historian Ivan Vlasovskyi provides us with contextualized evidence of Volodymyr's embrace of the metropolis of Kyiv under the patronage of the Patriarch of Constantinople and its continuation until substantiated by extant written evidence dating to the reign of Yaroslav 'the Wise' (1019-1054):

> When the historical data, coming out of the fog of ambiguity, become accurate, they tell us about the dependence of our Church in hierarchical management on the Patriarch of Constantinople. Given that such data date back to the time of Prince Yaroslav, son and successor to the princely throne of Volodymyr, it is quite correct, in the absence of other information, we must assume that this dependence of our Church on Constantinople was under Prince Vladimir, i.e., from acceptance by him and our ancestors of the Christian faith from Byzantium.[332]

Those surviving historical sources mention the first metropolitan of Kyiv being appointed by the Ecumenical Patriarch. He was a Greek, Archbishop Theopempt (1037-1048) whose enthronement as metropolitan of Kyiv coincided with the reign of Yaroslav 'the Wise'. The Kyiv Rus' stature within Christendom rose, given its connection to the Patriarchate of Constantinople. When kings scoured the land for suitable brides for their sons and heirs, they looked to Kyiv.

Yaroslav 'the Great's' female progeny married into royal houses that laid the foundation for modern Europe. His daughter Elisiv of Kyiv was betrothed to Harald 'Hardrada', Harald III of Norway. Anastasia of Kyiv married the future Andrew I of Hungary. Then there was his daughter Agatha. She was betrothed to Edward 'the Exile' of the royal family of England and became the mother of Edgar 'the Ætheling' and Saint Margaret of Scotland.

Anna of Kyiv, Yaroslav's favorite daughter, married Henry I of France. Arriving in France, Anna soon discovered she was the only literate person at court. Her temperament, literacy, education, and wisdom developed by the gymnasium in Kyiv, established under the auspices of the orthodox church, were so renown that when her husband, King Henry, lapsed into quarrels with Pope Nicholas II, the pontiff wrote to Queen Anna of Kyiv counseling her to guide her husband, the king, to govern by moderation. "…follow your conscience to right wrongs and intervene against oppressive violence."[333]

---

[331] 15 July by the Old School Calendar.
[332] Власовський, Іван. Нарис історії Української Православної Церкви. Том 1.—C. 35-37.
[333] Philippe Delorme, "Anne de Kiev: épouse de Henri Ier", *Pygmalion*. Paris, 2015.

After her husband's death, Anna of Kyiv served as regent of France throughout her son's minority.

The spiritual, cultural, educational, and unifying influence of the Patriarchate of Constantinople's guidance in the development of the Kyivan Rus', their capital at Kyiv and their nation across Ukraine cannot be underestimated. As Dr. Nadia Nikitenko asserts, and UNESCO accepts, Volodymyr 'the Great' laid the foundations for a grand edifice that would take its name from Constantinople's Hagia Sophia in 1011, just over a decade after the 'Baptism of Kyiv'. Kyiv flourished with Orthodox Christianity being celebrated under the authority of the Patriarchate of Constantinople.

It was to the Patriarchate of Constantinople, not Moscow, for whom the priests offered their patriarchal prayers—Moscow had no patriarch then. The *Laurentian Chronicles* inform us that Saint Michael's golden-domed monastery began to rise in 1108 during the reign of Sviatopolk II of Kyiv. By contrast, the first reference to Moscow doesn't arise until more than a century later, in 1147 where it is described as a mere: "minor town on the western border of the Vladimir-Suzdal Principality."[334]

While Saint Michael's golden-domed cathedral towered above Constantinople, Moscow's skyline was bereft of cultural, religious, or architectural achievements. Moscow's first stone church, the Assumption Cathedral, was not built until 1326.

The story of the restoration of the metropolis of Kyiv to the Ecumenical Patriarch is a long and complicated one. Any recital of the events will undoubtedly invoke criticism for either omissions, inclusions, or characterizations. It suffices, however, to acknowledge that Ukrainians have never been uniformly complacent to have their metropolis subordinated to Moscow. The close and enduring bonds that had arisen from hundreds of years of relations with the Ecumenical Patriarchate and Greek Orthodox polity were quashed by the translation of the metropolis of Kyiv to Moscow following the creation of the Moscow Patriarchate. The matter was complicated by the fact that the Ecumenical Patriarchate never consented to the metropolis of Kyiv being annexed by the Moscow Patriarchate.

According to Konstantin Vetoshnikov, the translation of Kyiv to the Moscow Patriarchate came about after the conquest of Ukraine in 1659: "The transfer of the Kyiv Metropolitanate, according to documents, took

---

[334] The assertion of Moscow's existence in 1147 has become ubiquitous and commonly accepted, seemingly by repetition on Wikipedia and numerous online information sites and articles that repeat it without citation. Despite an exhaustive search, we were unable to find any ancient or authoritative basis for this claim. It can be assumed, therefore, to be an apologist's device used to attempt substantiating a specific version of history and promote a Kyivan Rus' link that serves a geopolitical purpose rather than historical accuracy. Other extant ancient sources specifically contradict this assertion.

place at the request of the Russian monarchs, the Patriarch of Moscow and the Hetman of Ukraine with the consent of the Ottoman State."[335] The treaty with the Hetmanate included the following concerning the supremacy of Moscow over the Ukrainian Church: "and the Metropolitan of Kiev, as well as other spiritual leaders of Little Russia, shall be blessed by him... the Patriarch of Moscow...."[336]

There was no request by Kyiv to be transferred from the Ecumenical Patriarchate to the Moscow Patriarchate. The Ecumenical Patriarchate never recognized, adopted or endorsed the transfer. Canonically, the Kyiv Metropolis remained under the jurisdiction of the Ecumenical Patriarchate in Constantinople.

There was a contemporary protest over the Moscow Patriarchate's assertion of control over Kyiv. The locum tenens of the Moscow Patriarchate ordained Bishop Methodius of Mstislav to serve as locum tenens of the metropolis of Kyiv. The following year, in 1662, the new Moscow Patriarch, Nikon of Moscow, condemned the act because it lacked canonical authority. The Ecumenical Patriarchate did not recognize Bishop Methodius of Mstislav's appointment as metropolitan of Kyiv. The issue remained unsettled.

In 1667, the Moscow Synod elevated the Chernihiv diocese to an archdiocese. Again, this was done without permission or recognition by the Ecumenical Patriarchate. Moscow resolved to ignore the canons of the orthodox church, determined to flout the practice of conciliarity and do as they wish. From the time of its unorthodox inception as a patriarchate, Moscow remained obdurate with regard to Orthodox Christian principles dating back to the First Council of Nicaea in 325.

Through the years, the Moscow Patriarchate shared a difficult relationship with the Ecumenical Patriarchate. Part of it flowed from the conceit that they should be considered the 'Third Rome', given the diminishment of Constantinople in Ottoman Türkiye. Some of it arose from the political demands of tsars, commissars and presidents who were determined that Russia's interests were vested in the supremacy of the ROC. Undoubtedly, the difficulties were made more strained by the precepts of the Holy Rus' that God chose Russia to play a special role in Orthodox Christianity, and the Russian people were ordained to enlighten the world through the

---

[335] Konstantin Vetoshnikov, "La «concession» de la métropole de Kiev au patriarche de Moscou en 1686: Analyse canonique", *Proceeding of the International Congress of Byzantine Studies: Belgrade*, 24 August 2016.

[336] Collection of Chancery Documents, "Complete Collection of Laws of the Russian Empire: First Collection, Vol. I: 1649-1675", *St. Petersburg: In the printing house of the Second Branch of His Own Imperial Majesty's Chancery*, 1830.

ROC. The enduring refusal of the Ecumenical Patriarchate to accede to Russia's claims on the See of the Metropolis of Kyiv always served as a thorn in the side of the Moscow Patriarch.

With Ukraine achieving independence for periods of time throughout the centuries, the desire for the Church of Ukraine to be recognized as autocephalous arose repeatedly. Moscow was not inclined to grant Orthodox Christians in Ukraine their independence. As a last-ditch effort to retain their allegiance, on October 27, 1990, the Ukrainian Orthodox Church (Moscow Patriarchate) was created to replace the Ukrainian Exarchate of the ROC. The move only served to engender division and animus between patriotic Ukrainians and their Moscow master. The matter was made more pressing after Ukraine declared independence on August 24, 1991. The demise of the Soviet Union on December 25, 1991, made the eventuality of an autocephalous Ukrainian Church inevitable.

Russia's illegal invasion and occupation of Donetsk, Luhansk, and Crimea in 2014 made the situation unbearable for patriotic Ukrainian Christians who continued to suffer under the patronage of the Moscow Patriarchate. The very thought of participating in a liturgy where their bishops were required to pray for and commemorate their oppressor, the Patriarch of Moscow, became intolerable.

In response, primates of local orthodox churches gathered at the Phanar in Constantinople on March 9, 2014, "the first Sunday of Lent, the Feast of the Triumph of Orthodoxy" to discuss the state of pan-Orthodox affairs. In attendance and agreeing to the decisions of the primates were:

> The decisions of the Synaxis and the Message were signed by His Holiness Patriarch Bartholomew of Constantinople, His Beatitude Pope and Patriarch Theodoros II of Alexandria and All Africa, His Beatitude Patriarch Theophilos III of the Holy City of Jerusalem and All Palestine, His Holiness Patriarch Kirill of Moscow and All Russia, His Holiness and Beatitude Catholicos-Patriarch Ilia II of All Georgia, His Holiness Patriarch Irinej of Serbia, His Beatitude Patriarch Daniel of Romania, His Holiness Patriarch Neophyte of Bulgaria, His Beatitude Archbishop Chrysostomos II of New Justiniana and All Cyprus, His Beatitude Archbishop Ieronymos of Athens and All Greece, His Beatitude Archbishop Anastasios of Tirana and All Albania, and His Beatitude Metropolitan Sawa of Warsaw and All Poland.[337]

The participants in the meeting made several decisions concerning a convocation of the Holy and Great Council of the Orthodox Church. Despite objections by the ROC and its allies, it was decided: "The Holy and Great

---

[337] ROC—Department for External Church Relations, "Primates of Local Orthodox Churches celebrate Liturgy at the Cathedral of St George in Phanar on the Sunday of Orthodoxy", *ROC website* https://mospat.ru/en/news/51682/ (accessed 21 July 2025), 9 March 2014.

Council of the Orthodox Church will be convened by the Ecumenical Patriarch in Constantinople in 2016, unless something unexpected occurs."[338]

It is interesting to contrast the communique arising from the meeting with the language on the ROC website regarding the event. The communique reads:

> Above all, the Synaxis considered the prevailing situation in the Middle East and recent developments in Ukraine, as well as the ongoing uncertainty about the fate of the bishops, Metropolitan John of Aleppo, and Yuhanna Ibrahim of the Syriac Church, who were kidnapped by unknown persons a very long time ago.[339]

The Russian website version of the meeting wholly avoids any mention of Ukraine. It became the position of the Moscow Patriarchate and the Ukrainian Orthodox Church (Moscow Patriarchate) to deny the existence of the consideration of autocephaly for the Ukrainian Church in official statements.

The combination of the Russian state-ROC juggernaut proved persuasive and damned the meeting to near irrelevance. The first attempt by the ROC to frustrate resolving the Ukrainian Church crisis was to try to delay the meeting and deny that the matter was being considered:

> The Holy Synod, at its meeting on June 13, 2016 (Journal No. 40), having considered the situation that arose in connection with the refusal of a number of Local Orthodox Churches to participate in the Holy and Great Council of the Orthodox Church within the previously established timeframes—June 18-26 of this year—adopted a statement on this topic.
> The statement, which was sent on the same day to His Holiness Patriarch Bartholomew of Constantinople and the Primates of all Local Orthodox Churches, contained, in particular, a call to support the proposal of the Antiochian, Georgian, Serbian and Bulgarian Churches to postpone the dates of the Pan-Orthodox Council.[340]

Following almost two years of preparation, including the development of numerous documents for consideration, discussion, and action, it appeared Russia might choose to boycott the first council held in a millennium.[341] The Reverend Alexander Karloutsos, a member of the organizing committee of the Great and Holy Council, told the Associated Press: "There is no

---

[338] Chief Secretariat of the Holy and Sacred Synod, "Message dated 9 March 2014", *Synaxis of Primates of the Orthodox Church,* 9 March 2014.

[339] Chief Secretariat of the Holy and Sacred Synod, "Communiqué dated 9 March 2014", *Synaxis of Primates of the Orthodox Church,* 9 March 2014.

[340] ROC, Journals of the meeting of the Holy Synod of July 15, 2016, Magazine No. 48, *Holy Synod of the ROC,* 15 July 2016.

[341] The last canonical Pan-Orthodox Council prior to 2016 was the Council of Constantinople, held between 879–880.

mandate to change or postpone and we are going to proceed. They asked for a pre-conciliar meeting on the 17th and we expect to them to be here," he said. "We are the church of love and embrace everyone."[342]

Prior to the delegates' meeting on Crete, the ROC announced it would not attend the Holy and Great Synod. Without Russia's participation and that of Antioch, Bulgaria, and Georgia, the Holy and Great Synod took on the moniker, "The Council That Wasn't." The synod of the Church of Antioch took the extraordinary measure of releasing photos of their official documents showing their delegates had not signed them. In lieu of signatures, the Antiochians hand-wrote their objection to the format. Attempts to responsibly deal with the Ukrainian crisis by canonical norms were rendered useless by the ROC and its allies — not on matters of principle or substance — but by failing to participate whatsoever.[343]

Having defeated any constructive outcome from the meeting, Russia sought to relegate the Holy and Great Council to the dustbin of history. The following month, in July 2016, the synod of the ROC passed a resolution denying the validity of the council's authority for any of the decisions reached in Crete as being binding on pan-orthodox churches, declaring the Holy and Great Council to be simply: "an important event in the history of the synodal process in the Orthodox Church that was begun by the First Pan-Orthodox consultation in Rhodes in 1961.[344]

History records that when Russia and the ROC had the opportunity to promote conciliation and reconciliation in the hopes of stopping division and bloodshed, they instead elected to subordinate the ἔργον τῆς ἐκκλησίας [work of the Church] to the Russkiy Mir aspirations of Putin and the Russian state. The decision of the ROC to absent itself from responsible dialogue and decision-making calls us to consider the words of Saul Alinsky:

> Lest we forget at least an over the shoulder acknowledgment to the very first radical: from all our legends, mythology and history (and who is to know where mythology leaves off and history begins — or which is which), the very first radical known to man who rebelled against the establishment and did it so effectively that he at least won his own kingdom — Lucifer.[345]

---

[342] Associated Press in Moscow, "Russia will not attend historic meeting of world's Orthodox churches", *The Guardian*, 13 June 2016.

[343] Metropolitan Onufriy of the Ukrainian Orthodox Church (Moscow Patriarchate) took his instructions from Moscow and did not attend the Holy and Great Synod despite being invited.

[344] ROC Resolution, Journals of the meeting of the Holy Synod of July 15, 2016, Magazine No. 48, *Holy Synod of the ROC*, 15 July 2016.

[345] Saul Alinskey, "Rules For Radicals: A Pragmatic Primer for Realistic Radicals," *Vintage Books, New York*, 1971.

The ROC, like Lucifer, seemed determined to maintain its kingdom at the expense of Christian unity, peace, conciliation, and humanity. While the ROC may not be responsible for the wanton rape, pillage, torture, murder, and bloodshed in Ukraine today, it must admit its responsibility in failing to engage in dialogue that might have created a climate of peace, understanding, and reconciliation. Their choice to absent themselves from the first council in over a millennium will be cited for centuries as their enduring legacy of evil.

One of the most notable individual absences was that of Metropolitan Onufriy of the Ukrainian Orthodox Church (Moscow Patriarchate). Of all the delegates to the Holy and Great Synod, it was Metropolitan Onufriy who was the greatest stakeholder in the discussions surrounding autocephaly for the Ukrainian Church. His absence was not surprising—he had long been a Moscow apologist. It had not always been so.

Metropolitan Onufriy (born Orest Volodymyrovych Berezovsky) was born in 1944 in Ukraine's Chernivtsi Oblast. He was educated at the Moscow Theological Seminary and joined the monks of the Trinity Lavra, spending some 18 years in Russia. After returning to Ukraine, where he continued monastic life, he was consecrated a bishop by Metropolitan Filaret (Denysenko) on December 9, 1990, at Saint Volodymyr's Cathedral, Kyiv.

In 1992, shortly after the dissolution of the Soviet Union, the then ardent advocate for the Ukrainian Church to be made autocephalous enthusiastically added his name to a petition to Moscow Patriarch Alexy II seeking autocephaly for it. His hopes would be dashed. He should have known better. The proper form to request autocephaly is to petition the Ecumenical Patriarch in Constantinople. It seems, however, that the tsarist and Soviet practice of referring all things to Moscow guided their request for autocephaly. It would be denied. With his dreams of autocephaly dashed by Alexy II, Metropolitan Onufriy returned to Ukraine. Having taken stock of affairs, he gave himself over to the idea that 'might makes right' and abandoned his belief that autocephaly was in Ukraine's interest and part of God's plan for his nation.

In the aftermath of the petition being rejected, Metropolitan Onufriy has long sought to distance himself from the request. His decision to ally with Moscow over his homeland would come to haunt him. When pro-Russian President Yanukovych ordered the massacre of civil society protestors in Maidan Square, followed by Russia's invasion of Ukraine in 2014, Metropolitan Onufriy's fate was cast. He decried the bloodshed and made public prayers for peace. He did not, however, condemn Russia for the invasion. He certainly refrained from taking issue with the Moscow Patriarchate's promotion of the invasion as a necessity to protect Russian lives. By his own opportunistic actions, each proving misjudged, Metropolitan

Onufriy became a traitor to his people. He would later have his citizenship revoked for having hidden the fact that he possessed a Russian passport and citizenship.[346]

Metropolitan Onufriy's absence from the Holy and Great Synod of 2016 was undoubtedly the product of his misjudging the mood in Ukraine and adhering to the instructions of the Moscow Patriarchate in whose Synod he remained. The once vocal advocate for autocephaly had transformed himself into an advocate of the Moscow Patriarchate as a means of leaving open the opportunity for power and advancement. In the aftermath of Russia's aggression, Metropolitan Onufriy walked a tightrope, risking maintaining his balance with Ukrainian Orthodox Christians and his fealty to the Russian state and the Moscow Patriarchate.

Despite his Department of External Affairs projecting the aura of personal piety attaching to him, Metropolitan Onufriy became increasingly viewed by a growing body of Ukrainians suffering under Russia's invasion and occupation forces as a traitor to Ukraine, a Russia lackey. In the end, he was so tied to the Moscow Patriarchate that he had little choice but to obey Patriarch Kirill's instructions that he does not participate in the Holy and Great Synod. By contrast, Metropolitan Onufriy did, however, continue to take part in the Holy Synod of the ROC.[347]

Eventually, a growing number of Orthodox Christians in Ukraine found the situation intolerable. The Ecumenical Patriarch, Bartholomew I, resolved that he had exhausted all conciliarity-driven mechanisms available to him and that he would act in the hopes of providing a path forward for Ukrainians to resolve their conflict, given the ROC's shirking of its responsibilities and its vested interest in maintaining its control over Ukraine for Russian state purposes.

Frustrated with Russia's intransigence, in 2018, the Ecumenical Patriarch was left with no choice but to act. As stated by Metropolitan Ignatius of Demetrias, chairman of the Synodal Committee for Inter-Orthodox and Inter-Christian Relations, during the Extraordinary Session of the Holy Synod of the Church of Greece:

---

[346] Metropolitan Onufriy admitted he possessed a Russian passport and citizenship. He attempted to explain them away as a necessity of the age. He failed to address, however, why he did not disclose his Russian citizenship and passport from Ukrainian authorities when dual citizenship was prohibited then by law. See: Miceál O'Hurley, "An Injury to Religious Freedom in Ukraine?", *European Diplomat*, 4 July 2025.

[347] Wire Report, "Metropolitan Onufriy took part at the Holy Synod of the ROC", *Religious Information Service of Ukraine*, 8 March 2018.

We are dealing with millions of Orthodox faithful, who have historically suffered from policies of either Poland or Russia. Therefore, our focused discussions on the validity of Ordinations and the stance of Bishops must take into account the existence of millions of believers for whom we are responsible.... I think that it is also appropriate to explore the role of the ROC. And I insist on the term "ROC," inasmuch as experience has unfortunately demonstrated that our brothers give priority to the adjective 'Russian' over the adjective 'Orthodox'.... Indeed, not only did the ROC fail to present any solution, but its attitude during the preparatory process for the Holy and Great Council of 2016 was moreover completely negative. As we all know, autocephaly was among the questions discussed during this preparatory process. Thus, in the 1980s, the Ecumenical Patriarchate even appeared to consent to a relativization of its own privileges. Accordingly, adhering to a strict process, the Ecumenical Patriarchate requested pan-Orthodox consensus for the granting of autocephaly.[348]

In 2018, the Ecumenical Patriarch encouraged the factionalized Ukrainian Church, the Ukrainian Orthodox Church (Kyiv Patriarchate) led by Metropolitan Filaret (Denysenko), the Ukrainian Orthodox Church (Moscow Patriarchate) led by Metropolitan Onufriy (Berezovsky), and the UAOC led by Metropolitan Makariy (Maletych) to hold a Unification Council. It was within the gift of the Ecumenical Patriarch to grant a tomos (decree) of autocephaly, but consistent with the principles of conciliarity, the Ukrainians would have to work out their own issues—including selecting a head of the church.

At the time, the Ukrainian Orthodox Church (Moscow Patriarchate) had 52 dioceses and 12,000 parishes. The Ukrainian Orthodox Church-Kyiv Patriarchate claimed 35 dioceses and 5000 parishes. The Ukrainian Autocephalous Orthodox Church boasted having 14 dioceses and 1000 parishes.[349]

Metropolitan Onufriy, now irrevocably planted in the ROC camp, and with everything to lose having sided with Ukraine's invaders, vehemently opposed the Unification Council. He publicly railed against autocephaly and attacked the Ecumenical Patriarch for lacking the authority to act in Ukraine. He would have his comeuppance. The website of the Ecumenical Patriarchate in Constantinople exhibited two documents in response to these criticisms. The first was a copy of the resolution of the Local Council of the Ukrainian Orthodox Church (Moscow Patriarchate) of 1–3

---

[348] Panagiotis Georgakopoulos (Metropolitan Ignatius of Demetrias), "Ukrainian Autocephaly and Responsibility toward the Faithful", *Public Orthodoxy*, 23 October 2019.

[349] Інформаційні матеріали, підготовлені до чергового засідання постійно діючого Круглого столу "Релігія і влада в Україні: проблеми взаємовідносин", *Київ*, 26 квітня 2018р., за сприяння Представництва Фонду Конрада Аденауера в Україні.

November 1991 regarding the need for autocephaly for the Ukrainian Church in 1991. The second was the letter personally signed by Metropolitan Onufriy on January 22, 1992, pleading with the Moscow Patriarch not to delay in delivering autocephaly for the Ukrainian Church.[350] The documents were then shared on Facebook by Archbishop Eustratius (Zorya),[351] an advocate for the Ukraine Church autocephaly:

> These documents confirm that the UOC, including the episcopate, in 199-1992 officially raised the issue of the need for the UOC to be autocephalous and unanimously supported this until Moscow's actions brought division into the UOC.[352]

Metropolitan Onufriy was exposed as a hypocrite. It was revealed to the Ukrainian people and the world that the Ukrainian Orthodox Church (Moscow Patriarchate) had been prioritizing its relationship with Russia over those of Ukrainian Orthodox Christians. It was the beginning of the end for them.

The Ecumenical Patriarchate cleared the way for the restoration of the Ukrainian Church. On October 11, 2018, the Holy Synod of the Ecumenical Patriarchate declared that the 11th-century metropolis of Kyiv, which the Moscow Patriarchate attempted to annex in the 17th century, would be returned to the jurisdiction of Constantinople. In effect, Constantinople ended its toleration of the uncanonical usurpation by the ROC. The Orthodox Church of Ukraine, headed by the Metropolis of Kyiv and All Ukraine, would come into being. For the moment, it would still not enjoy autocephaly.

To ensure the council was canonically convened, those bishops whom the ROC had excommunicated for seeking an autocephalous Ukrainian Church were restored. The excommunication of two Ukrainian Orthodox leaders, Patriarch Filaret and Metropolitan Makariy, was lifted by the synod, restoring them to rank, but not office.[353] The ROC and the Ukrainian Orthodox Church (Moscow Patriarchate), which excommunicated the two hierarchs for seeking autocephaly, could no longer claim the actors were non-canonical in capacity or lacked authority within Orthodox Christian norms. The stage was set despite continued attempts by the ROC

---

[350] Staff Article, "The Ecumenical Patriarchate has published documents in support of Ukrainian autocephaly", *Gazetta. UA*, 14 September 2018.
[351] Archbishop Eustratius (Ivan Volodymyrovych Zorya) is now Metropolitan Eustratius of Bila Tserkva, Orthodox Church of Ukraine (Ecumenical Patriarchate).
[352] Євстратій Зоря, "Important: On the official website of the Ecumenical Patriarchate....", *Facebook: Post*, 14 September 2018.
[353] Staff Writers, "Ukrainian church wins independence battle", *Deutsche Welle (DW)*, 11 October 2018.

and Ukrainian Orthodox Church (Moscow Patriarchate) to frustrate progress toward Christian unity and peace in Ukraine.

In response to developments in Constantinople, Moscow Patriarchate spokesperson Igor Yakmichuk decried the development, claiming the Holy Synod of the ROC would meet to decide its next steps: "The response will be very decisive and harsh, it will be adequate to the situation that had developed."[354]

The ROC wasted no time in releasing its long response [excerpts]:

> With profound regret and sorrow the Holy Synod the ROC learned about the statement made by the Holy Synod of the Orthodox Church of Constantinople concerning the appointment of its two "exarchs" to Kiev. This decision was taken without an agreement with the Primate of the ROC and His Beatitude Metropolitan Onufry of Kiev and All Ukraine—the only canonical head of the Orthodox Church in Ukraine. It constitutes a flagrant violation of the ecclesiastical law and an intervention of one Local Church in the territory of the other. Moreover, the Patriarchate of Constantinople presents the appointment of the "exarchs" as a stage in the implementation of a plan aimed at granting "autocephaly" to Ukraine. This process, according to the statements of the Patriarchate of Constantinople, is irreversible and will be carried through…
> The reunification of the Kiev Metropolia with the Russian Church took place in 1686. It was done in a form of the Act signed by Patriarch Dionysius IV of Constantinople and members of his Synod…
> Until the 20th century none of the Local Orthodox Churches, including the Church of Constantinople, had disputed the jurisdiction of the Russian Church over the Kiev Metropolia. The first attempt to dispute this jurisdiction was made when the Patriarchate of Constantinople granted the autocephaly to the Polish Orthodox Church which at the time had an autonomous status within the ROC. The Tomos of the Autocephaly of the Polish Church, granted by the Patriarchate of Constantinople in 1924 and unrecognized by the Russian Church, groundlessly states: "The original secession from our Throne of the Kiev Metropolia and its dependent Orthodox Churches of Lithuania and Poland, and their joining the Holy Church of Moscow did not at all occur in accordance with the canonical regulations…."
> In the event that the Patriarchate of Constantinople will continue to carry out its uncanonical activities in the territory of the Ukrainian Orthodox Church, <u>we will be compelled to completely break off the Eucharistic communion with the Patriarchate of Constantinople</u>. All the responsibility for the tragic consequences of this division will lie personally with Patriarch Bartholomew of Constantinople and the hierarchs supporting him."[355] [emphasis added]

---

[354] Staff Writer, "ROC official vows 'firm and tough' response to Constantinople's move", *TASS*, 12 October 2018.

[355] The ROC Department for External Church Relations, "Statement of the Holy Synod of the ROC concerning the uncanonical intervention of the Patriarchate

The ROC's complaints of Constantinople acting without prior "agreement" and that it "constitutes a flagrant violation of the ecclesiastical law and an intervention" must be considered sui servientes. Russia did not reach any prior agreement when it usurped administration over the metropolis of Kyiv. Complaining that the Ecumenical Patriarch had ended its tolerance of the illicit act was nothing but an act of gross hypocrisy.

Given the very foundations of the ROC, with it declaring itself autocephalous, elevating a Metropolitan of Moscow without consultation or permission from the Ecumenical Patriarch in 1448 or coercing Ecumenical Patriarch Jeremias II to create the Moscow Patriarchate without allowing him conciliatory consultation with other hierarchs in 1589, Moscow had unclean hands. It has always been understood that one cannot benefit from one's own bad acts—*ex turpi causa non oritur action* [action does not arise from a dishonorable cause].

There was also the issue of the bishops whom the Moscow Patriarchate had deposed and excommunicated due to their agitation for an autocephalous Ukrainian Church. The ROC and the Ukrainian Orthodox Church (Moscow Patriarchate) referred to them in terms as wide-ranging as "apostates" to "self-ordained" and "non-ordained". Patriarch Kirill and Metropolitan Onufriy and those who asserted such claims knew them to be false.

There had been ample examples and serious consideration of like issues in numerous instances before both ancient and recent. In 246, Saint Cyprian of Carthage had adopted a strict posture regarding the readmission of heretics and schismatic clergy and bishops known as Lapsi, refusing to recognize their baptisms and ordinations. His decision was not unreasonable, though it was flawed. Saint Cyprian argued *Ecclesiam nulla salus*, [divine grace does not exist outside of the Church.][356] The church in council was not so absolute.

According to a masterful examination of the issues related to ordinations, canonicity, and the Ukrainian Church, Archimandrite Gregory Fragkakis writes:

---

of Constantinople in the canonical territory of the ROC" *Moscow Patriarchate: Moscow*, 14 September 2018.

[356] Saint Cyprian of Carthage, translated by John Henry Parker, "Epistle LXXIII, anno domini 256", *Oxford edition*, 1844.

In 691, the Quinisext (Fifth-Sixth) Council (Canon II) confirmed the Carthaginian canon but clarified that it applied only to the churches of North Africa. A milder position is seen in the 12th Apostolic Canon, which rejects the baptisms and ordinations of heretics but remains silent on schismatics.[357]

The outcry of non-canonical ordinations arising from the Moscow Patriarchate and their allies had nothing to do with church canons. The ROC had itself resolved the issue of the validity of ordinations in 1946 during the controversial reunification of the Ukrainian Greek Catholic (Uniate) clergy as Russian Orthodox clergy. At the time, Moscow Patriarch Alexy I himself recognized the validity of ordinations, even those carried out by Uniate clergy:

> The violation of this canon, namely re-ordination of Uniate priests along with the prior granting of permission to marry, would give the Catholic Church the opportunity to disparage the act of reception of the Greek-Catholic clergy and would justify this reception as arising from political, not ecclesiastical, motives. Furthermore, it would be uncanonical, since the validity of the ordinations of priests and bishops in the Catholic Church is recognized; re-ordaining unmarried priests who are being received for the satisfaction of the flesh would be improper.[358]

Certainly, if the ROC were to have accepted ordinations from Catholics (whom they deemed valid), they would be aware that they could not deny the validity of their own ordination of clergy and bishops. The Moscow Patriarch, Metropolitan Onufriy and their supporters, who claimed that ordinations by these bishops could not be canonical they again failed to adhere to orthodox church teachings and traditions:

> The non-reordination by the Seventh Council is also recognized by Archimandrite Hieronymus Kotsonis (1957):—...there is also the decision of the Seventh Ecumenical Council, which accepted the validity of the priesthood of those ordained by the Iconoclasts...
> If those from heresy (Iconoclasm was a heresy, not a schism) and ordained by condemned Iconoclasts are accepted into the Church without reordination, this applies even more to those ordained by schismatics or deposed bishops. It is worth noting that outside the Church there is no fullness of Grace; thus, the sacraments of the above are valid but incomplete. Upon the return of the misguided to the fold of Truth, God's Grace completes the deficiencies, and all is restored. The Apostolic Succession is not harmed.[359]

---

[357] Gregory (Emmanuel) Fragkakis, "The Justice of Grace in the Great Church of Christ: A Contribution to the Ecclesiastical Issue of Ordinations in Ukraine", *Leimon Publications, Athens*, 2023.

[358] Vladimir Latinovic and Anastacia K. Wooden, editors, "Stolen Churches or Bridges to Orthodoxy? Volume 2: Ecumenical and Practical Perspectives on the Orthodox and Eastern Catholic Dialogue", *Palgrave Macmillan, London*, 2021.

[359] Fragkakis, *ibid*.

Given the orthodox church canons and historical tradition of treating excommunication as a temporary measure meant to encourage a person to return to the fullness of communion with the orthodox church, the issue could not be one of excommunication. Nor could the Moscow Patriarch and Metropolitan Onufriy's objections to returning the clergy they excommunicated for seeking Ukrainian Church autocephaly be because they were "self-ordained" or "non-ordained." Their ordination of bishops was valid. As for the clergy they ordained, the Orthodox Christian tradition is that they are valid but "incomplete." The reconciliation of such persons with the canonical church renders the sacrament of ordination and all other deficiencies complete with no harm being done to the apostolic succession.[360] It has been the tradition of the orthodox church to embrace the axiom, "The priesthood is given by God; deposition is a human act."

The decision over whether to accept the reconciliation of excommunicated bishops and clergy remained, however, a matter of conciliarity. The tradition within orthodoxy of not intruding into the internal administration of another episcopal see generally prohibits one bishop from intruding into the affairs of another. In the church's infinite wisdom and mercy, however, an appeal to the patriarchal throne has always been recognized as a right of last resort.

Metropolitan Macarius (Maletych) was an example of such a bishop whose canonicity was in question, who desired to reconcile with the canonical church. Metropolitan Macarius had left the Ukrainian Orthodox Church (Moscow Patriarchate) only to be excommunicated by the Moscow Patriarchate for joining the UAOC (then considered non-canonical). When he, like other bishops and clergy, appealed to the Ecumenical Patriarch for reinstatement, it created a concern due to the principles not only of theology and canonicity, but also the role of the Ecumenical Patriarchate in matters of conciliation.

The matter concerning the reconciliation and readmission of deposed and excommunicated bishops and clergy weighed heavily upon Ecumenical Patriarch Bartholomew I and the Holy and Sacred Synod. Contrary to Russian Patriarchate propaganda, the matter was not predetermined as a matter of Russophobic action. Both the Ecumenical Patriarch and the entire Holy and Sacred Synod took the matter seriously.

Metropolitan Macarius's appeal to the patriarchal throne to be reinstated would guide decisions over the canonicity of bishops who could serve in the Unification Council or in the Orthodox Church of Ukraine (Ecumenical Patriarchate) that would be canonically recognized thereafter.

---

[360] *See* proceedings and judgments of the Seventh Ecumenical Council regarding the readmission of iconoclasts without the necessity of reordination.

Metropolitan Demitrius (Yerima), sometimes referred to as "Patriarch Demitrius" owing to his leadership of the UAOC, wrote to Ecumenical Patriarch Bartholomew I, urging him to allow Metropolitan Macarius to be reconciled and readmitted to the episcopal state:

> The Most Holy Throne of Constantinople has always shown understanding towards the enslaved Orthodox nations. The Ukrainians under Polish rule received from the Most Holy Throne the Tomos of Autocephaly in 1924. The Most Holy Throne of Constantinople also acted compassionately towards the Churches of those Ukrainians who were forced to emigrate to the West, to Germany, England, France, Canada, and both Americas, considering them canonical. For this reason, we now beseech you to hear our voice, to receive a delegation of our Bishops, to support us in becoming equal to other Christian nations, and to grant to our ecclesiastical hierarchy some opportunity for justification....[361]

The appeal was persuasive, but not dispositive. The Ecumenical Patriarch and the Holy and Sacred Synod were determined to consider the matter fully.

Tradition, the canons and history and the canons were to guide the decision.

> The Seventh Ecumenical Council (787), concerning bishops coming from the heresy of the Iconoclasts and who had been ordained by heretics, when the question arose whether they should be accepted with their rank, after a long investigation of many past examples and evidence from patristic and conciliar practice, accepted them with joy and restored them to their episcopal sees, granting only letters condemning the heresy. 'For ordination comes from God,' as the council declared through the head, Patriarch Tarasius, and 'because all the fathers agree, and there is no contradiction among them; only those who do not understand the economy and its purposes oppose them.' In the entire discussion, no objection was raised regarding someone ordained by a deposed bishop...[362]

The recent past also informed the decision, considering the reconciliation and restoration of bishops and clergy for justice, peace, and unity. Gregorios, Metropolitan of Chios and later Heraclea and Raidestos, provided the patriarchal throne and Holy and Sacred Synod with a richly resourced work, *Treatise on the Canonical Jurisdiction of the Ecumenical Patriarchal Throne over the Orthodox Churches in Bulgaria*. As noted by Archimandrite Fragkakis, none of the local churches objected to either the basis for granting the tomos of autocephaly or the jurisdiction of the patriarchal throne to do so.

---

[361] Fragkakis, *ibid*.
[362] Βασιλειος, Αρχιεπίσκοπος Σμύρνης, "Πραγματεια περί του κύρους της χειροτονίας κληρικών", [χ.ε.],1887.

A not dissimilar situation arose in the Church of Albania between 1927–1937. The canonicity of the ordinations of bishops and clergy and their role in the autocephaly issue arose. Again, as a matter of justice and economy, the Ecumenical Patriarch and the Holy and Sacred Synod embraced the "tradition of the Fathers" to heal the wounds of schism, reconcile the anathematized and provide pastoral care to the people in care of their souls reminiscent of the parable of the Prodigal Son[363]

> After all these events, and although the main instigator of the non-canonical acts had received ordination from hierarchs of another Church, and although everything had occurred entirely non-canonically, the Church of Constantinople, faithful to the tradition of the Fathers, in order to heal a great schism and to build up souls, forgave the sinners and recognized their ordinations.[364]

The Ecumenical Patriarch and the Holy and Sacred Synod were recognized in each of these and many other instances as having the authority to issue a tomos of autocephaly and act to reconcile and restore bishops and clergy to canonical status. Such information was available to the ROC, the Ukrainian Orthodox Church (Moscow Patriarchate) and others who claimed otherwise. Protests and objections and the eventual refusal by some within Orthodox Christianity to withhold recognition of the Orthodox Church of Ukraine (Ecumenical Patriarchate) on these grounds or in claiming the Ecumenical Patriarch and the Holy and Sacred Synod lacked the authority to grant the tomos of autocephaly to Ukraine were objecting on political, not theological or ecclesiastical grounds. Their injury to the unity of the Orthodox Christian church continues to mar Christ's prayer for Church unity.

The objectors to any reconciliation and restoration of bishops and clergy anathemized by the ROC and/or the Ukrainian Orthodox Church (Moscow Patriarchate) can only, therefore, be understood in the context of desiring to exclude them from participating in any Ukrainian Unity Council. Generally raising objections, weak, misunderstood, and misdirected as they were, additionally suited the Moscow Patriarchate's goal of undermining the credibility of the Ukrainian Unity Council and any tomos of autocephaly that the Ecumenical Patriarch might grant to the Ukrainian Church.

Beyond Metropolitan Macarius, great focus was placed on Metropolitan Philaret (born Mykhailo Antonovych Denysenko). The Ecumenical Patriarch and the Holy and Sacred Synod decided to restore Metropolitan Philaret, who had broken with the Moscow Patriarchate over the issue of

---

[363] *c.f.*, Luke 15:11–32.
[364] Great and Holy Synod, "Orthodoxia: Journal of the Ecumenical Patriarchate in Istanbul", *Ecumenical Patriarchate, Phenar,* 1929.

Ukraine's dignity and pleas for the autocephaly of the Ukrainian Church. Again, Archimandrite Fragkakis's opus on the Ukrainian Church ordination issues is instructive concerning the Ecumenical Patriarch's authority to restore clergy on appeal:

> The recent decision of the Ecumenical Patriarchate to restore Philaret is considered by some as inconsistent. However, this is not true, because the Patriarchate of Constantinople had, in principle, to accept the decision imposed by one of the local Churches upon one of its clergy (see, for example, Rules 32 of the Holy Apostles, Rule 5 of the First Ecumenical Council, Rule 6 of the Church in Antioch). Examination of the matter, whenever submitted, is a serious issue and differs from accepting the punishment. It requires reflection, study, and analysis of the parameters.
> Thus, the initial acceptance of a synodal decision does not exclude submission, acceptance, examination, or judgment of a case by the punished cleric on one hand, and by the Ecumenical Throne on the other.[365]

The patriarchal throne and the Holy and Sacred Synod's right of entitlement to examine such issues proved not only just and wise but were firmly rooted in the tradition of the orthodox church since at least the Seventh Council of Nicaea in 787.

Despite the ROC unilaterally breaking communion with the Ecumenical Patriarchate, on December 15, 2018, the Unification Council met at Kyiv's Saint Sophia Cathedral. The council was presided over by the Metropolitan of the Ecumenical Throne in Constantinople, Metropolitan Adamakis (born Emmanuel Adamakis). All bishops of the Ukrainian Orthodox Church (Kyiv Patriarchate) and the UAOC attended. Metropolitan Onufriy remained aloof, instead sending two bishops, but only to observe.[366]

The Orthodox Church of Ukraine was formed and would be autocephalous.[367] The bishops and clergy who appealed to the patriarchal throne for reinstatement had their petitions granted and participated in the proceedings on a canonical basis. In a demonstration of unity, the council elected, on the second ballot, the only candidate put forward by the Ukrainian Orthodox Church (Kyiv patriarchate) — Archbishop Epiphany (born Serhii Petrovych Dumenko).

His Beatitude Archbishop Epiphany, Metropolitan of Kyiv and all Ukraine, would lead the newly formed church into an uncertain, but unified epoch. Unified, that is, except for the Ukrainian Orthodox Church (Moscow Patriarchate), which rejected the Ecumenical Patriarch's call for

---

[365] Fragkakis, *ibid*.
[366] Штатний автор "Православная церковь Украины будет автокефальной — устав (полный текст документа)", *РБК-Україна*, 15 грудня 2018.
[367] Tadeusz A. Olszański, "Historic unification of Ukrainian Orthodox Church", *Ośrodek Studiów Wschodnich (Centre for Eastern Studies)*, 17 December 2018.

Christian unity and remained obdurate in its attachment to the Patriarch of Moscow.

The response was expectedly hostile. The Patriarch of Moscow claimed the Orthodox Church of Ukraine to be both non-canonical and heretical. He made good on the earlier threat of Moscow Patriarchate spokesperson Igor Yakmichuk, insinuating bloodshed would follow:

> The decision of the Patriarchate of Constantinople, with active participation of the Ukrainian government, to grant autocephaly to a new church structure is another political way to divide the peoples of Russia and Ukraine, which can lead to violence and bloodshed.[368]

As the pope once sent Jesuits to the shores of England in an attempt to assassinate the Tudor queen, the Patriarch of Moscow today employs his priests at home and abroad to do the Russian state's bidding. When Putin began to vest in himself the traditional powers of an autocrat, the situation required the Patriarch of Moscow to either stand in opposition to preserve the newly found sense of church autonomy or submit to making the governance of the Moscow Patriarchate co-align with his political master. The rapacious appetite for wealth and power, accompanied by assurances of tenure, Alexy II, Patriarch of Moscow, Supreme Leader of the ROC, submitted as a willing and loyal servant of Putin and the Kremlin.

Alexy had always been open to corruption in exchange for advancement. On February 28, 1958, only days after his 29th birthday, Alexy was given the code name "Drozdov" by the KGB. Within a couple of years, Alexy was elevated from the lower classes of priest to ordination as the Russian Orthodox Bishop of the Diocese of Tallinn and Estonia. Alexy would later deny he was a KGB asset. The denial was without merit.

According to Konstantin Kharchev, former chairman of the Soviet Council for Religious Affairs: "Not a single candidate for the office of bishop or any other high-ranking office, much less a member of Holy Synod, went through without confirmation by the Central Committee of the CPSU and the KGB."[369] The Soviets had their man in Alexy, and he repaid them in kind, immediately. Alexy suppressed rancorous monks who were opposed to communist organ oversight. In return, he was placed in charge of the all-important Pension Committee of the Moscow Patriarchate, where he made or unmade clergy by deciding their security in retirement.

---

[368] DECR Communication Service, "First Hierarch of Russian Church Outside of Russia: Constantinople's actions in Ukraine can lead to bloodshed", *Moscow Patriarchate: Moscow*, 18 December 2018.

[369] Yevgenia Albats and Catherine A. Fitzpatrick, "The State Within a State: The KGB and Its Hold on Russia—Past, Present, and Future", *Farrar, Straus and Giroux*, 1999.

So deft had Alexy become at politics that he was called upon by his KGB master Viktor Mikhailovich Chebrikov to help plan celebrations of the millennial anniversary of the conversion of the Kyivan Rus' by Saint Volodomyr. To be certain, the Communist Party and the KGB were not very enthusiastic about celebrating a religious event. However, times were hard. In 1988, the Soviet Union was facing increasing agitation for dissolution by its constituent states that felt the time was right to once again be free from the Kremlin's control. Finance Minister Boris Gostev reigned over an economy on the verge of collapse. The then eight-year-old invasion of Afghanistan was proving an unmitigated disaster with a corollary rise in discontent matching its casualty counts at the hands of the Mujahadeen.

Chebrikov and Alexey devised a plan to combine the secular, atheistic hardline communists and Russian Orthodox faithful based on being inheritors of a millennium of Russian history. By integrating divergent interests of secularists and the faithful across the Soviet Union through elaborate State-sponsored celebrations, the church and the KGB hoped to pull off a masterstroke of manipulation. Alexy and Chebrikov were assisted in their task by a young film student turned novice monk, Tikhon Shevkunov, who had recently joined the Moscow Patriarchate's publishing department. Later, as Archimandrite Tikhon, he would play a pivotal role as éminence grise to Putin, a role he continues to play as Metropolitan Vicar of the Moscow Eparchy, a position he owes to his special relationship with the Patriarchs of Moscow he has served, as well as his personal relationship with Putin.

In Kyiv, where freedom had always remained at the heart of Ukrainian identity despite being forcibly dragged into the Soviet Union 66 years earlier, KGB asset "Drozdov" convinced Chebrikov to have a local Communist Party apparatchik return ownership of the venerable Kyiv Pechersk-Lavra caves and monastic buildings to the church. The unexpected and startling move was well received by the Ukrainians, who were temporarily placated by the promise of change. It made the Moscow Patriarchate, then the canonical hierarch of the orthodox church in Ukraine, more appealing for having the appearance of national interests. Little did the faithful know that instead of liberating the Pechersk-Lavra from the communists, the exercise orchestrated by Alexy, Chebrikov and Father Tikhon was simply the trickery of accounting, transferring the asset from the Communist Party to the ROC, which itself was a virtual state, if not arguably a Communist Party asset.

Alexy was no fool, and he was already positioning the Moscow Patriarchate to become the intellectual and spiritual successor to the Communist Party in a Soviet Union that would barely survive for another three years. With the assistance of Father Tikhon, he quickly realized the church could be a player in shaping post-Soviet society through its own brand of propaganda. In distant Germany, Colonel Putin, an obscure KGB agent, was taking notes.

On May 3, 1990, Pimen I died. The Patriarchal See of Moscow and all the Rus' became vacant. To no one's surprise, Alexy was elected to replace him. In the 18 months he served as Patriarch of Moscow before the dissolution of the Soviet Union, Alexy had proven himself indefatigable in his efforts to cultivate close bonds with those clergy unquestionably loyal to the Moscow Patriarchate. From Kyiv to Kamchatka, Alexy fostered relationships with those who would become personally loyal to him. As patriarch in the post-Soviet sphere of nations, Alexy required that the clergy pledge their loyalty to him and demonstrated it in a like manner as they had shown their submission to the KGB and Soviet Union.

First on Alexy's agenda were new appointments designed to put 'yes men' in key positions while removing dissent. As patriarch, Alexy compelled the pension committee to revise pension award decisions he had himself made to reward those who now pledged their fealty to him. Conversely, those who opposed him saw their pensions diminished or terminated altogether. With a government in chaos, Alexy seemed driven to ensure there was no ambiguity as to who was now vested with authority as the dominant figure in social and religious affairs throughout the Russian Federation.

At 61 years of age, Alexy was abounding with energy, appearing everywhere and anywhere; he felt he needed to enhance his influence or assert the position of the Moscow Patriarchate. While enhancing his profile at the expense of the deeply troubled State Alexy nonetheless kept his KGB masters fully informed of all he knew, or at least what he wanted them to know.

When hardliners from the Central Committee attempted a coup d'état on August 4, 1991, an event timed to coincide with Mikhail Gorbachev's planned holiday in Foros, Crimea, Alexy started the day by biding his time. The still neophyte Patriarch of Moscow was at pains to neither offend his KGB masters nor ingratiate himself with the more liberal members of the Central Committee so vociferously steadfast in their support for Gorbachev's return. His decision to tarry before picking sides was not the product of inexperience or indecisiveness. Alexy was already too shrewd for that.

In any event, when informed of the coup, Alexy reportedly showed no emotion or surprise. The Soviet archives later showed the KGB had been planning to depose Gorbachev since 1990. As a Patriarch of Moscow and a provenly reliable KGB asset, it is unlikely that Alexy was unaware of the plotters' planning. Time, wisdom, and experience compelled Alexy to wait and see which way the wind blew before declaring his allegiance. After all, the church had not survived for two millennia by electing easily agitated bishops.

Late on the first day of the coup on August 19, 1991, Alexander Rutskoy, a Ukrainian by birth and a pilot distinguished by 428 combat missions over Afghanistan that saw him declared 'Hero of the Soviet Union', called on the patriarch. That Alexy took the meeting, knowing he was himself watched by the KGB, indicated he had already made up his mind as to where he would stake his flag. After Rutskoy asserted the strength of the numbers of high-ranking officials in opposition to the coup, Alexy was assured, yet still reticent to signify his position.

When news was broadcast that an Interfax poll showed 71% of Leningrad residents feared the return of repression, Alexy was confident enough of the eventual outcome to declare his support for Yeltsin. With the patriarch, the clergy and the Orthodox Christian faithful on side, the tide was turned. The last gamble by the KGB and communist hardliners to save the Soviet Union had been a bust. On the evening of August 22, Gorbachev arrived at Moscow's Vnukovo Airport dressed casually in a knit sweater. In a befuddling move, he traveled not to the Russian White House to reassert power but went directly to his dacha for rest. On August 23, Yeltsin welcomed Gorbachev back with personal applause.

Coup leader Gennady Yanayev was arrested shortly thereafter. His associate, Boris Pugo and his wife promptly committed suicide. Within another 48 hours, the other leading plotters, Pavlov, Starodubtsev, Baklanov, Boldin, and Shenin, would all be arrested. People wasted no time gathering outside KGB Headquarters on Lubyanka Square to topple the statue of the despised founder of the KGB, Felix Dzerzhinsky. A return to repression was now impossible.

Limited democratization, Perestroika, and Glasnost had not worked. In a few short days after the coup, Azerbaijan, Kyrgyzstan, and Moldova individually declared independence. Next, the Baltics asserted their sovereignty with Estonia, then Latvia and Lithuania each opting for independence. The floodgates were now wide open. Ukraine, Georgia, and other republics declared independence. On December 26, reality set in — the Soviet Union ceased to exist. The red flag emblazoned with the sickle and hammer was lowered from over the Kremlin for the last time, and a Russian tri-color flag was raised. It was not only the end of the Soviet Union, but it was also the end of an era. The Soviet Union and the KGB were no more. Democracy and religious freedom were the immediate winners. Patriarch Alexy and the ROC were left standing, possessing possibly the only authority and credibility still existing among the Russian people. While Alexy and the ROC's support for Yeltsin during the coup did not alone prove decisive in delivering Russia from communist hardliners, their importance cannot be diminished. By siding with Yeltsin, Alexy secured the ROC's central role as a pivotal and cohesive agent in the newly established Russian Federation.

With the collapse of the KGB, Putin was forced to leave Berlin. He resigned from the KGB but returned to St. Petersburg, where he remained in the reserves. He found his return humiliating. As if to rub his face in his reversal of fortunes, his beloved Leningrad even reverted to its pre-Bolshevik name, St. Petersburg. The old order was gone, and with it all the privileges Putin enjoyed as a KGB officer, functionary though he was. With work scarce and money even more so, Putin enrolled in a doctoral program at Leningrad State University (now St. Petersburg State University). While he labored on his doctoral dissertation, Putin toiled away as a taxi driver so he could feed himself. His faculty did, however, introduce him to Professor and Head of the Department of Common Law in Socialist Economics, Anatoly Sobchak. Sobchak would change Putin's life for the better.

The Russian state's and the orthodox church's threat to Europe does not rise and fall with its war on Ukraine. The traditional Russian sense of superiority that began with Catherine imposing a Russky Mir to build a Russian Empire and later saw Russian Bolsheviks subvert neighboring states beginning in 1917 did not come to an end on December 26, 1991, when the Kremlin last lowered the Soviet flag. The Russian Federation claims to be the successor state to the Soviet Union. Unsurprisingly, today's Russia Federation operates in much the same way as did the Soviet Union. Despite claims of democracy, Putin asserts the same unquestioned authoritarian power traditionally exercised by his Kremlin predecessors, be they tsars or premiers. The institutions of power are often exercised from the same locales as they had in recent history, be it Putin sitting in the throne room of the Kremlin as did Tsar Nicholas II Alexandrovich and the FSB operating from the same edifice in Lubyanka Square, like the KGB.

What has changed is not the ideology of extending Russian influence wherever "anyone speaks Russian or thinks in Russian," as Putin is fond of stating, but how the Russian state seeks to transform its neighbors. Putin believes it is necessary to transform those who have operated under Russian influence since 1991 into actual Russian control. A combination of muscular diplomacy, use of force, threat of nuclear holocaust, soft diplomacy, and cultural cultivation by the ROC has proven to be lethal, if not always effective, instruments in the Russian toolbox.

All former Soviet states and Warsaw Pact countries have voiced concern over Moscow's intentions to subvert their hard-won independence. This extends even to pro-Russian governments in Ljubljana or Bucharest. As late as March 21, 2024, Slovenia was forced to expel a Russian diplomat for what it called "activities incompatible with the diplomatic status". Viktor Orban, the reliably Kremlin-friendly prime minister of Hungary who has repeatedly claimed the west has nothing to fear from Russia, hedges his bets. After declaring on December 21, 2023, "[Hungary] looks beyond its borders with only one thought: the most important thing is that

Hungary should not share a border with Russia,"[370] Orban has stepped up his cooperation with NATO and agreed to abandon any efforts to block European Union aid for Ukraine further. He has remained resolute, however, on blocking Ukraine's entrance into either the EU or NATO, at least for the moment.

Instances of Russian espionage across Europe, by individuals, security service agents and even diplomats, are nothing new. Russia has been a bad actor for hundreds of years. What is new, however, is the extent to which European intelligence and policing services have exposed the role and activities undertaken by clergy and monks of the ROC in spy activities from the Baltic to the Mediterranean.

Europe's Wolves in Sheep's Clothing: The ROC and the Threat to European Security seeks to explore that intersection of Russian State activity with the Orthodox faith in Russia and how they have been used to undermine democracy, state security, church and interfaith relations across Europe. It is not an attack upon Orthodox Christianity, far from it. It is a warning of how the corruption of orthodoxy at the hands of the Moscow Patriarchate has injured communion within Orthodox Christianity, led the faithful astray and subordinated the church to the whims and will of Putin and the Russian state. This work provides not only insight into how the situation evolved, such that the church became a willing tool of Putin's political arsenal, but it has also collaborated with Russian state security services to engage in espionage all across Europe while simultaneously claiming religious persecution when exposed or caught.

Knowledge of these activities is insufficient to safeguard Europe, given the extent of the ROC's deep presence across Europe and further abroad. Western democracies must resolve that it is possible to oppose the ROC's state-related propaganda and espionage activities while preserving the inalienable right of religious freedom. This will require real courage to confront the evil—the genuine privation of due good—that reigns in the ROC under Patriarch Kirill.

Russian Orthodox clergy within Russia proper, throughout the Soviet Union, and by extension the ROC abroad were critical to Moscow's designs. Inserting spies and agents abroad could often prove tricky; sending Russian Orthodox clergy abroad extended the reach of the state that required their obedience, despite knowing that the Moscow Patriarchate was instrumental in placing clergy in "peace movements" from the late 1950s onward, even placing a young clergyman operating under the code name "Mikhailov" in the upper echelons of the WCC in Geneva. In the post-Soviet era, researchers exposed 'Mikhailov' as being none other than

---

[370] Staff writer, "Hungary does not want to share border with Russia—Orban", *TASS*, 21 December 2023.

one Vladimir Mikhailovich Gundyayev, better known today by his ecclesiastic name, Kirill—Patriarch of Moscow and all Rus'.

For just over two decades, a period coinciding with the elevation of Putin to the Russian presidency, the ROC has become ever more enmeshed in Wilson's aptly described 'militant theocracy'[371] that mutually permeates both the Russian state and the ROC. On a regular basis, media from the Baltics to eastern Europe report on the arrest and/or expulsion of Russian Orthodox clergy. While the Moscow Patriarch decries such arrests and/or expulsions as acts of religious persecution, intelligence agencies and prosecutors have relied on evidence establishing various grounds including being caught in arms and munition infiltration, espionage and surveillance, engaging in propaganda and efforts to undermine host states and being spy handlers of *Федеральная служба безопасности Российской Федерации* [Federal Security Service of the Russian Federation—FSB].

In Ukraine, where Russia continues to wage a more than decade-long war against its predominantly Orthodox Christian neighbors, ROC clergy and their Ukrainian counterparts of the Ukrainian Orthodox Church (Moscow Patriarchate) actively persecute the Orthodox Church of Ukraine. Some 1561 of the Ukrainian Orthodox Church (Moscow Patriarchate) parishes have joined the Orthodox Church of Ukraine since the December 2018 Unification Council established it. The greatest number of desertions from the Moscow Patriarchate church led in Ukraine by Metropolitan Onufriy occurred in 2022 after the Russian invasion.

According to the Carnegie Endowment: "63 percent of Ukrainians support a ban on the UOCMP, and 82 percent do not trust UOCMP head Metropolitan Onufriy."[372] Metropolitan Onufry of the Ukrainian Orthodox Church (Moscow Patriarchate) claims they are "schismatics". Russia has yet to come to grips with the fact that at the outset of the war, Moscow enjoyed significant influence over many Ukrainian legislators in the Rada and a soft, yet critical cultural influence over the population through the Ukrainian Orthodox Church (Moscow Patriarchate). If the Ukrainian Orthodox Church (Moscow Patriarchate) has troubles, they are of their own making.

Of course, being Moscow-oriented is not an assurance of mutuality of commitment nor a prophylactic against the ROC asserting itself in your jurisdiction. Even the supplicant Ukrainian Orthodox Church (Moscow Patriarchate), which claims to have separated itself from Moscow, yet still commemorates Patriarch Kirill in its liturgies, has discovered Moscow is

---

[371] Elaine Wilson, "Русская «самобытность»: попытки присвоить и переписать религиозную историю", *Public Orthodoxy*, 30 December 2024.
[372] Konstantin Skorkin, "Ukraine's Ban on Moscow-Linked Church Will Have Far-Reaching Consequences", *Carnegie Politika*, 4 September 2024.

replacing even their most vociferous pro-Russian bishops of Ukrainian heritage with Russian bishops. Russia's effective control of it deeply undermines claims by Metropolitan Onufriy that his church is autonomous. The Ukrainian people have taken note.

In temporarily Russian-occupied Ukraine, the ROC worked hand-in-glove with the Russian state to suppress religious liberty outside of Russian Orthodox communities. Orthodox Church of Ukraine parishes have been either confiscated or destroyed. All Greek Catholic temples have been shuttered, transferred to Russian ownership, and everything from storage facilities to barracks has been seized, and only one Roman Catholic parish continues to operate in Russian-occupied Ukraine. According to Archbishop Maksym Ryabukha, the Greek Catholic bishop of Donetsk:

> Those who openly call themselves Catholics disappear: Some are shot, others are imprisoned. There is no right to freely profess the faith. Our faithful keep saying: 'We're holding up, but it's like being locked up in a prison.'[373]

The faithful loyal to Epiphany I, Metropolitan of Kyiv and All Ukraine and therefore Bartholomew I, the Ecumenical Patriarch, as well as the Greek Catholic and Roman Catholic faithful to the Holy See, are not alone in being singled out for religious persecution by the Moscow Patriarchate and Russian occupation forces. Evangelicals, Baptists, Seventh-day Adventists, Jews, Muslims (especially followers of the Hizb ut-Tahrir movement), the Crimean Tatars who largely follow the Sunni Hanafi school, and other minority religious communities have also fallen under the yoke. Suppression isn't the greatest threat. Russian forces have been responsible for the death and/or extrajudicial killing of 67 clerics of varying confessions of faith since the full-scale invasion of Ukraine in February 2022.[374]

Despite Russia's unceasing claim that the West, pointedly through the Ukrainian government, is by the act of banning the ROC (Moscow Patriarchate) and the ROC from operating in Ukraine, "persecuting Christians," the claim is mislaid. It remains unequivocal that every Ukrainian, even those with pro-Kremlin leanings, has the right to worship in a canonical Orthodox Christian church—just not those actively undermining Ukrainian democracy, gnawing at its social cohesion and desirous of demanding allegiance to Moscow.

Russia's propaganda machine has been incessant in claiming an aggrieved status. A paid lobbyist for the Ukrainian Orthodox Church (Moscow Patriarchate) has gone so far as to claim Ukraine's law that would ban

---

[373] Eduardo Berdejo, "Church in Ukraine has lost half of its parishes in areas occupied by Russia, bishop says", *Catholic News Agency*, 29 October 2024

[374] Andreja Bogdanovski, "Russia is violating religious freedom in occupied territories, says Ukraine", *Church Times*, 17 April 2025

them and the ROC from operating in Ukraine is akin to "religious cleansing".³⁷⁵ It is not. Orthodox Christianity, the Greek and Roman Catholic faith, Baptists, Seventh Day Adventists, Evangelical Christianity, Islam, Judaism and other confessions of faith are freely practiced in Ukraine. It is only in Russian-occupied Ukraine that religious freedom is genuinely imperiled if not outright prohibited. One need only read Resolution 2540 (2024) adopted by the Parliamentary Assembly of the Council of Europe (PACE), which decries the 'holy war' declared by Moscow Patriarch Kirill.

All this simply illuminates how the Russian state and ROC combine both internally and externally to exploit the age-old colonialist tool of sowing discord and division among enemies to create a chasm that Russia then fills. While Russia forsakes its obligations in international law, it nevertheless appeals to the rule of law in the United Nations (UN), European Union (EU), Parliamentary Assembly of Europe (PACE), OSCE, WCC and other forums, pleading victimhood. For Russia, there is no greater benefit gained than celebrating when the very institutions they decry as being instruments of the "depraved Western world."³⁷⁶

---

[375] Dmytra Vovk, "International and National Responses to the ROC's Support of Putin's War in Ukraine", *Brigham Young University Centre for Law and Religious Studies*, 30 October 2024.

[376] Patriarch Kirill, "Sermon", Cathedral of the Holy Saviour, ROC, Moscow, 6 March 2022

Chapter Fifteen

Patriarch in All but Name
Vladimir Putin and the Russian Orthodox Faith

Over the last several years, the Moscow Patriarchate's authority has been called into question. The unorthodox behavior of Patriarch Kirill in declaring a 'holy war' on Ukraine has caused many to reconsider their once unbending respect for the ROC. In March 1992, theologians, scholars and clergy signed a declaration condemning the ethnophyletist and nationalist "Russian world" ideology of the ROC and Russian state. In it, the declaration's drafters and signatories cite the Moscow Patriarch's and Putin's promotion of the Holy Rus' and Russkiy Mir and its danger to Orthodox Christianity and the world:

> The support of many of the hierarchy of the Moscow Patriarchate for President Vladimir Putin's war against Ukraine is rooted in a form of Orthodox ethnophyletist religious fundamentalism, totalitarian in character, called Russkii Mir or the Russian world, a false teaching which is attracting many in the Orthodox Church and has even been taken up by the Far Right and Catholic and Protestant fundamentalists....
> Against this "Russian world" (so the teaching goes) stands the corrupt West, led by the United States and Western European nations, which has capitulated to "liberalism", "globalization", "Christianophobia", "homosexual rights" promoted in gay parades, and "militant secularism". Over and against the West and those Orthodox who have fallen into schism and error (such as Ecumenical Patriarch Bartholomew and other local Orthodox churches that support him) stands the Moscow Patriarchate, along with Vladimir Putin, as the true defenders of Orthodox teaching, which they view in terms of traditional morality, a rigorist and inflexible understanding of tradition, and veneration of Holy Russia.[377]

The declaration has to date garnered some 1560 signatures, including those of leading theologians, academics, and clergy. Given Patriarch Kirill's 'holy war' declaration on Ukraine, an Orthodox Christian proclamation without parallel, it is not surprising that his theological, philosophical and religious judgment and actions have invited rebuke. What is surprising, however, is

---

[377] Brandon Gallaher and Pantelis Kalaitzidis (Coordinators—Orthodox Christian Studies Centre—Fordham University), "A Declaration on the 'Russian World' (Russkii mir) Teaching", *Co-Published by the Volos Academy for Theological Studies*, 13 March 2022.

that a patriarch of the Holy Orthodox Church has given himself and the ROC over so entirely to the president of the Russian Federation at every turn. Putin has, in all but name, assumed the leadership of the ROC as the shadow patriarch commanding Patriarch Kirill's every move.[378]

Speaking to the General Assembly of the Orthodox Church of Finland on June 7, 2024, Archbishop Leo of Helsinki and All Finland used his final address before retirement to warn the world about the dangers posed by Putin controlling the mission of the ROC:

> The Orthodox family of churches is at present in crisis and badly divided. Our modern age has given rise to a new totalitarian myth and ideology in the guise of Orthodoxy which does not in reality represent Christianity at all. A few years ago I was still able to recognize some vestiges of Orthodoxy in the Patriarchate of Moscow, but they have now been replaced by a blend of Russian Messianism, Orthodox fascism and ethnophyletism. The last-mentioned heresy was condemned by the local synod of Constantinople 152 years ago.
> Russia now looks on itself as the only force for good in the world, with the task of opposing the West, which has lapsed into evil. This in turn represents a Manichean heresy in which the world is divided into opposites: light and darkness, good and evil, and so on.[379]

Patriarch Kirill's conduct speaks for itself as an attack upon fundamental Christian values of peace and unity. As we have already discussed his willingness to prioritize the Russian state over his ordination vows by aligning himself with the KGB in the Soviet era and subordinating himself to the Russian state since being enthroned in 2009, this topic won't be discussed further in this volume.

It is worthwhile, however, to explore how the Russkiy Mir's leader has been enabled to project the idea that Russia is "…the only force for good in the world, with the task of opposing the West, which has lapsed into evil." Putin's background and experiences tell us a great deal about how he acquired his political and religious ideology and both how and why it drives him to attempt to reshape the world.

Let us begin with Putin's worldview of order. Modernity's resort to the recognition of states being driven by consensus achieved in the UN should be the dispositive method of our determining independence and sovereignty.[380] From time to time, various entities have tried to assert statehood following the illegal use of force, but rarely have these entities gained

---

[378] Mansur Mirovalev, "'God of war': ROC stands by Putin, but at what cost?", *Al Jazeera*, 9 February 2024.
[379] Staff Report, "Archbishop of Helsinki: Not a trace of Orthodoxy left in the Patriarchate of Moscow", *Orthodox Times*, 11 June 2024.
[380] Christian Hillbruger, "The Admission of New States to the International Community, *European Journal of International Law, No. 9*, 1998.

widespread recognition.³⁸¹ For Putin, the issue is more complicated. The Russkiy Mir is not limited by geography but rather expanded based on interest. The concept of who is Russian and who "should be" considered Russian is rooted not in international law but in the ideas of ethnicity, language, and commonalities of history and religion. By presidential decree in 2024, Putin extended citizenship eligibility far beyond even what his revamped Russian Constitution provided, creating a path to citizenship for those lacking Russian heritage whose social and political ideology put them at odds with Europe and the west: "Applicants can request residency based on the rejection of what the decree describes as their home countries' 'destructive neoliberal ideals,' which it says differ from 'traditional Russian spiritual and moral values.'"³⁸² ³⁸³

Putin has shown scant regard for international law or norms within the sorority of nations. What drives Putin is his personal sense of humiliation. The collapse of the Soviet Union and the demise of Russia as a genuine superpower struck the former KGB colonel at his core. Putin believes the west purposefully engineered the collapse of the Soviet Union to carve up Russia and, in the process, divide the Russian people by fracturing their domain piecemeal:

> First and foremost it is worth acknowledging that the demise of the Soviet Union was the greatest geopolitical catastrophe of the century. As for the Russian people, it became a genuine tragedy. Tens of millions of our fellow citizens and countrymen found themselves beyond the fringes of Russian territory.³⁸⁴

Decrying what he described as 'Russophobia', Putin later said in 2023:

---

381 The list included Abkhazia, Northern Cyprus, South Ossetia, Transnistria, and Taiwan. Russia is also the only country to recognise the Taliban government in Afghanistan.

382 Chris Panella, "Putin has decided that Russia is going to be a 'safe haven' for people who want to trade liberal Western ways for Russian 'moral values'", *Business Insider*, 19 August 2024.

383 Offers of Russian residency and citizenship to those disaffected by the west have been celebrated by the Kremlin in the media to promote Russia's messaging on the failures of the liberal west. Citing "shared values", an American from Texas, Derek Huffman, moved his entire family to the settlement of Istra just outside Moscow in early 2025. Within six months, aged 46 (far beyond US military recruiting age), Huffman was inducted into the Russian Army and sent to the frontlines in Ukraine. His wife and children took to social media to complain they were misled, pleading for his release. See: Kieran Kelly and Louis Brady, "Father who moved family to Russia to escape 'woke' America is sent to front line", *The Telegraph*, 21 July 2025.

384 Владимир Владимирович Пу́тин, "*Ежегодное Послание Федеральному Собранию Российской Федерации*", *Кремль, Москва*, 25 Апрель 2005.

We are now fighting for the freedom of not only Russia, but the whole world," Putin said in a speech to participants of a meeting organized by the ROC....

Our diversity and unity of cultures, traditions, languages, and ethnic groups simply don't fit into the logic of Western racists and colonialists, into their cruel scheme of total depersonalization, disunity, suppression and exploitation....

If they can't do it by force, they will try to sow strife. Any outside interference, provocations with the aim of causing interethnic or interreligious conflicts as aggressive actions against our country, as an attempt to once again foment terrorism and extremism in Russia as a tool to fight us.[385]

Putin has never forgiven the west for the demise of all that he held dear. It is not within his character despite claiming to be a faithful Christian.[386] Here, Putin's eventual claim of enjoying a Christian identity comes into focus. Putin is the product of the Second World War which Russians call the "Great Patriotic War" in reference to their heroic defense against the NAZIs and fascism.[387] Born in 1952, he was the only surviving son of Vladimir Spiridonovich Putin, a staunch communist who served in the Soviet Navy's submarine service before finally joining a NKVD Destruction Battalion where he was gravely wounded in the liberation of Leningrad from the prolonged Nazi siege. His mother, Marina Ivanova Putina, was the very model of Soviet gender equality, a devoted mother and factory worker. He was a poster child for Leninist-Marxist ideology and the Soviet state.

His childhood was an unhappy one. Putin's contemporaries in Leningrad and the KGB recount how, as an adult, Putin often repeated the story of the death of his two older brothers. He is said to have dwelled on how his eldest brother died in infancy during the 1930s, and his other brother died of starvation and diphtheria during the Nazi's siege of Leningrad. Their deaths, and the demise of the Soviet Union in 1991, seemingly

---

[385] Associated Press Wire Story, "Putin accuses the West of trying to 'dismember and plunder' Russia in a ranting speech", *AP News*, 28 November 2023.

[386] Agence France-Presse, "What's Impossible to Forgive? Putin Was Asked in 2018. He Said...", *NDTV World*, 24 August 2023.

[387] Russia has long downplayed its role in instigating the Second World War by allying itself with NAZI Germany. The Molotov-Ribbentrop Agreement, which included secret protocols to divide Poland between Hitler and Stalin, served to instigate Europe's descent into widespread carnage, costing some 39 million European lives, including Russians. The photographs of the joint Russian-NAZI 'liberation' parades, such as that in Brest-Litovsk, remain as indelible records of the Soviet-NAZI plot to destroy Europe as part of their expansionist plans of domination. See: Serhii Pyvovarov and Yevhen Spirin, "The USSR and Nazi Germany held a military parade in Brest after the capture of Poland 84 years ago. Russia calls it a 'liberation campaign'. Then-reality in 15 pictures", *Бабель*, 22 September 2023.

defined Putin. While he could not bring his brothers back from the dead, he could, however, resurrect Russia.

Putin, then a colonel in the KGB, resigned and began to study law in St. Petersburg. Despite the pension he received from his service as a Russian spy, Putin drove a taxi to supplement his income. It was necessary. The ruble had collapsed. The newly independent Russian Federation was broke, limited by its Cold War economic legacy of heavy industry and the production of weapons the world no longer wanted. Having completed his education in law, Putin found a job in local St. Petersburg politics. He met Anatoly Aleksandrovich Sobchak, the mayor of St. Petersburg, who was immediately impressed with Putin. He gave Putin his first job in politics as a 'fixer' of local political problems.

Prior to their meeting, Sobchak had been an elected, independent member of the Congress of People's Deputies of the Soviet Union. His knowledge of jurisprudence catapulted him to critical appointments. Along with Boris Yeltsin and Andrei Sakharov, Sobchak became a co-founder of the Inter-Regional Deputies Group. He chaired the Parliamentary Commission on the Investigation of the events of 9 April 1989 in Tbilisi, which took the brave position of condemning the military's role in the deaths of demonstrators. So forceful and persuasive were the commission's findings that it made it extremely difficult for the military to use overwhelming force against civilian demonstrators, a move that would undermine those who shortly thereafter plotted a coup against Gorbachev.

In the final days before the Soviet Union's collapse, Sobchak no longer served as a legislator but served Gorbachev as a leading member of the President's Consultative Council, whose policies essentially supplanted the USSR State Council, which itself was dissolved on December 25, 1991. His 1991 election as mayor of St. Petersburg would also be Putin's good fortune.

According to Yury Shutov, a deputy of the St. Petersburg Legislative Assembly and one-time confidant of Sobchak, Putin scheduled a private meeting with the mayor. Shutov alleges that Putin used his position as a KGB reservist to access kompromat that, if revealed, would corroborate that Sobchak had monitored and informed on administrators, faculty and students while on the faculty of Leningrad State University. Allegedly, Sobchak succumbed to Putin's blackmail. Putin was immediately hired as a special adviser to the mayor. The humiliation of having to drive a taxi simply to eat was over.

To understand this pivotal event in Putin's life fully, it is necessary to understand what happened to Sobchak's one-time confident and Putin collaborator—Shutov.

Shutov had fallen out of favor. He had begun to expose what he believed was information that depicted serious corruption in St. Petersburg city politics. This put both Sobchak and Putin at specific risk. He was arrested and released. His ordeals were not yet over. In February 1999, Shutov was stripped of parliamentary immunity and arrested on charges of murdering two of his colleagues, both local St. Petersburg politicians. Mikhail Manevich and dissident politician Galina Starovoitova had both been murdered due to their knowledge of corruption in the St. Petersburg government. The court case was dismissed against Shutov as being politically motivated and unsubstantiated. As Shutov was leaving the courtroom, however, *Отряд мобильный особого назначения* [OMON, special military security service] personnel from Moscow arrived. They physically assaulted Shutov without any interference from court personnel. Shutov lost an eye and most of his hearing in the assault. OMON then arrested Shutov on dubious criminal charges.

The extent of the political nature of the prosecution against Shutov became clear when, despite the Russian Supreme Court finding his detention was unlawful. Despite having been re-elected to the St. Petersburg Legislative Assembly and enjoying immunity from such prosecution, Shutov remained in detention. Over the next seven years, Shutov was moved from prison to prison, living in depraved conditions, deprived of even a wheelchair, which necessitated him to crawl as a means of movement.

While the charges of killing Manevich and Starovoitova had been abandoned, in 2006, Shutov was convicted of murdering another local businessman. His lawyers launched an appeal to the European Court of Human Rights (Shutov v. Russia, ECHR Application No. 20922/08). Shutov, much like Alexandr Navalny years later, reportedly died in prison of natural causes in December 2014.

Putin is said to have orchestrated it all, first in his capacity as a special adviser to the mayor of St. Petersburg, then working as an adviser to Boris Yeltsin and then as president of the Russian Federation.

Whatever happened to Sobchak? In 1990, Shutov had allegedly obtained a tape recording of Sobchak engaged in corruption with a French intelligence officer. Shutov's apartment was raided, and he was arrested. None other than Putin himself intervened with the investigator, supposedly confiscating the tape. Sobchak was then even further indebted to Putin. Mystery still surrounds the event, and there is no evidence of a tape having ever existed. In 1997, Sobchak was himself arrested for allegedly having used his position as mayor to receive favorable treatment on the privatization value of his personal apartment, that of his daughter's and his wife's art studio. According to his daughter, Sobchak was the target of Moscow politicians who sought to turn those allegations of minor offenses into crimes that would keep him from higher office. Again, the insinuation was that Putin, deputy chief of the presidential staff and chief of the main control directorate of the Presidential Property Management Department, was pulling the strings.

Sobchak may have been incredibly corrupt, but he was no fool. In November, he flew to Paris with the pretense of requiring medical treatment, only to remain there in self-imposed exile for over two years.

Meanwhile, his former protégé turned blackmailer, Putin, had continued to climb the political ladder. With his sights set on becoming prime minister and one day president, Putin invited Sobchak to return from exile in Paris. Putin, ever conscious of public opinion and not yet able to control it, understood Sobchak could ingratiate himself with liberals and reformers to benefit Putin's continued rise to the top. Putin used his political cache to have prosecutors drop all charges against Sobchak, and he returned to Russia on June 12, 1999. Sobchak immediately became an active architect of Putin's continued rise to power. Putin became the prime minister of the Russian Federation on August 9, 1999. Sobchak had served his purpose.

Having achieved consequential power, Putin, who understood the dynamic of appropriation and extermination only too well, now needed to clean up his past to secure his ascendency to power. Exterminating Sobchak was at the top of Putin's list. He met Sobchak in private and tasked him with traveling to Kaliningrad to bolster his base of support in the upcoming elections. Traveling with two aides that doubled as a security detail, Sobchak suddenly died from what was then deemed a heart attack. His security team also suffered cardiac arrest. Owing to significantly divergent findings by two independent medical professionals, a criminal investigation was opened.

On May 6, 2000, the criminal investigation led to prosecutors declaring Sobchak likely died from "premeditated murder with aggravating circumstances."[388] There was significant concern that Putin would be implicated. That Sobchak and both of his security detail suffered 'heart attacks' simultaneously raised the specter of intentional poisoning—a method of political execution that would become a hallmark of Putin's reign and retention of power for years to come. Putin again intervened. The investigation was closed without issuing a finding. Putin need no longer fear any exposure from a man who once befriended him as a mentor, only to become a victim of his blackmail.

Having been elected prime minister, Putin realized he needed deeper public support. Donning his 'sheep's clothing,' Putin, ever the wolf, was on the prowl to satiate his hunger. He immediately realized the ROC, an institution he once so vehemently mocked and opposed as a colonel in the

---

[388] Masha Gessen, "The best theory for explaining the mysterious death of Putin's mentor", *Business Insider*, 2015.

KGB, was the inheritor of what trust the Russian public still had for institutions. The Patriarch of Moscow would become his prey.

Putin's life was truly a Dickensian *Tale of Two Cities*. From subsistence living by driving a taxi on the dangerous streets of Saint Petersburg to becoming prime minister in only nine years, Putin meteorically rose in the world while the fortunes of his country sank precipitously. Still, Putin found himself in a precarious situation. The lethargic Russian economy, rising crime, homelessness, and inability to provide adequate pensions for the elderly and veterans of Russia's nightmarish campaign in Afghanistan made for a restless public. His success was inextricably intertwined with that of the Russian state.

Change and transformation became the order of the day. As there was no time to build credibility organically, Putin needed to borrow that of others. Given Yeltsin's personal decline in health and popularity, there was only one place left for Putin to turn. As did the Empress Catherine and Stalin before him, Putin looked to the ROC in his hour of need. In Patriarch Alexy, Putin found an enthusiastic and willing collaborator, needing little prodding.

There was a problem, however, with Putin's image. Putin had sold himself to the communists and his KGB masters as a patriotic son of the state. After all, his grandfather had been a personal cook to both Lenin and Stalin. While such a pedigree made for a perfect story to bolster his chances of joining the KGB and serving the party, it was now anathema in the newly democratic, liberal Russia. It was doubly so for the ROC and her faithful. If he were to prosper in his new role and rise even higher to the presidency, Putin would need a new story. So it was that Vladimir Vladimirovich Putin, a native of Leningrad (now Saint Petersburg), once loyal son of the Soviet State, sought to cement his standing with the Russian people by embracing their ancient, Russian Orthodox Christian faith. It wouldn't be too difficult. Patriarch Alexey had himself been part of the KGB apparatus. The head of the ROC would not thwart Putin—he would be assisted.[389] [390]

The only question that remained was how to roll out this new 'wolf in sheep's clothing' charade in a way that the Russian people would embrace. Enter Archimandrite Tikhon (Georgiy Alexandrovich Shevkunov), abbot of Moscow's Sretensky Monastery. He would become known as "Putin's Confessor".[391] Archimandrite Tikhon instructed Putin in how the

---

[389] Yevgenia Albats and Catherine A. Fitzpatrick, "The State Within a State: The KGB and Its Hold on Russia —Past, Present, and Future", *Farrar, Straus and Giroux*, 1999.

[390] James Meek, "Russian Patriarch 'was KGB spy'", *The Guardian*, 12 February 1999.

[391] Timothy H.J. Nerozzi, "'Putin's confessor' named bishop of annexed Ukrainian territory", *FoxNews*, 12 October 2023.

primitive church had grown—it had a good story, artefacts, and eyewitness accounts. Putin mastered the lesson.

Shortly after being administered the oath of office as prime minister of the Russian Federation, Putin began to put Father Tikhon's plan into action. Under the approving eye of Patriarch Alexy, Putin began to share a new origin story. As the legend goes, Putin claims his mother had always retained her Russian Orthodox faith. She had practiced her Orthodox Christian faith in private, secreting it even from her husband, a staunch Communist Party Member. Shortly after his birth, Maria had taken her infant son Vladimir to Saint Petersburg's Cathedral of the Savior's Transfiguration of all the Guards.

By circulating this story, Putin was reinventing himself in the way Muscovy and the Russians had always done before him. Putin's claim of confraternity with the whole of Russian Orthodox Christianity helped him transform himself from being a feared, former KGB colonel turned politician into being a more relatable Russian—a human being. It was a political masterstroke. His newly created persona would help him avoid questions about having served in East Berlin as a monstrous member of the KGB who exploited Germans and manipulated the Stasi to keep them adherents within the Russian sphere. The new Putin, a masculine yet loving, compassionate and sincere person, would be cast as a humble Russian shepherd watching over his flock as did the leaders of the early church.

In what would later be dubbed the "Second Baptism of the Rus'", Putin told the story such: "My mother baptised me in secret from my father, who was a member of the Communist Party... It touched on me personally and my family."[392] [393] According to Archimandrite Tikhon's plan, Putin was now equipped with a moving and profound story of faith relatable to Russian voters and to be admired by world leaders. Putin still needed relics and witnesses to follow in the footsteps of the apostles. With the new adherents receiving the baptism narrative well, Putin repeated it often. In his first meetings with United States President George W. Bush, Putin made a point of stressing his Christian faith. For the Evangelical

---

[392] Staff Writers, "Putin Christened in Secret From his Father", *Moscow Times*, 23 July 2013.

[393] The context of the 2013 revelation about Putin's supposed baptism is noteworthy. It comes only the year before Putin invades Crimea, where Volodomyr the Great was baptized at Chersonesus (Korsun), Crimea, leading to the conversion of the Kyivan Rus' to Orthodox Christianity c. 988. The thematic emergence of faith and defending Russian Orthodox Christians playing a role in the decision to invade Crimea and Ukraine would soon loom large in Russia's propaganda narrative. Putin's emergence as a Christian would play a part in it, lending credence to the idea that the story is at least opportunistic and at most pure fabrication.

Bush, such an assertion curried favor. Entranced by Putin, Bush publicly pronounced his estimate of Putin's trustworthiness during a joint press conference at the 2001 Slovenia Summit: "I looked the man in the eye. I found him to be very straightforward and trustworthy…. I was able to get a sense of his soul."[394]

Even better than the recounting of Putin's virtues by President Bush, Putin had his mother to play the part of witness so central to the Christian story outlined by Archimandrite Tikhon. Marina Ivanova was, according to Putin's narrative, a deeply devout Russian Orthodox Christian. She braved persecution by the KGB and risked her marriage to her ardent Community Party Member husband, had it become known she had baptized her son, Vladimir:

> My mother told me how she and her woman neighbor took me to the church to be baptised. My father was a member of the CPSU. He was a strict and consistent person. They did that secretly so that he doesn't know anything. Anyway, it was considered to be a secret.[395]

Putin's assertion of faith was helpful but not enough to solidify his position with still semi-skeptical Russian Orthodox Christians. Putin needed corroboration. There was no record of his baptism. It didn't matter. Patriarch Kirill — ever helpful to his political master — would provide the missing verification.

Appearing on Russia 1 channel's documentary "Patriarch" (Saida Medvedeva films), Putin claimed Patriarch Kirill's father was the very priest who baptized him in secret in 1952 in Saint Petersburg (then Leningrad):

> The Russian leader spoke about how at the end of 1952 he was baptized in Transfiguration Cathedral, in secret from his father, a member of the Communist Party.
> According to Vladimir Putin, the priest suggested that his mother name him Michael in honor of the priest's own patron saint, but the mother of the Russian leader refused and named him Vladimir in honor of his father.
> Later, speaking with the patriarch, Putin asked how he came to the Church. Kirill answered that his father was a priest and worked in Leningrad in Transfiguration Cathedral.

---

[394] White House Transcript, "Press Conference by President Bush and Russian Federation President Putin *(Brdo Pri Kranju, Slovenia)*", *George W. Bush Presidential Library*, 16 June 2001.

[395] Commentary, "Putin says that as a child he was baptised in secret", *Commonspace*.eu, 7 January 2012.

> Putin asked the patriarch to clarify whether his father was the only Michael serving there in 1952. Receiving an affirmative answer, he told the patriarch about how it was his father who baptized him in childhood.[396]

Patriarch Kirill's alleged 'confirmation' of Putin's baptism seems as Miraculous as it was incredible. Still, Putin could not rely on it alone.

As if from stage left, Putin began to show the public a simple, unadorned cross made of simple aluminium. Putin introduced this 'relic' to the world in various interviews:

> In 1993, when I worked on the Leningrad City Council, I went to Israel as part of an official delegation. Mama gave me my baptismal cross to get it blessed at the Lord's Tomb. I did as she said and then put the cross around my neck. I have never taken it off since.[397]

Lore has it that Putin claimed his devout mother acquired the simple, unadorned cross for him at baptism, shortly after his birth.[398] She kept it for him for decades. Despite his 1993 claim, "I have never taken it off since," a fire at his mother's dacha in 1996 gives us reason to doubt the veracity of his story. According to various accounts he later gave, the fire destroyed the house in which his cross was kept. As if torn from the pages of the martyrology of Saint Nicholas, whose icon could withstand flames, the cross saved by his mother for Putin since his secret baptism and blessed in the Garden of Gethsemane survived while the intense flames and heat destroyed all other family possessions. Putin would have us believe it was a miracle! The transformation of the cross from artefact to relic was nearly complete. Putin expanded on the story, claiming a firefighter searching through the ashes and embers that had once been his mother's dacha found the cross and returned it to him. As the legend grew by repetition, the Russian Orthodox clergy and believers began likening Putin's cross to the Invincible Icon of Saint Nicholas, which had hung in the Kremlin's Nikolskaya Tower. The icon had proved imperious to destruction when Napoleon burned Moscow and when the Bolsheviks destroyed icons by the thousands. A cult belief arose noting how the aluminium cross, a metal which melts at much lower temperatures than brass, copper, silver or gold, somehow miraculously survived when everything else in the dacha was

---

[396] Social Media News, "Putin says father of Patriarch Kirill baptized him in 1952", *Orthodox Christianity*, 20 November 2016.

[397] Vladimir Putin, Nataliya Gevorkyan, Natalya Timakova and Andrei Kolesnikov, "First Person: An Astonishingly Frank Self-Portrait by Russia's President Vladimir Putin", *PublicAffairs*, 2000.

[398] No date has ever been clearly given for Putin's alleged Baptism. It seems incredulous that were Maria Putina a genuinely sincere Orthodox Christian, so passionate about her faith that she would risk the ire of the Soviet State by baptizing her child, she would have forgotten the date.

destroyed. Putin had achieved the trifecta: he could check off a good story, a witness, and a relic from his list, thereby completing Archimandrite Tikhon's list of requirements.[399]

Mark Twain once quipped, "Never let facts get in the way of a good story." He proved insightful. The divergence between Putin's claim that he had never taken the cross from his neck since it was blessed at the Tomb of Jesus in the Garden of Gethsemane and it having been inside his mother's dacha during the 1996 was ignored. Notwithstanding, the baptism and cross stories both reinvented and rehabilitated Putin, gaining him new admirers in the process, both domestically and internationally. The transformation from wolf to sheep was complete, at least for the moment.

Just as Putin had traded on his Russian heritage, his family's cult of communist patriotism and a mythologized Christian identity, Putin eventually realized he needed his devotees at home and abroad to be solidified. Putin masterminded citizenship and identity warfare as parallel components in Russia's hybrid-warfare campaign against the west. Aside from the poisonings, assassinations, attempted coups d'état, and general destabilization of European governments and economies,[400] Putin resolved to manufacture more Russians. The low Russian birth rate, alarming premature morbidity age of the Russian people, and, in time, the extraordinarily high casualty rates from his 'special military operation' in Ukraine were problematic. Putin[401] decided to culturally indoctrinate those with historic ties to Russia to place a higher value on that heritage.[402] This included citizens of neighboring states, especially those of Russian ethnicity or links to the Moscow Patriarchate and ROC, to self-identify as being Russian or at least become 'Russian-friendly.' The 'Near Abroad' strategy would be supported primarily by Russian troll farms, social media posts on TikTok and other influencer campaigns. The initiatives weren't limited to reaching those with Russian backgrounds but extended into Europe and the Americas.[403]

---

[399] The relic and supposed eyewitness account of the fireman took on unusual significance, given the absence of any record of Putin's baptism or his mother's inability to give the name of the priest who allegedly baptized him.

[400] Pjotr Sauer, "Twenty years of ruthlessness: how Russia has silenced Putin's opponents", *The Guardian*, 27 August 2023.

[401] We refer to Putin singularly, not the Russian government, as the country had ceased to be a 'managed democracy' and had become a kleptocratic autocracy.

[402] Luke Rodeheffer, "Kremlin Prioritizes Russian Language in Moscow's Near Abroad", *Eurasia Daily Monitor*, 31 October 2024.

[403] David Evans, "Russian Soft Power Cultivation in the United States of America: A Media Content Analysis of 'Russia Beyond The Headlines'", *Graduate Dissertation: West Virginia University*, 2015,

These would take their places as part of an overarching propaganda strategy that incorporated ROC clergy as direct 'soft power' projectors through their sermons, 'religious development' activities and their publications:

> Alongside representatives of the Russian diaspora scattered around the world, the Russian world encompasses all those for whom Russian tradition, the treasures of Russian civilization, and the rich Russian culture are the highest value and meaning of life.[404]

The goal is simple: cultivate an interest by citizens of other states once within the Russian sphere in claiming Russian affiliation or citizenship through the promotion of greater respect, esteem and affinity to 'Mother Russia'.[405] The diaspora would be defined in its most generous sense.

Recent changes to the Russian Constitution under Putin ensured that surrounding states are not the only arbiters of citizenship, even for their own citizens.[406] Russia's pursuit of the Russkiy Mir and embrace of the Holy Rus' ideology directly challenge internationally recognized mechanisms and claims of domestic authority for granting citizenship. The Russian practice of 'passportization' to impose its citizenship on people in Transnistria, Abkhazia, South Ossetia, Luhansk, Donetsk, Crimea, and other occupied territories extends well beyond international norms and represents a violation of international law.

Given Putin's revanchist policies, it is not only possible, but likely, that he will seek to have Russia's territorial footprint grow as quickly as possible. He is, after all, 72 years of age from a country where the average life expectancy for a male is only 68 years.[407] Russia's economic restructuring into a wartime economy and the battlefield experience Russia has gained in Ukraine have 'primed the pump' for re-expanding the Russian sphere of influence in Europe by force before NATO and European states

---

[404] Программы и документы конференций и форумов, "Наказ XXV Всемирного русского народного собора «Настоящее и будущее Русского мира»", *Всемирный русский народный собор*, 27 марта 2024.

[405] John T. Psaropoulos, "'Pragmatic manipulation': Is Russia playing with European voters' minds?", *Al Jazeera*, 5 June 2024.

[406] Russia does not have a recognized mechanism to renounce citizenship. In states formerly under the Russian sphere, difficulties have arisen in their quest to establish citizenship elsewhere due to many states having excluded dual-citizenship — more specifically, Russian citizenship — as a legal status for their citizens.

[407] UN Population Division, "Life expectancy at birth, male (years) — Russian Federation", *World Population Prospects, United Nations (UN)*, publisher: UN Population Division; Statistical databases and publications from national statistical offices, National statistical offices; *Demographic Statistics, Eurostat (ESTAT)*, 2023.

can finally ramp up their defense capabilities.[408] There is, in effect, a race currently being run between Russia and Europe.

Putin is anxious to achieve his military and political goals in Ukraine. Any move against NATO and Europe is contingent upon doing so before Europe can defend itself. Some analysts have expressed concern that Europe has been so generous to Ukraine with weapons and ammunition that it has left the continent vulnerable should Russia launch military operations in the near term.[409] Serious questions persist about the Trump administration's willingness to meet its Article 5 mutual defense commitments to NATO's allies.[410]

Putin has little time left to achieve his objectives. He has shown himself to be little interested in peace and remains undeterred by pressure from Europe or condemnation by the UN:

> President Putin has repeatedly spoken of his desire to bring the Ukrainian settlement to a peaceful conclusion as soon as possible. This is a long process, it requires effort, and it is not easy. The main thing for us is to achieve our goals. Our goals are clear.[411]

Despite pressure from Europe and, at times, some prodding by the Trump administration, Putin has resolved that peace in Ukraine can only come after his objective of removing the democratically elected government in Kyiv has been achieved. Reabsorbing Ukraine as part of Russia remains his goal. Europe's subjugation is certain to follow. If Putin can prevail in Ukraine before Trump leaves office and Europe has managed to ramp up its defense capabilities, given his age and objective, Russia may extend its footprint through military action in Europe before this decade ends.

Putin's tight grip on the ROC, acting as patriarch in all but name, continues to ensure he has 'soft power' access to Europe under the auspices of the liberal values of democracy and freedom of religion enshrined in the organizing documents of the EU and states across the continent. Putin's exercise of power and influence over the ROC by the autocratic leader of a belligerent state should greatly concern Europe and the west.

---

[408] Isabel van Brugen, "Four Signs Russia Could Be Preparing for War With NATO", *Newsweek*, 2 May 2025.
[409] David Genini, "How the war in Ukraine has transformed the EU's Common Foreign and Security Policy", *Yearbook of European Law*, 2003.
[410] Elena Davlikanova and Yevhenii Malik, "NATO is unprepared for the growing threat posed by Putin's Russia", *Atlantic Council*, 21 July 2025.
[411] Reuters, "Kremlin says Putin is ready to discuss peace in Ukraine but wants to achieve goals", *RTÉ News*, 20 July 2025.

Chapter Sixteen

Waging an Unholy 'Holy War'
Absolution for Rape, Torture, Summary Execution, and Attempted Genocide

It is the byproduct of that preternatural, militant, theocratic inclination that has disfigured the Moscow Patriarchate from its legitimate role in being an instrument of God and transformed it into a quasi-state political and intelligence apparatus that so often acts contrary to the teachings of Christ and the Orthodox church. Proof of this is manifest in the record of the ROC's involvement in Russia's drive to create a new empire spanning post-Soviet space.

That quest has often pitted the Moscow Patriarchate against the gospels, such as when Patriarch Kirill issued a decree during the March 2024 *Congress of the World Russian People's Council* declaring Russia's invasion of Ukraine a "holy war." That declaration of a 'holy war' now seems oddly incongruent with the earlier Russian assertion that it was acting to liberate the Ukrainian people from a fascist regime in Kyiv. As we see now, any 'liberation' by the Russian state has always occurred in tandem with the subjugation of local churches to the ROC or the abolition of churches altogether.[412]

The declaration of 'holy war' left the Christian world and humanity aghast. To the contrary, other religious leaders have roundly denounced Russia's war on Ukraine for being both a violation of the precepts of international law and an offense against humanity and civilisation.

Ecumenical Patriarch Bartholomew I called the invasion: "damaging to the prestige of the whole of Orthodoxy."[413] Later, in 2025, the Ecumenical Patriarch again addressed the issue of Russia's invasion of Ukraine with the full-throated support of the ROC:

---

[412] Kyriaki Topidi, "Religious Belief as an Existential Threat: How Russia Victimizes Religious Minorities in Russia and in the Occupied Territories of Ukraine; Series on Transnational Christian Nationalism, and its impact on politics, the rule of law, and religious freedom", *Canopy Forum on the Interaction of Law and Religion*, 2 November 2024.

[413] Peter Weber, "Russian Orthodox Patriarch Kirill's support for Putin's Ukraine war has fractured his church", *The Week*, 19 April 2022.

No nation has the right to force its will upon another, and no power can erase a people's history.... No force can extinguish the spirit of the people who refuse to be broken. Ukraine's sovereignty is not up for debate, nor can it be negotiated under the guise of diplomacy.[414]

The Holy See has also been vocal about Russia's invasion of Ukraine. During an Angelus address to the faithful in St. Peter's Square, Pope Francis stated: "Tomorrow marks the third anniversary of the full-scale war against Ukraine: a painful and shameful occasion for all of humanity.... I renew my solidarity with the martyred Ukrainian people."[415]

Patriarch Daniel of Romania, Patriarch Theodore II of Alexandria, and Archbishop Leo of Helsinki and All Finland, the archbishops of Canterbury and York and countless Protestant clergy joined in the condemnation of Russia's war on Ukraine. Lest it be misunderstood that this is a mere phenomenon of what Putin calls "a depraved Western world," some of the most vociferous condemnations emanated from within Russia itself.

Rabbi Berel Lazar, Chief Rabbi of Russia, condemned the Russian invasion of Ukraine by calling on the Kremlin to withdraw and end the war. The Chief Rabbi of Moscow, Rabbi Pinchas Goldschmidt, fled from Russia after refusing a demand from the Kremlin to declare his and Judaism's support for the invasion publicly. Evangelical Pastor Yevgeniy Peresvetov, who was once approached to act as an FSB spy in 2010, was eventually charged with sedition and banned from Russia for 25 years for his opposition to Russia's invasion of Ukraine and ministering to Evangelical Christians in Crimea.

There is no universal concept of holy war in orthodox theology, especially when wielded against fellow Orthodox Christians. The ROC's position is unique within Orthodox Christianity as well as the broader Christian community. It is difficult to comprehend, then, how Kirill, an Orthodox Patriarch, could be acting legitimately in his capacity as a Christian bishop by blessing religious violence in the pursuit of territorial acquisition of a neighboring Orthodox Christian country.

There are countless examples of Roman Catholic and Protestant nations going to war against each other for such purposes. However, in Orthodox Christianity, it is almost unique. Only one conclusion can be drawn by this 'holy war' and territorial dominion stance adopted by the Moscow Patriarchate—Kirill has abdicated his role as a Christian and bishop and embraced Russian state doctrinal values as being superior to the values of the Orthodox Christian church. For Kirill, the Russian elite and a majority

---

[414] Robert Badendieck, "Ecumenical Orthodox patriarch backs Ukraine's sovereignty in Mass marking 3 years of war", *National Catholic Reporter*, 24 February 2025.

[415] Deborah Castellano Lubov, "Pope on Ukraine: 'Painful and shameful' anniversary 'for all humanity'", *Vatican News*, 23 February 2025.

of the Russian hoi polloi, the union of the Russkiy Mir and Holy Rus' is absolute and indivisible.

There are theologians, clergy, and monks who argue that Kirill, as Patriarch of Moscow, is the supreme authority of Orthodox Christianity for the Russian peoples. While these authors concede the point as it extends to the wider claim of 'all the Rus'" being a pan-European See, (Putin and Kirill claim the Belarusians, Ukrainians and other Slavic peoples throughout the Baltics and Eastern Europe are their subjects by virtue of historically being related to the Rus'), Kirill does enjoy the canonical status of serving as Patriarch of Moscow and therefore the claim has legitimacy as it applies in its limited way to the Russian people. This is generally accepted without dispute. What is alarming for both orthodoxy and politics, however, is how the church has willingly submitted its spiritual role to Putin's political whims.

Putin has never tired of asserting that the Muscovy are heirs to the Roman Empire by virtue of Moscow being the 'third Rome' (the historical record is clear that that it is Kyiv, not Moscow, that would enjoy the greater position as the legitimate claimant of that mantle as the metropolis of Kyiv and all the Rus' predates the founding of Moscow and existed without interruption until was misappropriated by the Grand Prince of the Muscovy who broke communion with orthodoxy and the Ecumenical Patriarch in Constantinople in 1441).

Even by embracing the two-headed eagle, which signifies the unity of the Roman emperor's temporal powers of state and the authority of the church, Russia's and Putin's heraldry asserts that he is the successor of Constantine. It is argued by the clergy and monks of the Moscow Patriarchate that when Putin ordered the invasion of Ukraine in 2014, he did so in his dual capacity of head of state and the unofficial but still supernumerary empowered role as the ROC.

For the Orthodox Christian, war should be anathema. This is especially so when it is wielded without restraint in furtherance of nationalist goals and employed to subdue other Orthodox Christians. Nonetheless, Kirill dutifully declared that Russia's "special military operation" in Ukraine was a "holy war" during his sermon on 25 October 2022:

> The Church realizes that if someone, driven by a sense of duty and the need to fulfill his oath… goes to do what he is called to do and if someone dies in the performance of that duty, then he has undoubtedly committed something that amounts to a sacrifice. He will have sacrificed himself for others. And therefore, we believe that this sacrifice washes away all the sins committed by such a man.[416]

---

[416] Reuters, "ROC absolves Russian soldiers dying in Ukraine", *Jerusalem Post*, 26 September 2022.

Kirill's position is disconcerting for the average Christian in that it endorses war in opposition to Christ's moral teaching. It also does something uniquely unorthodox—it introduces ex nihilo a theological construct wholly foreign to orthodoxy—plenary indulgence. Cyprian of Carthage complained of this practice as anathema in his third-century treatise, "On the Lapsed":

> Man cannot be greater than God, nor can a servant remit or forego by his indulgence what has been committed by a greater crime against the Lord, lest to the person lapsed this be moreover added to his sin… But if any one, by an over-hurried haste, rashly thinks that he can give remission of sins to all, or dares to rescind the Lord's precepts, not only does it in no respect advantage the lapsed, but it does them harm.[417]

The depravity of Kirill, a patriarch of the Orthodox Christian Church, reaching outside orthodoxy into the juridical world of Catholic canon law to construct a mechanism to justify the kidnapping of children, wanton rapes, torture, summary executions, the indiscriminate killing of civilians and destruction of critical infrastructure such as hospitals and heat generation facilities by Russian forces in Ukraine demonstrates the extent to which Kirill has subordinated the church to the Russian State. Kirill and the ROC have prioritized pleasing Putin over pleasing God. Such fanatical submission to temporal power exercised by Putin has not been seen in Europe since millions of cultured, intelligent, and educated Germans gave themselves over with unparalleled zeal to an Austrian corporal who also believed his destiny and that of the state were inextricable.

This is not to say that orthodoxy has ignored the idea of justified or just use of force. In response to questions from Peter, James, John and Andrew about the end-times in Mark 13:7; Matthew 24:6; and Luke 21:9, Jesus speaks of "wars and rumours of wars", but in so doing, he does not imply any sanction of war but shares with the Apostles presage information that the church will endure trial, tribulation, and violence.

Undeniably, we have also received from scripture and tradition a circumstantial sense of acceptable use of force. Jesus' "sword" allusions in Matthew 10:34 and Luke 22:35-38 are indisputably militant. The Book of the Apocalypse is replete with imagery of war as written in Revelation 20. In the epistles, especially at 1 Thessalonians 5:8; Ephesians 6:10; 1 Corinthians 9:7; 2 Timothy 2:3-4, we receive ample literalist evidence that the use of force and Christianity need not be considered mutually exclusive. Such

---

[417] Saint Cyprian (Translated and Edited by Roy J. Deferrari), "Treatises (The Fathers of the Church, Volume 36), *Catholic University of America Press*, 1958.

instances and circumstances are, however, exceptionally rare when appropriately considered within Orthodox Christianity's moral and ethical framework, given the scriptural tradition.

Still, Kirill's declaration of a 'holy war' against Ukraine and her people is repugnant in Christian theology and philosophy. The New Testament gives us a solid foundation to adopt a thoroughly pacifistic posture toward war. Jesus' moral teaching opposing violence is firmly grounded in Matthew 5-7, 26:52 and Luke 2:14, 3:14, 6:29; et al. Kirill's submission of the church and the faithful to Putin's will and the Russian state's political ambitions stands in stark contrast to the legitimate exercise of religious activity and teaching a civilized person would expect from a church.

It remains an odd exercise in feigned surprise that Kirill and the Moscow Patriarchate claim that Orthodox Christianity stands in opposition to their call for an unbridled 'holy war'. Kirill and his ROC seem wholly oblivious to the immorality of their blessing for vicious warfare being inflicted on their fellow Orthodox Christians. The hypocrisy worsens when it is considered that they do so against a people they claim to be their 'brothers in race' (the 'Kyiv Culture' gives us archaeological proof that the Ukrainian people existed as a unique nation and people who thrived in antiquity for over a millennia before Ivan the Terrible transformed the Grand Duchy of Muscovy into the Tsardom of Russia in 1547). Ukrainians are not Russians.

It is not Kirill's 'holy war' alone that troubles and undermines Christian Orthodoxy. In June 2024, Archbishop Leo of Helsinki and All Finland used his speech before the General Assembly to claim that Kirill and the Moscow Patriarchate were promoting "…a new totalitarian myth and ideology" that has replaced Orthodox Christianity in Moscow. Leo pointedly accused Kirill of promoting a "Manichean heresy" to divide the world into good and evil by promoting a blend of "Russian Messianism, Orthodox fascism and ethnopyletism."[418]

The conflation of what should be the separation spheres of the Russian state and the ROC truly poses a threat to European security. Politically, it creates unique challenges that Europe must learn to confront.

---

[418] OCP News Service, "Finnish Archbishop Blasts Moscow Patriarchate: "No Trace of Orthodoxy Left"", *OCPS*, 11 June 2024.

Chapter Seventeen

Wolves in Sheep's Clothing
ROC Clergy and Their Role in Russian State Espionage

If the majority of this manuscript was spent on Russian history it is because we deemed it essential that readers fully understand all that drives Russia. Dealing with the ROC's threat to European security and democracy without the context of history would be akin to a doctor examining a tumor without understanding the human body. It would be an exercise in knowledge for the medical researcher but near meaningless to the treating physician treating the suffering experienced by the patient.

It is different for the Russian people and those who know the state all too well having suffered its colonialism, occupations, and their attending misery. Russians have always understood their government and the ROC's inclination to establish and maintain itself at the expense of others. In the 19th century, while the ROC was still undeniably, firmly entrenched as a creature of the Russian State, Mikhail Alexandrovich Bakunin wrote:

> Any honest thinking Russian is bound to realize that our empire cannot change its attitude to the people. By its very existence it is doomed to be its blood-sucker and tormentor. The people instinctively hate it, and it cannot help but oppress the people, since its whole being and strength are founded on the people's misery... The only worthwhile constitution from the people's point of view is the destruction of the empire.[419]

There were many Russians who shared that same point of view since Putin rose to power. Through general repression, including the 'Foreign Agents Act' that sought to ban civil society activities, dissent has all but disappeared in Russia.[420] A recent example of how forcibly Russia deals with dissent can be found in the case of 19-year-old Dariya Kozyreva.[421] Aside

---

[419] Geoffrey Hosking, "Russia: People and Empire 1552-1917", *Harvard University Press*, 30 September 1998.
[420] Miriam Lanskoy and Elspeth Suthers, "Putin versus Civil Society: Outlawing the Opposition", *Journal of Democracy*, Volume 24, Issue 3, July 2013.
[421] Staff Writers, "Russia: Activist Daria Kozyreva conviction for poetic anti-war protest exposes continued repression", *Amnesty International*, 18 April 2025.

from what in Europe would be considered innocuous criticism of government, Kozyreva was charged with hanging a quote from the Ukrainian poet Taras Shevchenko's poem "Testament" to his monument in St. Petersburg:

> Oh bury me, then rise ye up
> And break your heavy chains
> And water with the tyrants' blood
> The freedom you have gained.[422]

Like the Muscovy princes, tsars and Soviet premiers before him, Putin has not brooked criticism or dissent well. A whole generation of Russians and those coming of age today have never really known a leader other than Putin. Replacing Yeltsin, who left office in 1999, except for the term of office served by Dmitry Medvedev as president, with Putin taking a turn as prime minister to meet constitutional requirements, Putin has been firmly entrenched in power for 25 years and 75 days as of the writing of this chapter.[423]

The ROC has been much the same. Except for the period between 1917–1992 under Patriarch Tikhon, the ROC has either been a direct creature of the state (1721–1917) or chose to voluntarily subordinate itself to the Soviet state (1926–1991). The most senior hierarchs of the ROC today, including the Patriarch of Moscow, Kirill and Metropolitan Onufriy of the Ukrainian Orthodox Church (Moscow Patriarchate), had to be approved by the KGB to be ordained bishop.

There is solid evidence in the public domain that they were all Soviet collaborators.[424] In all, in the past 300 years, the ROC could only have been considered a church free of state control for a mere five years in that interregnum between the abdication of Tsar Nicholas II Alexandrovich and the rise of the Soviet government in 1922.

The total giving-over of itself to the Russian state has seemingly denied the ROC any ability at introspective discernment. It is fair to ask if, having been voluntarily enslaved to the Russian state for centuries, whether it understands how to function as a church as Europe and the world would understand one. Enduring evidence of the hierarchs and clergy continuing to function as part of the Russian state security apparatus

---

[422] Тарас Шевченко, "Заповіт", *Київ: Видавництво Глорія*, 2020.
[423] By comparison, Fidel Castro served as head of state in Cuba for 31 years, 2 months and 22 days—only six years longer than Putin. Changes demanded by Putin to the Russian Constitution on 4 July 2020 (by coincidence, American 'Independence Day') now allow Putin to serve as President for life.
[424] Roman Skakun, "The NKVD-MGB-KGB Agent Network in the Orthodox Episcopate of Ukraine (1939–1964): Formation, Functions, and Behavioral Models", *Ukrainian Catholic University Press: Lviv*, 2025.

indicates there is little interest or inclination to engage in critical self-reflection. The willingness of Moscow Patriarchate-aligned clergy to act in ways that can rightly be considered spies continues to challenge Europe's liberal democratic values and tradition of being disinclined to regulate the activities of churches and faith communities.

In Bulgaria, Latvia, Lithuania, Montenegro, North Macedonia, Sweden, and elsewhere in Europe, Russian Orthodox clergy, including hierarchs, have been arrested and/or expelled as persona non grata for their roles in subterfuge. This has included spying on NATO bases, collecting detailed engineering information about essential water treatment facilities, covertly recording conversations with foreign governments and diplomats, funding election interference activities, corrupting government officials with bribes and exploiting non-aligned clergy. The creation and or capture of kompromat used in blackmail operations as part of these activities by ROC clergy on behalf of the *Федеральная служба безопасности Российской Федерации* [Federal Security Service of the Russian Federation — FSB] constitutes a real and present danger for Europe.

The difficulty for Europe is not only how it responds, but if it will respond. Finland's president, Alexander Stubb, observed the insufficiency of Europe's willingness to adequately address the problem of Russia's and the ROC's revisionism and anti-European behavior concerning EU policy-making: "You go through three phases. First, you have a crisis, then you have chaos. And eventually you get a suboptimal solution."[425]

As Europe is home to countries that once fell under the Russian yoke, the consequence of these activities poses real and present dangers for Europe's security and democratic traditions. For years, Ukrainians have rightly claimed they are fighting a war so that Europe may not have to do so. In many ways, they are right. Given all that was discussed and detailed in previous chapters, the penchant for Russia continuing to experience elastic borders is not only possible but likely. The pundits who once claimed the conflicts in Georgia would be reconciled and Abkhazia and South Ossetia would be returned to Georgian control have sung a different tune since

Putin has shown no interest in the restoration of any Russian-occupied territories to their countries' internationally recognized borders. Consider the 2016 exchange between Putin and a young Russian boy. At a carefully managed televised awards ceremony for geography students, the following exchange occurred:

---

[425] Juraj Majcin, "Russia's threat to Europe goes beyond the battlefields of Ukraine", *European Policy Centre*, 28 January 2025.

[Putin] "Where does Russia's border end?"
[Boy] "At the Bering Strait!"
[Putin] "It doesn't end anywhere."

Realizing the implied threat and policy declaration, the audience was momentarily stunned into silence. With theatrical timing only the finest actors possess, Putin then quipped:

[Putin] "That was a joke!"[426]

The crowd erupted in laughter and applause. Intelligence experts, policy analysts, and leaders in the world's capitals, however, shivered. Russian conduct since has shown it was no joke. In that singular exchange, Putin appealed to the inalienable intersection of the Russkiy Mir and Holy Rus' in the hearts and minds of the Russian people. There are reasons Russians accept the despotism that the rest of Europe does not. After suffering post-independence malaise, poverty, economic and cultural banditry, which created an aggressive oligarch class, most Russians yearned for a reason to enjoy the pride of yesteryear. Putin gave it to them and did so often, although not always substantively. With symbolic parades and other ephemeral accoutrements of Russia's former glory, Putin appealed to populist enthusiasm and frenzy. Putin's exchange with the child served its purpose. He projected the idea that Russia is so invincible it can do as it wishes. He simultaneously began to plant the idea that he intended to re-establish what had once been a greater Russian empire.

Within Putin's reasoning are claims that the west is desirous of restraining the east from achieving advanced development within the Russkiy Mir. The ROC often echoes this theme. Using the theme of the Satanic West attacking Russia's 'traditional values', the Moscow Patriarchate constantly promotes the necessity of Russians maintaining their affiliation with the ROC as both an expression of identity and a defense against what are promoted as corrupted western values.

Intrinsic in this projection is the portrayal of the Russian state, nation and Putin himself as being deeply devoted to, and guided by, the only institution that survived all periods of their history—the ROC. It is often difficult to discern if the ideology of the ROC underlies state values or if Putin simply pretends it is so.

Putin's evocations about his early family life are, in essence, a mirror of what he believes should be the narrative of every Russian person. He is immensely proud of his father's patriotic devotion to the Soviet Union and

---

[426] Staff Writers, "Russia's border doesn't end anywhere, Vladimir Putin says", *BBC News*, 24 November 2016.

his fidelity to the Communist Party. He promotes those values of patriotism and fidelity to the state. Putin celebrates his mother's life of sacrifice and moral rectitude in her devotion to God and her Russian family. He encourages Russian women to do the same—contribute to the state while still having multiple children and forming families.

Putin lauds the ROC's promotion of the Holy Rus' ideology because it specifically claims God set aside Russia for the salvation of humanity and designated the Russian people to enlighten the world. The explicit raising of Russia as the salvific vehicle for humanity and not the church makes the Moscow Patriarchate's promotion of this ideology more of a political manifesto than a theological or ecclesiological dogma.

As much as these touchstones are meant to herald models of expected personal virtue and citizenship, they remain exercises in the ROC's thematic crafting of the Russian people to be obedient first to the state and then to the Moscow Patriarchate.

When considering the threat posed by the ROC to European security and democracy, it is helpful again to consider Joseph Nye's 'soft power diplomacy' definition. If it is, as he described it, the ability to co-opt rather than coerce (in contrast with hard power), it immediately appeals to reason that political grooming by ROC clergy can be particularly dangerous for Europe. It is the role of the clergy to co-opt humanity to believe in a faith rooted in pre-history, without much founding archaeological evidence, lacking in first-person witness or contemporary account and do so while encouraging the faithful to co-opt their family and friends to believe likewise. ROC clergy were tailor-made for being 'soft power diplomats.' This is what makes the ROC so vital to the fruition of the Russkiy Mir.

Under the authority of the Patriarch of Moscow, the ROC has undergone an expansive growth effort throughout the world. This includes significant development in Europe (the Patriarchal Exarchate in western Europe—Moscow Patriarchate), the Americas (ROCOR), and, of late, with rapidly accelerated development in Africa (l'Exarchat patriarcal d'Afrique). It is the ROC's global reach combined with its role in 'soft power diplomacy' that makes it so vital to the Russian state. In exchange, the ROC receives special favor from the state, with the Patriarch of Moscow being elevated to the status of an unofficial 'co-tsar' with Putin when it comes to the state's public persona.

The Moscow Patriarchate has not restrained its activities to moralizing and evangelizing or even exercising 'soft power diplomacy' abroad. Since the beginning of Russia's 2014 invasion of Ukraine, the Moscow Patriarchate has engaged in a pattern of punishing priests who remain faithful to the gospels and condemn war and violence.[427] Father Ioann Koval, a priest of the ROC in Moscow was charged by the Moscow Patriarch with "discrediting the Russian army," by substituting the word "victory" with "peace" in the Prayer for Holy Rus required by Patriarch Kirill to be recited by priests during the Divine Liturgy. Koval was stripped of his priestly rank by Moscow and fled Russia in fear. As a matter of justice, Ecumenical Patriarch of Constantinople, Bartholomew I, primus inter pares, received his appeal and restored him to the priesthood.[428]

The persecution of priests who condemned the violence of the so-called special military operation in Ukraine has become commonplace. Going beyond church tribunals, priests have been subjected to civil fines and even criminal charges. Father Nikandr Pinchuk, a priest of the ROCOR, was convicted of a crime for a social media post in which he claimed Russia's war on Ukraine to be a "mortal sin." Decrying his conviction, Father Pinchuk said: "I have committed no crime. I am a priest and have the right to denounce evil, regardless of who is involved in the political situation."[429]

Other priests have committed crimes, not against Russia, but in Europe. Invariably, they are related to infrastructure information gathers, the exploitation of individuals or other espionage-related activities. The last decade has seen an explosion in the number of ROC clergy having been caught in espionage. The response by the Moscow Patriarchate has almost become predictable—claim religious persecution by the west.

Evidence dismisses such a defense:

> An open-source investigation by the Molfar Intelligence Institute in late 2024 concluded that the ROC "continues to construct churches near strategic facilities, government institutions, and military bases across various European countries"—a systematic effort to use religious outposts for espionage. European security services are starting to heed the warnings: from Scandinavia to the heart of Europe, Orthodox churches aligned with Moscow are under intense scrutiny for their proximity to sensitive sites and ties to the Kremlin's security apparatus.[430]

---

[427] Sergei Chapnin, "An Act of Lighthearted Betrayal: How Moscow's Official Church Hunts Down Her Anti-War Priests", *Public Theology*, 12 May 2023.

[428] Associated Press, "Russian Orthodox Priests Persecuted for Supporting Peace in Ukraine", *Voice of America News*, 12 August 2023.

[429] John Burger, "Russian court fines priest for criticism of war", *Aleteia*, 21 October 2022.

[430] NDR Staff Writers, "ROCes in Europe: Espionage Outposts Under the Guise of Faith", *Nordic Defense Review*, 10 July 2025.

The Molfar Intelligence Institute's investigation was built on previous findings throughout Europe. The ROC's Head of Mission to the EU, Archimandrite Philip, has had his hands full trying to defend the spate of arrests or expulsions of ROC clergy from European States. Some of the more notorious of these events have included (non-exhaustively):

March 3, 2014, Crimea

Reshat Ametov, a 39-year-old father of three, was active in the Crimean Tatar community. Following Russia's February 20, 2014, invasion of Crimea, he came under intense scrutiny by occupation forces. He was known to defend his Muslim faith and his identity as both a Crimean Tatar and Ukrainian patriot. In broad daylight, he was abducted by Russian paramilitary personnel. It was the last time he was seen alive. Two weeks later, his body was discovered, badly mutilated with signs of prolonged and painful torture. Despite his abductors having been recorded on CCTV, Russian authorities did not pursue the case. Ametov would not be alone. Russia would continue to arrest Crimean Tatars, almost all Muslims, claiming they belonged to a terrorist organization (Islam). In a repetition of the brazen 'disappearing' of Crimean Tatars, Islam Dzhepparov and his cousin, 23-year-old Dzhevdet Islamov, would fall victim to Russian paramilitarists. When witnesses provided detailed descriptions of the abductors and the car registration plate information to Russian occupation authorities, nothing was done. Along with Ervin Ibragimov, Timur Shaimardanov and Vasyl Chernysh and countless others, Ametov would become victims of Russia's religious discrimination against those not adherent to the ROC.[431]

July 13, 2018 — New York

In the aftermath of a United States special prosecutor indicting 12 Russian intelligence operatives attempting to steal campaign information during the 2016 presidential campaign, an Associated Press (AP) investigation using Secureworks, a division of Dell Technologies for data mining, found Russia was using the FancyBear cyber phishing tool to exploit the computers of the world's top Orthodox Christian leaders:

> Among them were several senior church officials called metropolitans, who are roughly equivalent to archbishops in the Catholic tradition. Those include Bartholomew Samaras, a key confidante of the patriarch; Emmanuel

---

[431] Halya Coynash, "Reshat Ametov and 10 years of Russia's systematic torture, abductions and killings of civilians for supporting Ukraine", *Human Rights Ukraine*, 4 March 2023.

Adamakis, an influential hierarch in the church; and Elpidophoros Lambriniadis, who heads a prestigious seminary on the Turkish island of Halki. All are involved in the [Ukraine] Tomos issue; none returned recent AP messages seeking comment.[432]

Following the AP story, Russian intelligence analyst Dmitry Oreshkin told the AP: "Our church leaders are connected to the FSB and their epaulettes stick out from under their habits. They provide Vladimir Putin's policy with an ideological foundation."[433]

May 2021 – United States of America

The Federal Bureau of Investigation (FBI) charged a priest of the Moscow Patriarchate Department of External Church Relations, Dmitriy Petrovsky, with espionage. Documents on Father Dmitriy's computers showed he had hacked the computers of two "prominent" ROCOR clergy and developed kompromat to exploit them. The files seized by the FBI included detailed biographies of the clergy's family members created by Father Petrovsky, allegedly to use in coercion, blackmail, and exploitation on behalf of the Russian state. The data was being used, according to court filings, to blackmail other Orthodox Christian clergy in the United States to pressure them to join his espionage activities on behalf of the Russian Federation.

Petrovsky was stopped by US Customs and Border Protection officials in 2021 while attempting to enter the United States. His computer was searched. By 2023, data analysis led the FBI to warn orthodox church leaders across the United States about their concerns. The warning message included the following:

> The FBI decided to share the specific and sensitive Investigative information below to provide tangible examples to the Russian Orthodox and other Eastern Orthodox communities of the threat posed to them by the (RIS) Russian Intelligence Services....[434]

According to the FBI warning, Petrovsky was suspected of being:

> A Russian Intelligence Officer operating under nonofficial cover, as a lay person staff member in the Department for External Church Relations of the ROC (ROC)....

---

[432] AP News, "Sacrilegious spies: Russians tried hacking Orthodox clergy", *NBC News*, 27 August 2018.
[433] AP News, *ibid.*
[434] J.J. Green, "Crossroads of a Crisis: Spies use global chaos as cover", *WTOP News*, 16 November 2023.

> ... files obtained via the border search identified perceived vulnerabilities of ROC clergy and ROC employees very likely for use as kompromat, (compromising material) in an effort to blackmail employees into participating in Russian intelligence operations.[435]

The FBI was unusually candid in its contact warning:

> The Russian national was also carrying 'files regarding the source/agent recruitment process' as well as dossiers on church employees, including detailed biographical information about them and members of their families — information that the warning suggests could be used to blackmail employees of the church into participating in spy operations.[436]

As discussed earlier in this manuscript, the documents uncovered in the FBI's counterintelligence arising from the forensic examination of files on Petrovsky's computer and documents in his possession included a memorandum approved by Patriarch Kirill. The memorandum removed all doubt as to who authorized the espionage operation against persons in the United States and Orthodox Christian hierarchs and clergy involved in activities related to the tomos of autocephaly for Ukraine.

A "high confidence" intelligence conclusion was reached that the Moscow Patriarchate's Petrovsky was conducting espionage while using the ROC as a cover for Russian state intelligence services. Equally so, there was damning evidence that it was all authorized by Patriarch Kirill. The FBI and international intelligence community came to an inescapable conclusion — the ROC was continuing the role it played for the KGB during the Cold War. It could reasonably be concluded that the Moscow Patriarch is a security apparatus of the Russian state and acted with the blessing, if not direction, of Patriarch Kirill.[437]

The difficulty for the FBI was one Europe had grappled with for years. ROC clergy had been active in Russian state affairs in Europe for centuries. After 2021, the FBI had to start dealing with the rapid growth of the ROC in the United States in the previous decade.[438]

Following Russia's invasion of Ukraine in 2014, and noticeably during the COVID-19 pandemic, the growth of the ROC in the United States

---

[435] J.J. Green, *ibid*.
[436] John Jackson, "Russia's Trying to Recruit Spies From U.S. Churches: Report", *Newsweek*, 21 September 2023.
[437] Andrei Soldatov and Irina Borogan, "Putin's Useful Priests: The ROC and the Kremlin's Hidden Influence Campaign in the West", *Foreign Affairs*, 14 September 2023.
[438] Katherine Kaladis, "White Supremacy and Orthodox Christianity: A Dangerous Connection Rears Its Head in Charlottesville" *Religion Dispatches*, 18 August 2017.

far outpaced other religions.[439] Analysts believe that its popularity among young, right-wing, American, males seeking a "masculine" Christian experience with 'traditional values' are flocking to the ROCOR.[440] Their affiliation from social values at times puts them at odds with the sacramental life of Orthodox Christianity which many reject, yet remain in the ROC: "They're drawn to what they believe to be conservative views on things like LGBTQ rights, gender equality. Abortion is a really big issue for these folks, the culture wars issues, really." Aram Sarkisian, a postdoctoral teaching fellow at Northwestern University's Department of History, also said. "And so they leave other faith traditions that they don't believe to be as stringent about those issues anymore… I first started noticing this around 2010, 2011 on Orthodox blogs, where I started to see language and rhetoric that was subtly racist and was subtly engaging in what we would now know as the alt-right," Sarkisian said. "They bring it with them into the church because they see Orthodoxy as amenable to these goals, to these viewpoints."[441]

The 'conversion' of white nationalists, often evangelicals, with their other extremist views is not their desire to be changed by Orthodox Christianity but to change it.[442]

2022 – Ukraine

The *Guardian* reported an instance early in Russia's full-scale invasion of Ukraine of a pro-Russian monastery assisting Russian soldiers in combat operations. Due to martial law reporting restrictions at the time, Emma Graham-Harrison filed the following story:

> As war kicked off in Ukraine, soldiers at a military airstrip in the west of the country went hunting for the origin of a laser pointer they feared was marking out targets on their base.
> They found it in a nearby church. Behind the thick walls of the building in Kolomyia, run by monks loyal to Moscow, they also discovered a large stockpile of food and alcohol, and three guns.
> 'It's very, very surprising, because it was a monastery,' said Father Mykhailo Arsenich, army chaplain to the unit that searched the church. 'There was a big stockpile of food, packed for military use, designed to keep 60 to 65 people for a very long time.

---

[439] Kenneth R. Ross, Grace Ji-Sun Kim and Todd M. Johnson, editors, "Christianity in North America", *Edinburgh University Press*, 2023.
[440] Lucy Ash, "Young US men are joining Russian churches promising 'absurd levels of manliness'", *BBC News*, 25 May 2025.
[441] Terry Mattingly, "Concerning the new converts to Eastern Orthodoxy: Are they MAGA clones or worse?", *GetReligion*, 16 May 2022.
[442] Sarah Riccardi-Swartz, "Between Heaven and Russia: Religious Conversion and Political Apostasy in Appalachia", *Fordham University Press*, 2022.

> We found two pistols, and one hunting rifle which was converted from a combat Kalashnikov. They couldn't address the question of why priests needed guns.'[443]

The pre-positioning of large amounts of food packed for military use suggests the Ukrainian Orthodox Church (Moscow Patriarchate) monastery was known by invading Russian forces to be a supply depot. The presence of pistols and a weapon fashioned from a Russian-made Kalashnikov rifle in a monastery proved not to be an anomaly. Following Russia's full-scale invasion of Ukraine, numerous stockpiles of weapons were found in the possession of the Ukrainian Orthodox Church (Moscow Patriarchate) and the ROC clergy. In the autumn of 2023, a priest of the Ukrainian Orthodox Church (Moscow Patriarchate) was arrested as a profiteer for his role in the illegal arms trade.[444]

November 22, 2022 – Ukraine

The collaboration between the Ukrainian Orthodox Church (Moscow Patriarchate) and Russian security services has long been well known. In the autumn of 2022, Ukraine's security services, *Служба безпеки України* (SBU), launched a raid on the Kyiv Pechersk Lavra Monastery, the bastion of Metropolitan Onufriy's pro-Russian Church. According to the SBU:

> More than 50 people underwent in-depth counterintelligence surveys, including using a polygraph. Among them were not only citizens of Ukraine, but also foreigners, in particular citizens of the Russian Federation who were on the territory of the facilities.... [Some passports had] 'signs of forgery or damage.'[445]

In addition to pro-Russian propaganda and literature, including materials concerning the Russkiy Mir, the SBU also found exceptional amounts of cash in United States currency: "cash in various currencies worth tens of thousands of dollars was discovered."[446]

---

[443] Emma Graham-Harrison, "Ukraine's pro-Russian monasteries draw local suspicion", *The Guardian*, 7 March 2022.
[444] Staff Writers, "Priest with Moscow-affiliated church caught on illegal arms trade", *Ukrinform*, 26 September 2023.
[445] Staff Writers, "Ukraine says 'dubious' Russians found in raid on Kyiv monastery", *Reuters*, 23 November 2022.
[446] Staff Writers, *ibid*.

January 1, 2023 — Estonia

Estonia's Foreign Intelligence Service releases a public report based on redacted sources — "International Security and Estonia 2023". The report details Russian intelligence operations detected in Estonia and elsewhere in Europe using ROC clergy: "The Russian special services officers hide behind various 'covers'. A tried-and-tested cover organization used abroad is the ROC, which the Kremlin also operates as an instrument of influence against Ukraine and the West."[447]

September 18, 2023 — Macedonia

The government of North Macedonia banned Archimandrite Vasian (born Nikolai Valerievich Zmeev) from entering the country based on intelligence that he had been sent on numerous missions to the country previously to 'split' the orthodox church in North Macedonia on the orders of the Moscow Patriarchate.[448]

The North Macedonian Ministry of Foreign Affairs, which explained that in addition to Archimandrite Vasian, it was expelling three Russian diplomats from the country (allegedly, Archimandrite Vasian's 'handlers'): "This decision was made after receiving information from the competent authorities about actions committed by Russians that violate the Vienna Convention on Diplomatic Relations."[449]

September 21, 2023 — Bulgaria

Archimandrite Vasian, a frequent traveler to North Macedonia who was a resident of Sophia, and two other ROC clergy, were expelled under the authority of the head of the state Agency for National Security of Bulgaria (SANS):

> Measures were applied in connection with their activities directed against national security and the interests of the Republic of Bulgaria. There is information about the actions of these persons related to the implementation of various elements of the Russian Federation's hybrid strategy to purposefully influence the socio-political processes in the Republic of Bulgaria in favor of Russian geopolitical interests.[450]

---

[447] Estonian Foreign Intelligence Service, "International Security and Estonia 2023", *Cyber Vault Library*, 31 January 2023.
[448] Estonian Foreign Intelligence Service, *ibid*.
[449] Elena Konstantinova, "North Macedonia authorities ban ROC archimandrite from entering the country", *Union of Orthodox Journalists*, 18 September 2023.
[450] Igor Fedyk, "Espionage Scandal with ROC in Bulgaria, *New Geopolitics*, 25 September 2023.

Russia's ambassador to Bulgaria, Elenora Mitrofanova, stated at the time: "After being declared persona non grata, Wassian and the other two clerics were taken home under police supervision to pack up their belongings. Then they will be taken to the border with Serbia."[451]

Atanas Atanasov, a Bulgarian politician who headed the parliamentary committee for oversight of state intelligence services, spoke of his dismay that Archimandrite Vasian had not been expelled earlier:

> Everyone in the National Security Agency knows that this priest here is a representative of Russian intelligence in a cassock. I ask the Bulgarian counterintelligence — are they not ashamed that someone who lives and develops intelligence activities in Bulgaria was expelled from Macedonia, and here he lives in comfort.[452]

November 24, 2023 — Sweden

The city of Västerås is located approximately 100 kilometers from the Swedish capital of Stockholm. Situated on the shores of Lake Mälaren in the province of Västmanland would be unremarkable except for four things: its state-of-the-art water treatment facility, the presence of many advanced energy companies, its sizable former military airport and extensive runway reactivated after Sweden rejoined NATO and the decision of the ROC to build a new church, Church of the Holy Mother of God of Kazan only meters from the busy and extremely noisy runways at Västerås Airport. The presence of any new church in Västerås would not normally cause concern. With over 127,000 residents, a new church would normally be welcome. It was the decision to construct a ROC next to a reactivated dual-use civilian-NATO airfield, however, that raised eyebrows. The location is incongruous for a destination normally association with peace, tranquility and contemplation. Attendees at the church complain they can neither pray nor hear the liturgy with the roar of jet engines constantly overwhelming them. Other, more important considerations must have determined its location.

According to Swedish officials, the construction of the ROC parish just outside the gate of the airfield is no coincidence. It provides ease of access to monitor NATO flight activities and a nearby Swedish military communications center. According to Markus Göransson, a Swedish Defense University researcher focusing on Russia:

> The church offers a potential foothold that can be used for information-gathering, both directed at Västerås Airport and at industrial interests in the

---

[451] Katarzyna Skiba, "The ROC Has a Kremlin Spy Network — And Now It's Spreading Abroad", *WorldCrunch*, 4 January 2024.
[452] Staff Writers, "Russian priest also 'non-grata' has carried out 'counterintelligence'" in Skopje", *GeoPost*, 18 September 2023.

form of large companies involved in the energy sector. When Sweden's defense forces undertake exercises on or near the airport, as was done in June, they do so under possible surveillance from the church.[453]

Sweden's concerns are well-founded. In 2024, five Russian Embassy personnel were declared persona non grata and asked to leave Sweden immediately. In the aftermath of Russia's full-scale invasion of Ukraine in 2022, European capitals expelled hundreds of Russian diplomats associated with spying and espionage.[454] The mass expulsion of Russian diplomats tied to Russian state intelligence gathering and active operations represented a serious blow to Russia's espionage capabilities in Europe.

The reliance on ROC clergy, who are not generally vetted by their host states because of the religious freedoms specifically guaranteed by the European Charter of Fundamental Rights at Article 10, became ever more critical to Russian intelligence services like the SVU and FSB. The new ROC, built only 250 meters from the Västerås Airport control tower, is an exemplar of the role the Moscow Patriarchate is playing in shoring up Russia's long-arm intelligence operations.

Moscow Patriarch churches on Russia's periphery have become so vital to the Russian state's security operations and intelligence gathering activities that when a parish cannot be built to meet its espionage needs, Russians are mobilized to take over existing churches:

> But Father Angel says he's alarmed by Moscow's influence. His parish is affiliated with the Bulgarian Patriarchate, which is apolitical. Patriarch Kirill preaches war. He introduced a mandatory prayer. That priests must recite in every service for a Russian victory over Ukraine. That's outright heresy. Heretic!...
> Father Angel tells us that in 2019, the Moscow Patriarchate tried to infiltrate the parish. Around 50 newly registered parishioners attempted a coup. They tried to organize a vote to become the majority and take control of the parish to subject it to Moscow's authority. But the takeover attempt failed.
> One year later, another coup attempt in a neighborhood located in the hills above Stockholm. In 2020, to cover maintenance costs, they agreed to lease the church for just 2 months to an Orthodox congregation close to Moscow's St. George Parish. The newcomers did not pay the rent and tried to take over the church association by signing up new members. The attempt failed and the Russians resorted to drastic measures.

---

[453] Charlie Duxbury, "New Russian church raises suspicions in Swedish town", *Politico*, 11 November 2024.
[454] Kate Connolly, "EU allies expel 200 Russian diplomats in two days after Bucha killings", *The Guardian*, 5 April 2022.

This lock was changed three times. The third time they actually succeeded to have the church for themselves for almost 4 years. We couldn't come into our own church! They took it.[455]

The Syndigheten för stöd till trossamfund (SST), a Swedish state body that provides funding for religious groups, stopped funding for the Moscow Patriarchate-aligned churches in Sweden following consultations with the state security service, Säkerhetspolisen (SÄPO). Following a March 17, 2025, report by TV4 *Nyheterna*, Russia was recruiting people suffering from addiction problems to carry out acts of sabotage. SÄPO released the following statement:

> Foreign powers are using security-threatening activities and hybrid activities to destabilize Sweden and Europe. This involves illegal intelligence activities, influence, cyberattacks, theft of technology and knowledge, mapping, and threats against opponents. The Security Service can also note an increased Russian risk appetite with threats of sabotage also in Sweden.[456]

While not explicitly mentioning the ROC, SÄPO's timing of the statement coinciding with the cessation of funding from SST for Moscow Patriarchate-affiliated church activities suggests a connection.[457]

August 23, 2024 – Czech Republic

On August 20, 2024, the Security Committee of the Senate of the Czech Republic ordered the Security Information Service (BIS) to investigate the ROC (Moscow Patriarch) and its activities. The order came on the back of a running investigation by the Parlament České republiky (Czech parliament). According to the committee's chairman, Pavel Fischer:

> Foreign powers should not exploit concepts such as freedom of religion and the right of association to exert influence. The Russian Orthodox Church and the Orthodox Church in the Czech Republic must not be used as tools by the Russian Federation to act against the interests of the Czech Republic.[458]

---

[455] Reporters (Video), "Exclusive investigation: Is the ROC in Sweden a platform for espionage?", *France 24*, 4 July 2025.
[456] SÄPO, "Orolig omvärld skapar hot i Sverige", *Säkerhetspolisen*, 11 Mars 2025.
[457] In spycraft, the exploitation of those over whom you have kompromat or are otherwise compromised by their conduct or live with a poor social status make good candidates to "turn." ROC clergy would be prime candidates in identifying such persons as having both pro-Russian sympathies and being candidates to co-opt in such activities.
[458] Ahmet Gencturk, "Czech intelligence launches investigation into ROC's operations in country", *Anadolu Ajansı (AA)*, 23 August 2024.

The previous April, the Czech Republic moved to revoke the residence permit and honorary citizenship of a ROC priest, Nikolai Vasilyevich Lysenyuk, priest of a ROC in Karlovy Vary. Ostensibly, Father Lysenyuk was declared persona non grata and expelled for recruiting Czechs and other Europeans to create a pro-Russian successionist movement and for praising Russian aggression in his sermons. That same year, the Czech government added Patriarch Kirill of Moscow personally to its sanctions list along with Father Lysenyuk.[459]

To skirt Czech sanctions, the ROC transferred the Church of St. Peter and Paul in Karlovy Vary into the hands of the Kremlin-friendly Hungarian Orthodox Church.[460] Both the Czech Orthodox Church and the Hungarian Orthodox Church fall under the jurisdiction of the Moscow Patriarchate. Additionally, the Hungarian Government under Prime Minister Viktor Orbán has demonstrated itself as being hostile to the EU and marked itself as being clearly in the Russian camp. In June 2023, Patriarch Kirill awarded the First Degree of the 'Order of Glory and Honor' from the ROC to Orbán.[461]

June 23, 2025 – Estonia

Estonia has deemed the ROC and Moscow Patriarchate to pose such a security threat that it is seeking legislation to ban them from operating in Estonia as they represent a "threat to national security."[462] Despite ongoing efforts by the Riigikogu (Estonian parliament) to legislate a prohibition on the Moscow Patriarchate's continued presence and influence in Estonia, Russia's subterfuge and influence activities have not ceased.

In September 2024, the Estonian but Moscow Patriarchate-controlled Pühtitsa Convent joined the Estonian Orthodox Church of the Moscow Patriarchate (MPEÕK) in bringing legal proceedings in the Tallinn Administrative Court against the Riigikogu for their attempts to ban the ROC's activities in Estonia. Their complaint failed. The Moscow Patriarchate did not give up, however. They immediately appealed to Estonia's Supreme Court. On March 15, 2025, Estonia's highest court refused to hear the joint Pühtitsa Convent-Estonian Orthodox Church of the Moscow Patriarchate (MPEÕK) appeal.

---

[459] Daniela Lazarová, "Russia's Patriarch Kirill first name on Czech national sanctions list", *Radio Prague International*, 27 April 2023.
[460] Staff Writers, "Russian Church in Czechia Transferred into Ownership of Hungarian Diocese", *Hungary Today*, 11 February 2025.
[461] Hetzmann Mercédesz, "PM Viktor Orbán receives Russian Order of Glory and Honour", *Daily News Hungary*, 2 June 2023.
[462] Andreja Bogdanovski, "Russian Church branded security threat to Estonia", *Church Times*, 17 May 2024.

By the summer of 2025, Estonia's Pühtitsa Convent came under renewed scrutiny by the Estonian security service. Despite being in Estonia, as a demonstration of the ROC's outsized influence in states formerly under the Russian sphere, Patriarch Kirill appointed the convent's Abbess, Sister Filareta Kalatšova. In June 2025, Estonia's Ministry of the Interior's chief policy designer, Martin Tulit, spoke of the threat posed by the activities of the Pühtitsa Convent:

> The convent should be seen not simply as a religious institution, but also as a symbol of the Russki Mir ideology on Estonian soil — an ideology promoted by the Russian state and the Moscow Patriarchate that blends religion, nationalism, and imperial nostalgia.[463]

September 28, 2025 — Moldova

In the long run-up to Moldova's national elections in the autumn 2025, the country stood at the precipice of maintaining its pro-European orientation or lapsing back into the Russian sphere of influence. The stakes were extremely high. Moldova's highest courts had blocked the participation of the pro-Russian 'Heart of Moldova' party. It was barred from the election after Moldova's highest court ruled the party's activities should be restricted for at least one year after hearing evidence of vote buying, bribery, illegal party financing and money laundering. The police had carried out raids on multiple locations prior to balloting commencing after detecting sophisticated syndicates prepared to disrupt the democratic process. Russia denies it was engaged in assisting Heart of Moldova.

Notwithstanding such denials, the ROC, Russia's soft-power cadre, enmeshed themselves in election interference. An all-expense paid pilgrimage for Moscow Patriarchate aligned Moldovan Orthodox priests to visit Russia's holiest religious sites was arranged. While exiting Russia, the Moldovan priests were handed pre-paid credit cards by unidentified civilians unrelated to the tour group or its operators. They gladly accepted the funds. Reuters reported clergy were expected to promote pro-Russian candidates in exchange for the generosity of the Russian Orthodox Church.

Unconfirmed reports indicate Moldovan clergy were given 'talking points' and specimen 'sermons' to assist them in encouraging Moldova's faithful to reject Moldova's EU-oriented Party of Action and Solidarity and oppose EU policies. They were also given instructions on how to use their existing social media channels for election interference purposes and how to create more. The funds were meant to be a quid pro quo for the priests to encourage Moldovans to cast their votes for pro-Russian candidates. According to a report by TVP World:

---

[463] Anna Rees, "Estonian nuns accused of spying for Putin", *Christian News*, 23 June 2025.

> ...almost 90 new parish-led channels have appeared in the past year in Moldova, according to Reuters analysis. Many repost identical content from a central feed, Sare și Lumiña (Salt and Light), which pumps out messages about Europe corrupting Moldova's morals and threatening its Orthodox faith.[464]

According to Reuters:

> one of the Moscow Patriarchate aligned Moldovan Orthodox Church clergy, "Father Mihai Bicu, a priest in the Orthodox Church in Moldova, boarded the flight back home from Moscow with his head spinning from the unfamiliar attention lavished on him... Before they flew home, Bicu said he and many others in his group received debit cards issued by a Russian state bank which were handed to them in a monastery by non-church people whom he couldn't identify. They were told money would be transferred to them soon after they returned to Moldova.[465]

Father Bicu confirmed the Moldovan priests were told that in exchange for the money (he received about $1,200 upon his return to Moldova) they clergy expected to create social media channels for their parishes in Moldova to promote pro-Russian candidates and discourage parishioners from voting for pro-EU candidates and policies. Archbishop Marchel Mihăescu of the Moldovan Orthodox Church (Moscow Patriarchate), "dismissed claims of political interference, saying the trips were spiritual journeys and that new online channels were created locally."[466]

After the ROC scheme to sway Modlova's national elections away from its EU orientation, Stanislav Secrieru, national security adviser to Moldova's president said, "The most immoral feature of Russian electoral interference in elections in Moldova is the use of the most trusted institution – the Church." His observation about how the ROC masquerades as a church but operates as part of the Russian state propaganda mechanism is worthy of serious consideration in light of the Reuters Special Report:

> Almost 90 new Telegram channels have been established as the accounts of Moldovan Orthodox parishes over the past year, according to a Reuters review of social media data. Most channels have pumped out identical content on a near-daily basis, urging the faithful to oppose the government's pro-Western push in posts that have reached thousands of followers, the analysis found.
> When asked about the flurry of new channels, Telegram said it was a politically neutral platform that respects peaceful free speech.

---

[464] Reuters, "'To gay Europe I say no!': How Russia mobilizes Moldovan clergy ahead of elections", *TVP World*, 27 September 2025.

[465] Christian Lowe, Polina Nikolskaya and Anton Zverev, "Holy war: How Russia recruited Orthodox priests to sway Moldova's voters" *A Reuters Special Report*, 26 September 2025.

[466] Reuters, *ibid*.

The online activity has been ramping up as Sunday's election nears. The source for most of the content, a channel called Sare și Lumiña that is reposted by the parish accounts, published over 600 messages between May and August, almost triple the number posted over the previous four months of this year.[467]

The ROC's intrusion into Moldova's domestic electoral process was not surprising. A consortium of news organisations including VSquare and Frontstory, RISE Moldova, Expressen in Sweden, the Dossier Centre for Investigative Journalism, Yahoo News and Delfi revealed documents they had obtained outlining how Russia had plans to use the ROC as part of its 10-year plan to destabilise Moldova.[468] The all-expenses paid junket for Moldovan priests to visit Russia as guests of the ROC so they could receive funds and instructions on how to interfere in free elections in Moldova marked yet one more indelible mark of the ROC's willingness to place Russian state priorities above those of its character and mission as a church.

The disruptive and illicit activities of the Moscow Patriarchate's 'Wolves in Sheep's Clothing' is deserving of cataloguing and examination in a separate publication. This manuscript could have been devoted entirely to listing and examining the plethora of cases in which the ROC has manifested activities in which it has been exposed as posing a threat to European security and democracy. We have elected, however, to help readers better understand how Russian history and the ROC have collaborated and conspired in such a way as to not only create the threat but sustain it. The issue then turns to "How will Europe and the world respond?"

---

[467] Christian Lowe, Polina Nikolskaya and Anton Zverev, *ibid*.
[468] Tim Lister, "Secret document reveals Russia's 10-year plan to destabilize Moldova", *CNN*, 18 March 2023.

Chapter Eighteen

While Europe Sleeps
Will Europe Meet the Demands of the Age?

The question arises, "What will or can Europe do?" Both the question and the answer are complex. However, as Moldova proved in their 2025 national elections, Europe can be protected from the ROC's intrusions and Russian propaganda influence to safeguard itself against social disruption and pro-Russian subterfuge.

Western civilisation has developed a deep hostility to attempts by governments to restrain the exercise of free speech and religious liberty. In the Americas, Thomas Jefferson, the writer of one of the most universally recognized instruments of political and social genius expressed in prose, literature, and legal arguments in favor of liberty desired that his epitaph commemorate that he wrote the Virginia Statute For Establishing Religious Freedom (1786) and not that for which he is most famous—the Declaration of Independence (1776).

Equally so, the European Charter on Fundamental Rights waxes equally eloquently in Article 10 on the issue of religious freedom. The United Nations Declaration on the Elimination of All Forms of Intolerance and of Discrimination Based on Religion or Belief (1981) represents a powerful commitment to protecting each human being's right to worship (or not worship) as they see fit.

All these, and the body of related laws developed in Europe over the centuries to guarantee freedom of religion, speech, and expression, militate in the Moscow Patriarchate's and the Russian state's interest in thwarting efforts to stop their enduring misuse of the ROC's status as a religious entity. Any real examination of the ROC will find that when the church's theology and the Russian state's ideology are at odds (they rarely are), it is the Russian state that prevails. When it comes to establishing the Kingdom of God, the Moscow Patriarchate ensures that effort takes a back seat to establishing the Russkiy Mir.

While Europe slept, Russia remained active. In previous chapters, we have discussed the growth of the ROC abroad since the fall of the Soviet Union in 1991. Europe, anxious to encourage pro-western values and democratic norms sat on the sidelines while Russia tightened its grip of the ROC's control of the Russian population and ignored its intrusion into the religious affairs of the 'near abroad' in Europe. The lack of prior intervention on the part of Europe collectively and individually by willing states allowed the ROC to tighten its stranglehold on the faithful (willing and unwilling) and copper-fasten its physical and institutional foothold in Europe.

It is all understandable, even if regrettable. Orthodox Christians cannot deny Christ's presence in the ROC. There is much to be admired in its commitment to tradition. The difficulty, however, is the ROC's ability to distinguish orthodox tradition from political tradition.

As Europeans, democrats, and people committed to a rules-based world order, the lack of action in containing the ROC's threat to European security and democracy must be protested. The ecclesial nature of the ROC cannot avert attention from the fact that throughout its long history, from the time of the principality of Muscovy to today, the ROC has broken with the Russian State only once and only briefly, between 1917 and 1922. In 1926, the ROC renewed its relationship not with the Ecumenical Patriarchate in Constantinople, but with Stalin in the Kremlin. Indeed, the numerous times in which the ROC has broken communion with the Ecumenical Patriarchate by comparison survive as indelible proof that it prioritizes the Russian state before the church Christ Jesus left to his disciples at Pentecost.

We nonetheless understand that the ROC, given its embrace of Holy Rus' ideology and devotion to the Russkiy Mir, is undeserving of the deference normally afforded an institution of faith. Whatever good is done by the ROC does not mediate its declaration of a 'holy war' which not only blesses the rapine pillage, murder, destruction, and evils of war but promises martyrdom for those who fight in Russia's name and interests.

The brief, non-exhaustive list of ways in which the ROC and Patriarch Kirill have shown themselves intent on undermining Europe, its institutions, cultures, values, and commitment to peace should serve as an organizing tool to motivate European lawmakers to engage in mechanisms to restrain corruption of the west by the ROC and Russian State.

It will not be easy. It requires an examination of our understanding of the ROC and the courage to name it for what it is—a security apparatus of the Russian State. Only then can it be resolved that it needs to be regulated without fear of violating the precepts of religious freedom, rites and rituals.

After all, none of the legislation proposed or adopted to contain the misconduct of the ROC from Kyiv to Tallinn bans anyone's freedom of worship. No Orthodox Christian attending a ROC could claim they are being deprived of exercising their choice to worship in the Orthodox Christian faith.

The law has long recognized that what might be considered acceptable in an individual setting becomes illegal, even criminal, when conducted as part of an enterprise. For example, it is wholly lawful to conduct commerce as a sole trader. If, however, you join with other traders or become so large as to have the power to restrain other sole traders, you have crossed the line of acceptability and legality and engaged in restraint of trade or even market manipulation. It is no different for those who follow the Moscow Patriarchate.

There is no problem in believing in the catechism of the ROC. On the contrary, it is to be admired. However, when one gathers with others to do so under an organization, namely the Moscow Patriarchate, that seeks to prevent other free people in neighboring countries from worshipping freely as they choose, the adherent and the ROC cross the line. In such a situation, it can no longer be said they are exercising their rights of religious freedom but rather have become the oppressor seeking to prohibit others from worshipping freely.

Freedom of religion and the safeguarding of the inherent dignity of the human condition were at the heart of the justice done by restoring the Metropolis of Kyiv to the Ecumenical Patriarchate. The restoration of the metropolis of Kyiv and the erection of the autocephalous Orthodox Church of Ukraine were not acts intended to injure Moscow. To the contrary, the tomos of autocephaly was granted to liberate Orthodox Christians to worship in their own, genuinely autocephalous Orthodox Church of Ukraine, freed of the demand of participating in the Divine Liturgy in which their invader, including the Patriarch of Moscow, the very persons who had declared a 'holy war' on them, demanded he be commemorated by them. No right-thinking person could conclude that forcing victims of a 'holy war' to commemorate their centuries-long oppressor, who declared the 'holy war' against them, to be anything but a repugnant violation of their fundamental rights.[469]

Some would say that banning the Moscow Patriarchate from operating in Ukraine violates the freedom of religion rights of those who do wish to commemorate the Patriarchate of Moscow; they are wrong. This is nonsense. The Orthodox Christian faith does not require the commemoration of the Patriarch of Moscow. It is only the ROC that demands it. Every Ukrainian who wishes to exercise their right of freedom of religion and worship in the ancient Orthodox Christian tradition is guaranteed the right to do so.

---

[469] Metropolitan Onufriy declared the tomos, which restored the Metropolitanate of Ukraine to the Ecumenical Patriarchate, to be an act of "enslavement". See: Yekaterina Filatova, "His Beatitude Onuphry: OCU has the Tomos of slavery rather than autocephaly", *Union of Orthodox Journalists*, 11 July 2019.

What these laws do not provide for, and should not provide for, is the continued political oppression of others in the name of freedom of religion. Contrary to Russian apologists' claims, religious freedom endures in Ukraine and is far more robust than that which might still survive in Russia. When it comes to 'have' and 'have-nots' of religious freedom, Russia is firmly planted in the 'have-not' camp.[470]

The truth is that it is Russia and the ROC, not Ukraine, Estonia or any other country that seeks to defend themselves from the illiberality of those combined forces that offend the principles of freedom of religion. Consider the following testimony by the head of the United Kingdom's Delegation to the OSCE, Neil Holland, in Vienna:

> Father Stepan Podolchak, a 59-year-old priest of the Ukrainian Orthodox Church in Kherson Oblast, was known for his unwavering patriotism and insistence on conducting services in Ukrainian. Stepan resisted pressure from the Federal Security Services to align with the ROC. In February 2024, Russian authorities forcibly took Stepan to an unknown location. Two weeks later, Stepan's wife was summoned to identify his body. It's reported that Stepan was tortured to death.
> Madam Chair, Stepan's tragic death is not an anomaly but fits the brutal tactics of the Kremlin Playbook. Tactics used to subjugate the civilian population and eliminate diversity of religion, culture and identity.
> Two Greek Catholic priests, Father Ivan Levitsky and Father Bohdan Geleta, were unlawfully detained by Russian forces in Zaporizhzhia Oblast in November 2022. To this day, their families do not know where they are or if they will ever be released.[471] [472]

The two Catholic priests were later released. After 19 months of captivity, they were exchanged only after the direct intervention of Pope Francis, Pietro Cardinal Parolin, Matteo Cardinal Zuppi, and Archbishop Visvaldas Kulbokas.

Russia's targets have not been limited to Ukrainian Orthodox Christians or the 'Uniate' Greek Catholics whom the Moscow Patriarchate and the Russian state have long targeted. Evangelicals, Baptists, Anabaptists, Crimean Tatar Muslims and others have suffered as well.

---

[470] Elizabeth Lane Miller and Helene Fisher, edited by Kenneth R. Ross et al., "Religious Freedom." *Compact Atlas of Global Christianity,* 1st ed., *Edinburgh University Press*, 2025

[471] Neil Holland (Speech), "Russia is suppressing the freedom of religion or belief in Ukraine: UK statement to OSCE", *OSCE: Vienna*, 2 May 2024.

[472] Fathers Levitsky and Geleta were released from Russian captivity after having been arrested in Berdiansk in the region of Zaporizhzhia (neither was a Russian citizen, and their transport from occupied Ukraine to a foreign country for prosecution and detention was illegal in international law).

The following excerpt from *Time* magazine outlines only one such experience of repression inflicted on Evangelical Christians:

> Russia's invasion of Ukraine is accompanied with a strategic effort to repress, control, and crush religious groups outside of the Kremlin controlled Moscow Patriarchate, the ROC. There are over thirty cases of religious clergy killed and kidnapped. 109 known cases of interrogations, forced expulsions, imprisonments, arrests. 600 houses of worship destroyed. And these are just the confirmed numbers, with the real ones in information blackout of the occupied territories will much likely be higher.
>
> Evangelicals are targeted by the Russians disproportionally, and Azat's story is typical for Russia's systemic persecution of Protestants in occupied Ukraine. Protestants were the victims of 34 percent of the reported persecution events, and 48 percent in the Zaporizhzhia region where Azat was held. Baptists made up 13 percent of victims — the largest single group after Ukrainian Orthodox. Under Russian control 400 Baptist congregations have been lost, 17% of the total in Ukraine.[473]

The constant misdirection of attention that should be focused on the Russian state and the ROC for their role in destroying the precepts of freedom of religion in occupied Ukraine by blaming Ukraine's Rada (Ukrainian parliament) for restricting the operations of churches under foreign state influence is troubling. Consider the following, also an extract from the *Time* article: "'Your church has no right to exist, as it has connections with America and other Western countries' Russian authorities told the deacon of the Pentecostal church in Nova Kakhovka, Oleksandr Prokopchuk."[474]

The Russian authority's claim, "Your church has no right to exist," is understandable. Russian law provides for a special place for the ROC. From the time of Imperial Russia, the ROC clergy had the exclusive right to minister to ethnic Russians. Such privileges were renewed with Russian legislation, "On Freedom of Conscience and Religious Associations" in 1997.[475]

Putin claims Ukraine is not a country, and Ukrainians in occupied territory are required to accept Russian passports and thereby be rendered Russians, albeit against their will. The Russian authority claiming the Evangelical Church had "no right to exist" would be "right," albeit only in Russian law and in the eyes of the Moscow Patriarchate. For Ukrainians and Estonians constantly being accused by the ROC and far-right media as being religiously intolerant, the irony is palpable. Russian apologists like

---

[473] Peter Pomerantsev, "Russia's War Against Evangelicals", *TIME*, 20 April 2024.
[474] Pomerantsev, *ibid*.
[475] Arina Lekhel, "Levelling the Playing Fried for Religious "Liberty" in Russia: A Critical Analysis of the 1997 law "On Freedom of Conscience and Religious Associations", *Vanderbilt Journal of Transnational Law, No. 32 (1), 1999.*

Tucker Carlson and Marjory Taylor Green would have us believe Russia is a victim in this matter.[476]

What happened to Prokopchuk? He and his son, aged 19 years, were 'disappeared.' Their bullet-ridden bodies were later discovered in a forest, having been subjected to extrajudicial murder.

Under the Moscow Patriarch's declaration that Russians fighting in Ukraine are entitled to receive plenary indulgence for their acts[477] — the ROC did not consider such executions to have been sins, and if killed in the process, are to be considered martyrs to the faith:

> Many are dying in the fields of internecine warfare. The Church prays that this battle will end as quickly as possible, that as few brothers as possible will kill each other in this fratricidal war.
> And at the same time the Church is aware that if someone, moved by a sense of duty, by the need to fulfil his oath, remains faithful to his calling and dies in the performance of his military duty, he is undoubtedly committing an act tantamount to sacrifice.[478]

Patriarch Kirill's invocation of plenary indulgence for participating in his 'holy war' is not only unorthodox, it remains without foundation in Christian theology:

> 'The pronouncement of Patriarch Kirill is little different than the sort of indulgences that Martin Luther fought against in the Reformation,' said Andrew T. Walker, associate professor of Christian ethics at the Southern Baptist Theological Seminary. 'Whereas Luther was opposing indulgences for constructing buildings for Catholicism's empire, Kirill's indulgence is meant to bolster Russian empire.'
> It is also blasphemous to compare the meritorious sacrifice of Christ with the military operations led by a former KGB officer. Kirill's pronouncement is as unbiblical as it is absurd...
> It is the worst sort of example of the odious effects that come when church and state get too cozy with one another — false promises, a corrupt church, and an empowered state.

---

476   Stephen E. More, "Russia killing and torturing Ukrainian Christians, not 'protecting' them. Ignore MTG.", *USA Today*, 18 April 2024.

477   The ROC's theological development of this 'sacrifice' and indulgence remains unclear. Nothing like it has ever existed in Christian theology. It is uncertain if sins are forgiven simply by service in the 'holy war' against Ukraine, or if confession is still required, or if one must die in combat to be considered blameless and a martyr. Patriarch Kirill has not clarified the issue or otherwise published a treatise providing for the theological or biblical foundations of his 'holy war' declaration.

478   Peter Smith, "Moscow patriarch: Russian war dead have their sins forgiven", *The Hill*, 27 September 2022.

In this example and, virtually all others like it, the church ends up becoming a puppet for the state to consolidate its power. What's left is a church with little prowess apart from the subservience it renders to the state.[479]

The extent of Russia's anti-religious freedom ethos is made manifestly evident by the continuing persecution of Ukrainians in occupied territories. The extent of these efforts is difficult to either gauge or catalogue. Reliable information gathering and assessment are difficult in occupied Ukraine. Victims of Russia's campaign against religious freedom are often not detected for considerable periods of time.

Some facts, however, have become verifiable. The following analysis by *Вёрстка [Verstka]*, although now dated, is still illustrative of the problems:

> Key findings:
> 1. Verstka has discovered at least 109 acts of pressure on churches and religious figures against five religious denominations.
> 2. Most often, Orthodox Christians and Protestants were subjected to repression.
> 3. At least 43 clergy faced reprisals: eight were captured and five were killed.
> 4. In at least 66 cases, buildings of churches, mosques, religious centers and related organizations were confiscated, looted and destroyed. In their place, the military set up weapons depots, and pro-Russian authorities opened police departments, the Russian National Guard, and United Russia offices.
> 5. The reasons for the repressions included the Ukrainian language, refusal to support the pro-Russian authorities and the ROC.[480]

The ROC's discrimination knows no bounds. Their longtime Ukrainian creature, Metropolitan Onufriy's Ukrainian Orthodox Church (Moscow Patriarchate), has itself discovered it is the target of Russian state and ROC discrimination:

> Amid the systematic absorption of its parishes by the ROC, the Ukrainian Orthodox Church (UOC) has decreased in size by 140% in the past three years. The number of Protestant communities has shrunk by 360%, while the Catholic Church has been almost completely wiped out in the occupied territories: just one of 15 Catholic parishes remains, while not a single one of the 49 Ukrainian Greek Catholic Church parishes that existed prior to the occupation still does. Parishes of the partially recognised OCU have also completely disappeared.

---

[479] Brandon Porter, "'Odious effects' when church, state become too familiar with one another, Walker says", *Baptist Press*, 27 September 2022.

[480] Regina Gimalova, "OVD Instead of Church. How the Russian Army Persecutes Clergymen and Destroys Churches: Verstka's research on religious repressions in the occupied parts of Ukraine", *Вёрстка (Verstka)*, 6 July 2023.

> In total, the number of religious congregations independent of the ROC's Moscow Patriarchate has fallen fivefold since 2022.[481]

As with the ongoing acts of spying, espionage, and destabilization efforts undertaken by the ROC in Europe, the extent of Russia's attempts to extinguish religious liberty for non-adherents to the ROC faith is worthy of its own research and publication. This manuscript has outlined the issues in brief to highlight the problem and provide readers with an impetus to do their own further research. The dynamic has been established, however, through the information provided herein.

Europe has taken notice, even if it has failed to prioritize efforts to confront the problem or contain it sufficiently. Headway was made in 2025 when the European Parliament adopted a resolution condemning the political threat the ROC poses in Europe:

> Moscow's exploitation of Orthodox religion for geopolitical purposes, notably through the instrumentalisation of the ROC (Moscow Patriarchate) as a tool to influence and exert control over Orthodox populations in Ukraine, Georgia, Moldova, Serbia and other countries.[482]

The ROC's response to the European Parliament was predictable, following the Russian state policy of embracing the axiom, "a strong offensive is a good defense" when bad acts come to light.

The Moscow Patriarchate's reliable ally, the Serbian Orthodox Church, was also previously cited by the European Parliament in 2022 for its own role in inflaming tensions in the Balkans. Their response was almost a mirror image of the Moscow Patriarchate's position regarding attempts to affix responsibility for the perversion of the church in the service of state aggression. In a response that seems torn out of the ROC handbook, the Serbian Orthodox Church claimed the European Parliament's findings to be: "…based solely on deep historical prejudices and tendentious stereotypes is not surprising, but certainly deeply disappointing."[483] According to the responding statement of the hierarchs of the Serbian Orthodox Church:

> [It is] surprising to put in a negative context the issue of protection of traditional family values, which the Serbian Church stands for in the same way as the ROC and all other local Orthodox churches without exception, but not

---

[481] Maria Eherlich, "Soul occupation: The number of religious congregations in occupied Ukraine has halved in three years as Moscow cements its control", *Novaya Gazeta Europe*, 7 April 2025.

[482] European Parliament, "Resolution on Russia's disinformation and historical falsification to justify its war of aggression against Ukraine, 2024/2988 (RSP)", *European Parliament (Strasbourg)*, 23 January 2025.

[483] Serbian Orthodox Church, "On the Resolution of the European Parliament", *Serbian Orthodox Church*, 14 March 2022.

in the least different, and the Catholic Church, as well as some Reformation churches.[484]

The ROC and its aligned local churches invariably blame the west when under scrutiny. Cries of "prejudice" and claiming "persecution" arise when their complicity and involvement in state intelligence activities and belligerence are called into question. Refutations within the Russkiy Mir or about the Holy Rus' rarely, if ever, resort to a discernibly factual defense. Instead, Russia simply resorts to claims of "Russophobia" and "Western bias" to change the conversation.

Arguably, we live in an age when people often adapt their understanding of truth as mediated by their political ideology. Here, there can be no room for "alternative facts." Using the United States of America as an example, we can see that the once anti-communist, Russophobic Republican Party of Ronald Reagan is now overtly pro-Russian. This is true despite the documented increase of illiberal conduct on the part of the Russian Federation and its leaders. How can it be accounted for? The answer points to an acceptance that decision-makers, voters, and the media have chosen to be entirely selective in considering information in a way that only serves to reinforce their personal and corporate biases.[485]

Republicans elected to Congress, and now the White House, are increasingly dismissive of any criticisms of Russia. This is the only reasonable way to explain how, only a generation ago, United States Senator John McCain's scathing view that Russia was a "Gas station masquerading as a country" reigned supreme among Republicans who today eschew such a view.[486] The dynamic is not unique to the Americans. The consequence of this change in views is profound for Europe. Between January and February 2025, the United States' entire foreign policy outlook, developed over the last century, returned to a staunchly isolationist orientation. Europe can no longer rely on the United States as a partner on the world stage or in matters of collective defense.[487]

Europe must acquire the resolve and courage to learn to stand alone, or at the very least, be far less reliant on external partners like the United

---

[484] Dunja Arandjelovic (*Thesis*), "The Serbian Orthodox Church as a Transnational Political Actor: A Case Study of Regime Change in Montenegro Case Study of Regime Change in Montenegro", *Clemson University: Tiger Prints*, 2022.
[485] Paul L. Underwood, "Partisanship sways news consumers more than the truth, new study shows", *Standford Report*, 31 October 2024.
[486] Jonathan Mahler, "How the G.O.P. Fell in Love With Putin's Russia: What explains the Trump administration's radical reversal toward Moscow?", *The New York Times Magazine*, 12 April 2025.
[487] Aurélie Pugnet, "Four reasons Europe can't trust the US to protect it anymore", *Euractive*, 10 March 2025.

Kingdom and the United States, whose tendencies toward prioritizing self-interest are contrary to shared European values.

Some Europeans, too, have erred in adopting a political ideology that embraces Putin's Russian Federation. France's Marine Le Pen's far-right National Rally Party chose to discount facts on the ground regarding Russia. The party was only too aware that Putin's reign was marked by oligarchy, totalitarianism and the assassination of civilians on European soil using Russian state assassins (at times using proscribed chemical weapons). The Marine Le Pen Party, which had been cozy with Russia for decades, had become the focus of French ire over Russian aggression in Ukraine. Le Pen set up a parliamentary enquiry to investigate foreign interference in French politics. They earnestly believed the enquiry would serve to exonerate themselves from being labeled stooges of Russia. It resulted in being a self-damning exercise. The parliamentary enquiry report was tantamount to serving as a litany of Marine Le Pen's acts in collaboration and service to Russia as chief apologists in France and throughout Europe.

The infiltration of the European Parliament by far-right, pro-Putin, pro-Russia politicians is problematic. The rise of right-wing groupings like the Identity and Democracy (ID) group, which includes Germany's Alternative für Deutschland Party (ADF) and Austria's Freedom Party (FPÖ), only adds to pressure from states like Hungary and Slovakia, which can usually be found in the Russian camp.[488]

Reforms to European laws, especially at the corporate level of the EU, are unlikely given divisions within Europe. Even implementing sanctions against key players like Patriarch Kirill has become problematic thanks to opposition from quarters such as Hungary's Orbán.[489] The election of nationalist-conservative Polish President Karol Nawrocki in June 2025 has helped tilt Europe toward conservatism and Euroscepticism. While Poland remains divided between being pro-Europe leaning and simultaneously staunchly anti-European Union, its fundamental division between self-interest and European cohesion acts as a benefit to Russia.[490]

We can only hope those who have heretofore refused to accept the threat that Russia and the ROC represent to European security and democracy will take notice. If the ROC is allowed to continue in its indispensable role for the Russian state in tearing at Europe's social cohesion, it will do so. Europe must find a balance between liberal western democratic values

---

[488] Armida van Rij, "The pro-Putin far right is on the march across Europe — and it could spell tragedy for Ukraine", *The Guardian*, 11 April 2024.

[489] Alice Tidey, "Orbán criticises EU plans to sanction head of ROC", *EuroNews*, 5 June 2022.

[490] Editorial, "Polish far right's win is a thunderclap above Europe", *Le Monde*, 2 June 2025.

and providing for its security. Ukraine was far too late in addressing the divisive role the Ukrainian Orthodox Church (Moscow Patriarchate) played in dividing its nation. Estonia is attempting to address the problem. Europe should not tarry, as the consequences may prove dire.

The ROC's militant orientation and corrupted theological teachings remain at the heart of its *esse*. Their indiscriminate embrace of the Russian state at the expense of Holy Wisdom, the gospels and tradition represents an indelible stain on Orthodox Christianity and our shared humanity. It represents a direct challenge to the church fathers, deeply disfigures Orthodox Christianity in the service of the Russian state and breaks with the prayer of Jesus for Christian unity.[491]

Putting aside religious, theological and ecclesial considerations, there are compelling civic and political reasons for Europe to contain the Moscow Patriarchate's activities on the continent. The ROC cannot alone be judged by what it proclaims or does. Its peculiar and bellicose conduct, as referenced only so slightly above, speaks to its very character.

No amount of incense can mask the stench of hypocrisy from its conduct and declarations. Likewise, no number of clanging bells or chorus of melodic chants can drown out the cries arising from the 'holy war' it has elected to wage on its neighbors. Indeed, the voices of those fresh in their graves from the only war to plague Europe since World War II and the adoption of a rules-based order in Europe can still be heard in the tales about them by comrades, family, friends, and Ukraine's admirers. Their sacrifice for Ukraine is genuinely a sacrifice to buy Europe time. Europe must be wise enough to use it to its benefit.

It remains the ROC's sins of omission that are too often overlooked. Here, those disinterested in religion but concerned about civil society should take notice. The Moscow Patriarchate's resolute silence when condemnation should otherwise have been forthcoming from an institution supposedly devoted to goodness is disturbing. There are many such instances. Where was the outcry in its pulpits in the aftermath of Russia's 2006 murder of Alexander Litvinenko with polonium-210? Why was the Moscow Patriarchate silent after the 2018 poisoning of Sergei and Yulia Skripal in the United Kingdom, even after the FSB agents were positively identified and the chemical fingerprint of the outlawed nerve agent Novichok traced to Russia?[492] Following the conviction of Russian State Security Service assassin Vadim Nikolayevich Krasikov for the 2019 shooting of

---

[491] *cf.* John 17:20-23.
[492] Following the detection of the Novichok nerve agent and the identification of two FSB agents, Ruslan Boshirov and Alexander Mishkin, travelled from Russia to Salisbury where the Skripals lived before quickly exiting the country on false passports, Father Joseph Skinner, the director of Inter-Orthodox Relations for

dissident refugee Zelimkhan Khangoshvili in a Berlin park, in the presence of children, there was no detectable response from the ROC.

The silence did not endure, however, when it came to the arrest, imprisonment, torture, and eventual death in detention of Russian opposition leader Alexei Navalny. Here, the ROC broke with its usual silence, but not in a Christian manner. The Moscow Patriarchate denounced and punished Father Dmitry Safronov for conducting the burial service for Navalny, suspending him from clerical duties and sentencing him to "3 years penance."

By all appearances, the ROC is disinclined to practice mercy, even for the dead. It is undeniable that, among so many Russians subjected to violence and oppression, the ROC has become unrecognizable as a champion for those oppressed by state violence. By its very silence and overt acts of retribution for Orthodox Christians who became opponents of the state, the ROC has rendered itself indistinguishable from the Russian state security apparatus or serving as a state propaganda organ.

Until the ROC returns to the fullness of communion within Orthodox Christianity and chooses to renounce its loyalty to the Russian state above its fidelity to Christ, whose constant prayers were for peace and unity, no good can come of the quest for the Russkiy Mir to be realized or the Holy Rus' to be inaugurated at the expense of its soul.

The ROC's resounding failure to condemn the misconduct of the Russian state remains at the root of its problems. Having prostrated itself before tsars, commissars and now the authoritarian, kleptocrat that is the president of the Russian Federation, the Moscow Patriarchate seems incapable of understanding its complicity in Putin's ungodly adventurism. The Moscow Patriarch has blinded himself and caused the ROC to blind itself to its co-authorship of the scrolls recording the bloodshed, extrajudicial killings, poisonings, murders, rape, torture and mass graves it has not only collaborated in making possible, but also blessed the perpetrators of such abject evil.

As the co-author of evil with the Russian state, the ROC has rendered itself unrecognizable as a church as the world would understand one. European legislation should not favor the view it is a church in such circumstances. It is said that if a creature walks like a duck, talks like a duck and flies like a duck, it must be considered a duck, no matter what name it is given. Should it be any different for the Moscow Patriarchate? If it walks like a wolf, talks like a wolf and preys like a wolf, why shouldn't it be called a wolf instead of a Church? The ROC is a 'Wolf in Sheep's Clothing'.

---

the ROC in the United Kingdom resorted to the usual response of blaming investigators saying, "The climate, if you like, of developing Russophobia in the media is obviously something which is disturbing for people."

Reflections

Is Renewal Possible for the ROC

For the Christian community and the sorority of nations that are genuinely committed to the rule of law and pursuit of peace we can only muse over the prospects of the ROC reforming itself. That it desperately needs reform is undeniable. History militates against it.

The ROC's enduring bond with the Russian state from the time of the Principality of Muscovy through to its Imperial epoch and now in the era of the Russian Federation has been a constant. Eastern European nations with predominantly Orthodox Christian populations have always operated under a paradigm referred to as a 'Symphony' where both Church and state operate harmoniously for the common good. In reality, Russia has generally operated in a manner more akin to maestro directing his orchestra forbidding soloists from improvisation.

Church-state relations have always been attended by tension. In Constantinople the examples were plentiful. Patriarch Ignatius opposed Emperor Michael III who wished to banish his mother away to a convent. The people sided with the Patriarch and Michael III was humbled. Later, Patriarch Polyeuctus, excommunicated Emperor Nikephoros II Phokas for breaking church law and later Emperor John I Tzimiskes for gaining his throne by regicide. The support of the faithful allowed the Church to counter despotism and murder, even by its basileus. In England, when Thomas à Becket, Archbishop of Canterbury, challenged King Henry II over the rights and privileges of the clergy the king lashed out, "Will no one rid me of this turbulent priest?".[493] Believing it to be a call to action, four of the king's devoted knights stormed into Canterbury Cathedral and slew him with their swords. King Henry II claimed he never meant the Archbishop to be harmed. The outcry of the people was such that the king donned sack cloth and ashes to do penance at Becket's tomb and at St. Dunstan's Church. There are myriad examples in history where the will of the God-fearing faithful humbled kings and emperors alike.

If history provides numerous examples of the Church asserting its moral, ethical and spiritual authority for the good of the state and her people Russian history is almost devoid of it. The reason may lie in how the

---

[493] Jonathan McGovern, "The Origin of the Phrase 'Will no one rid me of this turbulent priest?'", *Notes & Queries*, Vol 68, Issue 3, September 2021.

Russian people and faithful have been conditioned to accept the authority of its rulers and the complicity of the ROC throughout its history. Russia's history catalogues its almost constant bellicose nature in waging war for its imperial ambitions. As the ROC has inextricably intertwined itself with princes, emperors and now Russian presidents the Russian people and faithful have been formed to embrace the imperial ambitions of its state as being synonymous with those of the ROC. This self-feeding loop may explain why Russians are so complacent with the policies of endless confrontation with the West and the sovereign states that once suffered under the Russian sphere.

The seeming indivisibility of the ROC from the state, and the state from the ROC results in a devaluation of acceptance for dissent. Opposition ruling parties and figures have fond favour in branding their opposition as traitors to the state—and therefore the ROC. It is not without reason that Russians have embraced the adage, 'Russia's democratic values end where Ukraine begins'. Unsurprisingly, opposition leaders like Alexei Navalny made public their belief that Russia's invasion of Ukraine was in Russia's best interests. And while Navalny may have changed his views on the subject of Ukraine's sovereignty while imprisoned by Putin the omission of some 100 pages from the Russian translation of Navalny's diaries sanitised any proof of his change of heart on Ukraine and Russia's revanchism because they realise their future as Russia's opposition depends on their not alienating the Russian masses who support the invasion of Ukraine and their attempts to annex Crimea and Donbas.

As we reflect upon ROC and its worldview, one decidedly driven by the Russkiy Mir and Holy Rus' ideology, it is undeniable that unless the ROC recover's a genuinely Christian ethos its future will continue to be subordinated to the whims and will of the state and the kleptocratic class that lead it.

Fundamental to any assessment of the ROC must be rooted in the individuals who make up the body by a candid evaluation of the individual Russian Orthodox who claims discipleship. Here, a quote from Saint Athanasius gives us insight into what we who confess Jesus as Christ should aspire to and to what we, as a church—the Body of Christ, should attain: "For the Son of God became man so that we might become God."[494] It is difficult to believe Russian Orthodox believers believe their apotheosis can be attained by embracing a Moscow Patriarchate and ROC that remains silent as its citizens are imprisoned for legitimate, democratic dissent, its sons are sent to Ukraine to kill their Orthodox sisters and brothers as part

---

[494] Saint Athanasius, "On the Incarnation of the Word", (first published *c.* 4th century), Athanasius of Alexandria, *Createspace Independent Publishing Platform*, 2007.

of a 'holy war' or embrace the heresy of ethnophyletism over the teachings of Christ.

Saint Athanasius' profound insight into God's promise for humanity has guided Christians for over 1600 years. While many in Europe do not ascribe to Christianity as a confession of faith, it is without question that European values are imbued in our understanding of what it means to be European.

I don't mean to assert that one should be, or ought to be, a Christian to be truly European. That is an absurdity. Europe's very strength is in its diversity and willingness to reconcile individual differences for the betterment of society, civilisation, nations and the community of states we know as the EU. We strive, and God knows, we certainly fail, but we at least still aspire to be better. This, if nothing else, is the inheritance which each European received from their share in Christianity's traditions and values that undergird western civilisation.

While we can decry the conduct of the church and have had good reason to do so, we cannot deny the church's role as the mother of European civilization any more than we can deny we are its children. There are, without doubt, many Europeans who are estranged from the church. Many reject it outright. We also enjoy the gift of our neighbors who share in other faith traditions — each with their own, precious contributions to our shared humanity and as Europeans.

What binds us all, however, Christian, Muslim, Jew, Buddhist, agnostic, atheist or other, is our central belief in each other. For most people, compassion, love, forgiveness, reconciliation, education for our children, health care for those in need, comfort for those who require care and consolation for those whose loss demands consolation are at the heart of our *esse* and are reflected in what we do. For all that is abhorrent about the tendency toward vitriol and scapegoating in public discourse of late, that it still upsets us is a sign that we have not lost sight of our moral compass. The arc of goodness and the progress of humanity remain bent in favour of kindness and humanity's well-being.

We ask the faithful of all faiths: "Do you recognise these hallmarks in the conduct of the ROC?" "Do you want the Moscow Patriarchate influencing your society, your nation and our Europe?" Or even, "Do you want to be made to worship as a Russian Orthodox 'Christian' and pay homage to the Patriarch of Moscow who declares 'holy war' on his neighbor and call Europe and the west, Satanic?"

We guess you do not. Our research leads us to conclude that we cannot discern these values prevailing in the ROC. Sadly, their belief in the nationalistic and messianic Holy Rus' ideology with its belief that Russia and the Russian people are predestined to save the world, leaves us no choice but to accept we living outside of Russia must either submit to living in the Russkiy Mir or cease to exist as free women and men. The ROC does not teach either the redemption of humanity or conversion of the human person but rather insists upon posing the existential question: "Will you submit to the Russkiy Mir and join the Holy Rus' or, well, or else?"

This is not the path Jesus Christ set for humanity. It is the road laid by centuries of willing servitude to the Russian state.

If we have, through Jesus Christ, the ability to realize the fullness of our humanity as children of God the Father, we cannot allow the indelible imprint of baptism upon our souls to be disfigured by a willingness to follow in the footsteps of the 'evil one.' We must not be willing to tolerate the silence of the ROC when its mission is "to be in this world, but not of it."[495]

And if Europeans believe that three generations of shared commitment to peace and prosperity are worth preserving (imperfect as it is — it is worth saving), we must not delay. It will be our regret, and that of generations to come, if we allow the status quo to prevail out of fear that we might offend our liberal democratic values. We should never discard them, but neither should we allow a lack of imagination to be an excuse for idleness. Our acts may not always be perfect, but errors can be forgiven — indolence and inaction cannot.

Having read this manuscript, we trust you now realise what truly confronts us — *Wolves in Sheep's Clothing: The ROC's Threat to European Security and Democracy* and will therefore decided to act.

An incoherent paradigm persists where Russian disinformation thrives despite access to knowledge and information. While Russia censors access to western media, Russians easily skirt it with the use of VPNs and other means.[496] If Russians claim they are unaware of the crimes of their state and people, it is a willing ignorance. The Kremlin and the Moscow Patriarch believe their security can only be achieved through the complete erasure of freedom, information, and knowledge on its borders, sustained through limiting access to Western information.[497]

The work of Russian propagandists has been made all the easier by the closure of Voice of America — Radio Freedom by the Trump administration, thereby forfeiting the airwaves to Russia and other entities hostile to Europe and the west.[498] The void in pro-democracy, fact-based news has

---

[495] *cf.* Jn 17:11, 14-15.
[496] Gleb Stolyarov and Lucy Papachristou, "Russia to spend over half a billion dollars to bolster internet censorship system", *Reuters*, 10 September 2024.
[497] Staff Writers, "Russia bans access to over 80 EU news outlets" *Deutsche Welle (DW)*, 25 June 2024.
[498] Sébastian Seibt, "Trump mutes Voice of America, makes space for Russian and Chinese influence", *France 24*, 19 March 2025.

been quickly filled by an already burgeoning cast of pro-Russian propagandists. Russian apologists in the west, like Tucker Carlson, disgraced and fired from FOX News for anti-democracy disinformation and defamation regarding US election coverage and Oleg Nesterenko, a 30-year resident of France and self-styled analyst appearing on news outlets across the globe, are examples of legacy media personalities who do Russia's bidding.[499]

Russia has also enjoyed spectacular success with using its propaganda channels to directly influence unwitting, naïve or willing social media influencers in the west. Copying a campaign previously deployed in Ukraine, TikTok influencer Cristina Horezlike and others assisted the pro-Russian presidential candidate Calin Georgescu in rocketing to the top of the polls in Romania in 2025.[500] His first-round election win was quashed by Romanian courts after it was revealed his election was engineered by Russia.

In preparation for the election, the Moscow Patriarchate, allied with and self-styled 'Orthodox Church of Romania', promoted the same disinformation from pulpits. The coordination between the Russian state intelligence and propaganda centers and the Moscow Patriarchate aligned the 'Orthodox Church of Romania' in their attempt to prevent civil society activist and pro-European centrist candidate Nicușor Dan from election, demonstrating the ROC's threat to European security and democracy.

Other influencers like Graham Phillips,[501] Lauren Chen, Benny Johnson, Tim Pool, David Rubin and Lauren Southern, among others[502] continue to do Russia's bidding not only on political matters, but those concerning the ROC. For as long as there is pay, there will be those willing to publish—whatever the content.

Over the last decade, far-right political entities across Europe began integrating religious messaging in their political manifestos and messaging. This has included ultra-conservative and far-right parties such as Austria's Freedom Party for Austria (FPÖ), the Nationalists and Conservative Party of Estonia (EKRE), France's Marine Le Pen, Germany's Alternative

---

[499] Arnaud Froger, Haïfa Mzalouat with contributions from Lesia Dubenko, "Conquering minds: A deep dive into the media offensive of a France-based Russian propagandist", *Reporters Without Borders*, 19 May 2025.

[500] Rowan Ing, "The TikTokers accused of triggering an election scandal", *BBC Global Disinformation Unit*, 30 April 2025.

[501] Peter Beaumont, "British pro-Kremlin video blogger added to UK government Russia sanctions list", *The Guardian*, 26 July 2022.

[502] Shannon Bond, Jude Joffe-Block and Caitlin Thompson, "How Russian operatives covertly hired U.S. influencers to create viral videos", *NPR*, 5 September 2024.

for Deutschland (ADF) and Italy's Lega Nord (LN). Domestically, the Russian Imperial Movement (RIM), an ethno-nationalist paramilitary organisation with international links to white supremacy groups, has also become an echo chamber for the ROC.

A religious turnaround has also been observed amongst several right-wing parties in Europe, from the Italian LN to the Austrian FPÖ. This was triggered on the one hand by immigration from Muslim-dominated countries, but on the other hand, as Stoeckl points out, it was about a narrowing of traditional values to set themselves off against the liberal world:

> Russia and the ROC play an important role in this context. Because unlike his two morally conservative predecessors the new Roman Catholic Pope Francis, who came into office in 2013, placed his pontifical focus on issues such as migration and the fight against poverty. The resulting morally conservative void was filled by orthodoxy.[503]

We recognise the complexity of the issues. We also admit the difficulty in balancing liberal values and national security interests. We are, nonetheless, inclined to agitate for the containment of the Russian Orthodox Church, given all that we have referenced and written in this manuscript. If the Moscow Patriarch's wolves in sheep's clothing continue to render the Russian Orthodox Church's threat to European security and democracy a menace to Europe, we must all either resolve to adequately confront the problem or be prepared to suffer its consequences. We urge containment for the ROC until it embraces a genuine Christian conversion.

---

[503] Kristina Stoeckl, "The role of religion in the Russian "culture war"", *Newsroom: Universität Innsbruck*, 2 June 2024.

Epilogue

Does History Provide a Way Forward?

The following story is true. Its lesson is that the situation isn't unanalogous to the situation the priests of the UOC of Ukraine (Moscow Patriarchate) or Moscow Patriarchate-aligned clergy across Europe face today. This story might well provide an example, and a way forward, for the orthodox church clergy now under the Moscow Patriarchate who want to remain Orthodox Christian priests and reconcile with their native kinspeople.

This allegorical story unfolds during the War of American Independence (1775-1783) by recounting the affairs of a Church of England clergyman who, not unlike the ROC priests of today, chose to conflate his religious obligations with what he believed were his duties to a temporal, political authority. In so doing, our young priest betrayed his native-born siblings in the North American colonies we now know as the United States of America.

By acts, deeds, and promoting propaganda that assisted a foreign power in its attempt to deprive the American people of the most essential of human rights—the Four Freedoms (freedom of expression, of worship, of want, and of fear), our colonial era priest became a traitor. He betrayed his parishioners' and neighbors' trust, confidence and gave secrets to the enemy. His knowledge of people, businesses, communities, roadways, and terrain gained from his travels around the colonies in the guise of a simple priest proved to be a clever way of collecting intelligence to betray to the enemy.

If this story sounds as though it was ripped from the headlines of this morning's news, it is for one reason: it could well have been. Like the priests of the ROC and the UOC (Moscow Patriarchate) in Ukraine, our colonial priest forsook his sacred oaths and subordinated himself to the temporal authority of a foreign autocrat, satisfying himself along the way that he was doing 'God's work'. He wasn't. As Mark Twain was fond of saying, "History doesn't repeat itself—but it often rhymes".

Our story unfolds 14 miles from New York's St. Paul's Chapel, located on Broadway in Lower Manhattan, the center of life for the 'established church' in the city. Our priest was the pastor of a well-heeled parish, established in 1693, in what is now Westchester Square, the Bronx. His grand stone church, St. Peter's, was newly constructed and the pride of the city, and yet, all was not tranquil in the parish as the faithful were split between considering themselves Americans and others adhering to the British Crown, calling themselves a 'Tory' or 'loyalist'. These were those heady days between 1774-1775 in which Americans earnestly began to debate the idea of establishing a new and independent nation in North America and free themselves from the established church.

Despite having been born in Connecticut, he fancied himself as an Englishman, as he believed any member of the Church of England should. Imbued with the sense of superior benevolence that comes from being a 'loyalist' and member of the established Church of England, our priest believed the political independence of the American people was a threat to their religious well-being, as it would divorce them from their sovereign, King George III, who had the dual role of head of state and head of the Church of England. To his mind, his fellow inhabitants were simply ungrateful for the privilege of being considered English and all it entailed.

Father Seabury had been taught since childhood to be obedient to his temporal master, the person of the king and the crown, which stands for the state. This ideology was reinforced during his theological education, along with being instructed that his ordination vows were indistinguishable from his oath of fidelity as a servant of the crown. Inasmuch as Henry VIII had established the Church of England by making himself the "Supreme Governor of the Church of England," Father Seabury simply could not reconcile Christian principles and his confession of faith without placing them within what he believed to be his higher obligation of fidelity, his older oath of loyalty to the crown. Nor could he imagine being a subject of the king without that circular fidelity to the Church of England whose head was, after all, his sovereign, the king.

Although born and raised in Connecticut, Father Seabury lived with the belief that he was mystically bound to England far more than to his native motherland. Being a member of the Church of England meant to him that he owed the crown his every loyalty. The unity of the triumvirate of king, country and faith appealed to Father Seabury intellectually, patriotically and spiritually, just as today the priest and the faithful of the ROC and UOC (Moscow Patriarchate) share the same view of the Russkiy triumvirate of Putin, Russia, and the Moscow Patriarchate.

It did not occur to our earnest but misguided priest that his view that Americans were, by virtue of being subjects of the crown and members of the established Church of England, graciously included by extension in English history and nationality by the crown. After several hundred years in North America, living alongside Native Americans, Spanish, French, Portuguese and others who settled in North America, our young clergyman didn't comprehend that his neighbors were in fact Americans, not English. After all, while claimed by the crown and the Church of England for the taxes and tithes they could give, Americans were deprived of representation in the parliament that made their laws, had no choice in who governed them or how, nor did they have any clergy that were not placed amongst them at the sole discretion of an archbishop 3461 miles away in Canterbury. Americans were kept in line by the militia and forced to quarter British soldiers in their homes despite considering them the enemy and the Church of England and its clergy who reigned over the American people and served to reinforce that repression.

For Father Seabury and his like-minded loyalists, any deviation from this binary state of conformity to king, country and church rendered persons voluntarily outside of the church—excommunicants and quislings as well. This reflected King George III's contention, "I wish nothing but good; therefore, everyone who does not agree with me is a traitor and a scoundrel".[504] George III was fond of saying, "we are one people—my people". Father Seabury and his fellow Church of England clergy, being both simultaneously both subject to the crown the head of the Church of England, the king, felt a natural antipathy towards their American brothers and sisters.

The king asserted his dominion over Americans, likening the relationship to being one of parent and child. This was accompanied, however, by his constant rants to his Foreign Minister, William Pitt the Younger, that Americans were "petulant children, biting the hand that feeds them", a misguided position shared today by Putin towards Ukrainians. George, ever imperious and convinced of that divine right, rendered his rule "Godly." He believed a firm hand and corporal punishment were required to keep the 'children' obedient. Americans by the 18th century were as different from the English as their ethnic background is from the Spanish, who also colonized America's shores. Americans were distinctly not English (just as Ukrainians are not Russian), albeit they shared commonalities in culture and religious expression during points in history.

Still, our priest believed himself to be a man of conscience. His misguided understanding of Christianity and being a subject of the crown left him feeling that his fealty to the king and his archbishop in another country seemed integral to his salvation. His confraternity with his fellow Americans or his discipleship as a follower of Christ, which he supposedly proclaimed each Sunday from the pulpit, were secondary to his obligations as a subject and ordination. Consequently, Father Seabury felt compelled to intervene in public discourse. He knew his decision would prove wildly unpopular to his fellow parishioners.

---

[504] Charles River Editors, "British Legends: The Life and Legacy of King George III", *Charles River Editors*, 2013.

Despite being born in America and enduring years of being treated as a lesser man by the king far away in England, Father Seabury felt compelled by his faith to mark himself as a Tory 'loyalist' to the King of England and thereby promote himself by so doing. His political passions, self-serving though they were, led him to pen the essays opposing what he saw as his fellow American brethren's dangerous, if not seditious, ideas of freedom, human rights, and independence. This included not only lifelong neighbours but his own parishioners.

To be fair, our priest was not acting out of solely political motives. He was genuinely convinced of the idea that he was obligated by both political and religious oaths that required a unified symmetry of conduct. After all, he believed his baptismal vows administered by the Church of England (for whom the King was the 'supreme head of the Church of England') bound him in all matters both political and religious. Our priest believed then, as do the majority of the clergy of the ROC today, that his profession of faith is inextricable from his state of being a subject of the traditional temporal authority that held itself out to have authority over him.

Opposing independence, religious pluralism, freedom of speech and political self-determination was, to his mind, contrary to the will of God. For political and religious zealots, the likes of Father Seabury, the same God who, by divine right, vested power and authority in the King of England, the titular head of the Church of England, must be obeyed above all else. The conflating of church and state by misguided hardliners, the likes of Father Seabury, is nothing new, but it always has tragic consequences for the individual, the Body of Christ and humanity.

It mattered little that the triumvirate of England, the crown and the Church of England were in perpetual breach of their obligations of fidelity to the American people. England claimed Americans as citizens, but without equality with English citizens. Parliament, sitting in London, or through their colonial governors in the colonies, subjected Americans to abusive laws. The crown imposed taxes without representation in parliament. Colonial assemblies were made purposefully toothless. Consequently, free speech and restrained fundamental liberties became the norm, despite the Americans and Englishmen purportedly being "one people". For 'loyalists' like A.W. Farmer, the inequalities suffered by American subjects of the crown were simply part of the price of being subjects of the United Kingdom of Great Britain and Ireland. God save the King!

As for the Church of England and its treatment of its American faithful, the Archbishop of Canterbury refused to provide Americans with their own bishop to ensure their spiritual needs were met. Sacraments often could not be administered. The archbishop forbade anyone in communion with the Church of England to ordain a priest or bishop lest the Americans acquire notions of autonomy. The archbishop even restricted who could be ordained a priest, ensuring the Church of England's powers were preserved far beyond the reasonable exercise of its authority. The Church of England made sure Americans' spiritual needs were always restricted by their reliance on the whims and will of the Archbishop of Canterbury, who held an iron grip on American religious life in concert with his master, the head of the Church of England, the king.

Without a bishop in the colonies, it was necessary for our priest to function through the Society for the Propagation of the Gospel (SPG), the Church of England's missionary arm in the colonies. He convinced himself that without fidelity to England, the crown and to the archbishop, he would live outside of the Grace of God. Whatever qualms Father Seabury had with the archbishop refusing to consecrate a bishop for America, he satisfied himself that he was fortunate to obtain appointments to several key colonial parishes in New Jersey, Long Island and Connecticut. Being an itinerant preacher or country pastor was not part of Father Seabury's constitution or plans.

It is said that, given his relative impecuniosity at ordination, Father Seabury pursued and married Abigail Mumford, the daughter of a wealthy Philadelphia businessman. Father Seabury quickly became indebted to his father-in-law and quickly found that his debts to him rendered his life one of being dutifully obliged to adopt and embrace his father-in-law's views and activities. Still, his indebtedness allowed him to lead a privileged life amongst his fellow native-born American neighbours, even if his allegiance to a foreign power and church put him at odds with their values and aspirations to live as a free people imbued with the equality they deserved. He would not be the first priest corrupted by wealth and position.

Writing under the pseudonym A.W. Farmer between 1774–1775, those turbulent few years leading up to the Continental Congress passing the Declaration of Independence, Father Seabury's authorship of a series of essays known as the "Letters of a Westchester Farmer," or more simply, the "Letters", brought his fame amongst his fellow Tories. Although seeking the anonymity that usually accompanies a pseudonym, Father Seabury ensured he told his secret identity to any fellow 'loyalist' with money and influence. Father Seabury had already determined that he would become the first North American bishop and was laying the groundwork by ingratiating himself with anyone who would make sure his fidelity to England was well known in faraway London.

The response to Father Seabury's "Letters" was immediate. The loyalists loved them. Americans despised them in equal measure. Quite quickly, A. W. Farmer's stature grew so great that the response to the essays was authored by none other than one of America's founding fathers, Alexander Hamilton. Though Hamilton could not be certain of the "Letters'" authorship, the feud between the two essayists would continue throughout their lives. As an antagonist, Father Seabury was superb. His essays were short, sharp, clear and well-organized. The "Letters" and Hamilton's responses were published throughout the colonies. Father Seabury may have been forgotten by history, but his memory was resurrected when he made a notable appearance in Lin-Manuel Miranda's iconic 2015 Broadway play *Hamilton,* in which he is portrayed as an avaricious, Tory opportunist. After all, it is true as they say—history is written by the victors.

Our Anglican priest turned political pamphleteer was not new to mixing his faith and politics. He had been one of the principal signatories of the White Plains Protest of April 1775, which railed against what the authors claimed to be "all unlawful congresses and committees", including the Continental Congress, which was debating a resolution to resolve the matter of American independence. His political activities reflected his deeply held personal view and fervent belief that his faith and his fealty to the crown were indivisible. Father Seabury preached the same to his congregation, ensuring that anyone who remained in the pews was 'loyalist' while patriots to the American cause were forced to worship outside of the Church of England or with priests who believed it was time to break with England, the crown and Canterbury. After all, fidelity to the faith should be more important than fealty to an archbishopric, historic though it was.

In modernity, priests of the Russian Patriarchate have followed in the same footsteps, conflating their faith with politics to the detriment of the Orthodox Christian faith, Russia and the world. The unified triumvirate of Putin, the Russian Federation, and the ROC functioned in very much the same way as did George III, England, and the Church of England, demanding unquestioned loyalty upon pain of penal servitude, execution or excommunication. Observing this dynamic, Winston Churchill wrote:

> George III had very clear ideas of what he wanted and where he was going. He meant to be King, such a King as all his countrymen would follow and revere. Under the long Whig regime the House of Commons had become an irresponsible autocracy.[505]

It is the same with Putin, who has styled himself czar in all but name, and the Duma, which has abdicated its constitutional authority to Putin, creating today's Russian autocracy. This perilous reality will unfold in the text of this book, but again, I'm getting ahead of the story.

Father Seabury's decision to carry out his propagandist advocacy and loyalist activities covertly is telling. He seemingly knew in his heart his conduct was wrong, but he chose to proceed with vigor. In his conduct,

---

[505] Winston Churchill, "A History of the English-Speaking Peoples, Volume Three: The Age of Revolution, "The First World War"", *Cassell, London,* 1957.

and a passing examination of priests and clergy who collaborated with regimes known then and proven since to have been on the 'wrong side of history', electing to conduct their collaborate affairs with the state and authoritarian henchmen is revealed as a uniform theme. History is replete with clergy who, like Father Seabury, collaborated clandestinely with oppressive and authoritarian states, even turning against their own people.

In 2007, the day after taking Canonical Possession of the See of Warsaw, Archbishop Stanisław Wielgus was compelled by Pope Benedict XVI to resign his appointment as Archbishop of Warsaw just hours before his installation was to be celebrated, based on the Vatican's discovery of Archbishop Wielgus' collaboration with the former communist regime in Poland.[506]. During World War II, Luxembourgish Father Robert Alesch secretly joined the Abwehr, using his position as a priest to infiltrate and betray the French Resistance, resulting in 80 arrests, including its Parisian leadership, many of whom were executed or met their demise after deportation to Buchenwald, Mauthausen or Ravensbrück concentration camps.[507]

There were also groups of priests who willingly aligned themselves with regimes steeped in the blood of their own people, such as the Catholic Clergy Association Pacem in Terris, which operated in the former Czechoslovakia until specifically banned under Pope John Paul II's prohibition against mixing politics and priestly duties in 1982.[508] Most recently, Father Seabury, like others before and after him who have embraced the strange bedfellows of faith and politics, has been judged harshly by history, and rightly so. Operating clandestinely to betray one's faith, sacred office, and neighbours is incompatible with the ordination prayer from the ordaining bishop:

> O God, great in might and inscrutable in wisdom, marvelous in counsel above the sons of men: You the same Lord, fill with the gift of Your Holy Spirit this man whom it has pleased You to advance to the degree of Priest; that he may become worthy to stand in innocence before Your altar, to proclaim the Gospel of Your kingdom.[509]

---

[506] Holy See, "Rinunce e nominee", *Holy See Press Office, Vatican City*, 8 January 2007.
[507] James Knowlson, "Samuel Beckett's biographer reveals secrets of the writer's time as a French Resistance spy", *The Independent*, 23 July 2014.
[508] *cf* C.I.C., can. 287 § 2; Sacred Congregation for the Clergy, decree *Quidam Episcopi* (8 March 1982), AAS 74 (1982).
[509] "*Liturgical Texts on Rites of Ordination in the Orthodox Church,*" Μωυσέως Ὠδή. Ἀφιερωματικὸς τόμος πρὸς τιμὴν τοῦ μακαριστοῦ Γέροντος Μωυσέως τοῦ Ἁγιορείτου, Ἱ. Μ. Μονὴ Βατοπαιδίου, Ἅγιον Ὄρος, 2017, 830-845.

Engaging in propaganda to promote war and political oppression, spying and betraying political opponents with knowledge, the penalty is invariably torture and imprisonment, and commonly execution would to the reasoned mind make such a priest particularly "unworthy" to "stand in innocence" before God's altar to proclaim the Gospel of His Kingdom. However, Father Seabury, the others, and so many priests of the ROC and UOC (Moscow Patriarchate) do that daily in Ukraine and throughout Europe.

By virtue of his sacred office as priest, Father Seabury was imbued with an inherent sense of trust and respectability. He regularly heard his parishioners' secrets and confessions. He knew them intimately, and when he chose to betray them in service to a foreign power and ecclesial hierarchy, he traded on this knowledge despite it having been shared with him for sacramental and pastoral reasons, not reasons of state and politics. What greater betrayal could a priest make than to exploit the human frailties and foibles of his flock for the sake of personal and political gain?

Inasmuch as Father Seabury exploited his parishioners and neighbours, he did the same by using his intimate knowledge of the parish, the region's roads, byways and highways. He knew his community and was known by them from his travels throughout the circuit. His visits to the faithful, clothed in the robes of a respectable churchman, allowed him to travel without suspicion. His status as a priest naturally imbued him with respect by most while carrying out his true mission—subverting the people's will to be free.

Far more than most, Father Seabury was well suited and situated to be a spy and theologically and politically formed as a loyalist to the crown. It was a deadly combination and proved devastating to American patriots, his neighbours and even family members who desired independence.

Father Seabury's background and knowledge predisposed him to be an invaluable intelligence asset for British forces in North America. Having rationalized away his decision to betray his parishioners and neighbors, Father Seabury felt no remorse when he presented himself to the Commander-in-Chief of British Land Forces in North America, William, 5th Viscount Howe. Having covertly made his loyalty to the crown known, General Howe received Father Seabury gladly. He was put to immediate and devastating use by divulging the secrets and knowledge he had garnered through his service to the church to benefit British Land Forces, the dreaded Redcoats. From his very first meeting with General Howe, Father Seabury sought to improve his personal position by aligning himself with the crown and all its resources by subverting his native land, his parishioners and fellow Americans who sought independence. Keeping his North American brothers and sisters under the thumb of the crown, albeit against their will and nature, was by contemporaneous estimates "the smart move" as conventional wisdom held that the Americans would surely be defeated by what was thought to be the greatest and strongest army in the world.

Father Seabury's first act was to advise General Howe to have the crown forces seize the newly completed St. Paul's Church and convert it into a British military hospital. Having resolved to betray his parishioners and neighbours, compromising their interests proved all too easy for him. That he had convinced himself he did so out of a sense of duty and obligation to the crown and the church relieved Father Seabury of feelings of guilt usually experienced by people who morally compromise themselves. His acts of betrayal were, to his mind, principled actions. That he expected to be amply rewarded by the king and church by being made America's first native-born bishop was merely a byproduct of 'right thinking'.

By debasing himself before General Howe, Father Seabury not only rendered his loyalty to the crown beyond question but intentionally elevated himself in the eyes of his fellow loyalists and parishioners. Depriving American patriots of the fruits of their labor, the impressive edifice of the very St. Paul's Church they scrimped and saved to build, was simply an added bonus.

As Father Seabury's diaries confirm, American patriots had offended the crown and, in so doing, committed a sin against the supreme governor of the Church of England. Serving the king and the church was a righteous act, and as a priest, Father Seabury was inclined to see his native countrymen and women, those "upstart lawless Committee-men"[510] punished for their haughtiness. Opposing their sovereign and God's appointed leader, the head of the Church of England, rendered all who followed them liable to being "gnawed to death by rats and vermin".[511]

Although held briefly by the Continental Army on suspicion of betraying the cause of independence, Father Seabury's position as a priest saved him from the imprisonment that attended others who aided the British. When American forces prevailed at Yorktown and Lord Cornwallis feigned illness to personally avoid the embarrassment of surrendering to the Americans, Father Seabury resolved that all he had done was in vain. He helped organize ships to evacuate loyalists leaving for British Canada, but imbued with a sense of opportunistic hunger the likes harbored by the fictitious Barry Lyndon, Father Seabury learned before boarding the last ship that Connecticut would be electing a bishop, and he intended it would be him.

The newly formed Episcopal Church (Anglican in faith, absent fidelity to the king) decided American independence compelled the new church

---

[510] Samuel Seabury, "Letters of a Westchester Farmer, by the Reverend Samuel Seabury", *White Plains: Westchester County Historical Society*, 1930.
[511] Seabury, *ibid*.

to have its own bishop. Having been born in Connecticut and educated at Yale, with a father who had served as a priest in the former colony, Father Seabury was a son of Connecticut despite his loyalist past having deprived him of the mantle of 'favorite son'. He wasted no time in attempting to ingratiate himself with the churchmen who were meeting to elect America's first Episcopal bishop. History records how Father Seabury prostrated himself before patriots, begging forgiveness for having been swept up in the wild abandonment of youth by defending the faith and loyalty his father had instilled in him. To his fellow reformed loyalists who now made their allegiance to the newly free United States, Father Seabury explained away his betrayals of his parishioners and neighbors as the necessary occupational hazards of having been bound to his ecclesial oaths from ordination, which subordinated his being to serving the church and crown. It didn't work.

Father Seabury expeditiously went about trying to convince his fellow clergy and co-religionists that his relations with General Howe, his appointment as chaplain to the King's American Regiment and loyalty to the British cause were being sensationalized. He denied authorship of the "Letters" to anyone in Connecticut who would listen. Father Seabury sought to end his long-running feud with one of America's founding fathers, Alexander Hamilton, leaving historians to ponder if his motives were a genuine reflection of his newfound pledge of allegiance to the United States he once vociferously opposed or if it was mere opportunism to win the good graces of the Connecticut electors.

The Connecticut synod of ten clergymen met at Glebe House in Woodbury on March 25, 1783, to elect America's first bishop. There were only two candidates: Father Jeremiah Leaming, a genuine patriot who had stayed loyal to his American brethren while remaining true to his priestly calling, and the former loyalist quisling, Father Seabury.

Father Leaming, an upright, intelligent and congenial priest, suffered from notoriously precarious health. In normal circumstances, his weakened constitution would have excluded him from being considered to serve as bishop. However, suspicion of Father Seabury ran so high that when Father Leaming was overwhelmingly elected on the first ballot, it spoke volumes about the electors' true view of Father Seabury. Much to the dismay of the electors, citing ill-health and incapacity, Father Leaming declined to accept election to serve as America's first bishop. As the synod had only two candidates from which to choose, fate's role in the election resulted in the only remaining candidate being elected. It was in this way that Father Seabury's avarice to be elected bishop finally paid off. Having betrayed his native American siblings by opposing independence and embracing the crown and Church of England, he just as quickly turned his coat again to reingratiate himself with the very Americans he had betrayed during the American War of Independence.

Father Seabury immediately set sail for the UK, where he expected bishops of the Church of England to ordain him to the episcopacy. He would be rebuffed. The English found him as expedient with his ethics and morals as did the Americans, but for different reasons. The English found his service as the Chaplain for the King's American Regiment was too easily abandoned when presented with the oath of allegiance to the newly formed United States, a requirement for election as bishop in Connecticut. In the end, after more than a year or prostrating himself before English bishops and finally claiming authorship of the very "Letters" he denied writing to his fellow clergy in America, Father Seabury was told in unequivocal terms he would never be ordained by English bishops.

He travelled to the UK to be ordained, but Father Seabury's desire to be elevated to the episcopal state was flatly rejected. It seems the English bishops were aware of his spying for the British Land Forces, but found his transient fidelity a barrier to being ordained, as his late oath of fidelity to the United States excommunicated him from the Church of England. Desperate to finally be invested with an episcopal miter, Father Matthews went begging to Scotland, where their centuries-old running resentment with the English allowed them to be more flexible and finally consecrate him as a bishop.

With his elevation to the episcopal state completed by consecration in Scotland on November 14, 1784, Bishop Seabury returned to the United States. Without the pull between faith and fidelity to his country, it cannot be said that thereafter Bishop Seabury did not faithfully discharge the obligations of his oath of allegiance to the United States. For the next 12 years, he served as Bishop of Connecticut, Bishop of Rhode Island and as the 2nd Presiding Bishop of the Episcopal Church (USA). His contributions to the American liturgy through his "Communion Office", which included the *epiclesis*[512] invocation is still included in the Episcopal Church's *Book of Common Prayer*. Bishop Seabury persuasively argued for a return to weekly celebration of the sacrament of Holy Communion each Sunday, a marked departure from the post-Reformation practice of only occasional celebrations by Protestant reformers.

Why recount this 250-year-old story? Again, referring to Mark Twain's quip, "History doesn't repeat itself – but it often rhymes," there is still a lesson to be learned. Father Seabury's story, told as an introduction

---

[512] Episcopal Church of America, "The Administration of the Lord's Supper or Holy Communion, Episcopal Book of Common Prayer", *Little Brown and Company, Boston*, 1868.

to *Wolves in Sheep's Clothing – The Russian Orthodox Church's Threat to European Security and Democracy*, may seem a roundabout way of addressing the current issue confronting Europe. It isn't. The parallels between the Father Seabury saga and modernity indicate that almost 250 years later, liberal democracies in the west still have not come to terms with how to inhibit the propensity of unscrupulous priests and bishops from exploiting the principle of freedom of religion for state-sanctioned, political subterfuge.

Presently, the insidious activities carried out by the ROC and the UOC (Moscow Patriarchate) on behalf of the Kremlin display significant parallels with the Father Seabury story. Inasmuch as he bowed to the unity of King George III, Britain and the Church of England, so too do today's priests and adherents of the Moscow Patriarchate show the same allegiance for the ideology and policies of Putin and the Russian Federation. The elevation of the triumviri, coalescing of powers of an individual autocrat, the Russian State and the ROC to an unquestioned unity, poses significant problems for individuals, societies, and other nations.

That Putin has taken all three identities onto himself, a president, Russian tsar in all but name and having been blessed as a *"Miracle of God"*[513] by Patriarch Kirill, Putin, like George III, who felt he possessed the 'divine right of kings', has made dissent tantamount to being a traitor and heretic. One need only look at Russia for the last 21 years of Putin's reign of terror to see how dissenters have been subjected to torture, being gunned down, blown up or poisoned.

Is it surprising then that Patriarch Kirill has acted to punish a Russian Orthodox priest for celebrating the funeral liturgy for the likes of the dissident Alexei Navalny[514] or de-frocked and imprisoned priests for speaking out against the invasion of Ukraine?[515]

Throughout Russia, in parts of Ukraine where the Ukrainian Orthodox Church (Moscow Patriarchate) operates, including temporarily occupied territories, and across Europe and the world at-large where the ROCOR functions, their pulpits are used not to preach the gospel but spread propaganda; the bulbous domes and Petrine towers of their churches and monasteries are not used for bells but as observation posts, and their invocation of religious persecution amounts to *sui servientes*

---

[513] Tim Costello, "Vladimir Putin: a miracle defender of Christianity or the most evil man?", *The Guardian*, 5 March 2022.
[514] Veronika Melkozerova, "Putin ally punishes priest who performed Navalny memorial service", *Politico*, 24 April 2024.
[515] Sofia Sorochinskaia, "Russian Priests Defrocked and Imprisoned for Their Anti-War Stance, Sofia Sorochinskaia", *Russian Post*, 22 January 2024.

pleas to deflect from being caught in activities incompatible with the security of the states in which they carry-out propagandizing, spying, and espionage.

The ROC and UOC (Moscow Patriarchate) operating domestically, in Ukraine or throughout Europe pose an existential threat to European security and democracy. The same is true in Estonia, Lithuania and countries throughout Europe. Black flowing robes of 'holy servants of God' aside, priests of the Moscow Patriarchate are wolves in sheep's clothing engaged in political activities under the guise of evangelism.

By spreading Russian propaganda, preaching criticism of Christians who do not see Putin and Russia as the "defender of Christianity,"[516] the Moscow Patriarchate, like Father Seabury did in America, strike at Europe's social cohesion. Coupled with Russia's bot-farms, hacking operations and Служба внешней разведки Российской Федерации (SVR) foreign security service, the Moscow Patriarchate's role in subverting Europe, NATO, and western security is robust and lethal in its effectiveness.

Following the June 2022 failure of the EU to reach agreement on sanctioning Patriarch Kirill, the most notorious religious operator that supports Russian aggression on the grounds that it might be injurious to Article 10 of the *European Charter of Fundamental Rights (Freedom of Thought, Conscience and Religion)* the need to expose the ROC for what it is — an intelligence apparatus of the Russian State — arises as urgent. The issues explored in this work should be sufficient to satisfy even the greatest of sceptics that this is not only true, but the necessity for action is compelling and acute.

This, at least, is one lesson from the Father Seabury saga that emerges as indisputably clear. Americans did not have to fret over the notion of impairing their adherence to their liberal values, including some of their most solemnly held core principles — freedom of worship and religion after being subjugated by the 'established' Church of England. America defeated the British, won the War for Independence and was therefore freed of the troublesome necessity of expelling their clergy and banning the Church of England from continuing to reign over the American people. Ukraine should be helped to do the same. The Baltics should be enabled to defend themselves so that war does not induce that necessity. Across Europe, the threat is real, and yet there seems to be a lack of the necessary resolution to fully meet the demands of this age. The west decries Russia's invasion of Ukraine yet funds the war with continuing energy purchases, sanctions derogations and third-party sales of technology that helps Russia

---

[516] Lt Col Dustin M. Hart and Dr. Robert S. Hinck, "The Unexpected Theologian: The Rise of Religious Messaging in Putin's Re-making of Russian State Identity", *Air University Online Journal*, 31 August 2023.

sustain its assaults on civilians, housing and the critical infrastructure necessary to sustain modern society and life.

Our consciences might best be relieved by seeing Russia defeated in Ukraine in the hopes of having the country returned to its sovereign, 1991 territorial borders. Absent Putin's willingness to negotiate a ceasefire, his call-up of additional reserve troops and the reorientation of the Russian economy to a war-footing we must resolve that Russia's abject defeat will prove the only way to end this carnage and deter Russia from further revanchism in its renewed imperial pursuit. It would be lawful, moral and constructive. Then, and possibly only then, will that brave yet imperiled country be freed of the presence of 'Wolves in Sheep's Clothing' who will, like their namesakes, watch and wait patiently for their next chance to strike, beginning with the weakest of their prey.

Bibliography

Abu Zaideh, Raïd, et al.. "In occupied Kherson, 'the Russians were destroying all books in Ukrainian'". *France 24*, Video, 5 December 2022.

Adamsky, Dmitry. *Russian Nuclear Orthodoxy: Religion, Politics and Strategy*. Stanford University Press, 2019.

AFP Staff Writers. "Putin vows that 'as in 1945,' Ukraine will be liberated from 'Nazi filth'". *Times of Israel*, 8 May 2022.

Agence France-Presse. "What's Impossible to Forgive? Putin Was Asked in 2018. He Said...". *NDTV World*, 24 August 2023.

Albats Yevgenia, and Fitzpatrick, Catherine A.. *The State Within a State: The KGB and Its Hold on Russia – Past, Present, and Future*. Farrar, Straus and Giroux, 1999.

Albert, Eric, et al.. "How the West is losing the international information war". *Le Monde*, 21 April 2025.

Alinskey, Saul. *Rules For Radicals: A Pragmatic Primer for Realistic Radicals*. Vintage Books,1971.

AP News. "Sacrilegious spies: Russians tried hacking Orthodox clergy". *NBC News*, 27 August 2018.

Arandjelovic, Dunja. "The Serbian Orthodox Church as a Transnational Political Actor: A Case Study of Regime Change in Montenegro Case Study of Regime Change in Montenegro". *Clemson University: Tiger Prints*, Thesis, 2022.

Archdiocese of Russian Orthodox Churches in Western Europe. *Archevêché des églises orthodoxes de tradition russe en Europe occidentale, Patriarcat de Moscou", Archevêché des églises orthodoxes de tradition russe en Europe occidentale*, 8 November 2024. https://archeveche.eu/en Accessed 5 July 2025,

Ash, Lucy. "Young US men are joining Russian churches promising 'absurd levels of manliness'". *BBC News*, 25 May 2025.

Associated Press in Moscow. "Russia will not attend historic meeting of world's Orthodox churches". *The Guardian*, 13 June 2016.

Associated Press. "Putin accuses the West of trying to 'dismember and plunder' Russia in a ranting speech". *AP News*, 28 November 2023.

Associated Press. "Russian Orthodox Priests Persecuted for Supporting Peace in Ukraine". *Voice of America News*, 12 August 2023.

Badendieck, Robert. "Ecumenical Orthodox patriarch backs Ukraine's sovereignty in Mass marking 3 years of war". *National Catholic Reporter*, 24 February 2025.

Bailey, Riley, et al.. "The Russian Orthodox Church Declares "Holy War" Against Ukraine and Articulates Tenets of Russia's Emerging Official Nationalist Ideology". *Institute for the Study of War Press*, 30 March 2024

Balmuth, Daniel. "The Origins of the Tsarist Epoch of Censorship Terror". *The American Slavic and East European Review*, Vol. 19, No. 4, 1960.

Baron, Samuel H. and Heer, Nancy (eds.). "Windows on the Russian Past". *American Association for the Advancement of Slavic Studies*, 1977.

Baum, Corinne and Sales, Ben. "'They're tearing the church apart': Putin targets Russia's 'godless' Jews at media conference". *The Jerusalem Post*, 20 December 2024.

Baumgartner, Frederic J.. *Behind Locked Doors: A History of the Papal Elections*. Palgrave Macmillan, 2003.

Beaumont, Peter. "British pro-Kremlin video blogger added to UK government Russia sanctions list". *The Guardian*, 26 July 2022.

Beglov, Alexy, et al.. *Osnovi Mirovih Religioznih Kultur*, Prosveshenie, 2012.

Bell-Fialkoff, Andrew. *The Role of Migration in the History of the Eurasian Steppe*. Macmillan Press Ltd., 2016.

Berdejo, Eduardo. "Church in Ukraine has lost half of its parishes in areas occupied by Russia, bishop says". *Catholic News Agency*, 29 October 2024

Bherer, Marc-Olivier avec Riabchuk, Mykola (Propos recueillis). "L'Occident est bien plus influencé par l'impérialisme russe qu'il ne l'admet". *Le Monde*, 15 Mai 2022.

Black, C.E. and Thompson, J.. *American Teaching About Russia*. Indiana University Press, 1959.

Black, Cyril (ed.). *Rewriting Russian History*. Vintage Books, 1962.

Blakkisrud, Helge. *Russkii as the New Rossiiskii? Nation-Building in Russia After 1991*, Cambridge University Press, 27 May 2022.

Blitt, R. C.. "Russia's Orthodox Foreign Policy: The Growing Influence of the Russian Orthodox Church in Shaping Russia's Policies Abroad". *University of Pennsylvania Journal of International Law*, 33, 363-460, 2011. https://doi.org/10.2139/ssrn.1725522 Accessed 18 July 2025.

Boeck, Brian J.. "The Performance of Forgery in Late Medieval and Early Modern Culture, Chapter 5, Prenatal Prophecies and Linguistic Ciphers: A Russian Political Forgery Devoted to the Autocratic Evil of Ivan the Terrible". *Brill, Intersections*, Volume: 84., 2022.

Bogdanovski, Andreja. "Estonian Parliament resumes efforts to cut ties between Church and Moscow Patriarchate". *Church Times*, 27 June 2025.

Bogdanovski, Andreja. "Russia is violating religious freedom in occupied territories, says Ukraine". *Church Times*, 17 April 2025.

Bogdanovski, Andreja. "Russian Church branded security threat to Estonia". *Church Times*, 17 May 2024.

Boncompagni, Ugo (Pope Gregory XIII). *Perepiska pap s rossiiskimi gosudaryami v XVI veke, naidennaya mezhdu rukopisyami, v Rimskoi barberinevskoi biblioteke. Izdana s perevodom aktov s latinskogo na russkii yazik [Correspondence of Popes with Russian Sovereigns in the 16th Century, Found Between Manuscripts, in the Roman Barberine Library, Published with the Translation of Acts from Latin into Russian]*. Sankt Peterburg: Akademiya nauk, 1834.

Bond, Shannon, et al.. "How Russian operatives covertly hired U.S. influencers to create viral videos". *NPR*, 5 September 2024.

Borrero, Mauricio. "Russia: A Reference Guide from the Renaissance to the Present". *Infobase Publishing*, 2009.

Buettner, Blake. "Breguet at Middle of Russian Patriarch's Photo Scandal". *Hodinkee*, 6 April 2012.

Burger, John. "Russian court fines priest for criticism of war". *Aleteia*, 21 October 2022.

Bushkovitch, Paul (ed.). *The State in Early Modern Russia: New Directions*. Slavica Publishers, 2011.

Βασιλειος, Αρχιεπίσκοπος Σμύρνης. *Πραγματεια περί του κύρους της χειροτονίας κληρικών*. [χ.ε.],1887.

Cao, Jiaqi. "Religious Origin and Political Extension of the idea of "Moscow – Third Rome"". *Advance*, 24 October 2023.

Cassiday, Julie A. and Johnson, Emily D.. "Putin, Putiniana and the Question of a Post-Soviet Cult of Personality". *Slavonic and East European Review, Modern Humanities Research Association*, Volume 88, Number 4, October 2010.

Chapnin, Sergei. "An Act of Lighthearted Betrayal: How Moscow's Official Church Hunts Down Her Anti-War Priests". *Public Theology*, 12 May 2023.

Charles River Editors. *British Legends: The Life and Legacy of King George III*. Charles River Editors, 2013.

Chief Secretariat of the Holy and Sacred Synod (Ecumenical Patriarchate). "Message dated 9 March 2014, Synaxis of Primates of the Orthodox Church". *Ecumenical Patriarchate*, 9 March 2014..

Chief Secretariat of the Holy and Sacred Synod (Ecumenical Patriarchate). "Communiqué dated 9 March 2014, Synaxis of Primates of the Orthodox Church". *Ecumenical Patriarchate*, 9 March 2014.

Chkhaidze, Nicholas. "Moscow Uses Russian Orthodox Church as Covert Foreign Policy Tool in Ukraine and the West". *Eurasia Daily Monitor*, Volume 21, Issue 55, 10 April 2024.

Christian, Gina. "Russia is killing clergy, banning religions in occupied Ukraine, says foreign minister". *OSV News*, 13 January 2025.

Chubarov, Refat Abdurahman oglu. "Interview with Miceál O'Hurley and Refat Aga, Chairman of the Mejlis of the Crimean Tatars at Antalya Diplomacy Forum, Antalya, Türkiye". *European Diplomat*, 2 March 2024.

Churchill, Winston. "A History of the English-Speaking Peoples, Volume Three: The Age of Revolution, "The First World War"". *Cassell*,1957.

Clark, Kenneth (presenter), Attenborough, David, (Developed by). *"Civilization: A Personal View, Episode 1, 'By the Skin of Our Teeth'"*. BBC Two, 1969.

Connolly, Kate. "EU allies expel 200 Russian diplomats in two days after Bucha killings". *The Guardian*, 5 April 2022.

Copilaş, Emanuel. "Cultural Ideal or Geopolitical Project? Eurasianism's Paradoxes". *Strategic Impact*, No. 3., 20 April 2018.

Costello, Tim. "Vladimir Putin: a miracle defender of Christianity or the most evil man?". *The Guardian*, 5 March 2022.

Coynash, Halya. "Reshat Ametov and 10 years of Russia's systematic torture, abductions and killings of civilians for supporting Ukraine". *Human Rights Ukraine*, 4 March 2023.

d'Amato, Raffaele. "The Golden Age of the Varangian Guard". *Medieval Warfare*, Vol. 1, No. 2, Karwansaray BV, 2011.

Daudze, Argita. "Why the notion 'post-Soviet' is obsolete, and not only for the Baltic states". *International Institute for Peace (IIP)*, 10 January 2022.

Daudze, Argita. "Why the notion 'post-Soviet' is obsolete, and not only for the Baltic states". *International Institute for Peace (IIP)*, 10 January 2022.

Davlikanova, Elena and Malik, Yevhenii. "NATO is unprepared for the growing threat posed by Putin's Russia". *Atlantic Council*, 21 July 2025.

Dellenbrant, Jan Åke. "The Integration of the Baltic Republics Into the Soviet Union". *Journal of Baltic Studies*, Vol. 18, No. 3., 1987.

Delorme, Philippe. *Anne de Kiev: épouse de Henri Ier*. Pygmalion, 2015.

Denysenko, Nicholas E.. *The Church's Unholy War: Russia's Invasion of Ukraine and Orthodoxy*, Cascade Books, 2023.

Dettmer, Jamie. "Putin: No More Color Revolutions". *Voice of America*, 10 January 2022.

Dibrova, Volodymyr. "The Valuev Circular and the End of Little Russian Literature". *Kyiv-Mohyla Humanities Journal*, No. 4, at p. 124, 2017.

Dixon, Simon. "Archimandrite Mikhail (Semenov) and Russian Christian Socialism". *The Historical Journal*: Cambridge University Press, September 2008.

Dmytra Vovk, "International and National Responses to the ROC's Support of Putin's War in Ukraine", *Brigham Young University Centre for Law and Religious Studies*, 30 October 2024.

Dreeze, Jonathon. "Russia's Lost Empire, Review of Lost Kingdom: The Quest for Empire and the Making of the Russian Nation, From 1470 to the Present, by Serhii Plokhy (New York: Basic Books, 2017". *Origins: Current Events in Historical Perspective*, November 2018.

Dusica Tomovic. "Montenegro PM Accuses Opposition Over 'Plot to Kill Him'", *Balkan Insight*, 10 November 2016.

Duxbury, Charlie. "New Russian church raises suspicions in Swedish town". *Politico*, 11 November 2024.

Eherlich, Maria. "Soul occupation: The number of religious congregations in occupied Ukraine has halved in three years as Moscow cements its control". *Novaya Gazeta Europe*, 7 April 2025.

Eisenhower, Dwight D.. "Address Before the General Assembly of the United Nations on Peaceful Uses of Atomic Energy". *General Assembly*, New York City, 8th Session: 463rd Plenary Meeting, New York (A/PV.463), 1 December 1953.

Episcopal Church of America. *The Administration of the Lord's Supper or Holy Communion, Episcopal Book of Common Prayer*. Little Brown and Company, 1868.

Estonian Foreign Intelligence Service. "International Security and Estonia 2023". *Cyber Vault Library*, 31 January 2023.

Euronews with Agence France-Presse. "Patriarch Kirill worked for the KGB in the 1970s, Swiss media reports". *EuroNews*, 6 February 2023.

European Parliament. "MEPs say no to Russian passports from occupied regions, stress right to asylum". *European Parliament*, Press Release, 20 October 2022.

European Parliament. "Resolution on Russia's disinformation and historical falsification to justify its war of aggression against Ukraine, 2024/2988 (RSP)". *European Parliament (Strasbourg)*, 23 January 2025.

European Union. "3rd EEAS Report on Foreign Information Manipulation and Interference Threats Exposing the architecture of FIMI operations". *European Union External Foresight: Strategic Communication*, March 2025.

Evans, David. "Russian Soft Power Cultivation in the United States of America: A Media Content Analysis of 'Russia Beyond The Headlines'". *West Virginia University*, Graduate Dissertation, 2015.

Fagan, Moira, *et al.*. "Republican Opinion Shifts on Russia-Ukraine War". *Pew Research Center*, 17 April 2025.

Fedyk, Igor. "Espionage Scandal with ROC in Bulgaria". *New Geopolitics*, 25 September 2023.

Fennell, John. *The Emergence of Moscow, 1304–1359*. University of California Press, 15 November 2023.

Filatova, Yekaterina. "His Beatitude Onuphry: OCU has the Tomos of slavery rather than autocephaly". *Union of Orthodox Journalists*, 11 July 2019.

Flier, Michael S. and Graziosi, Andrea. "The Battle for Ukrainian: An Introduction". *Harvard Ukrainian Studies*, Volume 35 (Number 1-4), 2017-2018.

Foreign & Commonwealth Office: United Kingdom. "Attempted coup in Montenegro in 2016: Foreign Secretary Jeremy Hunt notes the verdicts against 2 Russian GRU officers who plotted the coup". *Foreign & Commonwealth Office: United Kingdom*, Statement, 9 May 2019.

Fragkakis, Gregory (Emmanuel). *The Justice of Grace in the Great Church of Christ: A Contribution to the Ecclesiastical Issue of Ordinations in Ukraine*. Leimon Publications, 2023.

Froger, Arnaud and Mzalouat, Haïfa (with contributions from Dubenko, Lesia). "Conquering minds: A deep dive into the media offensive of a France-based Russian propagandist". *Reporters Without Borders*, 19 May 2025.

Gallaher, Brandon and Kalaitzidis, Pantelis (Coordinators—Orthodox Christian Studies Centre—Fordham University). "A Declaration on the 'Russian World' (Russkii mir) Teaching". *Co-Published by the Volos Academy for Theological Studies*, 13 March 2022.

Gaspar Mezger, Georg. *Memoria Hieronymi Wolfii Hieronymi*, Vol. I. Rieger, 1862.

Gavrilkin, Konstantin (McGuckin, John Anthony, ed.). *The Concise Encyclopedia of Orthodox Christianity*. John Wiley & Sons, 3 February 2014.

Gencturk, Ahmet. "Czech intelligence launches investigation into ROC's operations in country". *Anadolu Ajansı (AA)*, 23 August 2024.

Genini, David. "How the war in Ukraine has transformed the EU's Common Foreign and Security Policy". *Yearbook of European Law*, 2003.

Georgakopoulos, Panagiotis (Metropolitan Ignatius of Demetrias). "Ukrainian Autocephaly and Responsibility toward the Faithful". *Public Orthodoxy*, 23 October 2019.

Georgiev, Iordan. "Putin met with the Archbishop of Alaska ahead of the Summit". *Doxologia InfoNews*, 16 August 2025.

Gessen, Masha. "The best theory for explaining the mysterious death of Putin's mentor". *Business Insider*, 2015.

Gevorkyan, Nataliya, *et al*.. "First Person: An Astonishingly Frank Self-Portrait by Russia's President Vladimir Putin". *PublicAffairs*, 2000.

Gibbons, Edward. *The History of the Decline and Fall of the Roman Empire*. Strahan and Cadell, Published in 6 Volumes, 1776-1788.

Gilbert, Paul. *Nicholas II: Russia's Last Orthodox Christian Monarch: Russia's Last Orthodox Christian*. Self-Published, Kindle Edition, 2022.

Giles, Keir. *Moscow Rules: What Drives Russia to Confront the West*. Brookings Institution Press, 2019.

Gimalova, Regina. "OVD Instead of Church. How the Russian Army Persecutes Clergymen and Destroys Churches: Verstka's research on religious repressions in the occupied parts of Ukraine". *Вёрстка (Verstka)*, 6 July 2023.

Golubinskii, Evgenii. *Istoriia russkoi tserkvi, Vol. 2., Part 1.*. Moscow: Universitetskaia Tipografiia, 1900.

Graham-Harrison, Emma. "Ukraine's pro-Russian monasteries draw local suspicion". *The Guardian*, 7 March 2022.

Great and Holy Synod. "Orthodoxia: Journal of the Ecumenical Patriarchate in Istanbul". *Ecumenical Patriarchate, Phenar*, 1929.

Green, J.J.. "Crossroads of a Crisis: Spies use global chaos as cover". *WTOP News*, 16 November 2023.

Grey, Ian. *Ivan III and the Unification of Russia*. English Universities Press, 1964.

Gudziak, Borys A.. "The Creation of the Moscow Patriarchate: A Prelude to Patriarchal Reforms in the Kyivan Metropolitanate Preceding the Union of Brest (1595-1596)". *Logos – A Journal of Eastern Christian Studies*, Volume 37. (1996),

Gulubeva, Anastasia. "Rewriting history – the planned new school textbook accused of whitewashing Russia's imperial past". *BBC News Russia*, 1 September 2023.

Gundyayev, Vladimir Mikhailovich (Patriarch Kirill). "Appeal of His Holiness Kirill, Patriarch of Moscow and All Rus', to the Locum Tenens of the Kyiv Metropolitan See, Metropolitan Onufriy of Chernivtsi and Bukovina, the archpastors, pastors and all faithful children of the Ukrainian Orthodox Church in connection with the situation in Ukraine". *Moscow Patriarchate*, 2 March 2014.

Gundyayev, Vladimir Mikhailovich (Patriarch Kirill). "Sermon". *ROC, Moscow*, Cathedral of the Holy Saviour, 6 March 2022.

Gundyayev, Vladimir Mikhailovich (Patriarch Kirill). *The Statute of the ROC*. Department for External Church Relations of the Moscow Patriarchate, pt. I, § 3, ROC, 2008. http://orthodoxeurope.org/page/3/15.aspx) Accessed, 19 November 2011.

Gvindadze, Sandro. "Analysis: How Vladimir Putin defends 'family values' to mobilise voters". *BBC*, 27 February 2024.

Harary, Evan. "In Ukraine, Russian Passportization Generates Effective Denationalization". *OpinioJuris*, 4 January 2024.

Hart, Lt Col Dustin M. and Hinck, Dr. Robert S.. "The Unexpected Theologian: The Rise of Religious Messaging in Putin's Re-making of Russian State Identity". *Air University Online Journal*, 31 August 2023.

Hill, Fiona. *There Is Nothing for You Here: Finding Opportunity in the 21st Century*. Mariner Books, 5 October 2021.

Hillbruger, Christian. "The Admission of New States to the International Community". *European Journal of International Law*, No. 9, 1998.

His Own Imperial Majesty's Chancery (St. Petersburg). *Complete Collection of Laws of the Russian Empire: First Collection, Vol. I: 1649-1675*. St. Petersburg: In the printing house of the Second Branch of His Own Imperial Majesty's Chancery, Collection of Chancery Documents, 1830.

Hitler, Adolf (Manheim, Ralph, trans.). *Mein Kampf*. A Mariner Book, Houghton Mifflin Company, 1943.

Hoffmann, David L.. *Stalinist Values: The Cultural Norms of Soviet Modernity (1917–1941)*. Cornell University Press, 2003.

Holland, Neil. "Russia is suppressing the freedom of religion or belief in Ukraine: UK statement to OSCE". *OSCE: Vienna*, Speech, 2 May 2024.

Holy See. "Rinunce e nominee", *Holy See Press Office, Vatican City*, 8 January 2007.

Horne, B.D., et al.. "Generational effects of culture and digital media in former Soviet Republics". *Humanities and Social Sciences Communications*, 15 April 2025.

Hosking, Geoffrey. "Russia: People and Empire 1552-1917". *Harvard University Press*, 30 September 1998.

Hovrun, Cyril (edited by Moyse, Ashley John and Kirkland, Scott A.). *Political Orthodoxies: The Unorthodoxies of the Church Coerced*. Augsburg Fortress | Fortress Press, 2025.

Hrudka, Orysia. "Russian ideology: imperialism, militarism, and racism". *Euromaidan Press*, 5 April 2022.

Hughes, Lindsey. *Sophia: Regent of Russia, 1657-1704*. Yale University Press, 1990.

Ing, Rowan. "The TikTokers accused of triggering an election scandal". *BBC Global Disinformation Unit*, 30 April 2025.

Ivshina, Olga. "Ukraine war: Tuva and Buryatia pay the highest price, but latest BBC Russian casualty figures show poverty not ethnicity the key factor". *BBC News Russian*, 30 November 2023.

Jackson, John. "Russia's Trying to Recruit Spies From U.S. Churches: Report". *Newsweek*, 21 September 2023.

Jaffe, Greg and Dowsy, Josh. "A presidential loathing for Ukraine is at the heart of the impeachment inquiry". *Washington Post*, 2 November 2019.

Jančeveckij, Vasilij Grigorjevič. *Batu-kan : istorijski roman*. Prosveta, 1991

Jilge, Wilfried. "Russkiy MIr: "Russische Welt"". *Deutsche Gesellschaft für Auswärtige Politik* (DGAP), 3 Mai 2016.

Jochecová, Ketrin. "Moscow and Beijing rejoice at looming death of Radio Free Europe, VOA". *Politico*, 18 March 2025.

Jones, Seth G. and McCabe, Riley. "Russia's Battlefield Woes in Ukraine". *Center for Strategic and International Studies (CSIS)*, 3 June 2025.

Jones, Seth G.. "Russia's Shadow War Against the West", *Centre for Strategic and International Studies (CSIS)*. 18 March 2025.

Kaladis, Katherine. "White Supremacy and Orthodox Christianity: A Dangerous Connection Rears Its Head in Charlottesville". *Religion Dispatches*, 18 August 2017.

Kapral, Metropolitan Hilarion. "Appeal by Metropolitan Hilarion on the celebration of the 1,025th anniversary of the Baptism of Rus'". *First Hierarch of the ROC Outside of Russia*, ROCOR, 19 June 2013.

Kelly, Kieran and Brady, Louis. "Father who moved family to Russia to escape 'woke' America is sent to front line". *The Telegraph*, 21 July 2025.

Kelly, Walter Keating. *The history of Russia from the earliest period to the Crimean war: In Two Volumes*. Henry G. Bohn, 1854.

Kendall, Bridget. "Putin: Russia helped Yanukovych to flee Ukraine". *BBC News*, 24 October 2014.

Kennedy, John F.. *Why England Slept*. Wilfred Funk, Inc., 1940.

Kent, Neil. *A Concise History of the ROC*. Academica Press, 2021.

Khazin, Mikhail. "Их необходимо частично устранить". *YouTube*, Видео, 27 декабрь 2016.

Khromeychuk, Olesya. "Putin Says Ukraine Doesn't Exist. That's Why He's Trying to Destroy It". *New York Times*, 1 November 2022.

Knowlson, James. "Samuel Beckett's biographer reveals secrets of the writer's time as a French Resistance spy". *The Independent*, 23 July 2014.

Kolesnikov, Andrei., "Blood and Iron: How Nationalist Imperialism Became Russia's State Ideology", *Carnegie Russia Eurasia Center*, December 2023.

Kollmann, Jack. *The Moscow Stoglav ('Hundred Chapters') Church Council of 1551*. University of Michigan: Ann Arbor, (Ph.D. dissertation), 1978.

Kolstø, Pål and Blakkisrud, Helge. "Not So Traditional After All? The Russian Orthodox Church's Failure as a "Moral Norm Entrepreneur". *PONARS Eurasia*, 4 October 2021. https://www.ponarseurasia.org/not-so-traditional-after-all-the-russian-orthodox-churchs-failure-as-a-moral-norm-entrepreneur/ Accessed 3 August 2025.

Kolstø, Pål. *Strategic Uses of Nationalism and Ethnic Conflict: Interest and Identity in Russia and the Post-Soviet Space*. Edinburgh University Press, 2022.

Kongkini, Eirini. "*ROC: Spycraft and Statecraft Overlay Faith*". Grey Dynamics, 18 February 2025.

Kongkini, Eirini. "Russian Orthodox Church: Spycraft and Statecraft Overlay Faith". *Greydynamics*, 18 February 2025. https://greydynamics.com/russian-orthodox-church-spycraft-and-statecraft-overlay-faith/ Accessed 17 June 2025.

Konstantinova, Elena. "North Macedonia authorities ban ROC archimandrite from entering the country". *Union of Orthodox Journalists*, 18 September 2023.

Korenyuk, Maria. "Ukraine war: Russian schoolbook urges teenagers to join the army". *BBC*, 13 March 2024.

Kostoff, Stephen. "The Patron Saint of What?". *Orthodox Church of America: Reflections in Christ*, 3 January 2020.

Kozlenko, Svetlana and Heintz, Jim. "Troubled Ukraine Marks Year Since Protest Bloodbath in Kiev". *ABC News/Associated Press*, 21 February 2015.

Kozyrev, Andrei. "Boris Yeltsin, the Soviet Union, the CIS, and Me". *The Wilson Quarterly*, Fall 2016.

Kurti, Albin. "A concerning development emerged from yesterday's meeting between the Serbian Orthodox Patriarch and Vladimir Putin in Moscow". 'X', (formerly Twitter), Post of @albinkurti, 24 April 2025. https://x.com/albinkurti/status/1915478776873394523 Accessed, 9 September 2025.

Kuzenkov, Pavel. "The Third Rome": From Eschatology to Political Myth". *The ROC: Department for External Church Relations*, 20 July 2025. *https://mospat.ru/en/authors-analytics/86649/* Accessed 20 July 2025)

Laats, Alar. The Concept of the Third Rome and Its Political Implications. Kaitseväe Ühendatud Õppeasutused, 2009.

Langer, Lawrence N.. "Muscovite Taxation and the Problem of Mongol Rule in Rus'". *Russian History*, Vol. 34, No. 1/4, Brill, 2007.

Lanskoy, Miriam and Suthers, Elspeth. "Putin versus Civil Society: Outlawing the Opposition". *Journal of Democracy*, Volume 24, Issue 3, July 2013.

Lazarová, Daniela. "Russia's Patriarch Kirill first name on Czech national sanctions list". *Radio Prague International*, 27 April 2023.

Lekhel, Arina. "Levelling the Playing Fried for Religious "Liberty" in Russia: A Critical Analysis of the 1997 law "On Freedom of Conscience and Religious Associations". *Vanderbilt Journal of Transnational Law*, No. 32., (1), 1999.

Lenin, Vladimir Ilyich (Ulyanov, Vladimir Ilyich). *Letter*. Moscow: Collection, Translation by Library of Congress, 19 March 2022.

Letiche, John M. and Pashkov, Anatoliĭ Ignat'evich (ed.). *A History of Russian Economic Thought: Ninth Through Eighteenth Centuries*. University of California Press, 1964.

Levitsky, Ivan. *Brief information about the All-Russian Patriarchs*. Synodal type: Moscow, 1871.

Lewitter, Lucjan R. (1961), The Apocryphal Testament of Peter The Great", Polish Review, Vol. 6, No. 3.

Liivak, Arno. "Soviet Responses to Western Nonrecognition of Baltic Annexation". *Journal of Baltic Studies*, Vol. 18, No. 4, Taylor & Francis, Winter 1987.

Lipman, Masha. "Rewriting History for Putin". *Washington Post*, 22 March 2004.

Lister, Tim. "Secret document reveals Russia's 10-year plan to destabilize Moldova". *CNN*, 18 March 2023.

Loiko, Sergei L.. "Vladimir Putin says Crimea is part of Russia historically and forever". *Los Angeles Times*, 4 December 2014.

Lowe, Rebeca. "Ukraine: clear breaches of international law in Crimea". *International Bar Association,* 20 February 2015.

Lowe, Christian, et al.. "Holy war: How Russia recruited Orthodox priests to sway Moldova's voters". *A Reuters Special Report*, 26 September 2025.

Lubov, Deborah Castellano. "Pope on Ukraine: 'Painful and shameful' anniversary 'for all humanity'". *Vatican News*, 23 February 2025.

Lukyanov, Father Fyodor. "Defense of Family Values Is a Matter of National Security – Russian Church". *Global Orthodox,* 28 September 2022.

Luukkanen, Arto. *The Party of Unbelief: The Religious Policy of the Bolshevik Party, 1917-1929.* Suomen Historiallinen Seura, 1994.

Luxmoore, Jonathan. "Russian 'Holy War' declaration condemned". *Church Times*, 5 April 2024.

Mahler, Jonathan. "How the G.O.P. Fell in Love With Putin's Russia: What explains the Trump administration's radical reversal toward Moscow?". *The New York Times Magazine*, 12 April 2025.

Majcin, Juraj. "Russia's threat to Europe goes beyond the battlefields of Ukraine". *European Policy Centre*, 28 January 2025.

Martin, Janet. *Medieval Russia: 980–1584. Second Edition.* Cambridge University Press, 2007.

Martins, Janet. "Muscovy's Northeastern Expansion: The Context and a Cause". *Éditions de la 'EHESS', Cahiers du Monde russe et soviétique*, Vol. 24, No. 4., October-December 1983.

Mattingly, Terry. "Concerning the new converts to Eastern Orthodoxy: Are they MAGA clones or worse?". *GetReligion*, 16 May 2022.

McCain, John. "Relating to a National Emergency Declared by The President on March 13, 2020". *Congressional Record,* Vol. 168, No. 39, (Senate), 3 March 2022.

McGovern, Jonathan. "The Origin of the Phrase 'Will no one rid me of this turbulent priest?'". *Notes & Queries,* Vol 68, Issue 3, September 2021.

McNally, Raymond T.. "The Origins of Russophobia in France". *American Slavic and East European Review*, Vol. 17, No. 2., April 1958.

Meek, James. "Russian Patriarch 'was KGB spy'". *The Guardian*, 12 February 1999.

Melkozerova, Veronika. "Putin ally punishes priest who performed Navalny memorial service". *Politico*, 24 April 2024.

Mercédesz, Hetzmann. "PM Viktor Orbán receives Russian Order of Glory and Honour". *Daily News Hungary*, 2 June 2023.

Metzel, Mikhail. "Putin calls dissolution of USSR tragedy and 'collapse of historical Russia'", *TASS.* 12 December 2021.

Michaels, Daniel, et al.. "Europe Confronts Reality That Vance's Hostility Is More Than Just a Show". *The Wall Street Journal*, 26 March 2025.

Milbank, Sebastian. "Kiev and Moscow: a tale of two Russias (Ukraine threatens Putin because it offers an alternative version of Russia)". *The Critic.* 12 March 2022.

Miller, Elizabeth Lane and Fisher, Helene, Ross, with Kenneth R. (ed). *Religious Freedom." Compact Atlas of Global Christianity,1st ed.* Edinburgh University Press, 2025.

Milner-Gulland, Robin. *The Russians. The peoples of Europe.* Blackwell, 1999.

Mirovalev, Mansur. "'God of war': ROC stands by Putin, but at what cost?". *Al Jazeera*, 9 February 2024.

Mitchell, Amy, et al.. "Publics Globally Want Unbiased News Coverage, but Are Divided on Whether Their News Media Deliver Deep political divides in many nations on satisfaction with news media; greatest is in the U.S.". *Pew Research Center,* 11 January 2018.

Montefiore, Simon S.. *Stalin: The Court of the Red Tsar*, 5th Edition. Phoenix,2003.

Moore, Dene. "Schools' mission: take the Indian out of the child". *Toronto Star*, 6 March 2016.

More, Stephen E.. "Russia killing and torturing Ukrainian Christians, not 'protecting' them. Ignore MTG.". *USA Today*, 18 April 2024.

Moscow Patriarchate. "The complete transcript of the conversation between Patriarch Porfirije and Putin: Vučić is coming to Moscow". *Moscow Patriarchate*, Website, Transcript, 23 April 2025. http://en.special.kremlin.ru/events/president/transcripts/76775 Accessed 15 June 2025.

Moscow Times Staff. "Russian Priest Suspended After Navalny Memorial Service". *The Moscow Times*, 24 April 2024.

Moss, Vladimir. *How the Moscow Patriarchate Fell From Grace*. Vladimir Moss, 2012.

Muzikárová, Soňa. "Why some EU countries in the east are still pro-Russia". *Al Jazeera*, 6 February 2023.

NDR Staff Writers. "ROC Churches in Europe: Espionage Outposts Under the Guise of Faith". *Nordic Defense Review*, 10 July 2025.

Nechepurenko, Ivan. "Stalin's Image Returns to Moscow's Subway, Honoring a Brutal History". *New York Times*, 28 Mary 2025.

Necşuţu, Mădălin. "Council of Europe Designates Transnistria 'Russian Occupied Territory'". *Balkan Insight*, 16 March 2022.

Neplii, Anna. "Secret Fraternities, a Temple of War, and Espionage Globally. What Does the ROC Hide?". *United24 Media*, 23 June 2024.

Nerozzi, Timothy H.J.. "'Putin's confessor' named bishop of annexed Ukrainian territory". *FoxNews*, 12 October 2023.

Nikolaev, Sergei (Levitt, Marcus C., ed.). *Stefan Iavorsky – Early Modern Russian Writers: Late Seventeenth and Eighteenth Centuries*, Gale Research, 1995.

Nikolova, Vanessa. "Kremlin speaking: homophobia as geopolitics". *Factcheck.bg*, 1 June 2023. https://factcheck.bg/en/kremlin-speaking-homophobia-as-geopolitics/ Accessed 24 July 2025.

Nowak, Andrzej. *"The Empire That Catherine Erased"*. Pursuasion: American Purpose, 24 March 2023.

Nye, Joseph S. Jr., "Public Diplomacy and "Soft Power". *The Annals of the American Academy of Political and Social Science*, Vol. 616, Public Diplomacy in a Changing World, March 2008.

Nye, Joseph S.. "China's Soft Power Deficit To catch up, its politics must unleash the many talents of its civil society". *The Wall Street Journal*, 8 May 2012.

Nye, Joseph S.., "Unrevised Transcript of Evidence Taken Before the Select Committee on Soft Power and the UK's Influence". *House of Lords*, Evidence Session No. 10, (witness),15 October 2013.

O'Donovan, Oliver (Williamson, Roger, ed.). *War by Other Means: Some Corner of a Foreign Field*, Palgrave Macmillan, 1998.

O'Hurley, Miceál. "An Injury to Religious Freedom in Ukraine?". *European Diplomat*, 4 July 2025.

O'Hurley, Miceál. "In Conversation Interview with Harvard's George Soroka, Ph.D. on the Crimea Crisis—ICC Finds Basis War Crimes & Crimes Against Humanity Committed". *European Diplomat*, (Video), 25 October 2021.

OCP News Service. "Finnish Archbishop Blasts Moscow Patriarchate: "No Trace of Orthodoxy Left"". *OCPS*, 11 June 2024.

Olejnik, Lukasz. *Russian cyber and information warfare and its impact on the EU and UK*. Kings College, 15 April 2025.

Olszański, Tadeusz A.. "Historic unification of Ukrainian Orthodox Church". *Ośrodek Studiów Wschodnich (Centre for Eastern Studies)*, 17 December 2018.

Osborn, Andrew and Whalen, Jeanne. "Evidence in Georgia Belies Russia's Claims of 'Genocide'". *The Wall Street Journal*, 7 August 2018.

Ostrowski, Donald. "Was there a Riurikid Dynasty in Early Rus'?". *Canadian-American Slavic Studies*, No. 52, 2018.

Panella, Chris. "Putin has decided that Russia is going to be a 'safe haven' for people who want to trade liberal Western ways for Russian 'moral values'". *Business Insider*, 19 August 2024.

Parks, Michael. "Yeltsin Sheds Atheism, Gets Religion Again". *Los Angeles Times,* 15 June 1992.

Parmaksiz, Yagiz Efe. "Swedish agency cuts support to Russian Orthodox Church over intelligence concerns". *Türkiye Today*, 3 June 2024.

Parviainen, Sinikka. "War economy boosts life satisfaction for ethnic Russians and residents of military-industrial regions". *Bank of Finland Bulletin,* 4 June 2025.

Paul, Michael C.. "The Military Revolution in Russia 1550–1682". *The Journal of Military History*, Vol. 68, No. 1., January 2004.

Paxton, John. *Imperial Russia*. Palgrave Macmillan, 2001.

Pillay, Jerry (on behalf of WCC member churches). "WCC 'cannot reconcile' World Russian People's Council decree describing Ukraine conflict as a 'Holy War'". *World Council of Churches*, 12 April 2024.

Pipes, Richard. *Russia Under the Old Regime*. Charles Scribner's Sons, 1974.

Plokhy, Serhii. *The Gates of Europe: A History of Ukraine*, (Revised Edition). Basic Books, 2015.

Pomerantsev, Peter. "Russia's War Against Evangelicals". *TIME*, 20 April 2024.

Porter, Brandon. "'Odious effects' when church, state become too familiar with one another, Walker says". *Baptist Press*, 27 September 2022.

Porter, Tom. "Putin claimed a 400-year-old map proved Ukraine isn't a real country, not noticing it has 'Ukraine' written on it". *Business Insider*, 24 May 2023.

Prekup, Igor. "Baltic Rehearsal". *Russia in Global Affairs*, No. 2.1., June 2019.

Proekt Staff Writers. "New 'Proekt' investigation uncovers millions of dollars in real estate belonging to Patriarch Kirill and his family members". *Meduza,* 28 October 2020.

Pronina, Tatiana. "Teaching 'The Foundations of Orthodox Culture' in Schools of the Tambov Region: Achievements and Problems". *State Religion and Church*, Vol. 5, No. 2, 2018.

Psaropoulos, John T.. '"Pragmatic manipulation': Is Russia playing with European voters' minds?". *Al Jazeera*, 5 June 2024.

Pugnet, Aurélie. "Four reasons Europe can't trust the US to protect it anymore". *Euractive*, 10 March 2025.

Putin, Vladimir (Путин, Владимир Владимирович). "*Meeting of the Presidential Council for Interethnic Relations*". *Kremlin: Moscow*, Videoconference, 30 March 2021.

Putin, Vladimir (Путин, Владимир Владимирович). "Meeting of the Presidential Council for Interethnic Relations". *Kremlin: Moscow*, Videoconference, 30 March 2021.

Pyvovarov, Serhii and Spirin, Yevhen. "The USSR and Nazi Germany held a military parade in Brest after the capture of Poland 84 years ago. Russia calls it a 'liberation campaign'. Then-reality in 15 pictures". *Бабель*, 22 September 2023.

Raffensperger, Christian. "Ties of Kinship: Genealogy and Dynastic Marriage in Kyivan Rus'". *Harvard Series in Ukrainian Studies*, 2018.

Raffensperger. Christian. "Reimagining Europe: Kyivan Rus' in the Medieval World, 988–1146". *Harvard Historical Studies*, 2008.

Rahr, Alexander. "Yeltsin Campaigning", *Radio Free Europe/Radio Liberty*. 4 June 1991.

Ray, Charles A.. "Russia's Influence in Africa: The Role of the ROC". *Foreign Policy Research Institute,* 15 October 2024.

Rees, Anna. "Estonian nuns accused of spying for Putin". *Christian News*, 23 June 2025.

Reuters. "'To gay Europe I say no!': How Russia mobilizes Moldovan clergy ahead of elections". *TVP World*, 27 September 2025.

Reuters. "Kremlin says Putin is ready to discuss peace in Ukraine but wants to achieve goals". *RTÉ News*, 20 July 2025.

Reuters. "Orthodox Church leader says Russian soldiers dying in Ukraine will be cleansed of sin". *Reuters,* 26 October 2022.

Reuters. "ROC absolves Russian soldiers dying in Ukraine". *Jerusalem Post*, 26 September 2022.

Reuters. "Russians, opposition figures sentenced over role in 2016 Montenegro coup attempt". *Reuters,* 9 May 2019.

Reuters. "Ukraine says 'dubious' Russians found in raid on Kyiv monastery". *Reuters*, 23 November 2022.

Riasanovsky, Nicholas V. and Steinberg, Mark D.. *A history of Russia, (Ninth ed.)*. Oxford University Press, 2019.

Riccardi-Swartz, Sarah. "Between Heaven and Russia: Religious Conversion and Political Apostasy in Appalachia". *Fordham University Press*, 2022.

ROC – DECR Communication Service. "First Hierarch of Russian Church Outside of Russia: Constantinople's actions in Ukraine can lead to bloodshed". *Moscow Patriarchate: Moscow*, 18 December 2018.

ROC—Department for External Church Relations. "Primates of Local Orthodox Churches celebrate Liturgy at the Cathedral of St George in Phanar on the Sunday of Orthodoxy". *ROC*, Website, 9 March 2014. https://mospat.ru/en/news/51682/ Accessed, 21 July 2025.

ROC—Department for External Church Relations. "Statement of the Holy Synod of the ROC concerning the uncanonical intervention of the Patriarchate of Constantinople in the canonical territory of the ROC". *Moscow Patriarchate:* Moscow, 14 September 2018.

ROC. "Journals of the meeting of the Holy Synod of July 15, 2016". *Holy Synod of the ROC*, Magazine No. 48, 15 July 2016.

ROC. "Resolution, Journals of the meeting of the Holy Synod of July 15, 2016". *Holy Synod of the ROC,* Magazine No. 48, 15 July 2016.

Rodeheffer, Luke. "Kremlin Prioritizes Russian Language in Moscow's Near Abroad". *Eurasia Daily Monitor*, 31 October 2024.

Romanov, Pavel and Iarskaia-Smirnova, Elena, "'Foreign agents' in the field of social policy research: The demise of civil liberties and academic freedom in contemporary Russia". *Journal of European Social Policy*, 2015.

Ross, Kenneth R., et al. (eds). *Christianity in North America.* Edinburgh University Press, 2023.

Russia, *et al.. Treaty of Küçük Kaynarca*. National University of Singapore, Department of History, Faculty of Arts and Social Sciences, Archived and Translated Text), 1774. https://fass.nus.edu.sg/hist/eia/historical-texts-archive/ Accessed, 18 September 2025.

Russian Federation. *Constitution of the Russian Federation*, Russian Federation (As amended 2020). 12 December 1993.

Russkaia Pravoslavnaia Tserkov, Moscow Patriarchate. "Protokolle der Weisen von Zion", *Strafsache Schweizerischer israelitischer Gemeindebund und Israelitische Kultusgemeinde Bern gegen die Gauleitung des Bundes national-sozialisticher Eidgenossen und weitere Angeschuldigte ....* Jewish Culture Society: Bern, Microfilm Copy, Frames 001347, April 1958.

Ruud, Charles A.. *Fighting Words: Imperial Censorship and the Russian Press, 1804-1906.* University of Toronto Press, 1982.

S'Bunker. "The Serbian Patriarch calls for a 'Greater Serbia' with Putin's blessing". *Global Voices*, 11 May 2025.

Sacred Congregation for the Clergy. *Decree Quidam Episcopi.* Sacred Congregation for the Clergy, *cf* C.I.C., can. 287 § 2; AAS 74, 8 March 1982.

Safronova, Valeriya. "New Russian High School Textbooks Seek to Justify War in Ukraine". *New York Times,* 1 September 2023.

Saint Athanasius (Athanasius of Alexandria). "On the Incarnation of the Word". *Createspace Independent Publishing Platform*, First Published *c.* 4th Century, 2007.

Saint Cyprian (Deferrari, Roy J., trans. and ed.). "Treatises". *The Fathers of the Church, Catholic University of America Press,* Volume 36, 1958.

Saint Cyprian of Carthage (Parker, John Henry, trans.). *Epistle LXXIII, anno domini 256.* Oxford edition, 1844.

Saliashvili, Meagan. "Orthodox churches boomed during pandemic, study finds, but calls growth 'mixed bag'". *Religion News Service*, 23 August 2024.

SÄPO. "Orolig omvärld skapar hot i Sverige". *Säkerhetspolisen*, 11 Mars 2025.

Sauer, Pjotr. "Twenty years of ruthlessness: how Russia has silenced Putin's opponents". *The Guardian*, 27 August 2023.

Seabury, Samuel. "Letters of a Westchester Farmer, by the Reverend Samuel Seabury". *White Plains: Westchester County Historical Society*, 1930.

Seibt, Sébastian. "Trump mutes Voice of America, makes space for Russian and Chinese influence". *France 24*, 19 March 2025.

Serbian Orthodox Church. "On the Resolution of the European Parliament". *Serbian Orthodox Church*, 14 March 2022.

Shepherd, Jonathan. *Emergent Elites and Byzantium in the Balkans and East-Central Europe*. Taylor and Francis, 2011.

Shiltagh, Maggie. "Anti-American sentiment rises in Europe as Trump fuels anger". *Japan Times*, 2 April 2025.

Shkarovskii, Mikhail V.. "The ROC versus the State: The Josephite Movement, 1927-1940". *Slavic Review*, No. 54., 1995.

Shvab, Larysa and Tokarska, Yulia. "1580s Transfer Attempts of the Ecumenical Patriarch's Seat to the Ruthenian Lands of the Polish-Lithuanian Commonwealth (Rzeczpospolita)". *Codrul Cosminului*, XXVIII, 2022.

Sirhan, Yasmin. "Who is Vladimir Putin's Revisionist History For?". *The Atlantic*, 27 February 2022.

Skakun, Roman. "The NKVD–MGB–KGB Agent Network in the Orthodox Episcopate of Ukraine (1939–1964): Formation, Functions, and Behavioral Models". *Ukrainian Catholic University Press*, 2025.

Skiba, Katarzyna. "The ROC Has a Kremlin Spy Network — And Now It's Spreading Abroad". *WorldCrunch*, 4 January 2024.

Składanowski, Marcin, et al.. "Church of war: propaganda and disinformation in Patriarch Kirill's discourse on Russia's aggression". *Cogent Arts & Humanities*, 2025.

Skorkin, Konstantin. "Ukraine's Ban on Moscow-Linked Church Will Have Far-Reaching Consequences". *Carnegie Politika*, 4 September 2024.

Skutnabb-Kangas, Tove and Phillipson, Robert (Rannut, Mart, in collaboration with). *Linguistic Human Rights: Overcoming Linguistic Discrimination*. Muton de Gruytur, 1995.

Smelyansky, Eugene. *Medievalisms and Russia: The Contest for Imaginary Pasts*, Arc Humanities Press, 2024.

Smith, Peter. "Moscow patriarch: Russian war dead have their sins forgiven". *The Hill*, 27 September 2022.

Snyder, Rachel. "North Texas Congress members clash over the use of Nazi propagandist Joseph Goebbels quote at hearing". *WFAA*, 3 April 2025.

Social Media News. "Putin says father of Patriarch Kirill baptized him in 1952". *Orthodox Christianity*, 20 November 2016.

Soldatov, Andrei and Borogan, Irina. "Putin's Useful Priests: The Russian Orthodox Church and the Kremlin's Hidden Influence Campaign in the West". *Foreign Affairs*, 14 September 2023.

Soldatov, Andrei and Borogan, Irina. "Putin's Useful Priests: The ROC and the Kremlin's Hidden Influence Campaign in the West". *Foreign Affairs*, 14 September 2023.

Solzhenitsyn, Aleksandr Isaevich. *The Gulag Archipelago 1918-1956: An Experiment in Literary Investigation*. YMCA Press, 1973.

Sorochinskaia, Sofia. "Russian Priests Defrocked and Imprisoned for Their Anti-War Stance". *Russian Post*, 22 January 2024.

Soviet State Archives. *Interrogation of Vasily Ivanovich Bellavin*. Soviet State Archives (CPU), Transcript/Record, 1922.

St. Athanasius Academy of Orthodox Theology. *The Orthodox Study Bible. New American Bible, prepared under the auspices of the academic community of St. Athanasius Academy of Orthodox Theology*, Elk Grove, California. Thomas Nelson, 2008.

Stafford, Tom. "How liars create the 'illusion of truth'". *BBC,* 26 October 2016.

Stanley, Alessandra. "Church Leans Towards Yeltsin in Russian Vote". *New York Times*, 30 May 1996.

Stender-Petersen, Adolf. *Verangica*. Universitets Slaviske Institut, 1953.

Stezhensky, Alex. "Kremlin's propaganda machine: Who funds it, who runs it, and how it dominates Russia's media". *The New Voice of Ukraine*, 13 April 2025.

Stoddart, Kristan. "Russia's Cyber Campaigns and the Ukraine War: From the 'Gray Zone' to the 'Red Zone'". *Applied Cybersecurity and Internet Governance*, 19 June 2024.

Stoeckl, Kristina and Uzlaner, Dmitry. *The Moralist International: Russia and the Culture Wars*. Fordham University Press, 2022.

Stoeckl, Kristina. "The role of religion in the Russian "culture war"". *Newsroom: Universität Innsbruck*, 2 June 2024.

Stolyarov, Gleb and Papachristou, Lucy. "Russia to spend over half a billion dollars to bolster internet censorship system", *Reuters*, 10 September 2024.

Strzelecki, Jan. "Moskwa-Konstantynopol. Nowa schizma w prawosławiu?", *Ośrodek Studiów Wschodnich*. 17 Październik 2018.

Subtelny, Orest. "Russia and the Ukraine: The Difference That Peter I Made". *Russian Review (Wiley)*, Vol. 39, No. 1.,1 January 1980.

Sullivan, Helen. "Russia 'systematically' forcing Ukrainians to accept citizenship, US report finds". *The Guardian*, 3 August 2023.

Sullivan, Kevin and Rozsa, Lori. "DeSantis doubles down on claim that some Blacks benefited from slavery". *Washington Post,* 22 July 2023.

Sweeney, Lucy and Stein, Lucia. "With his luxury watch and murky Soviet past, Patriarch Kirill is Putin's spiritual leader and power broker". *Australian Public Broadcasting,* 21 January 2023

Terbush, Jon. "John McCain: Russia is a 'gas station masquerading as a country'". *The Week*, 8 January 2015.

Tidey, Alice. "Orbán criticises EU plans to sanction head of ROC". *EuroNews*, 5 June 2022.

Tishkov, Valery. "The Russian World—Changing Meanings and Strategies". *Carnegie Papers*, Number 95., August 2008.

Topidi, Kyriaki. "Religious Belief as an Existential Threat: How Russia Victimizes Religious Minorities in Russia and in the Occupied Territories of Ukraine; Series on Transnational Christian Nationalism, and its impact on politics, the rule of law, and religious freedom". *Canopy Forum on the Interaction of Law and Religion*, 2 November 2024.

Trevalyan, Mary. "Russian Orthodox priest faces expulsion for refusing to pray for war victory". *Swiss Info SWI*, 13 January 2024.

Troianovski, Anton and Safronova, Valeriya. "Russia Takes Censorship to New Extremes, Stifling War Coverage". *New York Times*, 4 March 2022.

Trump, Donald J.. *Restoring Truth and Sanity to American History: Executive Order*. White House, Washington, D.C., 27 March 2025.

Uncredited Amnesty International Staff Writers. "Russia: Activist Daria Kozyreva conviction for poetic anti-war protest exposes continued repression". *Amnesty International*, 18 April 2025.

Uncredited BBC News Staff Writers. "Russia's border doesn't end anywhere, Vladimir Putin says". *BBC News*, 24 November 2016.

Uncredited Civil Georgia Staff Writers. "Abkhazia, S. Ossetia Formally Declared Occupied Territory". *Civil Georgia*, 28 August 2008.

Uncredited Commonspace Staff Writers. "Putin says that as a child he was baptised in secret". *Commonspace*.eu, Commentary, 7 January 2012.

Uncredited DW Staff Writers. "Russia bans access to over 80 EU news outlets". *Deutsche Welle (DW)*, 25 June 2024.

Uncredited DW Staff Writers. "Ukrainian church wins independence battle". *Deutsche Welle (DW)*, 11 October 2018.

Uncredited France 24 Reporters. "Exclusive investigation: Is the ROC in Sweden a platform for espionage?". *France 24*, Video, 4 July 2025.

Uncredited Gazetta Staff Writers. "The Ecumenical Patriarchate has published documents in support of Ukrainian autocephaly". *Gazetta. UA*, 14 September 2018.

Uncredited GeoPost Staff Writers. "Russian priest also 'non-grata' has carried out 'counterintelligence'" in Skopje". *GeoPost*, 18 September 2023.

Uncredited Hungary Today Staff Writers. "Russian Church in Czechia Transferred into Ownership of Hungarian Diocese". *Hungary Today*, 11 February 2025.

Uncredited Insider Staff Writers. "When the "action" starts: Debunking 12 falsehoods from Vladimir Putin's "Direct Line"", *The Insider*, Analysis, 20 December 2024.

Uncredited Le Monde Staff Writers. "Polish far right's win is a thunderclap above Europe", *Le Monde*, Editorial, 2 June 2025.

Uncredited Moscow Times Staff Writers. "Putin Christened in Secret From his Father". *Moscow Times*, 23 July 2013.

Uncredited Orthodox Times Staff Writers. "Archbishop of Helsinki: Not a trace of Orthodoxy left in the Patriarchate of Moscow". *Orthodox Times*, 11 June 2024.

Uncredited RT Staff. "Russia-West clash not about ideology—Putin". RT, 13 July 2025.

Uncredited TASS Staff Writers. "Hungary does not want to share border with Russia—Orban". *TASS*, 21 December 2023.

Uncredited TASS Staff Writers. "ROC official vows 'firm and tough' response to Constantinople's move". *TASS*, 12 October 2018.

Uncredited Ukrinform Staff Writers. "Priest with Moscow-affiliated church caught on illegal arms trade". *Ukrinform*, 26 September 2023.

Uncredited UNIAN Staff Writers. "Приказ расстреливать митингующих отдавал Янукович—ГПУ [Order to shoot protesters was given by Yanukovych—GPU]". *UNIAN*, 2 April 2014.

Uncredited Wire Report. "Metropolitan Onufriy took part at the Holy Synod of the ROC". *Religious Information Service of Ukraine*, 8 March 2018.

Uncredited. *Anniversary of the establishment of patriarchate in Moscow. Metropolitan Job elected Patriarch*, Presidential Library of Russia, 1589. https://www.prlib.ru/en/history/619001 Accessed 19 July 2025.

Underwood, Paul L.. "Partisanship sways news consumers more than the truth, new study shows". *Standford Report*, 31 October 2024.

UNHCR Staff (27 January 2022), *Conflict-related civilian casualties in Ukraine*, Office of the United Nations High Commissioner for Human Rights.

Unidentified. *Въ лѣто 6694 [1186]—6698 [1190], Ипатіївський лїтопис [In the year 6694 [1186]—6698 [1190]*. The Hypatian Codex, in Church Slavic, 1908. https://litopys.org.ua Accessed 13 August 2025.

United Nations. *Charter of the United Nations*,1 UNTS XVI, 24 October 1945. https://www.un.org/en/about-us/un-charter Accessed, 21 February 2024.

United Nations. "Gross Average Monthly Wages by Indicator, Country and Year". *United Nations Economic Commission for Europe*, 2010.

United Nations. "Life expectancy at birth, male (years)—Russian Federation". *World Population Prospects, United Nations (UN)*, publisher: UN Population Division; Statistical databases and publications from national statistical offices, National statistical offices; *Demographic Statistics, Eurostat (ESTAT)*, 2023.

Valuyev, Pyotr. *Valuyev Circular*. Kremlin, Moscow, 1863.

van Brugen, Isabel. "Four Signs Russia Could Be Preparing for War With NATO". *Newsweek*, 2 May 2025.

Van Den Bercken, William (Bowden, John (trans.). *Holy Russia and Christian Europe: East and West in the Religious Ideology of Russia*, SCM Press, 1999.

van Rij, Armida. "The pro-Putin far right is on the march across Europe—and it could spell tragedy for Ukraine". *The Guardian*, 11 April 2024.

van Rubroeck, Willem (Rockhill William Woodville, trans.). *The journey of William of Rubruck to the eastern parts of the world, 1253-55, As Narrated by Himself with Two Accounts of the Earlier Journey of John of Pian De Carpine*, London: As Printed for the Hakluyt Society, 1900.

Velychenko, Stephen. "Restructuring and the Non-Russian Past". *Nationality Papers*, Vol. 22, No. 2., 1994.

Vernadsky, George. *Kievan Russia*. Yale University Press, 1948.

Vernadsky, George. *The Tsardom of Moscow, 1547-1682. Vol. 5 in A History of Russia*. Yale University Press, 1959.

Vetoshnikov, Konstantin. "La «concession» de la métropole de Kiev au patriarche de Moscou en 1686: Analyse canonique". *Proceeding of the International Congress of Byzantine Studies*, 24 August 2016.

Vladimir Latinovic and Anastacia K. Wooden (eds.). *Stolen Churches or Bridges to Orthodoxy? Volume 2: Ecumenical and Practical Perspectives on the Orthodox and Eastern Catholic Dialogue*. Palgrave Macmillan, 2021.

Vobejda, Barbara. "U.S., Soviet Textbooks Give Different Accounts of History". *The Washington Post*, 5 December 1987.

von Stählin, Jacob. *Originalanekdoten von Peter dem Großen: aus dem Munde angesehener Personen zu Moskau und Petersburg vernommen, und der Vergessenheit entrissen*. J.G.I. Breitkopf, 1785.

Vvedenskii, Alexander Ivanovich. Tserkov' i gosudarstvo (Ocherk vzaimootnoshenii tserkvi i gosudarstva v Rossii), 1918-1922, Unpublished Manuscript, 1923.

Walker, Sean (20 October 2020), *Angels and artillery: a cathedral to Russia's new national identity*, The Guardian.

Walker, Shaun and Grytsenko, Oksana. "Ukraine's new leaders begin search for missing billions". *The Guardian*, 27 February 2014.

Weber, Peter. "Russian Orthodox Patriarch Kirill's support for Putin's Ukraine war has fractured his church". *The Week*, 19 April 2022.

White House. "Press Conference by President Bush and Russian Federation President Putin (Brdo Pri Kranju, Slovenia)". *George W. Bush Presidential Library*, Transcript, 16 June 2001.

Whitmore, Brian. "Russia's Patriarch Increasingly Becoming Major Force In Politics". *Radio Free Europe/Radio Liberty*, 6 September 2009.

Wilson, Elaine. "Русская «самобытность»: попытки присвоить и переписать религиозную историю". *Public Orthodoxy*, 30 December 2024.

Wire Story. "Putin: Crimea is to Russia what Jerusalem is to Muslims, Jews". *Anadolu Ajansı (AA)*, 4 December 2014.

Wiśnicki, Jarosław. "History as an information weapon in Russia's full-scale war in Ukraine". *European External Action Service (EEAS)*, 14 July 2023.

World Russian People's Council. *Decree of the 25th World Russian People's Council: the present and the future of the Russian world*. World Russian People's Council, Plenary Session, 27 March 2024.

Yakovenko, Kateryna. "Russia's claim for 'Mother-of-Slavs' status". *International Issues & Slovak Foreign Policy Affairs*, Vol. 24, No. 1-2, Europe and Russia, 2015.

YouGov Wikimedia Foundation. "Women and Wikipedia: Summary of results from 2019 YouGov survey. Technical Report". *Wikimedia Foundation*, PDF, 2019. https://commons.wikimedia.org/wiki/File:Women_%26_Wikipedia_-_Summary_of_results_from_2019_YouGov_survey.pdf Accessed 11 August 2025.

Yurtaev, Vladimir and Klimenko, Anna. "Moscow as the Third Rome Concept: Its Nature and Interpretations in the 19th – Early 21st Centuries". *Revista de estudios sobre espacio y poder*, 2018.

Zagorcheva, Dessie. "Praying for Putin: Spies in Cassocks Threaten the West". *Center for European Policy Analysis*, 31 October 2023.

Zecher, Jonathan. "What makes a martyr? The proclamation of Patriarch Kirill and the question of sacred violence". *ABC Religion and Ethics*, 17 October 2022.

Zenkovsky, Serge A. and Keenan, Edward L.. "Prince Kurbsky – Tsar Ivan IV Correspondence. Reflections on Edward Keenan's The Kurbskii-Groznyi Apocrypha". *The Russian Review*, Vol. 32, No. 3., July 1973.

Zolotov, Andrei. "Orthodoxy, Oil, Tobacco, and Wine: Do They Mix?". *East-West Church & Ministry Report*, No. 5., 13 December 1996.

Zudenkova, Kateryna. "Oppression and Eradication: The Linguicide of Ukrainian by Russia". *Ukraine World*, 25 October 2024.

Ί. Μ. Μονὴ Βατοπαιδίου, Ἅγιον Ὄρος. "Liturgical Texts on Rites of Ordination in the Orthodox Church," Μωυσέως Ὠδή. Ἀφιερωματικὸς τόμος πρὸς τιμὴν τοῦ μακαριστοῦ Γέροντος Μωυσέως τοῦ Ἁγιορείτου. Ί. Μ. Μονὴ Βατοπαιδίου, Ἅγιον Ὄρος, 830-845, 2017.

Білінський, Володимир. *Країна Моксель, або Московія*. Видавництво імені Олени Теліги, книга 3, 4-е вид., 2012.

Власовський, Іван. *Нарис історії Української Православної Церкви*. Українська Православна Церква в З.Д.А., Нью-Йорк, Том 1, 1955, с. 35-37.

Воробьев, Владимир. *Следственное дело патриарха Тихона*. Сборник документов по материалам Центрального архива ФСБ РФ. Памятники исторической мысли: Москва, 2000.

Государственная Дума Российской Федерации, "Законопроект №1074945-7 «О внесении изменения в статью 128-1, Уголовного кодекса Российской Федерации»", *Москва, Кремль*, 30 декабря 2020 (Вступил в силу 10 января 2021).

Дашкевич, Ярослав. "Як Московія привласнила історію Київської Русі", Журнал Універсум, 11–12 (217-218), 2011.

Дашкевич, Ярослав. "Як Московія привласнила історію Київської Русі". *Журнал Універсум*, no. 11–12, 2011, pp. 217-218.

Зоря, Євстратій. "Important: On the official website of the Ecumenical Patriarchate....". *Facebook*, Post, Зоря, Євстратій,14 September 2018.

Издательский Совет Русской Православной Церкви. "Прием товарищем И. В. СТАЛИНЫМ Митрополита Сергия". *Журнал Московской Патриархии*, сентябрь 1943.

Інформаційні матеріали, підготовлені до чергового засідання постійно діючого Круглого столу "Релігія і влада в Україні: проблеми взаємовідносин". *Київ, за сприяння Представництва Фонду Конрада Аденауера в Україні*, 26 квітня 2018.

Кривова, Наталья Александровна. *Власть и церковь в 1922-1925*. АИРО-ХХ, 1927.

Летописец, Нестор. *Повесть временных лет*. Harvard Library of Early Ukrainian Literature in English Translation, Unknown binding, 1 January 1095.

Мельникова, Елена Александровна. "Skandinavskie runicheskie nadpisi: novye nakhodki i interpretatsii; teksty, perevod, kommentarii Скандинавские рунические надписи: новые находки и интерпретации; тексты, перевод, комментарии". *Vostochnaya literatura, Российская академия наук (РАН)*, 2001

Митрохин, Николай. *Ovčinnikov, O pravoslavnom obrazovanii*, Russkaja pravoslavnaja cerkov'. Moskva, 2004.

Никонов, Вадим. "Особенности вынесения приговоров Московским революционным трибуналом по делам духовенства и верующих в 1918-1920-е гг.". *Серия II: История. История Русской Православной Церкви, Вестник ПСТГУ*, 2022.

Пётр I Алексеевич. "Дело об издании писем и бумаг императора Петра Великого". *Дела по ученым учреждениям Департамента народного просвещения за 1863–1895*, 1672–1725.

Плотникова, Ольга Анатольевна. "История Одного Мифа. Легенда Династии Рюриковичей". *Гуманитарные науки Вестник Финансового университета*, No. 2, 2015.

Похлёбкин, Вильям. "Стреляющие котлеты". *Огонёк*, 4 май 1997.

Православіє в Україні. "Местоблюститель УПЦ митрополит Онуфрий направил письмо Президенту РФ В. Путину". *Orthodoxy.org*, 2 March 2014. http://orthodoxy.org.ua/data/vazhno-mestoblyustitel-upc-mitropolit-onufriy-napravil-pismoprezidentu-rf-vputinu.html. Accessed, 17 August 2025.

Программы и документы конференций и форумов. "Наказ XXV Всемирного русского народного собора «Настоящее и будущее Русского мира»". *Всемирный русский народный собор*, 27 марта 2024.

Прокопович, Феофан. Духовный регламент, тщанием и повелением всепресветлейшего, державнейшего государя Петра Первого, императора и самодержца всероссийского. Синодальная типография, 1856.

Путин, Владимир Владимирович. "Ежегодное Послание Федеральному Собранию Российской Федерации". *Кремль, Москва*, 25 апрель 2005.

Путин, Владимир Владимирович. *Об историческом единстве украинского и русского народов*. Кремль, Москва, 12 июля 2021.

Путин, Владимир Владимирович. Послание Президента Федеральному Собранию года. Москва, Кремль, 12 декабря 2012.

Путин, Владимир Владимирович. *Послание Федеральному Собранию Российской Федерации*. Москва, Кремль, 2005.

Путин, Владимир Владимирович. *Послание Федеральному Собранию*. Кремль, Москва, 3 декабря 2014.

Путин, Владимир Владимирович. Федеральному Собранию Российской Федерации Послание Президента РФ Федеральному Собранию. Кремль, Москва, 4 декабря 2014.

Рантанен, Терхи (Отв. ред. Вартанова Е.Л.). "Глобальное и национальное. Масс-медиа и коммуникации в посткоммунистической России". *Славянское обозрение,* январь 2022.

Русская Православная Церковь. «Настоящее и будущее Русского мира». *Наказ XXV Всемирного русского народного собора,* 27 March 2024.

Стародуб, Андрій. "Всеукраїнський православний церковний Собор 1918 року: огляд джерел". *Національна Академія Наук України,* 2010.

Филофей. Послание О Злыхъ Днехъ И Часѣхъ, Послание К Великому Князю Василию, В Немъже О Исправлении Крестнаго Знамения И О Содомском Блудѣ. Библиотека литературы Древней Руси, РАН. ИРЛИ; Под ред. Д. С. Лихачева, Л. А. Дмитриева, А. А. Алексеева, Н. В. Понырко, СПб.: Наука, Т. 9: Конец XIV – первая половина XVI века, 2000, с. 566

Шевченко, Тарас. *Заповіт*. Київ: Видавництво Глорія, 2020.

Штатний автор. "Православная церковь Украины будет автокефальной – устав (полный текст документа)". *РБК-Україна,* 15 грудня 2018.

Book Reviews

Russian aggression against Ukraine is far from being unprecedented. Rather, it is the latest in a long series of acts of aggression and coercion that stretches back to the Middle Ages. Vladimir Putin frequently invokes this deep historical narrative to justify his war against Ukraine.

This book critically examines and deconstructs the historical mythology that fuels and legitimises Russia's war narrative. It traces these myths back to their medieval roots, with particular attention to their religious dimensions. Approaching the subject from a religious perspective, the book reveals how spiritual and historical narratives are intertwined in the Russian propaganda machine.

For anyone seeking to understand the deeper, more nuanced layers of Russian propaganda and its efforts to rationalise war, this book is essential reading. Without grasping these subtleties, one cannot fully comprehend the motivations behind Russia's militaristic posture.

Archimandrite Cyril Hovorun, Ph.D.
Sankt Ignatios Folkhögskola, Stockholm

To truly understand the underpinnings of today's Russia and its toxic rulers, it is essential to explore the roots of a pillar of this autocracy as constructed by Vladimir Putin—the Russian Orthodox Church.

And in our search for how deeply implanted it is in this nation and its people, there is no more essential and riveting a work than Wolves in Sheep's Clothing: The Russian Orthodox Church's Threat to European Security and Democracy. Miceál O'Hurley and his writing partner Oksana Shadrina have provided us with a brilliantly conceived roadmap through this dark and arcane world to a threat that stretches far beyond the immediate confines of the Russian Orthodox Church, or for that matter, its Ukrainian homologue, to the boundaries of Europe and even further. Its roots are long and deep.

O'Hurley and Shadrina bring to their work a profound understanding of and sensibility to the history that has shaped the architecture that is today's Orthodox Church in Russia and beyond. With Russian Orthodoxy's efforts to co-opt its Ukrainian homologue and Putin's increasingly virulent attempts to blend religion and politics, an understanding of this complex landscape is indispensable. Start here.

David A. Andelman, former correspondent for The New York Times *and* CBS News, *creator of* Substack's Andelman Unleashed

The ideological dimension of Russia's invasion of Ukraine—marked by the active collaboration of the Russian Church (Moscow Patriarchate) with the Russian Federation—remains little known in the West outside specialist academic and Orthodox Church circles. O'Hurley and Shadrina explore how it is driven by a quasi-religious ethnonationalist vision synthesized by Patriarch Kyrill Gundyayev and his ecclesial underlings but having deep roots in today's Russian church and state, Vladimir Putin displays a sort of violent apocalypticism akin to that which fueled Nazism and the rise of Hitler. This volume begins the crucial task of exposing to a wider non-expert audience the two-headed monster of "Russkii Mir" and "Holy Rus'".

This rough 'beast' has not only deformed Orthodox Christianity (being a sort of 'heresy') but has also bound the Russian Church, as the largest Orthodox church in the world, to a brutal and devious regime bent on national conquest and the destruction of both the Ukrainian people and the West itself. Only when the secular West opens its eyes to the religious and historical dimensions of the war in Ukraine—and acknowledges Russian religious nationalism and fundamentalism as key motivations of contemporary Russia—will it be able to defend the democratic, humanistic, and religious ideals that underpin Europe and the West. One can only hope this awakening comes before it is too late...

Professor Brandon Gallaher
University of Exeter (UK)

When you think of the war in Ukraine, you may picture bombs, ruined cities, and the loss of life. But war is not only physical; it destroys much more than just material things. O'Hurley and Shadrina powerfully highlight the threat of a spiritual war, where even the most sacred—faith in God—is used as a weapon. It reveals just how ruthless the enemy is and helps you understand the scale of the aggression. If you understand this truth, you will have a chance to resist. Ukraine has paid a heavy price so that you can learn from its experience.

Serhii Kuzan, Chairman
Ukrainian Security & Cooperation Centre (USCC)

Russia is already at war with Europe. From sabotage in the Baltic Sea and election meddling in Moldova to the use of the Russian Orthodox Church as a tool of propaganda, aimed at undermining Europe's democratic fabric. Drawing on original research, Miceál and Oksana show how Orthodoxy is being weaponised in modern warfare, cloaked in soft power, traditional values, and the rhetoric of human rights. They trace how Russia's 2022 invasion of Ukraine was preceded by a religious conquest: denying Ukrainians their right to church independence (autocephaly).

This book is a vital wake-up call to European democracies, urging them to recognise the long-ignored security threats posed by militant and nationalistic religious ideologies.

Andreja Bogdanovski, Ph.D.
Journalist & Analyst Specialising in Orthodox Affairs

Wolves in Sheep's Clothing presents a growing body of evidence that the Russian Orthodox Church and its leaders often have acted and continue to act as agents of the Russian State, advancing its imperial ambitions by spreading the Russian World (Russkiy Mir] ideology to justify Putin's war in Ukraine. More alarmingly, the authors demonstrate that numerous parishes of the Russian Church located in other parts of the world, especially Europe, have engaged in intelligence gathering and other activities to undermine the security of their host countries. The authors persuasively argue that matters of state security should not be ignored out of the legitimate concern for religious freedom.

Paul Gavrilyuk, Ph.D., Founding President
International Orthodox Theological Association

O'Hurley and Shadrina will guide you through the pages of history rewritten by Russia, revealing real facts that are carefully hidden. The book uncovers how Moscow appropriated the legacy of Kyivan Rus', proclaiming itself the elder brother of the Slavs.

You will immerse yourself in the deepest recesses of the Russian Orthodox Church, which has served as an instrument of propaganda and state influence since ancient times. For centuries, the ROC has been subordinated to the state, from the reforms of Peter I to playing the role of an FSB branch under the leadership of Patriarch Kirill.

Today, ROC spreads its influence over Ukraine and the entire world. Agent-priests gather intelligence data, while church structures in Russia train mercenaries and conceal secret scientific facilities, including those related to nuclear research. This book is a profound analysis of the role of the ROC in destabilizing European security and democracy.

Anna Neplii, Ukrainian Journalist
United24Media, Podul.ro, Beta News

O'Hurley and Shadrina have performed a significant service by producing a fine work of research which, despite the dense topics, proves an enjoyable read. Their thesis that the weaponization of faith in service to the Russian State poses a threat to European security and social cohesion is supported by evidence detailed in numerous original source citations.

Defense, security and policy analysts should take notice of *Wolves in Sheep's Clothing* because it provides context for understanding how hybrid warfare, at times being carried out by clergy on behalf of the Russian Federation security apparatus, seeks to undermine neighboring states. The surprising number of Russian Orthodox Church clergy being expelled from states across Europe based on evidence of espionage and carrying out activities that undermine domestic security and democracy demonstrates the necessity of this work.

My experiences as an intelligence operator for several years, specifically in relation to Russian adversaries, tell me about the well-executed professional work that we find described in this book. I highly recommend this book for politicians, policymakers, defense and security specialists, journalists and all people concerned about the future of the European experiment in democracy.

O'Hurley and Shadrina have given us a wake-up call. We should take it.

Dr. Knut Normann Egeland, Ph.D.
Operations Research and Force Protection (retired)

This timely book by Miceál O'Hurley and Oksana Shadrina reveals a truth long known to most Ukrainians: The Russian Orthodox Church (ROC) is not an ordinary religious organization, but a powerful instrument of the Russian security apparatus and propaganda machine. *Wolves in Sheep's Clothing* argues that the ROC poses a threat to European security and democracy due to a dangerous combination of religious ideology and imperial ambition. The authors scrutinize the doctrines of "Russkiy Mir" [Russian World] and "Svyataya Rus" [Holy Rus'], exposing them as a justification for Russian expansionism, historical revisionism, and an "eliminationist policy towards its neighbors' identities". The ROC's role in spying, subversion, and justifying Russian aggression is exposed, including Patriarch Kirill's declaration of the invasion of Ukraine as a "holy war."

The book is an essential read for those who would like to understand how Russia abuses religious freedom, a fundamental European value, as a cover for its covert malign activities and why the ROC is an essential element of the Russian war against Ukraine and wider Europe.

Yuliya Kazdobina, Senior Fellow
Foreign Policy Council "Ukrainian Prism"

The Kremlin's most dangerous weapon is not always a missile. Sometimes it wears a cassock.

In *Wolves in Sheep's Clothing*, Miceál O'Hurley and Oksana Shadrina show what many have seen for years: the Russian Orthodox Church functions as a Kremlin instrument, built for intelligence, influence, and political warfare. It launders Moscow's ambitions in the language of faith and tradition.

Europe needs this book, illuminating how Moscow turns liturgy into a cover for subversion and uses piety as a passport for power. The full-scale invasion of Ukraine did not begin with tanks. It began in sanctuaries, where canon law was bent to deny a nation's right to exist. The authors trace the arc from medieval imperial myths to today's security threat, and the conclusion is blunt. Ignore these wolves in sheep's clothing and you invite a Trojan Horse through the cathedral doors. A vital read.

Jason Jay Smart
Security Consultant Specialising in Russia
& Special Correspondent, Kyiv Post

Russia remains an imperialist state at its core, willing to sacrifice lives, resources, and freedoms to preserve its delusional vision of 'greatness.' For centuries, the state has stood above the individual, demanding obedience while rewarding only the elite. In the XX century, this model started to break down—the USSR collapsed, and globalization opened Russia to world markets. However, its imperial mindset and endemic corruption never changed. Grand corruption corrodes every institution, stripping the country of the ability to modernize or innovate, precisely the requisites of dominance in the modern world. This weakness has left Russia unable to compete on equal terms, yet its desire for great power remained.

This contradiction has driven the Kremlin to develop a different arsenal—hybrid tactics designed to destabilize others rather than build strength at home. Cyberwarfare, propaganda, political interference, and corrosive investments all form part of this toolkit. Perhaps most insidious is the weaponization of religion. The Russian Orthodox Church has been reshaped into an instrument of state power, not a community of unity but a vehicle of influence, spreading ideology, justifying aggression, and reinforcing submission under the guise of faith.

This is the reality of Russia's power today: a failed state with imperial delusions, too corrupt to modernize, surviving only through deception, violence, and the desecration of faith itself.

Wolves in Sheep's Clothing offers a unique opportunity to learn and understand another tool in Russia's hybrid warfare arsenal.

Mariya Chukhnova, International Security Specialist, USA
& WFUWO Representative to the UNDGC/SOC

Russia's hybrid war is not fought solely with tanks or drones. The instrumentalization of the Orthodox Church as a psychological and propaganda weapon is part of a broader strategic offensive against Europe. Recognizing this invisible battlefield is as vital as defending our physical borders.

In *Wolves in Sheep's Clothing:* The Russian Orthodox Church's *Threat to European Security and Democracy*, Miceál O'Hurley and Oksana Shadrina clearly demonstrate that Russia's threat to Europe goes far beyond the military or political sphere: it is also spiritual and cultural. By turning religion into an instrument of manipulation and subversion, the Kremlin seeks to erode the very foundations of European democracy and social cohesion. To ignore this reality would be to abdicate our own security.

Fernando Figueiredo, Colonel (Ret.)
Portuguese Army

The Moscow Patriarchate in Ukraine has long ceased to be merely a religious institution. Its activities have turned it into an instrument of Russia's hybrid influence, aimed at undermining spiritual unity, fostering loyalty to the aggressor state, and justifying the war. Under the guise of pastoral work, narratives of the 'Russian World' are spreading—narratives that sow doubt about Ukrainian statehood and devalue the struggle for independence. At a time when Ukraine resists armed aggression, such structures are no longer a matter of faith but a matter of security. Recognizing the role and influence of the Moscow Patriarchate is therefore critically important: This is not religious competition, but a threat to national security that requires a clear response from both the state and society.

The Moscow Patriarchate has become not merely a religious institution, but a significant factor in the course of the Russian-Ukrainian war. Its structure is exploited by the Kremlin as a channel of propaganda, a tool to legitimize aggression, and a means of justifying violence under the guise of spiritual values. By blessing the weapons and army of the occupying state, and by spreading the ideology of the 'Russian world', it effectively takes part in the war against Ukraine. This influence undermines social unity, sows division within communities, and creates additional risks for national security. Recognizing this is key to protecting the state not only on the battlefield, but also in the spiritual domain.

Vladyslav Klochkov, Major General
Commander of the Directorate Moral and Psychological Support
Armed Forces of Ukraine (2021–2024)

With *Wolves in Sheep's Clothing*, O'Hurley and Shadrina highlight the importance of religious values and mythos for understanding why the post-Soviet Russian state and the Russian Orthodox Church advance a civilizational type of politics that seeks to forcefully expand its neo-imperial power both in Ukraine and elsewhere. Adding to a growing interdisciplinary conversation on the importance of religion in furthering post-Soviet Russian geo-politics, O'Hurley and Shadrina offer a crucial lens through which to focus on the entanglement of Christianity, political power, and globalized projects of moralization that result in war, continued violence, and policies of social control. In doing so, they reframe the geopolitical question of Russian power through the prism of Russian Orthodox metaphysical ideology, refracting key insights into questions of religious freedom/control and political authority. A timely and essential read given the growing embrace of Russia's illiberal and imperial politics by reactionary politicians and communities around the globe.

Sarah Riccardi-Swartz, Ph.D.
Assistant Professor of Religion and Anthropology
Northeastern University (USA)

Wolves in Sheep's Clothing demonstrates how the Kremlin has transformed the Russian Orthodox Church into one of its most effective instruments of hybrid warfare. By fusing ideology, religion, and state power, Moscow legitimises its expansionist efforts and destabilises Europe.

From the annexation of Crimea to the war in eastern Ukraine, the Russian Orthodox Church has provided both ideological cover and practical support, from propaganda and recruitment to acting as a channel for influence operations. As O'Hurley and Shadrina demonstrate, it now operates alongside Russia's disinformation machine, forming part of a hybrid campaign that stretches across the EU, North America, and Africa.

Having researched Russia's hybrid strategies for more than a decade, I see this book as a wake-up call to Western liberal democracies to recognise the Russian Orthodox Church not only as a religious institution but as an active instrument in Moscow's hybrid warfare against European security and democracy. It is also a warning that ignoring this dimension risks underestimating one of the Kremlin's most insidious tools, aimed at destabilising open societies from within.

Maksym Beznosiuk, MA, LLM.
Strategic Policy and Security Specialist on Russia and Ukraine

---

Russian aggression in Ukraine—especially its latest chapter following the full-scale invasion in February 2022—may seem to many like an isolated conflict over influence and dominance somewhere in Eastern Europe, at NATO and the EU's doorstep. However, such a perspective completely overlooks the ideological foundations of the entire enterprise and its messianic-imperial ambitions, which are now fully incorporated into the core idea of the Russian state and culture.

In this spiritual war against Western values of plurality and democracy, the Russian Orthodox Church plays a key role. Often quietly and covertly—but unfortunately very effectively—the ROC abuses the freedom of conscience to spread the influence of Russian imperial ideology, as if it were a legitimate European spiritual tradition. In this way, Russian Orthodoxy has once again become both the bearer and co-creator of an official dictatorship.

The book *Wolves in Sheep's Clothing* by Miceál O'Hurley & Oksana Shadrina is compellingly, insightfully, and comprehensively maps and describes this systematic operation of the ROC in support of Russia's aggressive ambitions. It represents a crucial contribution to understanding the very spiritual foundations of the ideology behind Russia's war of aggression. The publication thus opens the door to the much-needed deeper reflection on the possibilities of effective defense in the realm of modern Russian hybrid warfare.

Martin Kroupa, Chairman of the Board
Post Bellum
Member of the Presidium, Group D. – Drones Nemesis

In a world where geopolitical conflicts increasingly masquerade as religious and cultural narratives, Miceál O'Hurley and Oksana Shadrina's book *Wolves in Sheep's Clothing: The* Russian Orthodox Church's Threat to European Security and Democracy" emerges not just as an analysis, but as a beacon for understanding contemporary Russia. As an expert in international security and religious conflicts, I regard this work as critically important, as it unveils the essence of Vladimir Putin's authoritarian-totalitarian regime, where state power, propaganda, and religion intertwine into a single system of control. The authors brilliantly demonstrate how the Russian Orthodox Church (ROC) has transformed from a spiritual institution into a tool of hybrid warfare, threatening not only Ukraine but the entire Europe.

The essence of modern Russia cannot be grasped without delving into its historical roots. O'Hurley and Shadrina masterfully debunk the myths of the 'Russian World' and 'Holy Rus'', showing how Muscovite identity was shaped under the Mongol yoke, imperial expansionism, and Soviet totalitarianism. Russian mentality, as the authors convincingly argue, is rooted in an ideology of exceptionalism, where the state always dominates the individual, and the collective 'we' justifies aggression against 'others'. This mentality is not accidental: it has been cultivated for centuries through censorship, historical falsification, and suppression of ethnic identities, from Kyivan Rus' to modern occupations. The book emphasizes that ignoring these roots leads to underestimating Russian revanchism, which today manifests in the war against Ukraine as a continuation of medieval claims to dominance.

The authors pay particular attention to the role of the ROC in Russia's domestic and foreign policy. Under Patriarch Kirill, whom O'Hurley and Shadrina aptly call "patriarch in name but not in essence", the church has become part of the "unholy trinity" — an alliance with the Kremlin and the army. Domestically, the ROC legitimizes authoritarian control, promoting "traditional values" as a counterweight to democracy and human rights. Externally, it serves as a soft power tool: through diasporas, espionage under the guise of priests, and propaganda of "holy war" against the West. The authors provide compelling examples of how the ROC blesses the occupation of Crimea and Donbas, turning religion into a weapon of ideological expansion. This is not merely a religious structure — it is a hybrid actor that undermines European unity, sows division in societies, and facilitates disinformation.

A great danger lies in perceiving the ROC as a classical religious organization. Such an approach ignores its historical subordination to the state, from Peter I's abolition of the patriarchate to collaboration with the KGB in Soviet times. Today, the ROC is not a religious structure but a wolf in sheep's clothing, masquerading as spirituality to advance imperial ambitions and Putin's totalitarianism. O'Hurley and Shadrina warn: Europe, which "sleeps," risks becoming the next victim if it does not recognize this threat.

This book is a very important analytical work, grounded in meticulous research, archival data, and current events. The authors, combining academic depth with accessibility, offer not only a diagnosis but also prescriptions: sanctions against the ROC, support for independent churches like the OCU, and a critical rethinking of Russian history. Their work deserves the highest praise for its courage and relevance. I recommend it to all who seek to understand why Russia poses a threat to democracy and how to counter this shadow of totalitarianism.

Anatolii Pinchuk, Chairman of the Board
Eastern Europe Security Institute